D1233647

WILLIAM LYON MACKENZIE KING

The Prism of Unity

William Lyon Mackenzie King, 1935

William Lyon
MACKENZIE KING

✷✷✷

1932-1939

The Prism of Unity

H. Blair Neatby

UNIVERSITY OF TORONTO PRESS

TORONTO AND BUFFALO

© UNIVERSITY OF TORONTO PRESS 1976
Toronto and Buffalo
Printed in Canada

ISBN 0-8020-5381-5
LC 59-347

TO NICOLE, PIERRE, JACQUES

PREFACE

MACKENZIE KING died in 1950 but he has not been forgotten. The public image of the dull and cautious politician whose major claim to political fame was political longevity has been modified by the revelation of a private world where he indulged in a fascination for the occult and communed with the spirits of departed relatives and friends. The continuing interest in King, however, cannot be attributed solely to his personal eccentricities. Canadians have been reminded since his death that Canada is not an easy country to govern, that even after a century of federal union its cultural and regional divisions are still profound. This awareness of the fragility of national unity gives a different perspective to the career of a man who surmounted political crises and stayed in office for more than twenty years and draws attention to his political talents as well as to his personality.

The period covered by this volume gave King ample scope to demonstrate his talents. It begins in 1932 at the lowest point of the depression when many Canadians were desperately looking for a political solution to their economic problems. By 1935 the Liberal party under King's leadership had gained enough popular support to be returned to office. For the next four years his government responded to the depression and to the political alienation which it provoked in western and central Canada. In the process the nature of Canadian federalism was modified and the role of the federal government was significantly enlarged. During these years events in Europe threatened to disrupt the precarious balance at home, with Canadians sharply divided over the issue of participation in a European war. King's apparent indecision frustrated many of his compatriots but cautiously and gradually he prepared them for participating at Britain's side and in 1939 a united Canada went to war.

This volume continues the biography begun by R. MacGregor Dawson, *William Lyon Mackenzie King, I: 1874–1923: A Political Biography,* followed by my volume, *William Lyon Mackenzie King, II: 1924–1932: The Lonely Heights.* I was asked to write the biography for the interwar years by Mackenzie King's Literary Executors – then W. Kaye Lamb, F. A. McGregor, J. W. Pickersgill, and Norman A. Robertson. At no time did they inquire about my views on the man or the period; their only request was that I should try to maintain the high standard of scholarship established by Professor Dawson in his study of King's earlier years. They have never suggested any interpretations or questioned any of my conclusions. The final responsibility for this volume is mine alone.

Many others, however, have contributed to this study. Some years ago Professor James Eayrs prepared memoranda on Canada's external relations and Donald F. Forster, now President of the University of Guelph, produced extensive studies on economic issues. Both of them have long since gone on to other things, but the memoranda they left with me have been invaluable. I have also benefitted from long discussions with Professor Forster over lunch and coffee, with Professor F. W. Gibson who was long associated with the project, and with the late Frank H. Underhill who was curator of Laurier House when research on this volume began. Many of King's associates and contemporaries talked to me about their associations with Mackenzie King, including T. A. Crerar, R. Finlayson, J. G. Gardiner, C. D. Howe, N. P. Lambert, Malcolm MacDonald, F. A. McGregor, W. A. Mackintosh, Vincent Massey, C. G. Power, and E. A. Pickering. The documentary collections I have consulted are mentioned in the Note on Sources but I want to express my thanks here to the staffs of the Public Archives, the Queen's University Archives, and the Franklin D. Roosevelt Library for this generous assistance. Miss Frances Halpenny made suggestions on the organization of the volume and J. W. Pickersgill read the entire manuscript and spared me the embarrassment of some mistakes. Mrs Maureen Clermont cheerfully accepted handwritten drafts with all their revisions and transformed them into a neat typescript; Mrs Rosemary Shipton of the University of Toronto Press then edited the manuscript and imposed a consistent style and form.

My work was also facilitated by fellowships from the Guggenheim Foundation and the Canada Council as well as research grants from the Canada Council and Carleton University. Publication is now made possible by a grant from the Social Science Research Council of Canada, using funds provided by the Canada Council, and a grant from the University of Toronto Press Publications Fund.

The contribution of my wife Jacqueline merits a special paragraph. She discussed each topic before anything was written, read the successive drafts and suggested improvements on every page, and then selected the illustrations. In the Neatby home at least, Mackenzie King has long been a household word.   H.B.N.

CONTENTS

CONTENTS

Mackenzie King with Joan Patteson at Kingsmere *c* 1932

All photographs courtesy Public Archives of Canada

R. B. Bennett and Mackenzie King
at the Toronto centennial celebration in 1934

Mackenzie King and Mitchell Hepburn in Hepburn's office in 1937

TOP The ruins at Kingsmere in 1935
BOTTOM Mackenzie King at a political picnic
during his western tour of 1933

Mackenzie King and Pat in front of Laurier House in 1939

TOP Cordell Hull, Mackenzie King, and Franklin D. Roosevelt
at the signing of the Canada–United States trade agreement in November 1935
BOTTOM Mackenzie King and W. A. Riddell at Geneva in September 1936

TOP King George VI and Mackenzie King in a moment of royal informality
BOTTOM Ian Mackenzie, Charles Dunning, Raoul Dandurand,
Mackenzie King, Ernest Lapointe, and T. A. Crerar
on the way to the Imperial Conference of 1937

Mackenzie King with C. G. Power, Ernest Lapointe, and Norman Rogers
preparing to address the nation on September 3, 1939

WILLIAM LYON MACKENZIE KING

The Prism of Unity

INTRODUCTION

IN THE SUMMER OF 1932, Mackenzie King was already a veteran politician. He was one of the few survivors of the far-off Edwardian days of Sir Wilfrid Laurier, he had been leader of the Liberal party since 1919, and his ten years as Prime Minister was a record surpassed only by Laurier and Sir John A. Macdonald. Before the next election he would be sixty years old. Liberals might well assume that they would soon have to face the problem of choosing his successor.

A change of leaders seemed even more probable because change was the order of the day. The dust-storms and the bread-lines had shaken confidence in the old order. Three long depression years had passed and conditions, instead of improving, were getting worse. Men no longer talked confidently of a temporary recession. Many had concluded that instead of being a regrettably deep and prolonged swing of the business cycle, the depression marked the end of an era. Some argued that over-production and unemployment were the inevitable result of a free-enterprise system based on profits; others blamed democracy, in which politicians competed for power by catering to the gullibility and greed of the majority. For these people only the radical transformation of the economic or political system could end the depression. Those who rejected radical solutions were still forced to admit that something had gone wrong. If it was not the system it was logical to blame the leaders; new men with new policies might succeed where traditional leaders had failed. In a time when neither life nor property seemed secure, a politician who held out hope for a brave new world could achieve almost instant popularity. Even the more conservative Canadians saw the need for change. They watched the spread of radical ideas and feared social disorder or even revolution; the society they knew was in danger and strong and resolute leadership would be needed to preserve law and order and the values they cherished.

When Canadians looked abroad in 1932 the end of the old order seemed even more certain. Canada was not directly menaced by any foreign

3

power but it was part of an unstable world. European powers were fla-
grantly defying the reparations and disarmament clauses of the Treaty
of Versailles and the Japanese were brutally extending their control over
Manchuria. Communism, with its frightening overtones of conspiratorial
plotting and the dictatorship of the proletariat, was a reality in Russia and
a spectre which haunted even western Europe, where Communist parties
were winning more and more popular support. Europe's answer to communism was fascism. Would Canadians face a similar confrontation? In
an age when so many countries had turned to dictators, Canadians might
well turn to more dynamic or authoritarian leaders.

Mackenzie King was an unlikely leader in this troubled time. He was
not only elderly but he was also a notably cautious politician. As Prime
Minister in the 1920s he had extolled conciliation and compromise and
his policies had seldom gone beyond the balancing of conflicting pressures
and the piecemeal redress of grievances. As Leader of the Opposition since
1930 he had continued to be cautious and unimaginative, still emphasizing
the tariff as the major instrument of economic policy and insisting that the
expansion of international trade was the only effective remedy for the
depression. He gave little encouragement to those who favoured radical
forms of government intervention in business; he still equated economic
planning with totalitarianism and inflation with financial disaster. If the
old order had to give way to the new, King was an unlikely choice to
preside over the transition. For those who feared radical changes and
wanted a forceful leader who could rally the defenders of free enterprise,
King was also an improbable choice. A man who talked of co-operation
and made a virtue of placating the dissatisfied was not the fearless champion who would beat back the enemy. In an era of change Mackenzie
King seemed an old-fashioned survivor from the past.

And yet Mackenzie King would remain the leader of the Liberal party
for sixteen more years. Even more surprising, Canadians would return
him to office in the midst of the depression, would choose him to lead the
nation at war, and, finally, would elect him to preside over the post-war
reconstruction. When Canadians faced the challenges of economic and
international crises they voted for this cautious, aging, and apparently
indecisive politician.

Mackenzie King's improbable survival through these turbulent years
has no simple explanation. He was favoured by fortune—he was out of
office during the worst years of the depression and he was in office when
the war began. But good luck is not the full answer; he had the ability to
take advantage of his opportunities and to avoid the blunders of less able
rivals. In 1932 the political future might be obscure, but Mackenzie King

4

the political leader had already completed his political apprenticeship. His policies would be his response to changing circumstances but his fundamental assumptions about Canadian society, about the Liberal party, and about his role as political leader were already firmly established. Behind his unimpressive public image there were political talents and qualities of leadership which help to explain his longevity. A study of King's views on politics and political leadership in 1932 is a necessary introduction to his subsequent political career.

I

Mackenzie King had a coherent view of Canada and of Canadian politics. His guideline was the simple but fundamental conviction that Canada was a political association of diverse cultural, regional, and economic groups. He saw it as a voluntary association, a political partnership. He believed that these groups shared a sense of national community and an underlying commitment to national unity. They were as different as the colours of the spectrum but through his prism he saw them as bound together like a ray of light. His never-ending task as leader was to identify the policies which would maintain and strengthen the partnership, which would be acceptable to all even if no group was fully satisfied. His approach to political leadership was consciously designed to ensure that the Liberal party became the political embodiment of this partnership.

King's version of national unity was an extension of his earlier views on industrial relations. He knew that the interests of management and labour were not identical and that disputes over working conditions and wages were inevitable. But he rejected the idea of a class struggle, the belief that this was an irreconcilable conflict in which there must be a winner and a loser. He believed that both sides could win. Industry was for him a partnership to which both capital and labour contributed and from which both benefitted. Disputes could not be resolved by dissolving the partnership. Employers and workers had to become aware of their common interests, of their interdependence, and negotiate within this framework. Strikes or lockouts might sometimes be necessary to remind narrowminded men on either side that they could not survive alone, and to persuade them to modify the terms of a partnership which was no longer acceptable. The objective, however, was not victory for one side but the negotiation of a more satisfactory partnership. Industrial harmony depended upon the recognition that both employers and workers were partners; both would be better off if they learned to respect each other and to co-operate.

5

Canadian society, as King saw it, was also a partnership, albeit more complex. Cultural, regional, and economic groups had their own special interests and disputes between groups were a natural part of the political process. The conflicts, however, could never be resolved by the ultimate victory of one group or even by an alliance of a few groups. All sectors of Canadian society were interdependent; the welfare of each group depended upon the contribution of all to the partnership. He never doubted that there was a satisfactory solution to every political dispute or that a policy could be found which would restore social harmony.

No political crisis could shake King's conviction that an acceptable agreement was possible. He believed that most Canadians were "liberal-minded" men and women, who would respect the feelings and aspirations of their fellow-citizens when they became aware of them. By his definition liberal-minded Canadians were those who were committed to the national partnership, who would forgo their narrow and selfish interests when once they understood and appreciated the divergent views of their compatriots. Crises occurred because of a lack of understanding. When the broader interests of the community were recognized, King was convinced that the majority of Canadians would accept the necessity of compromise. His role as leader was to guide all groups to this understanding of their common interests.

Fundamental to this approach to leadership was the reliance on discussion to resolve conflicts. He could not intervene to impose a settlement; an imposed solution might end the debate but it would leave a sense of grievance. Even a policy which was eminently fair and eminently desirable was politically unacceptable if some group or region was not yet ready to accept it. The partnership had to be based on the recognition of common interests. King took it for granted that this could mean long and even acrimonious debates but he saw no alternative. Discussion was the only way to make liberal-minded Canadians aware of the interests of other groups in the national partnership. The method of reaching a decision was as important as the decision itself.

King knew that this could be a prolonged and exasperating process of education. He knew that even liberal-minded men thought first of their own narrow self-interest. Years before, in his book *Industry and Humanity*, he had described this limited perspective which made co-operation so difficult:

I believe I can say without exception, every dispute and every controversy of which I have had any intimate knowledge has owed its origin, and the difficulties pertaining to its settlement, not so much to the economic questions involved, as to 'this certain blindness in human beings' to matters of real significance to other lives, and to an unwillingness to approach an issue with any attempt at appreciation of the fundamental oneness of feelings and aspirations in human beings.[1]

But "this certain blindness" was not incurable. Liberal-minded men, because of their commitment to the social partnership, would eventually adopt a broader perspective.

King did not assume that all Canadians were liberal-minded. He conceded that some men were so blinded by their own self-interest that no arguments could broaden their horizons. Foremost among these were the men whom King classified as Tories. In King's lexicon there were two types of Tories: those who were colonials, looking always to Great Britain, blinded to the needs of the Canadian community by the Union Jack; and those who were committed to Big Business, heedless of the welfare of the less fortunate and determined to exploit political power for the benefit of this privileged group. The chosen agent of these Canadian Tories was the Conservative party, the party of British domination and the protective tariff. The Conservative party was thus a threat to Canadian unity as King understood the term.

In a two-party system this made the Liberal party the party of national unity. King believed it should include representatives from all groups, all regions, and all classes of Canadian society. Nobody was to be excluded, whatever his convictions or aspirations, as long as he accepted the implications of a national community. In this way the Liberal party would be a truly national party, the embodiment of the complex partnership in which he believed. The policies on which Liberals could agree would reflect the interdependence of all segments of Canadian society, and so would maintain and foster social harmony. Liberal-minded men might not always vote for the Liberal party. They might be frustrated by its apparent insensitivity to their grievances and turn elsewhere. One of King's aims as party leader was to convince such men that his party was responsive to their interests. In the 1920s King's major concern had been the Progressives. These men were not Tories according to King's definition because they favoured Canadian autonomy and a lower tariff. Their demands might be immoderate but their grievances were legitimate. The problem was to convince them that by joining with other liberal-minded men against the Tories they would accomplish more than they could as a third party. King therefore became a spokesman for the farmers within the Liberal party in order to win their confidence and bring the Progressives back into the Liberal fold. As he had explained to a correspondent in 1929: "The supreme effort of my leadership of the party has been to keep its aims and purposes so broad that it might be possible to unite at times of crisis under one banner those parties, which for one reason or another, have come to be separated from the Liberal party, though in reality belonging thereto, and to make the Liberal party such that, in the course of time, third parties would fade out altogether, and a united front be presented to a very determined foe by those who seek a larger liberty."[2] King had been remarkably successful. By 1932 most of the Progressives had rejoined the Liberal party. The party which he now led once more included representatives from all the major groups and regions of Canada.

Bringing liberal-minded men together in one political party was only the first step. The party had to provide an opportunity for these men to present their point of view and to appreciate the points of view of other groups and regions. King, as party leader, had the demanding task of guiding the discussions within the party. He had to be alert to grievances or to contradictory aspirations to ensure that significant issues were not ignored. He then had to ensure that all affected groups contributed to the discussion and that all points of view were adequately explained and understood. As leader he had to restrain the enthusiasts and placate the dissidents, distinguish between the essential and the peripheral, propose concessions and compromises, and keep the discussion going until agreement had been reached. He needed a sure judgment of men and of policies, an acute sense of timing, and a mastery of the arts of persuasion if his method of leadership was to succeed.

King's approach varied. On some topics he was sure he knew what liberal-minded Canadians wanted. They would always agree, for example, that Canada should affirm her autonomy in her relations with Great Britain. Autonomy was a complex concept because it did not mean independence but as a minimum it meant that Canada was not a colony, subservient to Great Britain. King believed that he knew when this autonomy was threatened and what the attitude of the Liberal party should be. Even then, however, he did not announce any decision until his party had been informed. Nor was this a mere formality. Members of caucus were free to question the decision or to raise objections, and the discussion would continue until everybody acquiesced. Usually there was no difficulty because most Liberals did agree on autonomy in principle and did not often differ on how to apply the principle in a given situation. If there was a debate King almost always had his way. He had a special status as an experienced leader who had attended imperial conferences and knew the leading politicians in Great Britain and the other Dominions. He was also respected for his political judgment in this area; no Liberal was likely to forget, for example, that it was King who had made Canadian

8

autonomy the central issue of the 1926 election against the advice of most of his followers, and had been vindicated by an unexpected victory. In any case, most Liberals were more concerned with domestic issues and attached less importance to international relations. Thus any individual who questioned King's proposal was unlikely to find much support in caucus. He might express his views at length but, unless he was unusually intransigent, the pressure to accept the position of the majority would help to bring him into line. The final consent might be given grudgingly but there would be consent. King's proposal would become the party line.

In other areas King was less sure that he knew where the national interest lay. Western and eastern Liberals regularly disagreed over the proper level of tariffs or freight rates. King took it for granted that liberal-minded men would not favour highly protective tariffs or freight rates which exploited western grain growers, but free trade or highly sub-sidized freight rates were also unacceptable. Agreement would have to be found somewhere between these extremes but no abstract concept of the national partnership could reveal what the ideal level of tariffs or freight rates should be. To reach decisions on such topics King relied on debate within the party. The frank exchange of views would clarify the different positions and moderate demands on both sides. Eventually, because these were liberal-minded men, a compromise would be found which would become the official position of the party.

King was less obtrusive in these discussions but this made his role even more demanding. The party caucus was the sounding-board. King's views might be affected by opinions expressed in his correspondence, in news-paper editorials, or in casual conversations, but the discussion in caucus was his major source of information on the political implications of the issue. Usually he listened, trying to assess the mood of the members and waiting until he felt the various points of view had been effectively presented. If he considered that the opinion of one region had not been adequately stressed, he might provoke a fuller exposition by directing a specific question to somebody from that region. At times he might even remind caucus of the views of a group which had failed to elect a Liberal to speak for it. When he felt that all points of view had been understood and when he sensed that agreement was possible, he would intervene, summing up the discussion and suggesting a compromise which he thought would be acceptable. If some members still disagreed, the topic would be reintroduced at the next meeting of caucus and the discussion would continue. On rare occasions, when King feared that debate would only confirm divergent points of view and make eventual concessions more difficult, he might speak first, outlining the difficulties and appealing for moderation. But if the technique varied, the objective was the same. King was guiding caucus to a decision on which all could agree.

King's approach to party leadership was thus a logical extension of his concept of national unity. The nation was a partnership of diverse groups bound together by their commitment to the national community; the Liberal party, by including liberal-minded men from all groups, was the political embodiment of this partnership. The terms of this partnership, however, had to be constantly modified and revised as the aspirations of each partner shifted or as new grievances were articulated. National unity, as King understood it, was an ever-shifting balance; the party caucus was the forum in which the partners negotiated the modifications. Because the Liberal party was composed of liberal-minded men, it would be able to agree, and because it represented the major elements of Canadian society, the policies it approved would redress any imbalance and help to maintain national unity.

The Liberal party thus provided the framework in which King operated. Leadership by consensus, however, is not a mechanical process; there were no political scales to weigh demands or to balance contradictory pressures. Even liberal-minded men might go on arguing indefinitely if they were not given some guidance and some direction. King relied on discussions within caucus but it was not enough to urge his followers to reach agreement. As party leader he had to be more than an impartial chairman or a judge; he had to make decisions and persuade the party to accept them. His contribution to party policy was not always obvious but it was often decisive. Over the years the cumulative effect of his leadership would shape the content of Liberal policies as well as the method of reaching agreement.

King's direct contribution to many decisions was difficult to assess because he had developed an approach to leadership which was appropriate to his personality. He had exceptional patience and self-control. He could accept prolonged discussions and delays even when the eventual decision seemed to him obvious and inevitable. Other leaders could operate more directly. Sir Wilfrid Laurier, his predecessor, could rely on his imposing presence and his pre-eminence as an orator to dominate his followers and on his personal charm to soothe his dissident followers. King had to be more subtle because as an individual he evoked less admiration and less affection. He might be tempted at times to rely on his position as party leader, to end the stress of indecision by imposing his will, but he rarely yielded to the temptation, sustained always by the conviction that eventually his followers would agree to the policies he approved.

His authority within the party depended more on respect for his political judgment than on personal loyalty. Even if his followers felt little affection for him they listened to him because they trusted his political wisdom and believed he could lead the party to power. He more than any other individual within the party would have to decide what issues were important and what solutions the party and the electorate would accept. His position as leader depended to an unusual degree on his judgment, on his capacity to assess and to respond successfully to changing circumstances.

Mackenzie King, like most politicians, arrived at his decisions almost intuitively. One of his outstanding qualities, however, was his exceptional sensitivity to political danger. He was constantly alert to political grievances which might threaten party unity and he sensed a potential risk long before most of his colleagues. His family background may account for his acute awareness of discord. In the King household strong opinions had been suppressed in the interests of family harmony. King's mother had dominated the household by indirect hints and by subtle manipulation. The young Mackenzie King had never rebelled; he had learned to interpret his mother's behaviour, to understand her unspoken wishes, and to conform to her will without any explicit directions. To all outward appearances it had been a harmonious and close-knit family but a boy nurtured in this environment might well develop an instinct for recognizing potential areas of conflict and an ever-present alertness to danger signals. Whatever the explanation, King's political judgment was marked by an acute sensitivity to friction within the Liberal party and an unusual capacity to forestall open conflict.

This sensitivity often saved King from political disaster but it also had its disadvantages. He saw the political process as a gradual readjustment of existing relationships, a sequence of decisions rather than any abrupt shift in policy. He could react quickly at a time of crisis but he did not react impulsively. He preferred to avoid mistakes, to minimize his losses, and to guard against defeat. If he believed a decision could safely be delayed or postponed, he could wait. His test for any measure was its effect on party unity or national unity and if this could be achieved by half-measures or by deflecting attention to less controversial topics, King felt no pressure to do more. It was not an approach which encouraged the analysis of fundamental social problems or the initiation of social change. Carried to the extreme, it could have led to a rigid comitment to the

11

status quo and an unwillingness to take any risks. His preference for avoiding controversy, however, was always subordinated to his awareness that strongly held grievances could not be ignored. His sensitivity to potential discord usually prevented him from being lulled into a false sense of security.

When political harmony seemed threatened, King's response was inevitably influenced by his philosophical assumptions. He was not a political philosopher but he did have political beliefs which shaped his assessment of political problems and guided him in his political decisions. He considered himself a liberal and although his definition of liberalism never went beyond platitudes, it did have some meaning for him. Liberalism, as King understood it, was social progress based on the expansion of liberty. Liberty was never precisely defined but in simple terms it meant the capacity of individuals or groups to influence the decisions which affected their lives. King often used freedom or autonomy as synonyms for liberty but the concept was the same. More important, he did not believe that the liberty of one group was necessarily extended at the expense of some other group. In an ideal society all would be free. Social harmony would still be possible because each group would freely recognize the autonomy of other groups and would voluntarily restrain its demands for the sake of a fuller liberty. If some men had grievances and threatened to disrupt the existing political harmony this meant to King that their liberty was too restricted and that their grievances had to be taken seriously. Liberal-minded men, representing all groups in society, could respond to this situation by removing some of the restraints and thus expanding the sum of liberty within the society.

It was easy for King's compatriots to overlook this philosophical basis for his political decisions because he himself was unable to articulate it. His own definitions of liberalism were so trite as to be almost meaningless: "Liberalism," he told the delegates to a Liberal convention in 1933, "is not any rigid set of doctrines or dogma; it is an attitude of mind, it is a way of looking at things, a broad generous attitude and outlook. I might have said that in its essence it is a thing essentially of the spirit, a spirit that loves liberty, not as a means of personal enjoyment, but as a means of the development of personality in one's self and one's friends, or for one's country, but for all mankind."[3] A few months later his liberalism had become even more abstract; it was now "the continuous releasing or unlocking of a great onward force—an energizing force, a vital force, a force that is forever serving all mankind."[4] Mankind, especially that portion of mankind which voted in Canadian elections, must have wondered what relevance this had to the urgent problems of the depres-

12

sion. When King described liberalism as "the principle of the future expressed in the general interests as against particular interests," and proclaimed that it was dedicated to "the cause of a larger freedom and a greater good for the masses of the people,"[5] few people took these platitudes seriously.

But if Mackenzie King seldom went beyond platitudes, his concept of liberalism nonetheless influenced his political decisions. It not only made him responsive to grievances but also helped to determine his response. He believed that a liberal should have a special concern for the less privileged groups. As an industrial consultant he had seen selfish and egocentric men on both sides of industrial disputes but he believed that management was better able to influence the decisions which affected it. If the industrial system had broken down, if a dispute had led to a strike or a lockout, the probability was that the worker's liberty had not been adequately respected. King, as a liberal, reacted in the same way to political crises. If the existing political arrangements were under attack, his instinctive sympathy was with the less privileged—the farmers, the workers, and the middle class, the men who needed some protection against the more powerful vested interests.

This was not a blueprint for social reform. King saw no need for political action when political harmony did not seem threatened. He accepted the broad framework of Canadian society; his objective was to adjust, to establish a new equilibrium when well-intentioned men found the existing partnership unsatisfactory. He paid little attention to underprivileged groups which were too small or too ineffective to disturb the political balance—he did little to improve the status of Indians or of women because in his day their grievances were not effectively articulated. Nor was he attracted to radical proposals which would alter the existing social structure. But if King's liberalism provided no utopian vision of an ideal society, it did assume that society would evolve, and that by favouring the less privileged groups Canada would become a freer and hence a better society. His liberal faith might be vague and imprecise but it did influence his assumptions about how political divisions ought to be reconciled.

Mackenzie King's leadership thus rested on solid foundations. His version of a national partnership was not the only possible definition of national unity but it was a logical definition, and his view of the Liberal party as representing the interests of all the major groups in Canada was a logical extension of this definition. His emphasis on frank discussions within the party and his insistence that prior agreement was necessary on all party decisions were consistent with his concept of party unity. His personality, his political judgment, and his liberalism had their limitations but they too were appropriate to the kind of political leadership which King exercised. It was a coherent structure, strengthened by the mutual reinforcing of its component parts.

There were some disadvantages to the structure. King could never become a popular leader by appealing directly to voters for their personal support. There could be no fireside chats, no public discussion of controversial issues, no campaigns to shape public opinion because King's approach forced him to resolve all controversies within the confines of the party. He might have to speak in the House or to the press before the party had agreed on a policy but he could only stress the complexity of the problem and appeal for tolerance and patience. He had to resort to generalities or platitudes because he could not take sides publicly until the party had approved a policy. Even then it was not easy to be forceful or dynamic because the decision was almost certain to be a carefully balanced compromise; he could explain it and defend it but it was not easy to dramatize it. King was essentially a party leader. He was a national leader only through his leadership of a national party.

Most Canadians underestimated King because they saw only the public image. His opponents convinced themselves that he was weak and indecisive. They grudgingly conceded that he got results; R. J. Manion, when comparing him with other Canadian leaders, described him as "the best politician—if by that term one implies skill in winning elections."[6] But Manion could not explain King's success. Here was a man who had "never been very popular in the House or country," a man who had apparently survived by a combination of good luck and opportunism.[7] King may have been favoured by events and by incompetent opponents but good fortune alone cannot explain political longevity. And to say that King was an opportunist is to say very little. King certainly wanted political power, and he could capitalize on the mistakes of his political opponents. But opportunism implies a willingness to say or do anything to win. A leader who is only an opportunist may gain office but he is not likely to build a stable party and enjoy a long political career. King's opportunism was guided and restrained by his concept of leadership and his own political philosophy. Critics who saw only his responsiveness to public opinion forgot that at times he could also resist popular pressures or advocate policies which were unpopular.

Even within the party there were doubts about King's capacity as leader during the years of opposition. In October 1932 R. J. Cromie, the maverick editor of the Vancouver *Sun*, openly insisted that King must go. He conceded that King was able and honest but argued that he had nothing to offer a nation in an economic crisis: "He is set. He is stodgy. He has got himself into a rut. Withdrawn within himself and living the intellectual life of a recluse, he is out of touch with trends and with people. He is living in a groove as deep and as narrow as a political grave."[8] Most Liberals were more circumspect in public but they sometimes expressed similar sentiments in private. Charles Dunning once argued that returning to active politics would be a waste of time because King, that "charming, polite, hospitable and inert mass," stood in the way of constructive action.[9] "Chubby" Power, who as a member of the Liberal caucus was closer to King, was less critical but even he had doubts about King's capacity to adapt to changing conditions. Emboldened on one occasion by Dutch courage, he told King frankly that he considered him an old-fashioned Whig and that he would eventually be replaced by some younger radical within the party.[10]

King paid little attention to these criticisms. He knew that he was not popular. He also knew that many Liberals wanted a more dynamic leader and wanted more positive and dramatic policies. But King could not change his personality or his style of leadership. He was sure that his approach was the only way to keep the party united and to respond responsibly to national needs. It was typical of King that he calmly shrugged off Power's outburst with the comment that "Opposition breeds unrest & discontent, it was ever thus."[11] In 1932 he was confident that the Liberals would defeat Bennett at the next election and that success at the polls would restore the confidence of his followers in his leadership.

King had good reason to believe that his position was still secure. His approach to leadership made it difficult for rivals to emerge. His major colleagues were forceful and influential men within the party but their role as regional spokesmen was also a handicap. Their success as the advocate of the interests of their region made them less acceptable in other parts of the country. King was the only Liberal who was not identified with one group or region. His role as leader was to balance regional interests, to respond to the aspirations or the grievances of all sections of the party. He might not be popular but he had become the only figure within the party who seemed to represent the national partnership. Unless he lost touch with some regions or lost the next election, his position as leader was secure.

In 1932 there was no assurance that any political leadership could be effective. King's approach was based on the conviction that all conflicts could be reconciled, but there was no certainty that the Liberal party or the country could remain united. If some regions became so alienated by the depression that they would no longer accept the half-loaf of compromise, the partnership might be dissolved. If the party was to survive it would require political judgment of a high order. King was by now a mature politician, with a coherent view of leadership, with more than a decade of experience as Liberal leader, who knew his colleagues and who knew a great deal about regional differences. But past experience might not be an appropriate guide in an unprecedented situation. In an era of social and political instability he would have to show a capacity for political leadership which his contemporaries had not yet discerned.

CHAPTER ONE

THE OTTAWA TRADE AGREEMENTS

IN THE SUMMER OF 1932 there were good reasons to question King's political judgment. He seemed almost oblivious to the growing conviction that the depression was more than a temporary recession and that radical changes in institutions and policies might be necessary. When other Liberals had suggested that the party advocate an expansion of social services, King had argued that the budget would have to be balanced before new expenditures could be considered.[1] When some of his followers had spoken in favour of inflation as a response to declining price levels, King had been shocked at such an immoral and irresponsible proposal.[2] The cause of the depression, according to him, was the decline in world trade. The solution, to the extent that the Canadian Government could solve the problem, was to increase trade by reducing tariffs and negotiating trade agreements with other countries. Radical measures were unnecessary and even to consider them was dangerous; they would divide the party. All would be well if Liberals would only concentrate on trade and tariffs.

King was insensitive to the changing climate of opinion because it did not seem important. He was already looking forward with confidence to the next election. He believed that Bennett had won the election of 1930 by irresponsible demagoguery, by his sweeping promises to end the depression, and that two years in office had exposed his dishonesty and his incompetence. The depression had progressively worsened because the Tory policy of higher tariffs had aggravated the crisis. By concentrating on trade policies the Liberals would be attacking the Conservatives at their weakest point and offering voters a positive and constructive alternative. This was the issue on which the party and the country could be united, which would reconcile east and west, and which would restore the Liberals to office. Success seemed so certain and so alluring that King saw no need to discuss other issues.

17

I

R. B. Bennett reinforced King's narrow view of the political situation because he too continued to stress the central importance of trade and tariff policies. He had raised the tariff to the highest levels in Canadian experience; his hopes now centred on the Imperial Economic Conference, scheduled to meet in Ottawa in July, where his objective was to establish a protected market in Great Britain for Canada's natural products. There was good reason to be optimistic. The coalition National Government in Britain had already taken the first step by imposing duties on most imports and by temporarily exempting Dominion products from these tariffs. Bennett expected to have this temporary preference confirmed during the negotiations at Ottawa.

Bennett had even higher aspirations for the conference. The meeting at Ottawa was also to be a significant contribution to the traditional Conservative policy of closer relations with the Empire. The economic crisis offered an opportunity to foster Imperial unity, to bind the mother country and its Dominions closer together by economic ties. "From that Conference may arise a power which will bring enduring harmony out of chaos," Bennett told the House of Commons when it prorogued in May. "Canada believes that the closer economic association of the British Empire will herald the dawn of a new and greater era of prosperity."[3] He greeted the delegates to the convention with the same rhetoric. "No one," he said, "can now deny that the time for action has arrived, and that the British Empire at last is to fulfil its long-time hope of real and helpful closer Empire economic association."[4]

Bennett's tariff policies were inconsistent with his high Imperial hopes, although he was probably not aware of the contradiction. Canada wanted non-Empire wheat and other natural products excluded from the British market by tariffs. This might benefit Canadian producers but it would also mean higher costs for British consumers. British negotiators would insist on equivalent advantages in the Canadian market for the textiles and machinery which were Britain's major exports. Would the Canadian Government be willing to forgo its protection for Canadian factories already operating below capacity? In the past the hopes for an Imperial trading bloc had foundered on the economic aspirations of each of the Dominions. This economic nationalism was, if anything, intensified by the depression. The delegates would not assemble at Ottawa to make sacrifices for an Imperial ideal but to find some solution to their own economic difficulties. For all the talk of Empire trade as a lofty ideal which could be an example to the world and lead humanity out of the slough of depression, the delegates would really come to bargain. For politicians facing an economic crisis, charity would begin at home. The strongest pressure for co-operation came, not from the Imperial tie but from the publicity which all Imperial governments had given to the conference. If negotiations failed and delegates returned empty-handed, some of them might soon be out of office. If new trading patterns were established it would be more from desperation than from idealism.

The harsh fact was that Imperial solidarity was a myth. It was obvious, for example, that trade agreements and preferential tariffs would mean little if any Dominion could subsequently alter the value of its currency unilaterally. A stable exchange rate was required. The delegates understood the importance of the monetary question but the interests of the different parts of the Empire were so divergent that nothing could be done.[5] South Africa, as a gold-producing country, wanted the restoration of the gold standard. Great Britain, however, had already devalued the pound, and the Australian and New Zealand pounds were at a discount to the pound sterling. The problem was referred to in the correspondence which preceded the conference but no constructive proposals were advanced.[6] None of the Dominions was prepared to sacrifice its control over its currency in the interests of Imperial unity.

Canada was no exception. The Canadian dollar was at a premium to the British pound because Canada had to borrow money in the United States and a sound dollar would maintain its credit-rating there. W. C. Clark, the Deputy-Minister of Finance and Bennett's adviser on monetary policy, bluntly argued that Canada's commercial and credit relations with the United States were more important than the corresponding ties with the Empire. His conclusion was that Canada must retain control over the exchange level of the Canadian dollar and so should reject any proposals that would bind the Canadian dollar to sterling.*

Nor was there much evidence of Imperial sentiment in the Canadian preparations for the tariff negotiations. Five months before the conference convened R. B. Bennett reassured frightened Canadian businessmen that their interests would not be sacrificed. "We will meet at the Imperial Conference," he wrote, "as practical men, not as visionaries, and will deal with our problems on a business basis or not at all. Of that you can be sure."[7]

*Bennett Papers, "Monetary and Financial Questions," pp. 112587–607. The memorandum is unsigned but is attributed to W. C. Clark in Bennett Papers, pp. 112697–711. In its final report the Conference admitted its failure to resolve the exchange problems: "While certain of the states here represented hold very definite views on the question of the most desirable [monetary] standard, the Conference refrains from making any recommendations on the subject in view of the fact that the question is shortly to be discussed at an international conference." Report of Imperial Economic Conference, 1932, p. 31.

He kept his word. The British Government had asked for an advance list of the items on which Canada was prepared to concede tariff reductions. The list was not produced until the British delegates reached Ottawa and even then the proposed concessions were so minor that it was almost insulting.[8] Bennett could hardly have been surprised because he had entrusted the task of drawing up the list to the Canadian Manufacturers' Association, which felt a natural reluctance to encourage manufactured imports from Great Britain. Even Bennett, however, felt some embarrassment at the result. "It is rather disheartening," he told the Secretary of the association, "to think that such a list should be submitted to intelligent men as indicating the extent to which Canada might be able to improve trade and commerce within the United Kingdom."[9]

This was an unpropitious beginning to a conference which was supposed to bring enduring harmony out of chaos. So much seemed at stake, however, that all governments sent impressive delegations. The British Government was represented, for example, by seven Cabinet Ministers and a much larger number of senior officials.[10] It was also a hard-working conference. There was the inevitable rhetoric about Imperial unity, the need for action, and the opportunity to lead the way to economic recovery at the first plenary session on July 20 but then the conference broke up into five committees to conduct the formal business. Each delegation also had to have informal meetings to discuss day-by-day developments as well as constant meetings with other delegations on specific questions. It was August 20 before the exhausted delegates met in the final plenary session and went home.

For Canada the most important negotiations were with Great Britain. Bennett was convinced from the beginning that the British delegates could not go home empty-handed, and he took full advantage of the situation.[11] He produced the Canadian Manufacturers' Association list without any apologies.[12] Canadian officials suggested that the concessions might increase British exports to Canada by as much as eighty million dollars. The British delegation was not amused; their estimate came to less than ten million dollars. Stanley Baldwin, always diplomatic, did protest that the proposals were hardly consistent with "the Imperial purposes of the Conference expressed by the Prime Minister of Canada,"[13] but Bennett was unmoved. He was quite prepared to offer preferences on items not manufactured in Canada, and so divert business from American to British manufacturers, but he made few concessions at the expense of Canadian enterprises. On the other hand, he insisted on a British preference for Canadian exports. One of his demands, for a tariff on foreign bacon which would benefit Canadian producers, almost split the British delegation. Bennett insisted, encouraged on this occasion by word from one of the British delegates that a firm stand would succeed.[14] He held out until the last possible moment; the ship carrying the delegates home had to be delayed for one day.[15] In the end his gamble succeeded; as Chamberlain put it, the conference could not be allowed to fail by their refusal to levy a duty on meat.[16] There was unconscious irony in Bennett's closing statement as Chairman of the conference when he extolled the spirit of co-operation and this "propitious beginning" to a "closer Imperial association."[17]

Neville Chamberlain, the dominant figure in the British delegation, was less impressed by the spirit of co-operation. He did not enjoy his visit; even the fishing in Canada seemed to him "a coarse, unscientific affair,"[18] and the business of bargaining in Ottawa was even more distasteful. His diary entry for the last day of the conference scathingly says of Bennett that "he alternately blustered, sobbed, bullied, prevaricated, delayed and obstructed, to the very last moment."[19] Chamberlain convinced himself, however, that in spite of Bennett the conference had been a major triumph: "The countries of the Empire have been drifting apart pretty rapidly. We have been in time to stop the rot . . . Most of our difficulties centred round the personality of Bennett. Full of high Imperial sentiments, he has done little to put them into practice. Instead of guiding the conference in his capacity as chairman, he has acted merely as the leader of the Canadian delegation. In that capacity he has strained our patience to the limit . . . That in spite of all this we should have won through, has been due to our unalterable patience, coupled with our complete confidence in one another."[20]

Canada, together with the other Dominions, would have advantages in the British market for wheat, apples, lumber, and for some meat and dairy products, based on a preferential tariff or a quota arrangement. The preference on wheat meant little because Dominion exports exceeded the requirements of the United Kingdom and so world market prices would prevail. Some regions of Canada, especially the Maritimes and British Columbia, however, would have a more secure market for their products. The total impact on Canadian exports might not be great but it would help. At the same time the Canadian tariff changes would cause little hardship for Canadian manufacturers. The British preference was to be increased either by reducing the tariff on British goods or by raising tariffs on foreign imports. In practice this meant diverting some trade from the United States to the United Kingdom but the amount would be an insignificant proportion of total British exports. The Canadian Government did also agree that the new tariff schedules would be low enough to allow

British manufacturers to compete on reasonable terms with their Canadian counterparts but, in practice, it tended to define any effective competition as unreasonable, and, even after reductions, the new schedules gave ample protection to domestic industries.[21] Bennett might exaggerate his achievement at the Conference but he could certainly claim that he had won some concessions and given very little in return.[22]

Mackenzie King had been sceptical about the results of the conference from the beginning. Bennett's rhetoric of Empire had no attractions for him because he objected to the infringements on Canadian autonomy which an Imperial trading bloc implied. He did not believe that Imperial unity depended on trade; as he would explain to one of the British delegates, "The political problem & the economic one are wholly separate & distinct, & the mistake the tories make is confusing them."[23] He was equally sceptical about the possibility of expanding trade. His analysis, in a conversation with Winston Churchill who visited Ottawa earlier in the year, was that "the tory party wd. never let Br. mffrs. compete in this country with Canadians, & it was Br. mffrs. England was alone concerned with. If Bennett tried to throw the mffrs., the mffrs. and the party wd. throw him."[24] During the budget debate in April he had also argued that even if trade within the Empire was increased it would have no impact on the depression if it was achieved at the expense of trade with other parts of the world. The objective must be to expand the total international trade. Any Imperial trade agreements which hampered negotiating future agreements with other countries would in the long run hinder economic recovery.[25] King had thought it wise to put this statement of the Liberal position on record, but he was not unduly worried about the outcome of the conference. Bennett, he was sure, would behave like a Tory and protect Canadian manufacturers at the expense of Imperial or international trade.

He avoided any public comments before and during the Ottawa meetings. If the conference failed, Bennett would not be able to accuse the Liberals of having undermined his position during the negotiations.[26] King was less restrained in private. He entertained many of the British delegates, heard a good deal of gossip about Bennett's behaviour, and freely expressed his aversion to such proceedings. He reminded two of the British officials that Bennett would soon be defeated and that the Liberals would be more generous when they returned to office; he might well comment in his diary that he "was perhaps a little too outspoken."[27] In any case, the strained relations between the British and Canadian delegates were encouraging. The British press would soon hear of Bennett's boorish behaviour and its comments would be helpful when the time came to attack the agreements.[28]

King remained reticent even after the agreements were signed. He was sure, even before detailed study, that they would be unacceptable: "What I feel about the Conference is that it was a wrong method—the bargaining—that the aim of greater freedom of trade was achieved in very small measure and that there is a lot of humbug about the whole business, a ballyhoo for nothing, with jingo emotionalism in evidence above all else. One sickens at the way different delegates try to make out it was a great success."[29] But King did not give vent to his disgust in public. As he wrote to one Liberal at the end of the conference: "Just now Imperial sentiment is at its zenith. Nothing is to be gained by antagonizing it unnecessarily."[30]

His caution was strengthened by his awareness that even some Liberals were influenced by this sentiment and also by the advantages which their region might derive from the British preference. Ian Mackenzie, for example, reported that many British Columbians felt that "a good beginning had been made" and suggested that the party, instead of attacking the agreements, should merely point out that the Liberals were willing to go much farther.[31]

A by-election in the rural riding of Huron South early in Otcober, six weeks after the conference, forced King to say something sooner than he intended. The former Liberal member had won by a majority of fewer than four hundred votes in 1930 but King had been looking forward to increasing this margin by stressing the unpopular protective tariff policies of the Bennett government. The Ottawa Agreements complicated the situation. The Conservatives were campaigning vigorously and, as was to be expected, the Ministers who spoke gave a glowing account of the results of the conference. "I feel," King wrote to Mitchell Hepburn, the provincial Liberal leader, "that there is nothing that matters quite so much as winning that particular contest. It is the first since the Conference, and whatever the results may be they will be viewed by the public generally as being significant of the way in which the country as a whole views the Conference."[32] Hepburn improved the Liberal chances by persuading the Progressive candidate to withdraw in return for a promise not to have a Liberal oppose the Progressive member in the next provincial election.[33] King prodded the Liberals in the constituency into activity, persuaded others to campaign there, and agreed to address two meetings himself. He would have to announce the Liberal position on the agreements.

King did not speak without first consulting some prominent Liberals. Early in September a small group met at Batterwood House, Vincent

23

Massey's home in Port Hope. In addition to King and Massey, as President of the National Liberal Federation, there was Norman Lambert, Secretary of the federation, Ernest Lapointe from Quebec, J. L. Ralston from the Maritimes, and J. W. Dafoe from Winnipeg. The informal discussions ranged over many topics. Of immediate concern, however, was the reaction to the Ottawa Agreements. The group seems to have been less inclined than King to challenge the results of the conference but eventually they agreed that the Liberals should promise to restore the tariff to the level of 1930, to offer a British preference of 50 per cent across the board, and to advocate reciprocal trade agreements with all interested countries.[34]

When King spoke in Huron South he was quite restrained. He merely deplored the Conservative insult to the intelligence of the voters when they asked people to endorse agreements before the detailed tariff changes had been announced, and explained the tariff measures which the Liberals would introduce.[35] The results of the by-election, however, strengthened his conviction that the Liberal party should attack the Ottawa Agreements openly, for the Liberal candidate was elected with a majority of almost two thousand votes. For King it was "a day to be remembered—a terrible day for the Bennett administration. It lets the Empire see what Canada thinks of Bennett."[36] It would also help dubious Liberals to see that the trade agreements were not as popular as they feared.

Parliament met early in October to ratify the trade treaties. The detailed tariff changes would not be known until the agreements were tabled in the House and so King, in the debate on the Address, concentrated on the errors and omissions of the government's domestic policies. He did condemn Bennett's style of bargaining during the conference but announced that if the agreements were consistent with the Liberal policy of increasing trade by lowering tariffs, his party would give its "wholehearted support."[37] Bennett, convinced that the conference had been a personal triumph, made a caustic reply. He denounced the rumours of bickering during the negotiations as no more than the fabrications of base journalists. He taunted the Leader of the Opposition for supporting the agreements with one breath and opposing them with the next. Criticism of the government's great achievement, Bennett concluded, could only be explained by jealousy; King was showing "his spleen that there should have been a successful conference in which he did not take part."[38] King dismissed Bennett's speech as "one of his tirades"[39] but he had other things to worry about. Some Liberals were still reluctant to concede that the agreements would have to be opposed.

King did not force the issue at the first meeting of caucus. According

24

to his account of the discussion he did not express any opinion. Lapointe, however, "made a strong appeal against approving the agreements." Others were less decisive. Motherwell, from Saskatchewan, wanted to see the detailed tariff changes first; Ian Mackenzie opposed the agreements in principle but favoured approval on grounds of expediency. King concluded that the majority wanted to oppose the agreements but he may not have been as confident as he sounded.[40] Certainly he was greatly relieved when Bennett announced the new tariff schedules. "It was clear before he had got very far—beyond the first paragraph, that we wd. have to oppose them."[41] Next day he conceded that many Liberals would want to approve them on the grounds of expediency, "popular sentiment and the press being for them," but his duty was clear. He would fight for Liberal principles.[42]

He convinced the caucus next morning. His diary entry describes the meeting:

The party made an all-important decision today. We had caucus at 11 and decided to oppose the approval of the Trade Treaty between Canada and Great Britain . . . I thought it well not to let the members get into a discussion so told Marcil [Chairman] to ask someone to explain the agreements knowing no one would be able to do so. I then told him to call on me, and I spoke for about half an hour giving a summary of the situation as I saw it—that their approval meant our endorsation of the principle of protection, of raising general tariff higher than ever, under cover of giving British preferences, of maintaining the tariff at a high rate for 5 years, thus restricting our power to make trade treaties or agreements with other countries, that it meant interference of one part of Empire in affairs of the other, creation of an imperial Zollverein, and an Economic unit, and above all that it made more difficult our securing wider world markets. I was given a most attentive hearing and great applause at the close. Malcolm followed endorsing what I said in principle, but not being sure whether we should vote against the agreement . . . Lapointe followed strongly endorsing my position. Mackenzie was favourable to the principles, but was fearful of B.C. resenting our opposing to the agreement. Illsley [sic] was the one person who said he wd have to support the agreement because of apples in his constituency . . . I had to intervene again for fear of our getting apart, made clear the broader principles were most important, that they could support items on the resolut'n. I then said I wd. like to say on Monday what I had said this morning. There was general approval. I added which meant that we could not approve the agreement. There was applause again & I took the matter as settled . . . It was really a remarkable achievement, having the caucus line up almost to a man in opposition to the agreement, with all the press propaganda, etc.[43]

Some Liberals were still uneasy, even after King's explanation. Ralston, for example, wrote to King after the caucus meeting to explain that, while he was opposed to the treaty in principle, *"our straight opposition to it will be construed and used not as a blow at Bennett but at our British relationship. I can see the cartoons now of the Liberal party slapping Britain in the face while Uncle Sam applauds."*[44]

King still took the matter as settled. His speech in the House took three hours to deliver but it was largely a repetition of the arguments he had presented in caucus. How, he asked, "can a party that hopes to be consistent in the matter of principle be expected to take a position which will completely deny all that it has been standing for in the past, and all that it stands for at the present time?" In his opinion the Conference was nothing more than "a tory conspiracy" to create a "protectionist zollverein." He did make one gesture to appease the worried Liberals. He admitted that many would like to support some features of the agreement, such as "those which in any way tend to increase the possibilities of greater demand for Canadian products." He then read a temporizing amendment although he did not introduce it as a motion.[45] This, as he noted in his diary, would give hesitant Liberals "something they could point to as being what some of them would like to have done."[46]

Mackenzie King's efforts did not end there. The Conservatives were quite unprepared for this opposition and were not ready for a prolonged debate.[47] King was determined to show that the Liberal criticism was more than a mere matter of form; if the Conservatives would not speak it was up to the Liberals to keep the House in session. "This morning another caucus was held," Norman Lambert reported to Dafoe two days later, "and under the advocacy of a strong deliverance from Mr. King, decided to carry on the opposition debate for the balance of the week."[48] The debate, in fact, continued for two weeks. Bennett could not believe that the Liberals really objected to the trade concessions he had so brilliantly negotiated. The only logical explanation must be King's resentment at his triumph. "Was it wounded vanity and pride?" he asked; "was it resentment that he was no longer in the spotlight but 'on the spot'?" Bennett then answered these questions in the affirmative.[49] But the Liberals at least had been convinced. When the vote was finally taken only one Liberal voted for the treaty. J. L. Ilsley, from the Annapolis Valley, was still worried about apples.*

When Parliament adjourned late in November King was more than satisfied. For two years Bennett had been promising that an Imperial Economic Conference would provide the answer to Canada's economic difficulties. But Bennett had remained true to his high-tariff principles. King

---

*In the treaty Canadian apples were guaranteed a tariff preference over apples from foreign countries of three shillings and sixpence per bushel.

was sure that the Conference had been a failure and that its failure would soon be recognized. It was now only a matter of time until Bennett and his government would be defeated. "I have never seen Bennett look more completely exhausted & worried than he did today & particularly to-night," he commented with satisfaction. "It wd. have taken very little to bring on a collapse. He has come to the end of his rope."[50]

The Liberal party and its leader had faced the challenge, had remained true to their principles, and King recorded in his diary his conviction that both party and leader would soon receive their reward:

I never felt more relieved, or more rejoiced, or a greater peace in my heart than I do today with what there has been of real achievement in the past two months. Like Paul I feel with respect to that period of time that I have fought the good fight, I have finished my course, I have kept faith, and I believe with him that henceforth there is laid up for me in the future of Liberalism in Canada the crown of victory. The battle in Parliament has been splendid. I have led the party with vigour, with insight & judgement, I believe. We should have fought more on the question of principle . . . The party too should have fought the tariff in detail & for a longer period—but one cannot compel men to do what they should, and they were persuaded to the limit. In any event we have made our position clear, & from now on it will continue to be justified from day to day & month to month, not only in Canada, but throughout the Br. Empire.[51]

Mackenzie King had good reason to be pleased with his leadership during these months—even if St. Paul might also have added a warning against the sin of pride.

In his last diary entry for 1932 Mackenzie King looked back with un-qualified satisfaction on his achievements: "I believe it has been the best year of my life," he wrote. Surely he was "being guided by Divine powers" and would be "their instrument in helping to bring about conditions on earth more in accord with what they are in the Kingdom of Heaven."[52] The triumph of liberalism and of the Liberal leader seemed assured.

27

CHAPTER TWO

THE NEW LIBERALISM

MACKENZIE KING was confident but he had not been lulled into a false sense of security. In a two-party system a Conservative defeat would mean a Liberal victory. A new party, however, would disrupt this simple equation. The first steps had already been taken in the summer of 1932 to form a third party, the Co-operative Commonwealth Federation. The delegates would meet at Regina in July 1933 to approve the party platform, better known as the Regina Manifesto, and to confirm the choice of J. S. Woodsworth as leader. The formation of the C.C.F. coincided with the lowest point of the depression; its socialist philosophy provided an explanation for the economic crisis and its platform offered solutions. Many Canadians, frustrated by their own impotence in the face of spreading unemployment, or of crop failures and disappearing markets, were increasingly sceptical of politicians who still argued about tariffs and balanced budgets. In a world where the capitalist system seemed to have collapsed, the socialism of the C.C.F. could have a wide appeal.

King saw the danger. In January 1933 he told a friend:

If we had an election tomorrow, we would, without question, sweep the country. I doubt if Mr. Bennett's fate would not be equal to Mr. Meighen's when we came into office in 1921 and [he] did not have a single seat in six provinces out of nine. Unfortunately, we would meet to some extent with the same kind of misfortune as we did in 1921, through the inroads of a third party—a combination of farmer and labour—the Co-operative Commonwealth Federation they call themselves. Inflation of the currency and freeing society of the capitalist system is, at the moment, their main objective. Western Canada, in particular, where the farmers have suffered terribly through low prices, appears to be ready to support anything which promises to increase the nominal values which they are called upon to meet.[1]

King would continue to oppose the Conservative government but in 1933 he would also direct his attention towards this new threat. By the end of the year the Liberal party had responded to the "thunder on the left."

28

I

Socialism, as a political philosophy, had no attractions for King. It was inconsistent with his version of liberalism because, like Toryism, it rejected his ideal of a social partnership. Conservatives wanted to exploit political power for the benefit of capitalists; socialists wanted to exploit political power for the benefit of the working class. By accepting the concept of the class struggle they threatened national unity as King understood the term. This meant that socialists, unlike the Progressives of the 1920s, were not misguided Liberals who could be reunited with the Liberal party. As he explained to an advocate of a conciliatory policy: "The C.C.F. movement to my mind, is something wholly different from the old Progressive movement. The distinguishing feature of the Co-operative Commonwealth Federation is that it stands for the nationalisation of industry, land, banking, etc. Moreover, leading members of the C.C.F. have declared that their antagonism to the Liberal party is as strong as their antagonism to the Tory party. In the circumstances, they cannot be regarded in any sense as allies."[2]

Socialists, however, even if they were not Liberals, were somehow not as immoral as Tories. Their heart was in the right place because their sympathies were on the side of the less privileged groups in society. Their sentiments were admirable even if their solutions were unacceptable. King thought of R. B. Bennett as a narrow-minded and arrogant demagogue, but he admired J. S. Woodsworth for his idealism, for his "real conviction and vision."[3] Woodsworth might be mistaken but King never questioned his sincerity and his integrity.

This distinction between socialist aims and socialist policies shaped King's response to the C.C.F. party. Socialism was not the answer but King was ready to admit that it could be attractive to well-intentioned men. Liberal-minded Canadians, driven by desperation or by concern for those who were suffering, might support the C.C.F. if no other party offered an alternative. The Liberal party would have to criticize the co-operative commonwealth as a solution but it would also have to show its concern for the underprivileged. "Opposition to socialism or a socialist state," King stressed, "is not to be regarded as opposition to so-called social or humanitarian legislation."[4] The Liberals must appeal to potential C.C.F. supporters by showing that they too had a policy of social reform.

King had never been enthusiastic about a Liberal programme which included specific promises. As he explained to a western Liberal in January 1933: "There are always dangers that anything in the nature of a platform may become a target for opposing parties. It would be said that anything not included had been left out by design, and with respect to what is included there is bound to be the assertion that it goes either too far or it does not go far enough, depending upon the point of view of the audience to be addressed." But the emergence of the C.C.F. could not be ignored. Liberal principles and Liberal expressions of social concern might no longer be enough to retain the support of men trapped by the depression. The same letter continues: "However, the value of something definite outweighs the risks in other particulars and, if sufficient care is taken with the wording, I see no reason why we should not be able to get out a statement of policies sufficiently comprehensive to cover everything that is essential at the present time."[5]

One essential issue, and the one that most concerned King, was the question of inflation. The broad outlines of Liberal policy on trade, tariffs, and railways were clear enough, and King foresaw no serious difficulties in drafting a policy statement on which the party could agree. Monetary policy was different. The Ginger Group—the United Farmer and Labour M.P.s who had played a leading role in the formation of the C.C.F. —had moved an amendment during the budget debate of 1932 advocating the printing of money to depreciate the Canadian dollar. But support for inflation had not been confined to this group. Many of the Liberals from the prairies and from British Columbia had favoured supporting the Ginger Group amendment.[6] King had avoided a split within the party at the time but it was not an issue which could be ignored much longer. Western members in the House of Commons, whether Farmers, Labour, or Liberal, were acting as spokesmen for a region in which monetary policy had displaced the tariff as the central issue in politics. "There were two ways one could become popular in the west," according to J. G. Gardiner; "one was to hammer the banks and one was to hammer the Tories."[7] Hammering the bankers, who appeared to control credit and currency, became an even more satisfying outlet for western frustrations as the prestige of the Conservative party declined. Early in 1933 Norman Lambert reported to King that " 'inflation' has swept like a fire over the prairies."[8] It was a fire that would burn many fingers before it was put out.

Orthodox financial theories made no distinction between inflation and theft. Investors who provided funds for loans and mortgages would be robbed if they were repaid in depreciated currency. Contracts would mean nothing if the value of money could be deliberately manipulated. The uncontrolled inflation in Germany after the war was still a frightening spectre, with its stories of paper money in wheelbarrows to pay for a loaf of bread. Economic recovery, it was assumed, depended on financial stability and the confidence of lenders that Canadian governments and Canadian businessmen would pay their debts in honest money. Bennett was among the orthodox and his view of financial integrity was reinforced by his reliance on the sale of Dominion of Canada bonds to meet federal deficits. He had bluntly announced that his government "will stand for sound money. Let there be no mistake about that."[9]

Prairie farmers, however, were no longer impressed by the morality of the existing system. In December 1932 the price of wheat had dropped to below forty cents a bushel, the lowest price in Canadian history. For farmers, sound money meant that even if they harvested a crop, it now took three or four bushels to buy what one bushel used to buy. Interest rates on old mortgages did not decline—a contract was a contract—and so crop failures and price levels made it impossible for honest farmers to pay their debts. Land values had also declined and arrears of interest alone often exceeded the probable selling price of a farm. Loans for machinery repairs or replacements were out of the question; banks wanted adequate security and there was no security in farming in the 1930s. Something was obviously wrong with an economic system in which hard-working and honest men across the prairies were going bankrupt. For a debtor community, inflation offered some hope. If more money was put into circulation prices would rise. Farmers would get more money for their wheat and could buy what they needed and pay off their debts. The government had printed money to pay the cost of the war. Surely the depression was an even greater emergency? Whenever there were discussions of the economic crisis there was talk of credit and currency and their role in economic recovery. Inflation was an idea in search of a political party.

Mackenzie King was as orthodox as Bennett; he too saw inflation as a threat to the economic and social fabric. As he explained to an apprehensive T. A. Crerar in January 1933: "Confidence in the soundness of our national institutions lies pretty much at the foundation of all else that pertains to the nation's stability. If that were shaken, I do not know what might happen to the country as a whole."[10] In private he would commend "the determination of the Prime Minister not to yield to the inflationists' demands."[11] But inflation was not the only threat to national stability. A confrontation between east and west over monetary policy would also be disruptive. The attitude of western Canada, misguided though it might be, was nonetheless a political fact which could not be ignored. "I fear we are going to have a difficult time in reconciling the views of some of the members of our party on currency and credit problems,"[12] King confided to Crerar. But reconciled they must be if the Liberal party was to survive as a national party.

King had already prepared himself for the discussions. The small Liberal gathering at Batterwood House in September 1932 had discussed more than the tariff question. The Liberal position on unemployment and on railways had been on the agenda, and also the question of monetary policy. No record was kept of the discussions but a letter by J. W. Dafoe does give some impression of the informal procedure:

Most of the discussions were initiated by members of the group who were not actually in politics. Mr. Massey opened up most of the subjects, and the discussion in the earlier stages was pretty much carried on by him, Mr. Lambert and myself with Colonel Ralston taking a considerable part. Both Mr. King and Mr. Lapointe later came into each discussion after they had heard our views, and in the main they were acquiescent, subject to a reservation here and there suggested by their political experience. On the whole, the group was in fairly complete agreement on the various points that came up for discussion.[13]

The agreement on monetary policy was far from precise. Massey's summary was that "Canada requires the establishment of a Central or National Bank of Rediscount, and possibly of Issue." It went on to note that interest rates on Canadian Government bond issues were higher than necessary and that "the control of rediscount rates by a properly organized central bank might be a corrective to this evil."[14] Agreement on this should not have been too difficult. Most countries had the equivalent of a central bank, and an institution which "possibly" would issue currency and "might" reduce interest rates on government bonds was hardly a radical innovation. Nor should too much importance be given to King's agreement at this stage. His version of the decision as recorded in his diary was: "a national central bank of discount, get low rate of interest on securities, credit available at low rate of interest, like Bank of Eng.—issue currency by paying interest rate for."[15] It is obvious that King had only the vaguest idea of what a central bank could or should do.[16]

Shortly after the meeting King began to study the problem. The first step was to consult an expert and King turned to Norman Rogers for information. Norman McLeod Rogers was an intense intellectual, now in his late thirties, who had long aspired to a life of public service. He had been impressed by Mackenzie King's high principles and, almost a decade earlier, had written him an adulatory letter: "My object in writing to you now is simply this," he had explained, "if you have some hard task to be done, you will find me ready and happy to undertake it. Indeed, I shall not be quite happy until I have thrown myself into the work for which I have planned."[17]

King was more than willing to take advantage of such idealism. Rogers had come to Ottawa to work as King's secretary for two years. In 1929 he had joined the faculty of Queen's University but had volunteered to assist King from there if he could be of any help. When King became Leader of the Opposition he sorely missed the memoranda and draft speeches which O. D. Skelton had produced and was soon asking Rogers for material on a wide range of topics. Rogers had a tremendous capacity for work and needed only a hint to produce a memorandum or to come to Ottawa.

His influence on King is not easy to assess. He seems never to have doubted King's commitment to humanitarian ideals or to have questioned King's political judgment. He had a more youthful zest for social reform, however, and laid more stress on the need for positive government action. "We shall probably have to use the power of the State through Parliament to effect a drastic curtailment of the anti-social practices which have developed under economic individualism, and to bring about a closer approximation to an equal distribution of the national income," he argued in one of his letters.[18] Rogers was also more of a centralist and frequently warned King against any statements which might prejudge "the future question of widening the sphere of federal action in the field of social and economic relations."[19] King was pleased to have a devoted assistant to draft speeches for him but he also listened with respect to a young man whom he considered almost a protégé and for whom he felt an almost paternal pride.

Rogers had already stressed the importance of monetary policy. "The currency question," he had explained in April 1932, "is likely to bulk large in the general task of economic reconstruction." He had no specific policies to propose but he had tentatively supported the idea of a central bank and had warned King not to appear indifferent to the possibility of monetary reform.[20] It was natural for King to turn to Rogers now for further details on central banking. The response was a long memorandum on the subject prepared by Professor C. A. Curtis, a Queen's University economist.[21]

The memorandum was of great help to King. Curtis explained that the amount of money in circulation, combined with the amount of credit, affected the general price level. In Canada the chartered banks could influence price levels by their lending operations and by their limited right to print money. Bankers, however, were not primarily concerned with prices or the level of economic activity in the country; they lent money when they had some assurance that it would be a profitable transaction. The sum of these private transactions did not necessarily add up to a total of credit which conformed to the national interest. Curtis cited the uncurbed expansion of credit before 1929 as an example of how unregulated private banks could affect the national economy. In 1932, when economic prospects seemed less favourable, banks were less inclined to lend money to businessmen and farmers and so tended to reduce the level of economic activity even further. He concluded that a central bank was needed to regulate the total volume of credit, allowing the commercial banks to operate freely within prescribed limits. "Such a central bank, in handling rediscounting and bank reserves, would exercise its powers to give us a maximum of social control of credit for the welfare of the nation." There was also another reason for the control of credit: "the strength of the political agitation for inflation must be reckoned with as a fact of the utmost political significance." Some inflation might be desirable but, without the control which a central bank could provide, a policy of inflation could get out of hand. Curtis's conclusion was cautiously phrased:

The Liberal party can reasonably take the position that it believes the monetary function of our economic life is so important in its social implications as to justify a more ample measure of control in the national interest. Consistently with this view, it can advocate the establishment of a central bank in which the public interest shall have adequate representation. . . . Assuming that we are ever to pursue a policy of inflation for social ends, it can be demonstrated that such machinery is absolutely indispensable if we are to avoid the disasters of uncontrolled inflation and the perils of nominal control which is solely political in character.[22]

Mackenzie King was delighted with this analysis. The details were not important but he quickly saw the possibility of reconciling eastern and western Liberals. A central bank was an institution, not a policy. Opponents of inflation might be persuaded to support the idea of establishing a central bank because it could provide some control over credit without interfering unduly with private enterprise and would not necessarily inflate the supply of money. The advocates of inflation, on the other hand, would favour a central bank because it provided the necessary machinery if a policy of controlled inflation was to be adopted. King saw no chance of immediate agreement on the issue of inflation but agreement might be possible on the more equivocal policy of establishing a central bank.

King had made up his mind but this was only the first step. The Liberal caucus would have to be consulted and any statement of party policy would have to have its prior approval. Vincent Massey protested the delay would be disastrous because many voters would be impressed by the C.C.F. argument that neither of the two major parties had a platform and because a policy statement emerging from caucus would involve so many compromises that the final result would be of little use.[23] King refused to issue any statement in his own name. "You know," he reminded Massey, "how strongly I believe that a party which is liberal and democratic cannot afford, even in appearance, to be dominated by a single individual."[24] For him the consent of the party was essential, even if it involved regrettable delays and compromises.

The House reconvened late in January 1933. King wasted no time; at the first meeting of caucus he "spoke of the necessity of considering immediately the major issues, and of defining our position." It was only a preliminary meeting but King still used the occasion to guide the party in what he believed to be the right direction. He noted in his diary that "On the banking & currency issue I prepared the way for reconciling extreme views, by concentrating on a Central Bank—but we left that discussion over."[25] When caucus met again the next week King reported "a first class discussion on currency, credit and banking, during which from all sides men were much more moderate than they have previously been. The Central Bank idea seemed to furnish the point of convergence of the many views." Caucus had at least agreed on the need for a statement on policy and the broad outlines of its platform were emerging.

The Liberals had been spurred on by Woodsworth, who had already introduced a resolution recommending that "the government should immediately take measures looking to the setting up of a cooperative commonwealth."[26] The absence of Liberal speakers in the debate on this resolution was a serious embarrassment. King encouraged the caucus to move quickly:

I was able by waiting till the end to point out we were in agreement as to the need of a statement of our position on principal issues and to have it ready soon. I then produced the tentative draft the office had prepared, and read it to caucus, saying it seemed to embody those principles & policies on which we were already agreed. I suggested it be referred to a committee which had been named to frame a policy on currency, credit, etc. and that power be given the Committee to add any Lib. persons from either House of prlt. who wished to be present.[27]

The committee met next day, with twenty-five Liberals in attendance. King did not record the details but he took some credit for the progress that was made: "I had to do a lot of careful navigating to get along as rapidly and as unanimously as we did." He was also pleased that Vincent Massey had attended and was "able to see how necessary conferences of the kind were."[28] The committee met again the next day but still there was "such diversity of view, e.g. between those who want to help labour by cutting down hrs. etc. & rural members who seek in vain for something that will help the farmers." It was left to King to revise the original draft on the basis of these discussions. It was not easy, he noted. "They all seem

35

keen on making the man who had yield up to him who has suffered. There is an element of justice but also of injustice in much that is proposed. The problem is to balance the two as nearly as may be."[29]

King's version of the proper balance was presented to the full caucus at its next meeting. The proposed platform was largely a consolidation of the policies to which the party was already committed. It advocated tariff reduction, increased British preferences, and trade agreements with foreign countries whenever possible. For unemployment it proposed a national commission to co-ordinate the administration of relief and to initiate work projects. The federal budget was to be balanced by eliminating inefficiency and duplication within the public service. There were also familiar items such as restoring the rights of Parliament—no more arbitrary control over relief funds by the executive—and restoring the rights of the individual by repealing Section 98 of the Criminal Code. The only radical departure from traditional liberalism was the commitment to establish "a properly constituted national central bank to perform the function of rediscount and the control of currency issue." The purpose of the bank would be to manipulate the money supply on the basis of "public need" and "the domestic, social and industrial requirements of the people."[30] There was no explicit reference to inflation but the door was open. The party would no longer be committed to the principle of sound money or the integrity of the dollar. King had moved a considerable distance when he could agree that the value of money should be determined by social needs.

King read the draft to caucus, "making clear that every member had been free to sit in on the discussion." His account of the meeting also makes it clear that many Liberals were still unhappy with a statement that went too far, or, for others, did not go far enough. The party, however, would have to respond to the Woodsworth motion: "I finally told caucus I appreciated the confidence they expressed, that I would be willing to make the speech provided they would agree to what was in the statement, & follow me within those limits. This was agreed to unanimously. Someone suggested a committee to counsel further, but I objected to that, said I wd. be glad to get any suggestions but there must be finality; this was approved."[31] There might not be enthusiasm but at least there was agreement. The party had a platform and that platform had been approved by the caucus. King was more than satisfied; he described it as a "splendid" meeting.

King gave his speech on the Woodsworth resolution late in February. He was convinced that his statement was of crucial importance. The formation of the C.C.F. was the major political development during the Bennett administration and the Liberal response might determine the results of the next election. The Conservative response was clear. A succession of Conservative speakers denounced the new party as a revolutionary threat to democracy; the recurring theme was that "the cooperative commonwealth is communism and communism is the cooperative commonwealth."[32] Bennett had already bitterly attacked the C.C.F. outside the House: "What do they offer you for dumping you in the mud? Socialism, communism, dictatorship. . . . And we ask every man and woman to put the iron heel of ruthlessness against a thing of that kind."[33] He did not deliver a prepared speech on Woodsworth's resolution but his interjections in the debate, usually with caustic references to Russia, showed that he still equated the C.C.F. with communism. King saw the debate as more than an opportunity to put the new Liberal platform on the record. He wanted to seize the middle ground, to reject socialism but to avoid the Conservative condemnation of the new party.

His speech was predictably long—he spoke for two hours. As usual King felt that he could have done better if he had had more time. He did stay up until five o'clock the next morning revising the Hansard report to improve the style. But if it was not a good speech, it was one, he was sure, that would "have to be reckoned with."[34] The Liberal party, as King described it, was in general agreement with the C.C.F. on many points. It certainly conceded that economic conditions were bad and that "the great question of the day is the social problem, the problem of how masses of people are to live."[35] Thus Liberal aims differed little from socialist aims. But the Liberal party disagreed with the C.C.F. solutions. Who could believe that the state could manage all the economic activities of the country? The present government could not even operate a railway efficiently; an expansion of the bureaucracy would only lead to chaos.

The Liberal party, King argued, had a better solution. "Opposition to socialism or a socialist state is not to be regarded as opposition to so-called social or humanitarian reform."[36] Unrestricted competition could be controlled without suppressing individual initiative. Public ownership was possible without socialism; instead of doctrinaire policies, the Liberals advocated "considering each proposed measure on its merits, in the light of conditions as they exist at that particular time." In answer to the critics who alleged that the Liberals had no policies for existing conditions, he then produced the platform which the party had adopted. It was not a final solution; there would be no finality until individuals forsook their greed and were converted to the spirit of Christian service and sacrifice. A Liberal government would not bring the millennium but King did imply in his peroration that liberalism was strongly influenced by the Sermon on the Mount.

The speech did not end the debate within the Liberal party but it did end the formal discussions of a platform. To one Liberal, who felt that a broader appeal was needed, King explained that "there is a great deal of difference between broadening out a platform and falling off one end over a precipice."[37] Vincent Massey had a different interpretation. As President of the National Liberal Federation he made some speeches on "the new liberalism" in which he argued that the platform was a prelude to a new and more radical Liberal party. In his eagerness to attract left-wing support, Massey was even prepared to admit that some of the present members of the party were not truly liberal. When right-wing Liberals protested against this heresy, King was more convinced than ever that he had struck the necessary balance.[38] King's House of Commons speech was reprinted as a pamphlet with the platform itemized in fourteen points. In future, when correspondents criticized the party for having no clear statement of its policies, King merely mailed them a copy. He was not prepared to run the risk of reopening the debate. The pamphlet would be one of the major items of Liberal literature in the election campaign in 1935.

King was prepared to extend public control and even public ownership when it seemed necessary but he was disturbed by the number of Liberals who talked of economic planning as the panacea for the depression. Planning for him had become synonymous with a bureaucratic state, the antithesis of liberalism. Even his reaction to the Roosevelt administration in the United States was coloured by his suspicion of social blueprints. He had been delighted by Roosevelt's election and the defeat of "the protectionist forces in the U.S."[39] Roosevelt's inaugural address seemed to King to embody liberal sentiments and with a style which he could not hope to rival.[40] But he soon had doubts about the New Deal. The National Industrial Recovery Act, for example, with its trade associations and trade unions under government regulation, was a contradiction of liberalism by King's definition; Roosevelt, he commented, was "on wrong line re Labour & industries—use of arbitrary power to make artificial agreements."[41] The President, he feared, was becoming as much of a dictator as Bennett. King continued to sympathize with the aims of the New Deal; he even believed that he had outlined the ideas long ago in *Industry and Humanity*.[42] It was the head-long eagerness to impose bureaucratic solutions which disturbed him.

Vincent Massey still wanted to go "full steam ahead."[43] In the summer of 1933 he organized a conference at Port Hope for "the discussion of present-day problems by liberal-minded men and women of all parties."[44] King resented Massey "trying to force the pace," and read into the conference an implied criticism of his own leadership.[45] He did not look forward to the meeting—"Massey will be for planning—with young Liberals and University radicals etc."—but he saw some advantage in associating the Liberal party with the public discussion of new ideas. Despite his reluctance he stayed for the entire week and even persuaded some of his colleagues to attend.[46] The Liberal platform might be drafted but the Liberal image could not be neglected.

The conference confirmed his suspicion of men who wanted to direct the economy according to a plan. Raymond Moley, a New Dealer, horrified him when he blithely boasted that New Deal measures had ignored the federal constitution and by-passed Congress.[47] King tried to express his misgivings in his closing address at the conference. Experts, he conceded, might have special and very valuable knowledge but no specialist could solve the complex social problems of the present. "I say that no plan can be devised which is sufficiently comprehensive to meet all the situations that have to be met by a political party or by the State."[48] He believed in a statement of broad principles and objectives but not in rigid commitments to preconceived social remedies. The liberal way was to advance from discussion to agreement before acting. He could admire men in advance of their time but as a political leader he believed that enduring reform depended upon moderate opinion which would "carry the great body of a nation with him."[49]

King was cautious but he had not been immobile. He had responded to the economic crisis when it threatened his political hopes. The formation of the C.C.F. had forced him to go beyond trade and tariff issues and to consider other forms of economic intervention by government. A central bank which could control the supply of currency and credit might not seem radical to ardent inflationists but it was potentially a major instrument of economic planning. Cautiously and even reluctantly a new liberalism was emerging, and both leader and party had moved forward together.

II

R. B. Bennett was still the impatient man of action. The ever-worsening economic disaster dominated his arduous days; at times he even feared that if the depression continued for another year it would "break the whole capitalist system."[50] Mackenzie King, with his talk of dictatorship and his unctuous references to the Sermon on the Mount, was only a bothersome gadfly to a man who had the onerous burden of saving Canada from possible bankruptcy and revolution. Unfortunately, in the spring of 1933 Bennett had no panacea for the nation. He had already raised the tariff to prohibitive heights. The Ottawa Agreements would surely increase Canadian exports. But these remedies would not take immediate effect and, in the meantime, the government faced enormous deficits and social unrest. Bennett, with nothing new to offer, concentrated on balancing the budget and maintaining order.

Bennett had good reason to worry about the financial problems of his government. For the fiscal year ending in March 1933 the federal government would have a total revenue of some three hundred and ten million dollars. Federal expenditures, including relief and the Canadian National Railway deficit, exceeded four hundred and sixty million dollars. In Bennett's terms, here was a business enterprise earning six million dollars a week and spending nine millions. Either the deficit had to be drastically reduced or the federal government would go bankrupt.

Edgar Rhodes, Minister of Finance, introduced the budget in March 1933. He gave a depressing picture of the decline in world trade and world prices, of war in China, of political upheavals in Europe, and of the closure of banks in the United States. Considered in the light of world conditions, Canada had an enviable record for which the government deserved great credit. Inflation would only have made matters worse; a government which depended on heavy borrowing could not risk destroying confidence in the Canadian currency. He paid tribute to the contribution of the chartered banks to Canada's financial stability and saw no immediate need for a central bank. The one concession was the announcement of a Royal Commission to study the problem. Despite this impressive record, however, the government did have a deficit. Even if the extraordinary expenditures for relief and railways were set aside, expenditures exceeded revenues by eighty million dollars. Rhodes promised to eliminate this deficit. Fourteen million dollars would be saved by reducing departmental expenditures; the rest would be covered by increased taxation, mainly from higher corporation and personal income taxes and from excise taxes. Leaving aside the unpredictable costs of relief and the railway deficit, the result would be a balanced budget.[51]

The Liberals, as was to be expected, were not impressed. It was easy to criticize a government which admitted to an unprecedented deficit. It was also easy to denounce a government which proposed not to reduce expenditures significantly but to levy taxes which would bear most heavily on those who were already in distress. J. L. Ralston, speaking for the party, showed no sympathy for the government as a victim of a world-wide depression. It stood condemned by its deficit, by its inability to do what was necessary. The budget should be balanced, not by raising taxes but by reducing expenditures and encouraging economic recovery. His amendment merely deplored the failure to introduce the "changes in existing policies regarding trade, credit and employment which are required to cope with the present situation."[52] The C.C.F. were more forthright; their amendment called for "controlled inflation" and increased expenditures "by the direct use of our national credit."[53] Mackenzie King showed no concern. The Conservative budget was so unpopular that he saw no need to participate in the debate;[54] the C.C.F. amendment, he believed, had only clarified the differences between the three parties.[55] The government, he was sure, was discredited by its own statistics. A deficit of one hundred and fifty million dollars spoke for itself.

The government's major efforts at retrenchment would have to come not in the budget but in its relief measures and its railway policy. For Bennett the frustration of such a staggering deficit was aggravated by the fact that these two major items, accounting for almost a hundred million dollars, were almost beyond his control. Relief was administered by the provincial governments but the federal government was providing a large proportion of the funds.* If there were economies to be made, the federal government would have to exercise more control over the provincial administration of relief.

Bennett was tempted to take drastic measures. At a Dominion-Provincial Conference in January 1933 he threatened to cut off all aid unless the provincial governments balanced their budgets or at least reduced their deficits to less than a million dollars. The alternative, he stated, was to appoint a federal comptroller to supervise all provincial expenditures.[56] In a letter to the western Premiers, apparently drafted at this time, he argued that he had no alternative: "It is with regret that I find myself obliged to write to you in these terms but the fact is that the credit of the Dominion is just now the most vital factor affecting the welfare of the people of Canada, and I dare not omit any step necessary to protect that credit."[57] Vital as the credit of the Dominion might seem, provincial autonomy was not so easily ignored. Bennett took no further action; his startling proposal was no more than the threat of a man almost driven to despair.

The government's Unemployment and Farm Relief bill was introduced late in February. The discussion showed the impact of the depression in Canada and again underlined the impossibility of cutting relief costs significantly by budgetary restraints. As the Minister of Labour explained, more than one million three hundred thousand Canadians were on relief in March 1933; this out of a total population of just over ten millions. He

---

*The federal contribution to relief in 1932–3 was some thirty-five million dollars. In addition the federal government lent some seventeen million dollars to the western provinces to enable them to meet their share of relief costs.

unconsciously revealed the preoccupation of the government when he found encouragement in the fact that federal expenditures on relief had not increased over the year before, even though more were on the relief rolls. Some savings had been achieved by discontinuing public works projects; it was less expensive to make direct relief payments than to pay both wages and other construction costs. The government saw no way to improve on existing arrangements. Its legislation merely proposed to extend the provisions of the Relief Act of 1932 for yet another year.[58]

The opposition was critical but it could hardly be described as constructive. King was shocked at this "orgy of public expenditure" but at the same time he criticized the resort to direct relief and argued that if men were willing and able to work, the state should provide work for them. His solution was still a national commission to supervise the administration of relief. His major criticism, however, was that the government was again asking for a blank cheque; the bill did not specify how much the federal government would spend or on what it would be spent.[59] Bennett finally agreed to set the maximum expenditure at twenty million dollars but that was his only concession.

One aspect of the bill had more to do with Bennett's fear of revolution than his concern for balancing the budget. A Conservative amendment reintroduced the "peace, order and good government" clause which would allow the government to deport undesirables without the inconvenience of legal proceedings. This section had appeared in the Relief Act of 1931 but had been dropped in 1932 after King's prolonged objections.[60] King again protested at every stage of the bill. Under the guise of dealing with distress "we are being asked to establish a dictatorship in this country," he declaimed.[61] Unlike the debate in 1932, however, the Liberals did not prolong the debate and force the government to resort to closure; some Liberals were reluctant to oppose any relief measure too strenuously.[62] On the final vote all the Liberals voted in the negative, as did Woodsworth. The farmer members in the C.C.F., however, voted with the government. Woodsworth was having more trouble than King in keeping his party united.

Bennett hoped to be more successful in reducing the operating deficit of the Canadian National Railways, which was accumulating at the rate of more than a million dollars a week. A Royal Commission on Transportation, under the chairmanship of Lyman Duff, had reported in the fall of 1932 and the government now introduced legislation on the basis of its recommendations. The commission had drawn attention to the growing competition of road transport but had concentrated on the wasteful duplication of railway services as the major problem. It reluctantly

42

rejected the amalgamation of the two railway systems as politically impossible. Voluntary co-operation between the two lines offered little hope. The two Presidents paid lip-service to co-operation but neither showed much willingness to make concessions or curtail operations. The commission's solution was an independent tribunal to arbitrate disputes and compel co-operation. It also stressed "the red thread of extravagance" running through the administration of the government railway.[63] It blamed the management and, indirectly, the politicians for responding too easily to public pressure for increased services. Its recommendation was to replace the unwieldly Board of Directors by three trustees who would restrain the General Manager and presumably resist any political pressures.

The legislation which adopted these recommendations provoked a lengthy and bitter debate. The bill itself scarcely justified the vehement opposition. Behind much of the verbiage in Hansard was King's conviction that Bennett was opposed to a government-owned railway on principle, and his fear that this legislation was somehow designed to eliminate the Canadian National system. Some of the economy measures already forced on the railway seemed deliberately designed to divert traffic to its rival,[64] and King credited the government with "self-evident sabotage."[65] A tribunal, appointed by Bennett, which could impose co-operation was consistent with this apparent pattern; King immediately concluded that the legislation was "a clear case of the Govt. destroying the C.N.R."[66] But King also knew that "the country feels, & rightly so, something must be done with the railways to effect necessary economies."[67] Rather than challenge the function of the tribunal he concentrated on the Board of Trustees which, he argued, could "deprive Parliament almost entirely of some of its fundamental rights."[68] This had the advantage of being an issue which could keep the party united, for many Liberals who were reluctant to criticize a policy of railway co-operation would defend this high principle. King carried the party with him; seven Liberals did support the bill on second reading but even they voted against it on third reading.

There were some grounds for believing that Bennett was hostile to the government railway. He had been a solicitor for the C.P.R. and was a poker-playing crony of its President, Sir Edward Beatty. Bennett was a businessman and his criterion for the efficiency of any enterprise, public or private, was not whether it was providing a public service but whether it was making a profit. For this reason, as he candidly admitted, he favoured amalgamation.[69] But Bennett was also a politician. He knew that amalgamation was politically unacceptable in western Canada, where the memory of the C.P.R. monopoly was still fresh. His legislation was a compromise and it must have been difficult for him to understand the prolonged debate it provoked. He was certainly exasperated by the impassioned defence of the historic liberties of Parliament; he coldly replied that "this House in its power to vote money has complete control over that board of trustees."[70]

It was ironic that, after all this debate, the legislation accomplished almost nothing. The Board of Trustees proved unworkable. The chairman, as the only full-time trustee, dominated the board and, because of his authority, became the President in all but name. The rivalry of the two railways still prevented voluntary co-operation. And because neither railway would submit disputes and no government, federal or provincial, would take the initiative of proposing that certain services be reduced or certain branch-lines be abandoned, the compulsory power of the tribunal was never invoked.[71] The railway deficits continued.

Bennett had failed to bring the costs of unemployment and railways under control. His efforts to maintain social order, while more dramatic, were probably no more effective. It was true that in addition to the "peace, order and good government" clause of the Unemployment and Farm Relief bill there was also Section 98 of the Criminal Code, which made it a criminal offence to advocate the use of force to achieve reform, and that Tim Buck and seven other Communists were therefore in jail as members of an unlawful association. In the session of 1933, however, both the C.C.F. and the Liberals urged the repeal of Section 98. Conservatives might wax eloquent over the menace of communism; the Minister of Justice could even claim that "if ever there was a time in the history of this country when section 98 was justifiable as part of the criminal law of this country, this is certainly the time."[72] It is noteworthy, however, that no more arrests were made.

Bennett did introduce one novel measure during the session to strengthen Canada's threatened social fabric. In a world where the ruling classes were under attack he decided to redress the balance by once again granting titles to deserving Canadians as a reward for their services to the state.[73] The House of Commons had passed a resolution against the conferring of titles in the troubled year of 1919, and in 1933 it was easy for King to discourse on the theme that aristocracy had no place in a democratic society in which all men were equal. He even suggested as an ulterior motive that Bennett wanted a life peerage.[74] This was doubtless unfair. It would not be unfair, however, to suggest that the restoration of titles in this, the worst year of the depression, showed an extraordinary lack of political judgment.

The events of the session strengthened King's conviction that the Bennett government would be resoundingly defeated at the next election. King saw danger, however, in the certainty of defeat. The Conservatives, in a desperate attempt to escape this merited punishment, might propose a coalition. The National Government in England had already provided an example. Nobody could deny that there was an emergency, and the appeal for statesmanlike co-operation instead of partisan opposition would find many supporters. King knew that he and Bennett could never be in the same government. It was more than a question of temperament. Governments, even national governments, had to have policies. What would such a government do about the tariff? "What Canada needs today," he explained to one Liberal, "is not a neutralizing of all policies, much less any covering up or perpetuating of Tory policies, but an application of Liberal principles and policies more definite and far-reaching than we have ever had before."[75] His concern was one of tactics. How could he refuse an offer to enter a coalition government without appearing to put the interests of his party ahead of the interests of his country?

King was not opposed to all coalitions. He had even encouraged the coalition between the provincial Liberals and Progressives in Manitoba in 1931.[76] But this was because he saw no ideological differences between these two parties. His comment when John Bracken led the coalition to victory in the Manitoba elections in 1932 was that "it shows what a union of democratic forces can effect."[77] It was a different matter when the Conservative premiers of Saskatchewan and British Columbia proposed coalitions to the provincial Liberal leaders. For King these would not be unions of democratic forces and he heartily approved when J. G. Gardiner and T. D. Pattullo in turn rejected the proposals.[78]

King interpreted these provincial Conservative overtures as a prelude to a coalition proposal at the federal level. There is no evidence that Bennett had seriously considered the idea although there were many rumours. Most of the pressure came from those in the business community who believed that only a national government could impose railway amalgamation. King tried to forestall any such move by insisting that the Liberal party would never support amalgamation.[79] He was relieved when Bennett's railway legislation also rejected this policy. King probably exaggerated the danger. Neither Liberals nor Conservatives looked back with much satisfaction to the coalition experiment of 1917; as one correspondent put it, "the odor of Union Government is still in their nostrils and they don't want another such."[80] In any case, by the end of the session King was no longer worried. Bennett might yet propose a national government but he was now so discredited that King was sure it would be interpreted as no more than a desperate attempt to avoid defeat at the next election.[81]

King also worried about another possible move by the government to improve its chances at the next election. The election of a Democratic administration in Washington raised the possibility of a reciprocity agreement with the United States. The Liberals, in an attempt to embarrass a government committed to Imperial trade, proposed that Canada initiate negotiations for a Canadian-American trade agreement.[82] Bennett countered this move by expressing his willingness "to negotiate on terms that are fair and reasonable."[83] At the time King conceded that Bennett had made "a very plausible speech" but was sure "that he had no thought whatever to enter into any agreement."[84] A few months later, however, Bennett visited Roosevelt in Washington and gave the impression on his return that serious negotiations would soon begin.[85] King was still sceptical about Bennett's sincerity but even the remote possibility of a trade agreement could not be overlooked.* He resolved to stress Liberal trade policies that summer, "to declare for a reciprocal treaty at once . . . drive the Govt. to it—if it is to be done."[86] Even if Bennett negotiated a treaty, the Liberal party would be able to claim the credit.

III

Even before the session ended, King was making plans for the summer. He explained to Norman Rogers in March that he intended "to make a real campaign this summer in the interests of Liberalism which will save Canada from Fascism on the one hand, and Socialism leading to Communism on the other. I believe this is the great need of the day. Bennett is heading as rapidly as possible in the one direction and Woodsworth and his group at an equal pace in the other."[87] It was not enough to have a new platform; "the important task of the Liberal party," as Crerar told him, "is to convince the people of its good faith."[88] This was especially true in the west, where the radical proposals of the C.C.F. were being widely and favourably discussed. King was now more worried about Woodsworth than Bennett; he decided to go on a western tour.

*There was some justification for King's scepticism. Bennett had told a American official in Ottawa that he was still committed to protection for Canadian manufacturers. Unless international trade improved, however, he might be forced into "a number of untried social and economic experiments" which might include "the abandonment of Canada's present determination to pay its foreign obligations." This dire warning was followed by the suggestion that "even a small partial agreement" with the United States would be helpful. *Foreign Relations of the United States, 1933*, II, 46–8, Chargé d'Affaires in Canada to Under Secretary of State, April 14, 1933.

The trip was carefully timed. The C.C.F. met in Regina in July, where it adopted the Regina Manifesto, and King's first speech on the tour was delivered the day after the convention ended. King was also concerned about a by-election in the Saskatchewan constituency of Mackenzie. The riding had returned M. N. Campbell, a Progressive, in every election since 1921 but Bennett had appointed Campbell to the Tariff Board. The by-election would be the first test for the new party and King believed that "if, for any reason, the C.C.F. candidate should win in Mackenzie, the west will be on fire with C.C.F. enthusiasm at once." A Liberal victory, on the other hand, would show that the socialist party was too radical for most western voters, and would be "a signal for the waverers in all parties to rally to our standard."[89]

The arrangements for the tour were carefully planned to show the concern of the Liberal party for the plight of the western farmers. Instead of visiting the cities, King met villagers and farmers at rural picnics across the prairies. Softball games and races were interrupted to hear King expound on the tariff and the central bank, on the bankruptcy of Toryism and the abyss of socialism. King was driven by car from one gathering to the next, often giving three or four speeches in one day, shaking hands before and after the meeting, and usually having lunch and dinner with the prominent local Liberals. He enjoyed the informality and was stimulated by the close contact and the responsiveness of his audiences. He even participated in some of the softball games and proudly recorded facing Gardiner as pitcher and getting a three-base hit.[90]

Political picnics were a fading tradition in Canada. King was exhilarated by the experience but after a month he was also exhausted, and he never undertook a tour of this kind again. He was certain, however, that much had been accomplished. He had visited his own constituency of Prince Albert and, more important, had paid special attention to the Mackenzie by-election, visiting the constituency on the way west and making a special detour for a second visit on his way back.[91] He could take some credit for the results, for on October 23 the Liberal candidate won, with a decisive majority of sixteen hundred votes. The by-election also appeared to justify King's emphasis on the C.C.F. as the major obstacle to a Liberal victory at the next federal election. The C.C.F. candidate came second and the Conservative candidate lost his deposit.

Two other by-elections were held on the same day. The Conservative member for Restigouche-Madawaska in New Brunswick had died and a Liberal member from Yamaska, in Quebec, had been unseated for irregularities. Yamaska presented serious difficulties for the Liberals, for the party was split by local rivalries and at the last election had only held the seat by a majority of one. Arthur Cardin wanted to avoid an election and proposed a saw-off by which the Conservative in Restigouche-Madawaska and the Liberal in Yamaska would be elected by acclamation. New Brunswick Liberals, however, expected to win and insisted on running a candidate. King was delighted—"my heart filled with blood as this word came"—and opposed any deal with the Conservatives.[92] He felt vindicated by the results. The Liberals won both by-elections, by a majority of over six thousand in New Brunswick and by eighty-four in the Quebec riding. The voters had clearly registered their disapproval of the Bennett administration.

Two provincial elections in this year also encouraged the Liberals. The Liberal party in Nova Scotia defeated the provincial Conservative government decisively. Much of the credit went to the young Liberal leader, Angus L. Macdonald, who had great personal charm, spoke with Celtic warmth and vitality, and had conducted a vigorous campaign. It was generally admitted, however, that provincial Conservatives had suffered from the unpopularity of the federal Conservative party and what one observer described as the "tremendous feeling of hostility to Bennett."[93] The two C.C.F. candidates lost their deposits. In the Maritimes at least a Liberal victory at the next federal election seemed assured.

The provincial election in British Columbia was somehow less encouraging. Here too the provincial Liberals under Dufferin Pattullo won a sweeping victory, with the Conservative representation almost eliminated and with seven C.C.F. members forming the official Opposition. Federal issues, however, had played a more minor role than they had in Nova Scotia. Premier Tolmie had alienated many of his followers by advocating a coalition and officially the Conservative party had not even contested the election, with former Conservatives running as Unionists, Non-Partisans, and Independents.[94] The popular support for the C.C.F. party was also ominous. Before the election King had referred to "this latest political fledgling, which, like most infants, appears to be creating a maximum of disturbance with a minimum of intelligent utterance."[95] But the evident popularity of the C.C.F. had brought the federal Liberals into the campaign and on election day 30 per cent of the voters in British Columbia had opted for this fledgling.

King was also less cheered by the results because of his misgivings about T. D. Pattullo, the provincial Liberal leader. Duff Pattullo and King had been acquainted since boyhood and both came from genteel, middle-class Presbyterian and Liberal families.[96] But there the resemblance ended. King had gone to Toronto and Harvard and then into the civil service; Pattullo had gone to the Yukon and had lived in the frontier communities of Dawson and Prince Rupert. Pattullo's victory owed little to federal Liberal support. "It is no exaggeration to say that the election was won by the courage and accepted honesty of Mr. Pattullo rather than by the Liberal party as such," warned one reliable observer.[97] But King's major reservation was that Pattullo had competed with the C.C.F. by presenting a comprehensive programme of economic planning with the catchy slogan of "work and wages." To King this was almost a socialist platform. He wired his congratulations to Pattullo and followed this with a letter in which he commented on "how pleased your mother and father, and mine, would have been to see us both at the head of the Liberal party in our respective spheres of action,"[98] but in private he warned Liberals that "the slogan of work and wages is a good one for a campaign but it will be a very difficult one, conditions being what they are, for the Government to bring about." His advice to his followers in British Columbia was to stress only federal issues so as not to be too compromised if Pattullo became a handicap to the party.[99] Despite these misgivings, however, it had been a Liberal victory and this augured well for the future. "The year now drawing to a close has been an exceptionally good one for the Liberal party in Canada" was King's conclusion.[100]

The Tory party, he was more convinced than ever, was finished. It might even disappear entirely, as it had in British Columbia. Some Liberals might be tempted to "keep more to the right in the hope of bringing the Conservatives into our ranks," but King was resolved to resist this temptation. He had no intention of leaving "the centre of the stage and the middle of the road."[101] Even the C.C.F. no longer seemed such a serious threat. The Mackenzie by-election showed that they "have not by any means captured the membership of the old Progressive party to the extent we have." Most important of all, the Liberal party was united and had unanimously adopted a new platform.[102] The year ended with King in the library of Laurier House, praying for guidance and looking forward to the new year which "it would seem will bring great changes—possibly a change of government & the return of the Liberal party."[103]

CHAPTER THREE

PRE-ELECTION MANŒUVRES

MACKENZIE KING looked forward to 1934 with confidence. There would be problems—politics was a never-ending succession of problems—but the unity of the party now seemed assured and only continuing vigilance and patience would be needed to ensure a Liberal victory when the election came. The political developments during the year would only confirm his assessment. The government did introduce some new legislation, including the Bank of Canada Act and the Natural Products Marketing Act, and the Liberals found it difficult to agree on a party line for these measures, but King managed to avoid any public airing of these differences. Two provincial elections and a number of federal by-elections produced a series of Liberal victories which convincingly showed the unpopularity of the Conservative party and the readiness to turn to the Liberal party as an alternative. King was on his guard as always but as far as party policy was concerned he saw no need to go beyond the platform of the year before. He was wrong about the date of the election, which he expected in the fall of 1934. Bennett's decision to wait, however, was at least further evidence that the government was in trouble, for it meant that Bennett was not optimistic about his chances of winning. To King the delay seemed no more than a postponement of the inevitable.

I

The year began with many Conservatives in despair. They still had a great deal of respect for R. B. Bennett, for his administrative ability, his knowledge of government affairs, and his talent as a political campaigner. But Bennett, who had been such a dominant figure in the election of 1930, seemed to have lost interest in politics. As R. J. Manion told his son, the party desperately needed a programme and some organization or "in the near future most of us will be looking for another job." "It seems a pity," he continued, "that a man like the Chief, who could probably put a scheme like this over better than anyone else if only he would, seems simply to be satisfied to wait for good fortune to do everything for him."[1] A few months later Manion was more discouraged than ever. Bennett was clearly letting the party drift and the only explanation seemed to be that he intended to resign and was just awaiting a convenient occasion.[2]

The House met late in January for what might be its last session before the election. The Speech from the Throne, however, gave little evidence that the government had any new policies to propose. It contained the usual assurances that conditions were improving and gave full credit to the administration for its efforts but, apart from the promise of legislation on banking and on marketing, it was almost a repetition of the Speech of the year before. King took four hours for his reply, but he did no more than denounce the failure of the government to cope with the depression. His concluding motion—"that Your Excellency's advisers do not possess the confidence of the country"[3]—aptly summed up the shift from criticisms of specific policies to a partisan attack on the government and all its works. Bennett replied in an even longer oration but he too seemed more concerned with the past record than with future measures. "If the electors are not grateful, and I have every reason to believe that they will be when the appropriate time comes, we are content because we have had the great privilege of serving the people."[4] Three weeks later, after some fifty members had contributed their comments on the Speech, one Cabinet Minister quite aptly described the entire debate as "the dullest, the most destructive and the most useless debate I have heard."[5] The parties were rehearsing for the next election.

For the Relief Act of 1934 the principal actors already knew their lines. This Act was again an extension of the previous legislation, but with no limitation on the amount which the federal government could spend on relief, and included once again the controversial "peace, order and good government" clause. The Minister of Labour found some encouragement in statistics; the number on relief had declined from the year before. The government was clearly on the defensive, however. It could hardly boast when more than 1,200,000 Canadians had depended to some extent on government charity in February 1934.[6] In an effort to limit a debate which could only embarrass the government the necessary legislation was introduced late in March, little more than a week before the previous Act would expire. If the Liberals insisted on a prolonged discussion, they would run the risk of being blamed for delaying the distribution of relief after the end of the month.

Mackenzie King was not intimidated. He insisted on a prolonged debate, in spite of the reluctance of many of his followers, and when no

51

Liberal was prepared to intervene, he himself took up the time of the House, repeating the same old arguments against blank cheques and arbitrary powers.[7] Liberal obstruction delayed the final vote until mid-April.

The budget provided further evidence that the government had nothing new to offer. It was a stand-pat budget, with only minor administrative changes in taxes. The Minister of Finance had figures to prove that conditions had improved since the last budget: "What was then a hope can now be asserted with confidence as a fact of experience. The fiscal year that has just closed has been a year of recovery—recovery that is unmistakeable."[8] It was true that conditions had improved from the disastrous conditions of the previous winter but even so government revenues fell short of ordinary expenditures by some twenty-four millions and, when relief expenditures and railway deficits were added, the total deficit was one hundred and thirty-five millions. The efforts of the previous year to limit relief costs and railway losses had been ineffectual and for the coming year the government had no solution except to wait for the depression to end. Ralston once again presented the Liberal alternative of promoting international trade[9] but the debate was little more than a parliamentary ritual. King did not even consider it necessary to speak on the budget.

The government, however, could not ignore the many pressures for action. Bennett might still think that recovery depended upon sound fiscal policies; "Canada," as he explained to one correspondent, "has not the money to buy its way back to prosperity as the United States is doing. The economic burdens of our national and railway debt place a limit on our further borrowings."[10] But even if Bennett saw no alternative to retrenchment he could not ignore the immediate plight of those to whom the depression meant disaster. Gradually and reluctantly the government had had to intervene in areas which had formerly been left to private enterprise. Only a few years before the major instruments of economic policy had been tariffs and taxes. By the session of 1934 the balance had clearly shifted; the most important economic measures were separate from the budget and involved the establishment of government agencies to regulate private business.

Early in the session the government introduced legislation to establish the Bank of Canada. A year earlier the government had defended the banking system and had denied any need for a central bank but it could not ignore the political pressure from western Canada or the inclusion of a central bank in the Liberal platform. In the summer of 1933 it had named a Royal Commission on Banking and Currency, with Lord

MacMillan as Chairman; in September the commission had recommended the establishment of a central bank. Bennett was still dubious. Privately he had denounced the chartered banks for "driving customers to the wall who are unable to liquidate their liabilities under existing economic conditions" and had menacingly reminded the banks that he would be responsible for the revision of the Bank Act in 1934.[11] But if Bennett was critical of some bankers, he still had confidence in the Canadian banking system. In 1934 he reminded one correspondent that "the fact is admitted on all sides that banks have served this country fairly well during this depression."[12] What had convinced Bennett that Canada needed a central bank? His explanation to the House stressed the problems of international exchange and his discovery at the World Economic Conference that Canada relied on Wall Street for international operations.[13] The proposed Bank of Canada would improve the regulation of foreign exchange but, as the Minister of Finance insisted, it was not intended to introduce any major changes in domestic credit or monetary policies.[14]

The new institution was carefully designed to ensure that inflationary pressures would be resisted.[15] The bank would eventually have a monopoly of the issue of bank notes and would be able to influence the availability of credit by the rediscount of bills, but the decision to expand or restrict credit would not be entrusted to the government. The Bank of Canada was to be a private bank, owned by private shareholders. The government would appoint the first Governor and the directors but in the future the shareholders would elect the directors and the directors would appoint the Governor. This cumbersome arrangement was designed to ensure that the government would not be able to dictate the policies of the central bank. What would happen if the government and the bank disagreed? "Unquestionably," the Minister of Finance replied, "the authority of the governor and the board of directors of the bank would prevail."[16] Governments presumably could not be trusted to resist inflationary pressures; monetary policy was too important to be left to politicians. The governor and the directors, as responsible businessmen, would protect the public interest by protecting the value of the dollar. Some Conservative spokesmen did talk of managing credit for the benefit of society but their arguments clearly implied that society would best be served by the sound monetary policies which had characterized Canadian banking policies in the past.

Mackenzie King also feared reckless inflation. If the central bank was an agent of the government, a future prime minister might be urged to manipulate the supply of credit without a proper regard for sound principles and would be criticized if he refused to give way. His first reaction was that "the act is an exceedingly good one, and I am more in favour of its provisions than some of the changes being suggested by some of our party." He worried about "the terrible position a govt. would be in with no buffer against the provinces & its own followers in the H. of C."[17] But King also knew of the intense resentment against commercial banks and financiers; the Liberal party would never be united in support of a privately owned central bank. And however suspicious he might be of backbenchers on monetary matters, he never questioned the principle that public policies must ultimately be determined by governments. If the central bank and the government disagreed, the will of the government should prevail; anything else would be a contradiction of parliamentary sovereignty. Some middle way would have to be found between a monetary policy dictated by the government and one determined by a privately controlled central bank.

King knew that many of his followers would oppose any compromise. "Some of the members are very decided in their views," he reminded one financier, "and it is not going to be an easy matter to influence their judgement, no matter how sound the arguments presented may be."[18] The first step was to play for time until the party could agree on a compromise which would be consistent with sound policies and also with parliamentary sovereignty. He persuaded caucus not to oppose the bill on second reading:

I was able to present the considerations of the moment . . . — the dangers of a publicly-owned & Govt. appointed bank vs. the dangers of a purely privately-owned, the former with danger to Govt. as such—the institution of government itself—and the latter dangerous to the political party that supported it. The thing to be done lies somewhere between the two. The aim this morning was to get the measure to the banking committee without disclosing the divisions in our own ranks till after it reaches there. This I got unanimity on eventually.[19]

King's solution was a mixed institution in which the majority of the directors would be appointed by the government but with the rest elected by private shareholders, thus permitting government control without complete government ownership. Some Liberals found this compromise unacceptable and there was a heated discussion in caucus early in March:

Member after member spoke in favour of a government-*owned* & controlled bank, a publicly owned bank. Several members, notably Charlie Stewart, Euler & others said that nothing would stop them advocating both, everyone was falling into their way of speaking. . . . I had to strike out boldly, first on the politics of the thing, the folly of imagining this wd. be the issue in a campaign (probably trade with the U.S. & waterways, etc.) bank forgotten (un fait accompli) save for our amendments re control—the merits of the question— Liberalism for control by subordination of special interest to the general, Toryism general interest subordinated to special, Socialism or State Ownership & control. This as thin edge of wedge to govt. in business. Govt. I said shd. control business, freedom for ind'l initiative, self-reliance etc.—finally present action—needed for a united party etc. I told them as leader I could not support state ownership of a bank, knowing what it would mean in way of pressure by members & provinces on govts. etc. We had a duty as trustees to the nation, greater than consideration of party, to see that credit of ctry. was not impaired etc.—pointed out how sensitive credit was, how good our banking system etc. & danger of frightening capital, saving etc.

When I got through I had carried caucus to the extent of their agreeing to move no amendment on 2nd reading, to vote against any progressive [C.C.F.] amendment, & to leave to me to make the statement on the House of our position on the second reading. It was a strong appeal & a bit impassioned—I dislike fighting our own men—but the men themselves for the most part seemed to enjoy it & to feel the truth of what I was saying.[20]

No Liberal could feel aggrieved by King's statement in the House for he did no more than pledge the party to the principle of a central bank without committing it to government ownership or government control.[21] Fortunately the C.C.F. motion was ruled out-of-order and the bill was safely referred to committee without any public revelation of the differences within the Liberal party.

The Standing Committee on Banking and Commerce held meetings for the next three months. The witnesses provided little guidance for they ranged from such conservative magnates as Sir Herbert Holt and Edward Beatty to convinced inflationists like G. G. McGeer and Major C. H. Douglas, the Social Credit theorist. Liberal and C.C.F. members of the committee repeatedly tried to amend the bill to establish government control or ownership; Bennett warned the committee of the danger of the bank becoming a "political football," and refused to compromise.[22] Some minor amendments were adopted but on the question of private ownership the legislation remained unchanged.

King never convinced all his followers that government control was sufficient. He did make his own position clear in the House[23] and his appeals to party unity did temper the speeches of more radical Liberals, but the best the party could agree on for third reading was an amendment for either government control or ownership.[24] When this was ruled out-of-order, the Liberals did at least present a united front by voting unanimously against the bill.

There were other minor but contentious issues raised during the debate.

In at least two cases the Opposition amendments were defeated but, politically, the government was embarrassed. One Liberal motion proposed that the Governor and the directors of the bank should be Canadian citizens. Bennett might ask "what experience any banker in Canada has had with regard to central banks,"[25] but his blunt refusal was seen as evidence of a colonial attitude. Even more controversial was the issue of bilingual currency. Now that Canadian currency would be issued by the Bank of Canada, what language would appear on the bills? Bennett was prepared to recognize French to the extent that while most bills would be printed in English, some would be printed in French for circulation in Quebec. He defended this concession vigorously as equitable and just but many French Canadians drew the logical inference that the government preferred not to have French appearing on money circulating in the rest of Canada.

French-Canadian Liberals bitterly resented the implication that the French language should be restricted to a Quebec ghetto and insisted on bilingual currency as a symbolic recognition of linguistic equality. King feared some English-Canadian backlash—"The French are apt to push this side too far," he noted in his diary[26]—but when Lapointe insisted, King allowed him to introduce an amendment to have all currency bilingual. When Bennett denounced this presumptuous proposal King went even farther and spoke in support of Lapointe's motion.[27] The amendment was defeated but some French-Canadian Conservatives voted for it and in the French-Canadian press the position of the Liberal party was widely applauded.[28]

The prolonged debate on the Bank of Canada could hardly be described as constructive. Little attention was given to the powers and responsibilities of this new financial institution. And on the issue of immediate concern—whether or not there was to be inflation—there was still no decision. The central bank could use its authority to issue currency and rediscount bills in order to expand the money supply but neither the government nor the major opposition party had made it clear what it hoped or expected the Bank of Canada to do. The debate, however, was more than a partisan competition for political advantage. The ultimate question was whether businessmen or politicians should control monetary policy. Bennett obviously believed that the integrity of the dollar was safer in the hands of businessmen. Mackenzie King was not in favour of inflation but for him the overriding principle was that governments must be ultimately responsible for policy, even for monetary policy. He had not managed to resolve the division within the Liberal party over government control or government ownership, but this was not a difference over the fundamental issue.

56

King characteristically assumed that any controversy between business-men and politicians over monetary policy could be resolved by frank discussion and he saw a mixed Board of Directors as an appropriate forum for discussion. His version of government control, by a government-appointed majority on the board, might delay the implementation of controversial policies but it would, like outright ownership, ensure that governments and not businessmen would have the final say on policy. As it happened the Bank of Canada only began operations in the following year and the question of ultimate control was never posed during the Bennett administration.

The financial problems of some Canadians could not be resolved by monetary policies, no matter who devised them. Canadian farmers, for example, needed more income, and this depended upon better crops and higher prices for their products. The government could do nothing about the weather but it could do something to help farmers stay on their land until conditions improved. The total debt of Canadian farmers was over one billion dollars, mainly in the form of mortgages.[29] Low prices and successive crop failures had meant that many farmers had made no mortgage payments for some years and the accumulated interest alone sometimes exceeded the present value of the farm. Mortgage companies rarely foreclosed—repossessed farms would only remain untilled—but for many farmers the growing burden of debt destroyed any hope of ever gaining title to their farm. If the family farm was to survive in western Canada, mortgages would have to be scaled down, even if it meant that the sanctity of contracts would be compromised. The Farmers' Creditors Arrangement Act established a procedure by which the courts could determine the farmer's ability to pay and could reduce the mortgage payments to this level.[30] Nobody opposed the legislation in the House but nobody was very optimistic about its effect. The Act would prevent mortgage arrears from accumulating but the financial plight of farmers would not be improved until farms could produce an adequate income.

The Natural Products Marketing Act was more radical, at least in principle, because it involved controlling prices by regulating the marketing of natural products. The initiative had come from fruit and dairy co-operatives in British Columbia, which had not been able to prevent independent producers from dumping perishable produce such as strawberries on the market and forcing prices to absurdly low levels. The co-operatives had successfully appealed to the provincial government to compel the minority to conform to their grading and marketing regulations; when the provincial legislation was declared *ultra vires* by the courts, the co-operatives appealed to the federal government. The provinces had no jurisdiction because some of the products were sold outside the province but federal intervention in marketing within a province was also of doubtful validity. The Natural Products Marketing Act was designed to avoid this constitutional problem by allowing provincial marketing boards to act as federal boards as well. Each local board would have the power to determine the quantity and quality of a produce to be offered for sale, and the time and place it could be marketed. By their control over marketing the boards could maintain higher prices for producers.

This proved to be the most controversial legislation of the session. The federal government was taken by surprise because it attached little importance to the measure. At first it had intended only to legislate for some specific commodities but, because of the difficulty of drafting legislation to cover the wide range of possible provincial marketing boards which might be set up, it had opted for a broad authority with the details to be left to administrators.[31] The bill was consistent with Conservative policies to the extent that, like the tariff, it gave some protection to producers, but only local markets for small fruits and some dairy products would be affected. Regulating the price of strawberries in Vancouver would not have much effect on the national economy. Broadly interpreted, however, the act would allow the government to control the production and sale of most of the raw materials and food produced in Canada. The debate focussed on the theoretical issue of government intervention in the economy.

King had to take the legislation seriously because once again the unity of the Liberal party was threatened. The C.C.F. welcomed the bill because in principle they saw it as a step towards a planned economy. There were also enthusiastic Liberal supporters, especially those from western Canada who, like W. R. Motherwell, the former Minister of Agriculture, had been active in co-operatives and had waged a long battle for the "orderly marketing" of prairie wheat. Other Liberals, however, were equally vehement in their opposition to this interference with private enterprise. The Natural Products Marketing Act might have only a marginal impact on marketing but King could not ignore the political repercussions if the Liberal party revealed that it was divided over the issue of economic planning.

King, as usual, managed to focus attention on an aspect of the bill on which all liberal-minded men could agree. The issue, as he described it, was not planning but the delegation of parliamentary authority to appointed boards. "It is a shameful measure," was his immediate reaction to the bill. "We shall have neither liberty nor government in a little while. It creates a lot of self-appointed soviets to manage affairs, and destroys the power of parliament altogether."[32] In caucus Liberals who suggested that their constituents wanted some form of marketing legislation were over-ruled by this appeal to the higher law of liberalism. King ended his lecture to his followers by "speaking of grandfather having been prepared to sac-rifice home life etc. for principles, liberty for his fellow men & I was pre-pared if need be to do the same."[33] He then carried his crusade to the House where, in a two-hour speech, he showed that democracy was in danger and managed to work in three separate references to Magna Carta.[34] The following speaker might well ask what this had to do with the price of strawberries.

The bill had a difficult passage through the House. King was more careful in subsequent interventions to express his wholehearted support for the principle of orderly marketing[35] but, in spite of warnings from prominent Liberals,[36] he continued to denounce the legislation. The government offered only a half-hearted defence. Bennett took almost no part in the debate and H. H. Stevens, Minister of Trade and Commerce, lamely explained that in these trying times the people demanded "some-thing out of the ordinary"[37] and that the government could not be more specific because nobody knew what should be done.[38] Some amendments were adopted which did restrict the powers delegated to the boards al-though the broad outlines remained unchanged. On the final vote the C.C.F. supported the bill but all the Liberals, with the exception of Motherwell, voted against it. King considered it "an excellent afternoon's performance."[39]

During the session of 1934, however, government legislation and oppo-sition criticism received far less publicity than did the proceedings of a select committee of the House, a committee appointed to investigate price spreads. Stevens, the Chairman of the committee, had achieved some prominence by his disclosure of the Customs scandals nine years before, but in twenty years of public life he had remained a secondary figure within the Conservative party. He seemed an unlikely champion of social reform and an even more unlikely critic of the government. But Stevens, like many Conservative members, had been nurtured in the tradition of the local businessman, the retail merchant, and the small manufacturer, the men who embodied the virtues of thrift and hard work and who epi-tomized the system of free enterprise. The depression was disastrous for many of these small entrepreneurs, and it was widely believed that large enterprises—mail order and chain stores, meat-packing firms, and major manufacturers—were exploiting the advantages of size to drive small firms into bankruptcy. Large firms, it was claimed, could force down the prices for the goods they purchased, undersell their smaller competitors, and still make a handsome profit. Stevens, like many of his compatriots, was sympathetic to the plight of the smaller entrepreneurs. What brought him to prominence in 1934 was that he went beyond generalities and implicated specific firms. In the depression atmosphere, when soulless corporations were a popular scapegoat, Stevens attracted wide-spread attention. Within a few months he became a popular national figure and a potential rival to R. B. Bennett.

The Price Spreads Committee had an innocuous beginning. Bennett had been scheduled to speak at a convention of retail shoe merchants in Toronto early in January 1934 and at the last minute had asked Stevens to take his place. Stevens in his speech had accused large firms of using their dominant position to extort price concessions from their suppliers, thus provoking sweat-shop conditions among manufacturers, and then of underselling local businessmen and so crushing those who were "probably the finest expression of democratic life to be found anywhere."[40] He mentioned no names but his accusations were too pointed to be ignored. Officials of Eaton's and Simpson's, the major mail-order firms, promptly denied the allegations.

Stevens was probably surprised by the publicity he received. His speech was widely reported and his desk was soon piled high with letters of approval. He seems to have been impressed by his sudden popularity; the response certainly strengthened his conviction that the evil influence of department and chain stores had to be destroyed.[41] When the Prime Minister criticized him privately for his irresponsible statements, he threatened to resign. Bennett was not prepared to dismiss a minister who had suddenly emerged as the champion of small businessmen. Instead, he appointed Stevens as Chairman of a Select Committee to investigate the effects of mass buying and the reasons for the spread between the prices received by producers and those paid by consumers.

If Bennett thought the investigation would end the agitation, he was wrong. Witnesses alleged that department stores and meat-packing and tobacco firms had made huge profits and that their executives were paid munificent salaries while their employees were on starvation wages. Representatives of these firms denied any unfair practices but their evidence was often disputed by Stevens himself, who made no attempt to hide his conviction that the companies were guilty of nefarious practices. The hearings of the Special Committee were well attended, the press coverage was extensive, and, although the evidence of guilt was far from conclusive, the public was eager to believe the worst. Successful corporations were obvious scapegoats at a time when so many were suffering privation, and the bias of the committee reinforced this popular prejudice.

The Stevens committee had not completed its hearings by July when the session ended. Public opinion, however, had already rendered a verdict of guilty and any attempt to delay further hearings until the next session would have been widely interpreted as an attempt to suppress the investigation. Bennett took the unusual step of transforming the Select Committee into a Royal Commission, and the hearings continued after prorogation. For the moment nobody could assess the political impact of the investigation. Large business enterprises were obviously more vulnerable and the pressure for government regulation was intensified. Stevens had acquired a sudden popularity as a crusader and, as a member of the government, his prominence might benefit the Conservative party. It would depend upon whether Bennett took advantage of the opportunity and capitalized on the popular sentiments with which his colleague was now identified.

Mackenzie King paid little attention during the session to the Stevens committee. He felt no need to get involved until a report was tabled and the government had announced its policy, and he expected the election to be held before then. He ended the session on a confident and, indeed, a belligerent note. He asserted in the House that the government "has lost completely the confidence of the country and that it should no longer continue in office." If it persisted in desperately clinging to power, and if it called yet another session of the present Parliament, he stated bluntly that his party would "do all in its power" to obstruct the government and force an election. This, King announced, "is not a threat, it is a duty."[42]

II

King's conviction that the Conservative government would not survive the election had been strengthened by some political developments at the provincial level. There had been two provincial elections in June 1934, in Ontario and Saskatchewan. In each province an incumbent Conservative government had been decisively defeated and a Liberal administration had taken over. These elections had been fought on provincial issues but the unpopularity of the Bennett government had also been a factor.

The most startling Conservative setback had come in Ontario where the Liberals under Mitchell Hepburn won a sweeping victory. Ontario had long been dominated by the Conservatives; who had been in office at Queen's Park for all but four of the last thirty years and had consistently won a majority of the provincial ridings in federal elections. The party seemed almost invulnerable; in 1929 the provincial government had been returned with the largest majority in the history of the province and in

61

1930 more than two-thirds of the Ontario members sent to Ottawa were Conservatives. The Liberal victory in the provincial election of June 1934 was therefore a dramatic upset. Even more surprising was the decisiveness of the victory, with the Liberals winning seventy of the ninety seats. Even in Tory Toronto six Liberal candidates were successful. A surprising number of the usually reliable voters of Ontario had shifted their political allegiance.

The result was widely interpreted as a protest vote. As Manion commented, "General discontent and general depression [are] two great leaders for any opposition." The unpopularity of the federal Conservative government was certainly a factor although the provincial Conservatives had also been on the defensive because of a series of alleged scandals. For the Liberals, however, it was reassuring that most of the dissatisfied voters had turned to the Liberal rather than to the C.C.F. party. By 1934 the C.C.F. in Ontario had been weakened by serious internal divisions. From the beginning the United Farmers of Ontario had been uneasy about their association with labour. When the Labour Councils had been discredited by communist activities, the United Farmers had withdrawn leaving the C.C.F. completely disorganized.[43] Most of the protest votes went to Liberal candidates.

Mere protest, however, can hardly explain the extent of the Liberal victory. Mitchell Hepburn had been a major factor. He had been chosen as provincial leader in 1930 and over the next four years had broadened the base of the party. He himself had once been a member of the United Farmers of Ontario and when Harry Nixon, leader of the provincial Progressives, gave his support to Hepburn, the Liberal party regained much of its traditional rural support. Arthur Roebuck, a prominent labour lawyer, and David Croll, the mayor of Windsor, helped to consolidate the support of both labour and ethnic groups in urban areas.[44] By 1934 the Liberal party had a positive appeal for a wide range of voters who no longer had confidence in the Conservative administration.

"Mitch" Hepburn's personality may have been as important as his political strategy. Political leadership in Canada had traditionally come from the respectable middle class, from men whose style and values resembled those of successful businessmen. In the 1930s many Canadians, the victims of economic conditions over which they had no control, no longer trusted the traditional leaders of society. Hepburn offered them an alternative because he was different. He was aggressive and flamboyant and young—he was only thirty-seven in 1934. He could be reckless in his denunciation of the public or private activities of his opponents and reckless too in his promises of what he would accomplish. He gave an impression of virility, which was enhanced by his homespun metaphors, his brashness, his lack of dignity, his impulsiveness, and his quick temper. He had also rejected some of the most obvious middle-class virtues. He consorted with gamblers and prostitutes and drank to excess—as one old-fashioned Liberal complained to King, "Hepburn is too wet to burn."[45] But even his intemperance did him little harm. People, and especially younger people, had learned that poverty could never be genteel and that middle-class leaders had no answers to the depression. For those who had suffered, a vote for a man like Hepburn was a symbolic rejection of the old order. This rejection of traditional middle-class leadership had also been a factor in the election of Pattullo in British Columbia, as it would be in the support for Aberhart in Alberta and for Duplessis in Quebec.

Mackenzie King and Mitchell Hepburn had little in common except membership in the same party. It was typical of Hepburn that when first elected to Parliament in 1926 he had objected to being relegated to a seat in the back row in the House and had blamed one of the Ministers for this personal affront. It was typical of King that he took the time to soothe Hepburn's ruffled feelings. King found Hepburn brash and irresponsible but recognized his enthusiasm and tolerated his volatility.[46] He did not like such men but he knew they could be useful.

Mackenzie King could tolerate Hepburn as a backbencher but he had showed less detachment when Hepburn became a candidate for the leadership of the provincial party in 1930. King took no official part in the leadership contest and did not attend the convention but he did intervene privately. Hepburn was not his choice; the provincial party might well be compromised under the erratic Mitch and even the reputation of the federal party might suffer by the association. Of more immediate significance, Hepburn would be expected to resign his federal seat if he became provincial leader and the Liberals might lose the by-election. King invited Hepburn to a small gathering at Laurier House and, as he later recorded, tried to dissuade him from running:

Quite clearly Hepburn is flattered by the approaches made to him & would like to be given the leadership. We pointed out the dangers, no seat in the Legislature, no funds for organization, Tory attacks in Fed. & Prov. House, riding two horses & falling between, the affront to Sinclair [the actual leader of the Ontario Liberal party] etc. etc. I was frank in saying we did not want to lose him from the Federal House, that I believed it wd. be Hepburn's undoing etc.— later we discussed his danger of drinking & getting mixed up with women, at his young age this wd. be fatal to success. I doubt too if he is sufficiently broad gauged.[47]

King even tried to persuade another Liberal to contest the leadership, a man whose major qualification was that he was not erratic and whose selection would at least avoid a by-election.[48] When this effort failed, King suggested as a temporary solution that the convention merely appoint a committee to lead the party with Hepburn as a member. But, as one Liberal commented, the Ontario Liberals "wanted a young man of colourful personality, decision and courage, who can also as a leader appeal to our rural people."[49] The convention, tired of cautious leaders who always lost elections, chose Hepburn on the first ballot.[50]

Mackenzie King never brooded over setbacks. He promptly wired Hepburn his "heartfelt congratulations . . . Your selection as Liberal leader for Ontario does honour to us all."[51] This was followed next day by a long letter in which he commended Hepburn for his ability and enthusiasm, explained his reluctance to see Hepburn leave federal politics but promised his full co-operation and offered some sound advice on party organization.[52] Over the next few years he was careful to treat Hepburn as a respected colleague, to give him credit for his achievements in Ontario, and to encourage other Liberals to support his efforts.[53]

Hepburn, for his part, was in no position to spurn offers of co-operation from the federal Liberals and he too behaved like a loyal party member. In his acceptance speech at the convention he had referred warmly to King, even declaring that "I love that man."[54] Whatever his true feelings may have been, he co-operated by campaigning vigorously in federal by-elections in Ontario and by retaining his federal seat until just before the provincial elections in June 1934. By then the two men were on confident enough terms that King could give Hepburn fatherly advice about campaigning: "Again, let me implore you, in your own interests and that of the party to do everything in your power to avoid discussion other than on a public platform and, no matter how difficult it may be, do not yield to the wishes of others to share with them all kinds of social obligations in addition to the imperative and all important demands of the campaign."[55] Hepburn showed no signs of following this advice but apparently he did not resent it. Two days after the election he announced that he was going to Ottawa to consult with the leader of the federal Liberal party.

King was quick to see the danger of becoming involved in provincial affairs. He immediately announced his willingness to discuss problems with Hepburn but explained that he would not interfere in any way. Hepburn alone would have to take the final responsibility for choosing his colleagues and deciding on the policies of his government. When Hepburn arrived, King avoided specific issues but did offer general advice, such as the importance of able colleagues and "also stressed re drinking, not to take or appoint anyone with that habit."[56] In a subsequent letter he repeated his advice "to be increasingly non-communicative as far as the press is concerned and to reserve your pronouncements for public meetings and the legislature." He also suggested discussing all decisions with his colleagues before making any announcements; "adoption of this course will save you many pitfalls."[57] But he was careful not to go beyond this paternal counsel. He consistently refused to intercede with the new government on behalf of any of his friends.[58] He still did not trust Hepburn and now that Hepburn was in office, and less dependent upon federal support, King was more prudent than ever. He commented in his diary after meeting Hepburn that the newly-elected Premier "seemed intoxicated in a love of publicity . . . I confess to a real concern as to his ability to keep away from 'the gang' around him, & exercise the needed judgement in matters of government. He needs prayer to aid him I told him to pray for strength and guidance."[59] Until he was sure that the prayers had been answered, King would be on his guard. As he explained to a correspondent, he was "anxious to avoid being, directly or indirectly, under obligation for even the slightest favour."[60] He was delighted by the Liberal victory in Ontario but intended to keep a safe distance from the unpredictable Hepburn.

On the same day as the Ontario elections, June 19, there was a provincial election in Saskatchewan. The Liberal victory there was less of a surprise but it was even more decisive. J. T. M. Anderson, the Conservative Premier, had been in difficulty from the time he took office in 1929. He had depended on the support of Progressives in the legislature for his majority and had had the additional burden of governing the province which had suffered most severely from the depression. J. G. Gardiner had directed his talents towards reorganizing the Liberal party and in his campaign had criticized the government without committing himself to new or radical policies. The Liberals won fifty seats, with the other five seats going to the C.C.F. Not a single Conservative was elected. Federal tariff policies had been a major issue in the campaign, which augured well for the next federal election,[61] and Gardiner was a leader who could be relied on to be responsible, cautious, and loyal. King's satisfaction with the Saskatchewan results was unqualified.

The federal Liberals interpreted the two provincial victories as defeats for R. B. Bennett. "Today has been [one] of the very best days in the H. of C.," wrote King. "The Govt. is cowed before the blow it has been struck by the two provincial elections. One can see it has taken the last hope from them."[62] He gave full credit to Hepburn and Gardiner in his press release but did point out that federal issues had been discussed. "The country," he concluded, "has served notice on the Prime Minister, Mr. Bennett, that his administration has long since ceased to enjoy its confidence, and that the government's future continuation in office is without a shadow of a justification."[63] The victories in Ontario and Saskatchewan, combined with a successful session at Ottawa, seemed to ensure that the federal Liberals would soon be in office.

III

In July Bennett announced five federal by-elections to be held in September. King was disappointed because this made it almost certain that there would be no general election until after another session but he decided to treat the by-elections as "a miniature general election" and to provide more proof of the unpopularity of the Bennett administration."[64] If the government won in even two of the constituencies, Bennett would probably brazen out another session and hold the election the next fall.[65] Should the Liberals win all the by-elections King did "not see how he can possibly face Parliament again. If he does, however, it should be an easy matter for us to refuse him supply and force a general election."[66]

A Liberal victory could well be interpreted as a rejection of the government. All of the five seats were in Ontario. Two of them were Liberal ridings, opened when Hepburn and Peter Heenan had resigned to run in the provincial elections. The other three seats, however, were traditionally Conservative, vacant in each case because of the death of the sitting member. North York, now a part of metropolitan Toronto, had elected a Conservative ever since King's defeat there in 1925. Toronto East had always been Conservative although the labour vote gave the C.C.F. some hope of winning the seat.[67] Frontenac-Addington was one of a bloc of Conservative constituencies in eastern Ontario and had never returned a Liberal.

The Liberals had high hopes, not only because of the declining fortunes of the federal Conservatives but also because Hepburn was now in office in Ontario. His government had already introduced some popular measures and his support might be decisive. Hepburn did not disappoint them. He behaved with his usual vigour and actually attracted more publicity than Mackenzie King.[68] Indeed, Hepburn was so active that some federal Liberals became concerned about his motives. His personal dislike of Bennett and his hope that a Liberal government at Ottawa would bear a larger share of relief costs provided only a partial explanation for his enthusiasm. His insistence that the provincial Liberal organization should collect and distribute the campaign funds was especially disquieting; he seemed to assume that Ontario was his bailiwick and that even the federal

66

Liberals should accept his authority. Vincent Massey, President of the National Liberal Federation, explained to King that he could hardly refuse Hepburn's help. The federal party was little more than a federation of the provincial parties; the provincial organizers and the provincial fund raisers would be needed for the federal election. The status of the National Liberal Federation needed to be affirmed but its dependence on the Ontario organization made it vulnerable.[69]

King made a special trip to Toronto to try to arrange a satisfactory compromise. His aim was to persuade the provincial financial committee to act as a committee of the National Liberal Federation for the by-elections and the coming general election. His arguments were those of a politician who soon expected to be in office:

I spoke out very frankly and fully about the relations of several groups to the existing situation, the jealousies between the Ontario office and the federal parliamentary group—urged making Lambert [Secretary of the National Liberal Federation] the centre through which all should operate, a link with Quebec and other provinces as well, with myself a court of last resort to approve or disapprove important steps. I made it clear I would make no promises to anyone, also that if in office, my view would be that other things being equal, wherever the matter was not one of contract to be settled by tender, supporters of the Government should get the preference, and between supporters, those who helped most to make the party's principles and policies prevail—those who helped now in days of need and opposition.

King's proposal was accepted, to his great relief. "Ending the meeting I said 'How blessed a thing it is for brethren to dwell together in unity.'"[70] This, however, was as much an admonition as a benediction. The future role of Hepburn was still unclear and King suspected that he "might be seeking to build up a little machine of his own." There were already rumours that Hepburn was trying to have his own candidates nominated for some federal ridings. But King could live with uncertainty. "Be this as it may," he concluded this entry in his diary, "sufficient unto the day is the evil thereof."[71] The immediate objective was to win the by-elections.

H. H. Stevens threatened to disrupt the Liberal plans. The Parliamentary Committee had now become the Royal Commission on Price Spreads but Stevens, in spite of his role as Chairman, made no effort to be either judicial or objective. His first step at the end of the session had been to write a pamphlet giving his observations on the committee hearings. There was nothing tentative about the title, *Deplorable Conditions in Some Businesses Revealed*, and the entire pamphlet was a tirade against "the strange and, I was going to say, incomprehensible disregard for ethics that has characterized some of the leaders in industry and finance in this country." Stevens mentioned some of the firms by name and went on to say that he, for one, would not condone their activities. The true conservative could not accept dictation from financial interests. "I believe that this Conservative party must readjust itself, get a new orientation of its views on some of our political policies and fix them upon the well being of the farmer first, and on the large body of industrial workers in the second place."[72] Bennett was not pleased. He insisted that the pamphlet, with its unsubstantiated allegations, be suppressed, but he apparently accepted Stevens' explanation that it had only been intended for private circulation and took no further action.[73]

The pamphlet had already been mailed to a number of newspaper editors—Stevens had an unorthodox view of private circulation—and could not be suppressed.[74] One can only guess why Stevens had written this extraordinary document. J. W. Dafoe thought the most plausible explanation was that Stevens saw himself "as a great popular hero; and perhaps the leader of a Tory party transmogrified into a radical outfit. It is probably not a matter of calculation; he is an emotional fellow, who easily works himself into a state of moral indignation."[75] Partisan Liberals took a less tolerant view; they favoured Ian Mackenzie's explanation that it was "a bare faced attitude by Stevens to save his own political neck when he sees his party already wrecked."[76] Bennett's reaction was also puzzling. The pamphlet was a harsh criticism of his administration and yet Stevens was not asked to resign from the government or from the Royal Commission. Either Bennett was procrastinating or he wanted to capitalize on Stevens' popularity for the by-elections before taking action.

During the by-election campaigns the Conservatives did try to take advantage of Stevens' role as champion of the oppressed. Bennett was in Geneva and did not return until after the elections but Stevens played a prominent part in the campaign. The Liberal response was to point out the contradictions between Stevens' position and the policy of the Conservative administration. As Mackenzie King explained it, the Conservative tariffs had made nefarious trade practices possible· and so were to blame for the evils which Stevens decried; the Tories had lost the confidence of the public and were now losing confidence in themselves.[77] Hepburn was more colourful: Why had Stevens not resigned? Because he was like a sign-post; "he points the way but is not prepared to go." He dismissed the pamphlet as no more than a Tory plot with Stevens and Bennett in collusion to hoodwink the people.[78] The debate may not have enlightened the citizens of Ontario but it did make politics more interesting for them; at one meeting the hall was so crowded that King had to enter by a window to get to the platform.[79]

The results of the by-elections did show that the government was in serious political difficulty. King was disappointed that Toronto East had re-elected a Conservative. T. L. Church, the successful candidate, had not received a clear majority, however, and in any case he was not an orthodox Conservative and was an independent in fact if not in name. The Liberals did win in the other four constituencies, and in each case the majority was over two thousand votes. As Mackenzie King told the press: "the popular verdict goes far beyond being one merely of lack of confidence. It is one of no uncertain hostility to the Bennett administration."[80]

For King the "little general election" seemed decisive. Bennett was so obviously discredited that the Liberals could now attack with impunity. At the next session they could obstruct the business of the House and refuse to vote supply, confident that popular opinion would approve. Late in September, a few days after the by-elections, King left for a two-month holiday in Europe, his last chance to relax before the next session of the present Parliament and the campaign that would follow. Bennett left London shortly after King arrived. He returned home to a party facing defeat and to a divided Cabinet in which Stevens had emerged as a critic if not a personal rival. There would be no holiday for Bennett before the next session.

CHAPTER FOUR

BEYOND POLITICS

MACKENZIE KING was now in his sixtieth year. He was remarkably healthy for his age. He suffered from arthritis but he could still endure the physical strain of a political campaign and could stay on his feet to deliver a four-hour speech and then spend the next five or six hours revising the text for Hansard. When physical effort or concentration were required, he could still respond. Age, however, had taken some toll. He was less resilient than he had been; he felt more tired after a trip or a speech and more impatient during caucus discussions. If there were no pressing political demands on his time he was more inclined to isolate himself at Kingsmere and to indulge in non-political distractions.

His distractions were those of a lonely and self-centred old man. He seldom attended symphonies or plays, had no interest in popular sports—he paid no attention to the Grey Cup or the Stanley Cup play-offs—and he was not tempted by the increasingly popular game of bridge. He did have an annual outing to watch the Minto Club figure-skaters and he occasionally saw a film, often because he was appearing in the newsreel. In his years as Leader of the Opposition politics absorbed less of his time and he was therefore more free to yield to his fascination for the many manifestations of the spirit world; his ventures into the occult helped to dissipate his loneliness and also to reassure him of his significance as a person as well as a public figure. Politics would continue to be his major occupation but in this less hectic interim he could allow himself the luxury of a private world.

I

The summer of 1934 was for King a peaceful interlude after the long session and before the September by-elections. It was also likely to be the last summer of relative freedom because the session of 1935 would be followed by the general election. As he explained to a colleague in mid-July:

I have not given myself a real rest for twenty or more years, and as you know, some of the years have been exceptionally strenuous and anxious ones. I want to be in the best of shape for a political campaign, when it comes on, and for the years of strenuous effort which I believe are ahead, let the result of the campaign be what it will. I have, therefore, made up my mind this summer, regardless of what others may think, to take all the rest I possibly can, and avoid speaking as well as other engagements, for at least the remainder of this month and the month of August.[1]

King felt the need for a rest because he had been very concerned about his health. During the winter he had been seriously bothered by arthritic pains in his leg and although he had not been confined to Laurier House he had had to forgo his regular walks along the Rideau Canal.[2] Massages and mild electric shock treatment in Ottawa and a visit to an osteopath in New York had provided only partial relief. His annual visit in November 1933 to a doctor in Baltimore had at least reassured him that his general state of health was excellent. The doctor had linked the arthritis to two abscessed teeth, which King had had extracted on his return to Ottawa.[3] Possibly more important was his insistence that King must go on a very restricted diet, since his weight had gone up to almost two hundred pounds. King had taken the warning seriously and, being a man of exceptional self-control, had kept to the diet rigidly. There are surprisingly few references to the rigours of his diet in the diary for the next few months but the results were soon apparent. By July King had lost forty pounds.*

King was in remarkably good health but he had the usual apprehensions about the approaching frailties of old age. Some of his outings during this relatively quiet summer were visits to Dr Locke, a popular doctor some fifty miles south of Ottawa who believed that most pains were caused by pressure on the nerves and who treated almost all physical ailments by manipulating the bones of the feet. King privately expressed some scepticism—he was perceptive enough to suspect that his arthritis was largely the result of worry and emotional strain—but his eagerness to believe that Locke was a "healer" suggests a hidden fear of growing old. He might be sceptical but he did visit Williamsburg five times during the summer.[4]

Age also deepened King's feeling of loneliness. He had a deep personal need for affection but he had never been able to sustain a close relationship which imposed any obligations or which required any concessions or sacrifices on his part. As a politician he attended many social functions and he did have some personal contacts outside of politics but none of

*Diary, July 24, 1934. King also required stronger glasses for reading at this time although he did not yet need bifocals; Diary, Jan. 9, 1934.

these associations could fulfil his compulsive need to feel that people loved him. The need was always there but for King, who was determined not to let friendships interfere with his political decisions and who suspected that most people had ulterior motives, it was not easy to resolve his problem.

His solution was to find reassurance in another world. He had become intrigued and fascinated by psychic experiences. He recognized the political risks involved and also had some misgivings about the moral implications of communicating with the spirit world but he had come to depend on the solace of messages from the dear departed. He eased his conscience by keeping a record of his experiences and by telling himself that he was doing psychical research but this was a transparent rationalization. As he once explained to a woman who was deeply involved in psychical phenomena:

The time I give to it, however, is rather by way of diversion and relaxation, and I should add, inspiration, than anything in the nature of serious study and research. I recognize that my real work is in Parliament and in dealing with present day affairs, and, in particular, the problems of the people. Nothing, however, has helped me quite so much in the prosecution of my day to day work than what I have gained, and continue to gain, from the time I am able to give at odd moments to reading and reflection along psychical lines.[5]

King's contacts with the spirit world were so important that in spite of his uneasiness and his ambivalence he found it impossible to live without them. As part of his summer holiday he invited Etta Wreidt, a medium from Detroit, to visit Kingsmere.[6] The visit was planned for mid-August but was abruptly cancelled when King heard that a magazine article had appeared which referred to his interest in psychic matters. The article proved to be an innocuous criticism of his political opinions but King at first felt that he should "heed the warning." It was not long, however, before King's caution gave way to his desire, and the visit took place at the end of the month.

Mrs Wreidt was a guest at Kingsmere for four days. She did her part by going into a trance and her interlocutors from beyond did speak but for two of the days the results were very disappointing. Whatever the reason, whether it was ectoplasmic interference or that King was not in a properly receptive mood, Mrs Wreidt's contacts had no messages from the people to whom King wished to speak. On the other two days, however, communications were established and King did hear from his parents, from William Lyon Mackenzie, Wilfrid Laurier, and a number of other friendly souls. King was thrilled by this evidence that he was not

72

alone although it was an exhausting four days and he was not unhappy to see Mrs Wreidt leave.

For the next few days, however, his diary records his growing doubts about what he had heard. The communication from his father, for example, had given the impression that John King was an authoritarian businessman, and King "felt certain it was not his soul and spirit that was reaching me." Nor could he reconcile the boastful William Lyon Mackenzie with his own image of his grandfather as a dedicated Christian, or the assertive and dominating Wilfrid Laurier with the generous gentleman he had known. Most disturbing of all, his mother had not spoken at all at the last session and the interlocutor had even said that she was not there.[8] King knew that this was inconceivable; it was enough to convince him, for the moment at least, that séances were an unreliable means of communicating with the departed. The problem must lie with the reliance on an intermediary, who had obviously intervened in some way and distorted the messages. His doubts did not extend to questioning the existence of the spirits or their eagerness "to guide and to guard him" but, as he explained it, "spiritualism is the lowest plane" and the most reliable communications were those which came to him directly from the loved ones.[9]

Fortunately King had already discovered how to receive messages from beyond without having to rely on a medium. Dr Arthur Doughty, the dignified Dominion Archivist, had introduced him to the parlour-game of table-rapping in the winter of 1933. Many Canadians, at one time or another, had spend an evening seated around a table with hands touching and, if all went well, having the table leg tap out answers to their questions. For most of them it was no more than an intriguing experience but for King it was a confirmation of what he wanted to believe. "It was an amazing evening," he recorded. "The first time I have seen table-rapping and having messages come thro' to me from father, mother, Max and Bella. There can be no shadow of doubt as to their genuineness."* This new form of contact with the spirit world had the added advantage that it did not require the presence of a medium. It was also fortunate that King's friend, Joan Patteson, shared his fascination for the occult and when he felt the urge he could drop in at the Pattesons and sit down at the table.

Joan Patteson was an unusually discreet and sympathetic woman, always ready to share King's interests, to listen to his account of the events of the day, to read and discuss the books he was reading, and to respond to his different moods. She was much more than a passive listener, however. She was widely read, a woman of good taste, sensitive and percep-

---

*Diary, Nov. 13, 1933. Max was King's deceased brother and Bella his deceased sister.

tive, and King respected her opinions on all the subjects they discussed.[10] Her husband, Godfroy, was a banker and an ardent gardener but as far as King was concerned he was an unobtrusive presence. He was important only because as Joan's husband he eliminated the risk of scandal. The Pattesons' apartment on Elgin Street and their cottage at Kingsmere were havens for King whenever he felt the need for companionship. The initiative for the visits and telephone calls came from King but Joan was always there and he took full advantage of the Pattesons' hospitality. It was an indication of his insatiable need for reassurance that Joan's friendship was not enough and that King still needed messages from beyond.

One of the frequent occasions when King felt the need to hear from the dear departed was on his fifty-ninth birthday, in December 1933. It was remarkable, if not uncanny, how responsive the loved ones were and how often they told King what he wanted to hear. On this particular evening he and Joan felt they were given amazing evidence of "the tenderness and love" which surrounded them. A long procession of King's relatives and ancestors sent messages of "love" or "happy birthday." The session ended when King, after three hours of greetings, was abruptly told to "go home." King commented in his diary that he was indeed very tired but by then he had also realized with some embarrassment that all the messages had been for him and that Joan had been ignored. He insisted on redressing the balance and Joan's dead daughter Nancy did send her love. "I asked any other message—Answ. Go to bed." King thereupon yielded to this higher authority and went home.[11]

The messages King received almost always gave him the reassurance which the living could not provide. In March 1934 he gave a speech in Toronto which he felt had been a disaster. His train arrived in Ottawa late the next day but instead of returning directly to Laurier House he stopped off at the Pattesons and sat down with Joan at the table. "It was midnight," he noted, "but I felt I wanted at least just a word which would help me to know what those beyond thought of Friday night." To his great relief Sir Wilfrid Laurier told him that he had done "exceedingly well last night."[12] Coming from Laurier this must have been most reassuring.

Even table-rapping, however, had its hazards. There was nothing clandestine about his friendship with Joan—she even acted as hostess at some of his dinner parties—but it would have been unusual if King at times had not felt some physical attraction to Joan. He would never have admitted to such a natural feeling, even to himself, but on one occasion a session at the table gave some hint of what lay behind the self-control. One of the messages they received was in praise of love and King recorded that both he and Joan sensed they were being tempted by earthly passion. Joan wanted

74

to end the session immediately but King persuaded her to go on "for scientific reasons." The messages then "became very personal and direct, so much so that I would not write down what was said."[13] Both of them found it was a very disturbing experience but they could not resist the temptation to try again next evening. This time the messages restored stability by making it clear that the praise was for spiritual rather than physical love. According to King's diary, both he and Joan were much relieved and reassured.[14]

There were no hints of illicit passion in subsequent sessions but King's early enthusiasm for table-rapping became more restrained for other reasons. He began to pose questions about future events only to receive answers that later proved to be wrong. He tried to explain away minor discrepancies as "difficulties & possible errors in transmission" but it was not so easy to minimize some of the more glaring mistakes. For example, King naturally wondered whom Bennett would recommend for knighthood for the King's birthday list in 1934. He had prepared his own list of probable recipients and, at a table-rapping session, his list was confirmed. When the honours were announced on 3 June, however, none of King's choices were included.[15] King was puzzled but he quickly thought of an explanation. He had not asked when the titles would be conferred; there would probably be a special Dominion Day honours list which would include the names confirmed by the table.[16] While waiting for this vindication of his ethereal informants, King and Joan had yet another session and learned, this time from Laurier, that the Conservatives would be re-elected in Ontario in the June election by a slim majority. This again coincided with King's own expectations. He was so confident that he told Ernest Lapointe what the honours list and the Ontario elections would bring, although he did not reveal his sources.[17]

Hepburn's sweeping victory was a matter for rejoicing but it forced some second thoughts about table-rapping: "I felt an anguish of mind and heart, in discovering that this 'prophecy' had failed, that Sir Wilfrid had not had the knowledge evidently required and had seen only so much of the whole. I did not want to have any feeling of disloyalty to him, nor to doubt it was he who was speaking, as in fact I did not. I believe it was he, but that he was unable to foretell, had based his knowledge on what he had foregathered, but the knowledge was insufficient."[18] The long awaited knighthoods might still re-establish the reliability of his sources. King recorded that at a table-rapping session on July 1st, Sir Wilfrid even "told us that the titles had been granted, that the recipients knew 'now'." Even if Laurier's prophetic powers might be inadequate, he could surely be relied on to know what had actually happened.[19] Unfortunately there was no list of honours for Dominion Day. Had the announcement been delayed? A few days later King had to admit the blunt fact that Laurier had been wrong and there would be no additional knighthoods. He and Joan puzzled over the implications; "we were either using our own sub-conscious thoughts, or an evil spirit was creeping in."[20]

Table-rapping might well have ended with this incident. But King was not primarily concerned with the opinions or prophecies of his contacts. The question he had posed had been about events over which he had no control; he had never thought of asking advice about his own decisions. He now knew that he could not rely on the information he received but even this was not important. What he wanted most of all was some contact with those who had been close to him, some assurance that they still watched over him and still loved him. It was not political advice he wanted but some sign of the presence of the departed. The table could still provide this even if it could do nothing more. Mrs Patteson and King agreed that they could not believe the messages but that very night they sat down once again at the table.[21]

The sessions continued but they became less frequent and less remarkable. King noted in his diary the occasions when he had "conversations" at the table but after the incident of the titles he seldom bothered to record what the messages were. It was enough to have had contact with the departed. Table-rapping seems to have become no more than one of the many ways in which their reassuring presence was confirmed. Almost any incident might have the same effect—even the accidental spilling of ink and then seeing some references to spilt ink would become "one of those many 'coincidences' which remind one of our friends being about & letting us know in this way."[22] Table-rapping, like these other incidents, helped to dispel King's feeling of loneliness and to buttress his conviction that he was not really alone.

King also believed that his dreams were messages from the other world. For him these messages had the advantage that there was no interlocutor and therefore no risk of evil intervention. He had frequent dreams, as many as two or three a week, which he carefully recorded the next morning. All of them seemed significant but those in which relatives or former friends appeared had a special meaning and were usually identified as visions. King had heard of Freud and knew of the significance he attached to dreams,[23] but he remained naïvely unaware of what they could reveal about himself. When he interpreted his own dreams he ignored the possible psychological revelations and saw them as the voice of conscience or a confirmation that his motives and his actions were beyond reproach. Even when he could not interpret a vision, however, he was not disturbed. It was enough to have received a sign that he was not alone or forgotten.

76

His dreams do reveal the central place of his mother in his private world. It was not only that she appeared frequently; he often dreamed of Joan and other women as well. It was much more significant that these other women were sometimes explicitly identified with his mother. In one almost classic illustration of an Oedipus complex, King dreamt one night that he saw the face of Mrs Wreidt change directly into the face of his mother.[24] On another occasion he recorded that in his dream his mother had "the kind of look Joan had when I scolded her last night . . . a look that meant everything was understood."[25] King, however, was blissfully unaware of the interpretation that might be placed on this transfer of identity. It was enough for him that his mother had appeared. For the first dream he recorded "a joy in my heart that was indescribable"; for the second, "a delight indescribable in my heart at being with her." He felt no need to probe more deeply into the meaning of such visions.

King's dreams also hint at his ambivalent feelings for his father. John King had been a kindly but ineffective man who had never been able to live up to his wife's financial or social aspirations. Mackenzie King was aware of his father's shortcomings but as a dutiful son he could never admit that he had ever lacked filial respect and affection for him. This unresolved conflict had affected his relations with other men. As a younger man, for example, he had been a great admirer of Sir Wilfrid Laurier and had looked to him as he would to a father for guidance and advancement. Like most fathers, however, Sir Wilfrid had frustrated the younger King at times, sometimes appearing to ignore him or to pay too much attention to others.[26] Their relationship became even more complex in 1917 when Laurier had opposed conscription and rejected King's efforts to find some compromise. There was also the rumour that King had even considered betraying his leader by entering the Union Government.[27] King's interpretations of the dreams in which Laurier appears suggest the strain of this relationship. He did not recognize Laurier as a substitute father but like a son he did look for confirmation that Laurier still loved him and that Laurier at least had no doubts about King's loyalty to him.[28]

King's dreams at this period also suggest a subconscious response to encroaching old age, to the fear of declining virility. In one of his dreams he recorded, in March 1934, for example:

I seemed to be in a very large building, a very high one, and to be looking out to the roof. There I saw a woman I knew of refined nature and good character, standing naked on a pedestal, also posing in different positions. I could not make out why she was there & thought it first the modern craze for sensation. Then I found that some guests at the hotel came out and dropped money into a sort of tambourine she was holding and I noticed that it was poverty that had driven her to expose her nakedness. What impressed me was the beauty of her form—her natural beauty—and quite evident chastity and purity. Then I seemed to go into a room where there were four young persons, two ladies at one table, a young woman and a young lad in bed in the same room, the latter might have been brother and sister. There was no suggestion of immorality of any kind.

Mackenzie King, however, did more than record his dreams. He also interpreted them. He showed no awareness of the possible psychological explanations; for him his dreams were reminders of his obligations and duties, strengthening his resolve to catch up on his correspondence, to be more sociable, or to dedicate himself even more completely to the cause of humanity. In the dream just referred to, for instance, he saw no significance in the nudity or the couple in bed. The dream had come on the eve of the unveiling of a memorial to William Lyon Mackenzie on the hundredth anniversary of his election as mayor of Toronto. King was to be the principal speaker on this momentous occasion and he was busy preparing his speech. "It is clear," he concluded, "that this vision has been sent to help me in what I am preparing on my grandfather." The naked figure symbolized poverty; the dream was therefore a reminder that he should stress the privation which his grandfather and his mother suffered in exile after the rebellion.[29]

Dreams also provided confirmation for King's views on political leadership. He once found himself trying to board the engine of a train but somehow the engine was so crowded that he despaired of getting on until at last he found a place reserved for him. "It might mean," he concluded, "that I was party Leader, my business was to start the train moving, that also I should as Leader not get separated from the party but we should all keep together."[30] King scarcely needed a dream to remind him of the importance of keeping the party united; as usual, the message he discovered was a confirmation of what he already believed.

The source, however, was more significant than the actual message. For this reason, he considered his dreams—or visions—to be the most reassuring form of contact with the spirit world. Dreams required no intermediary; he actually saw his loved ones and their spiritual presence was unmistakeable. Any noctural message came to him directly, without any distortion and without the possible intervention of evil influences. And although King did not mention it, his dreams had the further advantage that they could mean what he wanted them to mean. His loved ones offered no specific advice or prophecies for the future; the message was what King drew from them. Even if subsequent events somehow contradicted his interpretation, he merely reinterpreted the dream without questioning the authenticity or the authority of the source.[31] Whatever happened, nothing could shake his conviction that the dear departed had made their presence known.

This faith in the immanence of the spirit world was unorthodox, and even eccentric, but without it Mackenzie King might not have survived. His unresolved conflicts, his ambivalent feelings about his parents, had led to an insatiable need for proof that he was important to others, that some people cared, and that they were aware of his problems and properly appreciative of his virtues and his dedication. No living human being, not even Joan Patteson, could give him the assurance he needed. This emotional insecurity might well have destroyed a less resourceful man. Mackenzie King, however, found the reassurance he needed in the almost daily signs of the presence of loving spirits. It was almost paradoxical that this faith in the occult, which some might have interpreted as evidence of emotional instability, gave King the stability to cope with the strains and stresses of a long political career.

CHAPTER FIVE

THE NEW CONSERVATISM

MACKENZIE KING returned from Europe in November 1934 convinced that the political situation was well under control. He intended to challenge the government as soon as the House met and force an election. He saw no warning signs of political danger; the Liberals were united and eager for battle whereas the Conservatives were in turmoil, with a chastened and discredited leader. King did not even make any public appearances in the eight weeks between his return to Ottawa and the opening of the session in mid-January 1935.

R. B. Bennett did nothing to undermine this confidence. He talked of amending the constitution to give the federal government jurisdiction over social legislation, presumably as a preliminary to introducing some reform measures, but when the provincial governments were unco-operative he did nothing more. He approached the United States about a trade agreement but again this came to nothing. Then suddenly in early January, only a week before the beginning of the session, Bennett gave five radio speeches. The New Deal broadcasts, as they were called, dramatically altered the political situation. Bennett once more became the man of action, the leader who would end the depression. The government had again seized the initiative and its new programme might give it another five years in power.

I

The Conservatives knew they were facing disaster. Something had to be done if the fortunes of the party were to be retrieved. Their problem was that Bennett was the dominant figure in the party, the man who almost single-handed had won the election of 1930, who had initiated all the measures introduced by his government, and to whom his followers looked for leadership. They were worried about his health and disturbed by rumours that he intended to resign; he so overshadowed his colleagues that he seemed irreplaceable. And yet if Bennett did not do something soon, the party was doomed. As R. J. Manion had told his son as early as May 1934:

Very confidently again, a fully reasoned opinion is that the Chief is anxious to quit around the King's birthday and is hoping for something to turn up that will permit him, without his being accused of running in the face of the enemy. Anyway, I am convinced, whatever is in his mind (if anything in this regard), he is gradually letting the Party drift towards the rocks, and I am almost beginning to wonder if it is not too late to turn the boat upstream.[1]

The Conservative defeats in Ontario and Saskatchewan made shipwreck seem even more certain. Manion had plaintively told Bennett that without intensive political activity "nothing in this world can save us from complete rout."[2] Bennett's absence during the Ontario by-elections did nothing to reassure his followers; there was even talk of calling a party convention to "ditch the man they claim is sulking in his tent."[3] Manion who, with Stevens, was mentioned as a possible successor, was not encouraging; he replied that he had "no desire to take over a job that has been pretty nearly wrecked."[4]

Bennett did deal with H. H. Stevens late in October but his action did nothing to restore the popularity of his party. The Prime Minister bluntly demanded from his colleague a public apology for the false and misleading statements in his pamphlet, which Bennett claimed had damaged the reputation of the firms that had been named and which had prejudiced the work of the Price Spreads Commission. Instead, Stevens resigned and took advantage of the occasion to denounce Bennett for trying to suppress the investigation. The last sentences of his letter of resignation threw down the political gauntlet:

But, Sir, when you refer in your closing words to 'British justice and fair play,' I cannot but bring to my mind the countless thousands of citizens of Canada who are patiently suffering while others whom you champion in such eloquent terms have been reaping rewards far beyond that which any citizen might reasonably expect to win. It is for those inarticulate sufferers that I have been striving with the hope that remedial measures might be found.[5]

Stevens' dismissal made him a more popular figure than ever. The Liberal Toronto *Star* speculated that in a public poll he "would today probably take ten votes to each one for Bennett"[6] and even the Conservative Ottawa *Journal* conceded that he had left the government with "the sympathy of a majority of the people of the country."[7] By dismissing him

81

Bennett appeared to be defending the heartless corporations, with Stevens as the persecuted champion of the oppressed. Nobody knew what Stevens intended to do. Clearly he was not going to remain silent; in a tour of central Canada he was even more outspoken than before. He saw "too much fiddling while Rome burns; too many human souls being crushed; too much demand for patience and fortitude; while those who could ameliorate the suffering have been enjoying unusual prosperity in the last few years."[8] His remedies were vague—a federal trade commission to protect the public against unfair trade practices and a huge programme of public works financed by "national credit"[9]—but he continued to draw large and enthusiastic crowds. Was he planning to found a new political party or did he hope that the Conservatives would choose him to replace Bennett? Stevens himself probably did not know. He did say that he was not yet seeking the leadership of any party, but he was obviously weighing the possibilities.[10]

His growing popularity worried even the Liberals. Many of them warned King that too many people saw Stevens as "a great political evangelist"[11] or even as a "saviour."[12] King still considered him "a demagogue, pure and simple—ambitious for power & catering to the trends he knows are popular today."[13] But until Stevens made his move he decided it would be wiser to ignore him. King did promise that the Liberals would make a full investigation of the charges of profiteering.[14] Beyond that, a discreet silence would leave the ring to Stevens and Bennett without exposing the Liberal party to any blows.

King's assumption that Stevens was an embarrassment to the Conservative party was amply justified. Bennett was in poor health and might have resigned as party leader but Stevens' defection made this impossible. He too viewed Stevens as a demagogue, a man who had betrayed his leader and who was now denouncing the policies of his party. And yet if he resigned Stevens might be chosen as his successor.[15] Bennett would have to stay on and fight for the sake of the party and the country.

Bennett's problem was that he did not know what to do. He was convinced that he had done everything that could be done, and that the protective tariffs, the Ottawa Agreements, and his rigid economies had saved the country from complete collapse. During the session of 1934 he had referred to the necessity of revising the British North America Act so that the federal government would be "enabled to embark on those improvements in our legislation which the circumstances clearly necessitate,"[16] but what these improvements were he did not say. Nor did he give the impression that he saw any immediate prospects of accomplishing anything. He had later admitted that any amendments to the Act would require the co-operation of the provinces and made the partisan but legitimate observation that Taschereau, the Liberal premier of Quebec, was not likely to give his consent.[17]

Bennett, however, had taken a tentative step in August when he had proposed a federal-provincial conference before the end of the year to discuss possible constitutional amendments. This time he had been more specific. In his letter to the Premiers he asked: "Are the provinces prepared to surrender their exclusive jurisdiction over legislation dealing with such social problems as old age pensions, unemployment and social insurance, hours and conditions for work, minimum wages, etc. to the Dominion Parliament? If so, on what terms and what conditions?"[18] In effect, Bennett was asking the provinces to yield much of their authority to the federal government—his etcetera was especially tactless—and he could hardly have expected an encouraging response. The Premiers' replies had made it painfully clear that his proposal was not welcomed and that any conference would be protracted and probably abortive.[19] When Bennett returned from England in September he had tersely announced that the conference was indefinitely postponed.

Another possible measure was a trade agreement with the United States. W. D. Herridge, the Canadian Minister in Washington and Bennett's brother-in-law, had been urging Bennett to consider such an agreement for more than a year.[20] Nothing could be done until the Reciprocal Trade Agreements Act was passed by Congress in June 1934. This Act allowed the President to negotiate carefully circumscribed trade treaties without having to submit them to Congress for ratification. The Roosevelt administration, however, had little interest in a trade agreement with Canada. The Secretary of State, Cordell Hull, insisted with evangelical fervour that freer international trade would save the world from chaos but many of Roosevelt's other advisers were more interested in driving hard bargains that would expand American exports.[21] Neither point of view gave a high priority to a trade agreement with Canada; politically it would be preferable to begin with countries whose imports and exports were complementary rather than competitive. Herridge therefore got little encouragement when he raised the matter in Washington in August 1934.[22]

In November 1934, however, Bennett decided to take the initiative. He authorized Herridge to tell the American Secretary of State that "the Government of Canada believes that the time has come for definite action" and to propose "the freest possible exchange of natural products between the two countries," with specific reference to farm products, lumber and fish.[23] American officials were suspicious of Bennett's tardy conversion.

"The Canadian note appears to have been written with an eye to eventual publication and political use by the Conservative party of Canada," warned the American Minister in Ottawa.[24] This suspicion was confirmed when Herridge refused to withdraw the specific proposals, which would be useful campaign material in the Maritimes and on the prairies, and conceded that Bennett would probably want to table the proposal at the next session.[25] Since the negotiations could hardly produce an agreement before the summer of 1935, the Americans might well conclude that Bennett was more interested in a campaign issue than a treaty. They also saw some advantage in waiting until after the election; there might be a change of government and Mackenzie King, in the opinion of the American Minister, "is inclined far more than the other party to play the game with us."[26]

By the end of the year the Conservatives seemed stymied. There would be no revision of the constitution and no trade agreement with the United States, so the government would have to appeal for support on its past record. Manion told King a week before Christmas that "he was not aware of any business of importance which the government had on its programme for the coming session."[27] C. H. Cahan, the Secretary of State, publicly warned against false hopes for any sweeping social reforms; "no purpose could be served," he declared, "by an illegal attempt by either parliament or the provinces to exercise powers vested in one or the other."[28] Even Bennett declared early in December that the major issue in the coming election would be the Ottawa Agreements.[29]

Mackenzie King drew the logical conclusion from these developments: the government would have to campaign on its record, and that meant its certain defeat. In mid-December he had explained his position to the Governor General. Bennett, he argued, had lost all popular support and should resign. If he intended "simply to call Parliament together, get the necessary supply and avoid controversial measures . . . we might be able to reach some agreement as to the time at which an election would take place." Otherwise, he implied, the Liberals would have to resort to obstruction. King made a specific reference to the possibility that Bennett would want to attend King George V's Silver Jubilee celebrations and the Imperial Conference, scheduled in London for May. The Liberals would oppose any adjournment for this because Bennett had no right to be making decisions on Imperial matters. Bennett, according to King, did not even have the right to be consulted about the name of the next Governor General. He was still Prime Minister in name but King saw himself as the heir-presumptive and intended to claim his inheritance. The conversation made the transfer of power seem very close:

84

I felt . . . as if the harness were already being put over my body and that an enormous weight had been added to my back. From now on I will have to cease to think in terms of freedom for myself. Opportunity for reading, rest, Kingsmere, everything, seemed as if it were to vanish for years of the most strenuous activity. Nothing in the world would cause me to assume what I see ahead in these times but a sense of duty in the way of public service, and that almost an imperative demand.[30]

Other observers drew the same conclusion. J. W. Dafoe, at the end of December, concluded that Bennett had no policies and his only hope would be to outdo his demagogic campaign of 1930: "The whole play," he wrote, "will be on emotions, prejudices, appetites, hopes and what-not, with promises of a new Jerusalem for them as the reward for electors if they vote right. R.B. will be in the coming campaign the outstanding demagogue of Canadian history. Poor Harry Stevens will have to go way back and sit down, his ineffectual fires paling in contrast with R.B.'s effulgence."[31] Bennett would go down fighting but, as the year ended, it seemed certain that he would lose the battle.

II

Bennett upset everybody's calculations by a series of five half-hour radio speeches early in January. The impact of these broadcasts owed something to the fact that radio provided a new forum for political leaders. Radio had been used before by Canadian politicians but by 1935 there was a national network and there were radio sets in most communities. Bennett could speak directly to the people. And Bennett exploited the new medium with consummate skill. The short, staccato sentences, the striking metaphors, the sweeping generalizations, and the dramatic affirmations held the attention of the listeners. The credit for this should go to Herridge, who drafted the speeches, but Bennett's oratorical style added to the impact. He had been brought up as a Bible-reading Methodist and he delivered his speeches with the rapid-fire intensity of a preacher extolling temperance or threatening hell-fire.

But there was more to the speeches than style. Bennett had not consulted any leading Conservatives, not even his Cabinet colleagues, but he now announced his own political conversion and promised that his government would introduce new and radical measures that would transform Canadian society. Radio listeners could believe that they were participating in an historic occasion; even his Ministers tuned in each night to hear his revelations. As a political event the New Deal broadcasts were unique.

The suggestion for the broadcasts came from Herridge, who had been urging Bennett for a year to save the political situation by a dramatic appeal to the people. Herridge, in Washington, had seen Roosevelt's New Deal in action and, although he had not been impressed by the New Deal measures, he was aware of the political benefits to the Democratic party. The President had accepted the idea that the government must take the initiative to restore prosperity, and Americans looked to him "as a leader, who, in some way not wholly revealed, will lead them out of the wilderness of the depression." Little had been done to end the depression but "the spirit of the New Deal is what has really mattered. . . . The hope and promise of a new heaven and a new earth remain." Bennett, Herridge continued, had already accomplished a great deal but he had failed in psychological terms. The Canadian people must be "persuaded that they also have a New Deal, and that that New Deal will do everything for them *in fact* which the New Deal here has done *in fancy.*"[32]

For Herridge it was merely a question of public relations. Mackenzie King and his party were the champions of laissez-faire. Bennett and the Conservative government had already accepted the logic of state intervention in the economy. Package this message dramatically and "the new Tory party" would win the support of disillusioned Liberals and even of those who might otherwise support the C.C.F.[33] Herridge was not concerned with details. His strategy was to have Bennett proclaim his commitment to government intervention, to sell this by showing how far he had already gone along this road and by referring to the measures still to come. King would obviously denounce this New Deal when the House convened—he had already promised to refuse supply. Bennett could then dissolve Parliament and go to the people as the champion of reform.[34]

Bennett may have hesitated but he had no alternative. He would soon be meeting the House, facing a militant opposition which had already promised to obstruct. The prospect was for a frustrating session in which little would be accomplished and almost certain defeat in the election which would follow. His only hope was to seize the initiative. And so, early in January, the Conservative Prime Minister, the millionaire corporation lawyer who only two years before had wanted to crush socialism with "the iron heel of ruthlessness," announced to a startled Canadian audience that "the old order is gone. It will not return":

If you believe that things should be left as they are, you and I hold contrary and irreconcilable views. I am for reform. And, in my mind, reform means government intervention. It means the end of *laissez-faire.* Reform heralds certain recovery. There can be no permanent recovery without reform. Reform or no reform! I raise the issue squarely. I nail the flag of progress to the masthead. I summon the power of the State to its support.

And then, in what seemed to some to be a clarion call to revolution, Bennett affirmed that "the dole is a condemnation, final and complete, of our economic system. If we cannot abolish the dole, we should abolish the system."[35]

But Bennett was not advocating the overthrow of capitalism. The rhetoric of reform overshadowed the qualifications and may have misled many listeners, but the qualifications were there. He would go as far as necessary to "reform the system" and this might mean, as "some advanced thinkers claimed," that "the old capitalist system would be changed out of all knowledge." But Bennett was not yet convinced; "I cannot bring myself to agree that there is anything radically wrong with the system which adjustment and reform will not remedy. But that has yet to be decided." He would only promise to do what was necessary without fear or favour.[36]

There was more rhetoric to come. The Conservative government, by its careful husbanding of resources, had saved the nation from disaster. The time had now come to go forward: "Our recovery measures have had good results. You all know that. They have kept our ship afloat during the storm. The first fury of the storm has abated. It is time to thoroughly overhaul and repair the ship and to set it on its new course."[37] There were some specific references to what the government had done and what it would do. Bennett reminded his listeners of the Farmers' Creditors Arrangement Act and of the Natural Products Marketing Act, and promised that these measures would be extended. He also referred to the Bank of Canada, that "powerful instrument of social justice." Workers had a right to a secure and adequate income; Bennett announced that government would bring in legislation to provide unemployment insurance, minimum wages, and maximum hours of work. He also declared war on corrupt business practices. "Selfish men, corporations without souls, those fearful that this Government might impinge on what they have come to regard as their immemorial right of exploitation, will whisper against us. . . . We fear them not."[38] He had already established the Price Spreads Commission and would bring in the appropriate legislation when the Commission had reported.

The final broadcast was more frankly partisan. Bennett explained that he had been speaking as the Prime Minister; it was now his painful duty to speak as leader of the Conservative party and to warn his fellow-citizens of the potential disaster if the laissez-faire Liberals returned to power. "Liberalism," he explained, "is Toryism in the reactionary sense of the term, just as present-day Conservatism is Progressivism in the best and most constructive sense of the term," and he warned his listeners that the

Liberalism of Mackenzie King, dominated as it was by the ethics of Big Business, carried with it the danger of fascism.[39]

The New Deal broadcasts were open to a number of interpretations. Herridge had argued for a dramatic gesture and the rhetoric and partisan exaggerations were consistent with this aim. The speeches, however, went beyond this. Bennett was proposing more extensive government intervention in economic affairs. As he later explained to one Conservative, the New Deal was a modest attempt to introduce some of the social reforms which an industrial country like Great Britain had long taken for granted.[40] More significantly, he was proposing that the federal government introduce these reforms. He was promising to do unilaterally what he had assumed only a few months before would require an amendment to the British North America Act. The full implications of Bennett's New Deal would not be known until it was presented in the form of legislation but, if it meant anything, it meant a larger role for the federal government in economic and social policies.

The reactions to the broadcasts were understandably mixed. Bennett's colleagues, who had neither been consulted nor informed, were divided. Manion, who had been encouraging Bennett to take action, had no objections. As he wrote to his son on January 10, after the fourth broadcast:

> The big item of interest in Canada at the present time is the series of addresses put over by the Chief. They were well staged and the whole country was listening in, so far as I know . . . He still has another one to give on Friday night coming—that is tomorrow night—and I imagine it will be the last of the series. I haven't any idea as to what he will cover tomorrow, as he has done this stuff off his own bat entirely, at least so far as we are concerned.[41]

Some of Bennett's colleagues were less tolerant. Cahan, as spokesman for St. James Street, later described how shocked he had been to hear his leader "espouse the economic fallacies of Karl Marx."[42] The Conservative Montreal *Gazette* was openly hostile. It, for one, was not prepared "to fly the flag of Socialism side by side with the historic banner under which Conservatism heretofore has always made its appeal to responsible, sober-minded Canadians."[43]

The Liberal response was more consistent. They interpreted the broadcasts as no more than a desperate, last-minute effort by Bennett to delude the public. Mackenzie King was shocked by such irresponsible demagoguery. "If the country stands for this kind of bombast," he wrote after the first broadcast, "I shall feel like dropping out of public life—but I have no fear of the reception it will get."[44] The following broadcasts intensified his disgust without modifying his view of their impact, as he commented on the fourth speech:

It was really pathetic the absolute rot and gush he talked—platitudes—unction & what-not, a mountebank and a hypocrite—talk of my reforms, wishing to see it all underway before passing off the scene, etc.—no mention of the Government, or colleagues, or Parliament—sickening and disgusting. If the people will fall for that kind of thing there is no saving them, they will deserve all they will get. It amazes me men of substance in the Conservative Party from coast to coast put up with it and with him as they do.[45]

It was indeed amazing what the Conservatives would accept. Some of them may have been shocked but no Ministers resigned. They may have been influenced by the popular response which was generally favourable. Bennett might yet keep the party in office. They may also have been waiting to learn what the New Deal really meant and for that they would have to wait until the legislation was presented. They would not have long to wait. The House reconvened a week after the last broadcast and the Speech from the Throne promised a series of measures "as part of a comprehensive plan designed to remedy the social and economic injustices now prevailing, and to ensure to all classes and to all parts of the country a greater degree of equality in the distribution of the benefits of the capitalist system."[46] Bennett had donned the garments of reform and, although the full portent of his new guise was not clear, he had certainly won the attention of his party and of his compatriots.

CHAPTER SIX

DEALING WITH THE NEW DEAL

THE PARLIAMENTARY SESSION of 1935 was really the beginning of the election campaign. The members knew that Parliament was in its fifth year, with a mandatory election to follow and, in this session, partisan considerations were accentuated because the Conservative party faced probable defeat. It could not hope to restore its fortunes by campaigning on its past record and so it would have to take the initiative. Bennett's New Deal broadcasts had opened the Conservative campaign. He had announced that he was for reform, for government intervention to provide economic security, and his tactics during the session would be designed to establish the reform image of the Conservative party.

Mackenzie King also concentrated on political tactics. He did not believe that the Conservative party had changed its spots. The New Deal was therefore no more than a desperate effort to deceive the electorate and the Liberals would have to take advantage of the session to expose the government's hypocrisy. From the beginning of the session King made it clear to the Liberal caucus that Conservative legislation could not be considered on its merits but must be seen as no more than election promises. The Opposition must not fall into the trap of appearing to be against reform or of revealing any internal divisions. It could criticize but it could not obstruct. And because this was so largely a question of day-to-day tactics in the House, caucus must allow King to make the tactical decisions. If the Liberal party could keep united the insincerity of the government could be exposed and the election could be won.

I

When the House met in mid-January, Bennett had not committed himself to a specific date for the election; like most Prime Ministers he preferred to delay the decision until the last minute. May was the earliest possible date because an amendment to the Franchise Act the year before required the preparation of permanent electoral lists and these lists would not be ready until April. Any delay much beyond April would require further revision of the lists and would postpone the election until September or October. There can be little doubt, however, that Bennett was thinking of an early election. King had already made it clear that the Liberals intended to obstruct and force an early election. Bennett's plan was to encourage the Liberals to denounce the government during the debate on the Speech from the Throne, and then to dissolve the House and ask the people to vote for the New Deal. Herridge saw the New Deal broadcasts as the first stage of the election campaign, with dissolution late in February and the election sometime in May. According to his later, almost conspiratorial outline of this strategy: "We started off with Phase 1. It accomplished precisely what it was designed to accomplish. You will agree that it had a marked, if not revolutionary effect on the public sentiment. And at that Phase 1 had been hurriedly arranged and appropriate legislation to support it was not available. According to the predetermined plan, Phase 2 would have been launched toward the end of February."[1]

Phase 2 was not launched because King revised his tactics. Eager as he was to have Bennett given the electoral punishment he deserved, his feelings did not impair his political judgment. Bennett might be a "bounder"[2] but his New Deal speeches had had a political impact which could not be ignored. Instead of obstructing and forcing an election, King concluded it would be wiser to embarrass the government by shortening the debate on the Speech from the Throne and asking Bennett to produce his vaunted reforms. He explained his shift in tactics to his senior Liberal colleagues on the first day of the session:

I outlined at once what I had in mind—no amendment re want of confidence—call Bennett's bluff—ask for legislation in nature of Reform & promise cooperation in putting it through—criticizing measures on their merits etc. To say nothing to caucus of this decision but have word given to trust Headquarters, that we are now in the campaign & must not hand over our tactics to the enemy. I favored leaving all private members motions & supply, to get on at once with Reform of Capitalistic system. To end debate on Address on Monday, so far as we are concerned. They were unanimous on this.

King and his colleagues then went directly to the first caucus meeting of the session, where King spoke "of the present situation, said we were now in Gen'l election, prlt. being used for a stage. . . . The caucus agreed to leave the final word to me."[3]

Mackenzie King was therefore the only Liberal to speak on the Address. His speech began with a partisan reply to the New Deal broadcasts. He contrasted the government's four-year record with its present promises of reform. The Liberal party, on the other hand, had a proud record of reform legislation, from the Industrial Disputes Investigation Act to old-age pensions. It was true that the Liberals had sometimes sponsored laissez-faire policies but the party had also favoured government intervention when it had been necessary to protect the public interest. The Liberal platform of 1933 was at least "no death-bed repentance on the eve of an election."[4]

Finally he came to the Address itself. The Liberals, he explained, had not introduced more social legislation in the past because "until within the last few weeks, it has been understood that practically all legislation of a social character came exclusively within the jurisdiction of the provinces."[5] If the government was sincere in its promises, how did it propose to overcome the constitutional obstacles to its reforms? Had the Prime Minister secured legal opinions which would justify federal legislation? Or was he trying to delude the citizens of Canada? King was careful to express his desire for social reforms and his hope that the constitutional difficulties could be overcome, but he deplored any unilateral action by the federal government. A conference with the provincial governments was a necessary preliminary step. But since the government must somehow have resolved the constitutional problem, "let us therefore . . . take as first measures those dealing with problems of unemployment and social reform and give to them our undivided attention from day to day so that, working together, we may, if at all possible, produce something in the way of a solution."[6]

The Conservatives were not impressed by this talk of working together. King talked of co-operation, as Manion said, "when of course his whole object is to embarrass."[7] And he had succeeded; the government was embarrassed because it had no legislation prepared and could only stall for time. The debate on the Address, which would normally have lasted for three or four weeks, took only three days. Taken by surprise, the government floundered. A Conservative backbencher had to fill in time on the fourth day by moving the adoption of a Canadian flag. Bennett, frustrated by the Liberal tactics and infuriated by Liberal demands to bring on his reforms, angrily reminded King on one occasion that he was "still in control of this House; get that in your mind."[8] He might be in control of the House, but King's tactics had disrupted his plans for a dissolution.

The government was not completely unprepared for the session. Unemployment insurance had been promised before the New Deal broadcasts and Bennett introduced the Employment and Social Insurance bill in the first week. A commission would supervise an insurance scheme based on contributions from employers and employees, with the federal government paying the costs of administration. Bennett frankly admitted that in the past he had had grave doubts about the constitutional power of the federal legislature to introduce such a measure but he assured the House that these doubts had now been dispelled. Two recent judgments by the Judicial Committee of the Privy Council had upheld federal jurisdiction over radio and aviation on the basis of Section 132 of the British North America Act, which gave the federal government the authority to carry out treaties between the British Empire and foreign countries. Bennett explained that he was relying on "this widening sense of the power of the central authority."[9] As a signatory of the Versailles Treaty Canada had agreed to secure humane conditions for Canadian workers and Bennett now argued that this justified federal legislation on labour matters even though the provincial governments normally had exclusive jurisdiction in this field.

Mackenzie King was sure that the legislation was unconstitutional but he did not want to oppose it because this might be interpreted as being against labour reforms. His response in the House was to point out that the bill would do nothing for those who were already unemployed and to underline the fact that the government had not and did not intend to get a legal opinion on the constitutionality of the measure before enacting it. He convinced caucus next day to go no farther: "I outlined tactics to be followed on the measure, no opposition to 2nd reading, no amendment to improve the bill unless obvious, draw out all the information possible—state position, seek to hurry through & leave discussion of limitations etc. for hustings—making clear our position re having jurisdiction question settled, & agreement with provinces etc. beforehand as in case of Old Age pensions."[10] To strengthen the impression that the Opposition was not being obstructive, the caucus even agreed that all Liberal resolutions should be dropped from the Order Paper—including King's cherished resolution against the granting of titles.

The second reading of the Employment and Social Insurance bill was delayed for two weeks because the bill was not yet printed. Many Liberals were unhappy about voting for such an obvious encroachment on provincial jurisdiction and King had "difficulty in having Cardin & some others support 2nd reading, tho' this had been agreed upon."[11] The question was raised again in caucus: "It was left to me as on previous occasions," King recorded, "to go all over the ground again, to remind them we were already in the battlefield, and that tho' discussing principle they had already voted favorably to it. I pointed out what the effect of division in the ranks would be so far as the public were concerned, drew attention to the unity in the ranks of the tories."[12] Ernest Lapointe followed this with an appeal for loyalty to King and caucus once more acquiesced. King made one concession to reluctant Liberals by moving that the bill be referred to the Supreme Court for an opinion on its constitutionality but he was not sorry when Bennett rejected the proposal.[13]

The government was certainly not setting a hectic pace. Two days were spent debating a Conservative motion that the Ottawa Agreements merited the approval of the House, a motion designed to embarrass the Liberals by bringing out their differences on this issue but not calculated to advance the New Deal. King again persuaded his followers to keep silent and let him speak for the party.

The next reform legislation, when it appeared, included bills to establish an eight-hour day, a forty-eight-hour week, and minimum wages in industrial enterprises. These measures were based on labour conventions approved years before by the International Labour Organization, of which Canada was a member. Bennett again argued that the recent decisions of the Judicial Committee established the right of the federal government to enforce these international conventions.[14]

The constitutional validity of these measures was even more doubtful than that of the Employment and Social Insurance bill. King grappled with his conscience. On previous measures, such as "the peace, order and good government" sections of the Relief Act, he had defended the constitution on the grounds of high principle. To oppose this legislation, however, would give the appearance of opposing reforms which he himself had long favoured. He was sure that Bennett and Guthrie, the Minister of Justice, knew that the legislation was invalid but hoped to win the election on the strength of their "reforms" before the courts had time to expose their hypocrisy. Under the circumstances King convinced himself that his duty was to outmanœuvre the government:

My first impulse was to fight it outright as an invasion of provincial rights—fight it on the ground of its hypocrisy and deceit. I now feel that it would be best to point out its deceit and hypocrisy & that we believe it to be ultra vires, but allow the Courts to decide on the constitutional point & that the Government take the responsibility for presenting a bill of the kind without settling this point first. To do otherwise is to be drawn into the trap set for us, the public will be impatient of and not understand our constitutional objections, but when they find they are deceived, they will turn and rend Bennett. We can afford to let the provinces raise the question of the evasion of their rights. It may be difficult to get Lapointe & others to agree but I expect to be able to carry caucus.[15]

King was able to carry caucus but it was a continual strain. Liberal members, with the election imminent, were influenced by the situation in their own constituencies. Some of them, especially those from Quebec, were apprehensive about voting for measures which encroached on provincial rights and would have preferred open obstruction. Others felt that the party had already said enough about the constitutional problem and that further criticism would give the impression that the Liberals were opposed to any reforms. King could only insist again and again that this was an election campaign and that his tactics would keep the party united and bring victory.

By the end of February it was obvious that the Liberals had won the first round. The legislation introduced by the government had fallen far short of the promised New Deal and there would be no snap election. The Conservatives were further embarrassed because Bennett had a mild heart attack late in February, and without him the government drifted. As Manion explained to his son early in March:

The Chief has been ill for about a week but I understand he is out today, though I have not seen him. The paper says he will have to go south for a while. It will be somewhat embarrassing if he has to get away for any length of time, because his reform program (whatever it is) has been kept largely in his own hands, and so far the only thing we have had is the Eight-Hour Day, the Six-day Week and the Unemployment Insurance which, while all to the good from a reform and progressive standpoint, could not quite fulfill his suggested plan.[16]

A week later Bennett was still absent. There were so many rumours about his condition that a reassuring medical report was read in the House, explaining that there had been "some disturbance of cardiac rhythm" which while "not serious in itself necessitates further rest."[17] This was little help to his colleagues. Until Bennett recovered or resigned, the government could only mark time. King expressed his deep regret at the Prime Minister's absence and generously offered "to facilitate and expedite the business of the House"[18] but privately he was greatly encouraged. The end was in sight. If the Liberals continued their tactics of formal co-operation the session might only last another five weeks and the strain would be over.[19]

The next month produced no surprises. The budget was introduced late in March but it followed the pattern of the previous year. Once again the Minister of Finance had to report a deficit of more than one hundred million dollars, largely accounted for by relief expenditures and railway deficits. Again however, the Minister was optimistic. By forgoing any significant tax reductions and by some increases in income taxes, he hoped to produce a twenty million dollar surplus over "Ordinary Expenditures," and improved economic conditions were expected to reduce relief and railway costs.[20] Even though it was a pre-election budget, there was no attempt to win votes by tax concessions. J. L. Ralston replied for the Liberals. He offered no alternative to the policy of continued retrenchment; his solution was merely a change of government.[21] The other Liberals kept silent and the week-long debate would have been even shorter if some twenty Conservatives had not kept it going.

Two other bills were debated but they too fell short of the major reforms which Bennett had promised. The Prairie Farm Rehabilitation bill was intended to develop and publicize better farming practices in the drought areas. Within a few years the Prairie Farm Rehabilitation Act would provide for large-scale federal assistance to western farmers. In 1935, however, with an initial budget of less than one million dollars, the legislation would do little more than encourage the planting of windbreaks and the construction of farm dug-outs. The bill was passed with almost no discussion. The second bill was more controversial because it authorized the expenditure of some forty-five million dollars on public works projects. Even Bennett had misgivings about this "pork-barrel legislation."[22] King saw it not as a stimulus to employment but as a fund which would be used by the Conservative party, and the Liberals did oppose this bill.

By mid-April, however, the budget and most of the bills before the House had been passed but the sense of urgency of the New Deal broadcasts was gone and the government now decided to adjourn the session for a month. As Sir George Perley, the Acting Prime Minister, told King, "Bennett had in mind one or two measures he wished to put through himself" and the House would have to wait for his recovery.[23] The official reason for the adjournment was to allow the Prime Minister to attend the Silver Jubilee in London. The Liberals took the opportunity to belabour the government once more for not yet having produced the promised New Deal,[24] but King rather welcomed the interlude. He had no doubt that the first part of the session had gone extremely well. As he told a friend in England: "I do not recall a more extraordinary or baffling kind of session than that which we have had in the last few months. We completely out-manœuvred our opponents by adopting an attitude of non-resistance towards all social reform legislation. It was heralded with a blare of trumpets through the medium of a series of nation-wide broadcasts on the eve of the reassembling of Parliament. Today the whole business is as flat as a punctured tire." There was a possibility that Bennett would resign, King went on, but he was now so confident of victory that he hoped Bennett would recover; "we are all hoping he will continue to lead," he explained, "for he is the one who deserves defeat."[25]

The Conservatives would not have disagreed with King's assessment of the session. Even a new leader would make little difference. As Manion commented, "God help the someone who would have the present condition handed to him."[26] And from Washington Herridge saw only disaster: "The colour has faded from the reform picture. The promise of performance is gone. The prospect of achievement is forgotten. . . . There was invested in us a short time ago, certain curative powers. We commenced to employ them with some measure of success. Then we broke off. Unless we have been vouchsafed as well, the magic of reincarnation, there is little use beginning again. For I fear our big, beautiful reform child is dead."[27]

II

Mackenzie King did not devote his full time to politics during the adjournment but he found it difficult to relax. A motor trip to New England with the Pattesons was not a success. It was a strain to have to be sociable and to adapt his schedule for the convenience of others even though neither Joan nor Godfroy was demanding. King fretted about his accumulating correspondence and the speeches he should be preparing and after five days he decided to cut his holiday short and return to Ottawa.[28] He was relieved to get back to Laurier House and to his dog Pat, who showed affection but did not interfere with King's own self-centred activities.[29]

Even in Ottawa King could not concentrate on politics. He could not prepare for the rest of the session because the initiative for any new measures would come from Bennett. His conscience told him he should be drafting material for the election campaign but so much would depend on the coming legislation that it was difficult to concentrate on speeches which would almost certainly have to be revised. He did not undertake a political tour because he wanted to husband his energy for the campaign. Nor did he concern himself with party organization; he did not believe that this was his responsibility. And so, almost without any conscious decision, King found his time taken up by editorial work on two books and by the supervision of some major improvements at Kingsmere.

King had already spent most of his weekends during the session arranging for the publication of his own biography. A decade before John Lewis had produced a campaign biography and King had initially suggested to Norman Rogers that Rogers might add a few chapters to bring it up to date. Rogers must sometimes have regretted undertaking the task because King insisted on supervising every detail. Not surprisingly, King had found the first draft "inadequate and disappointing"; somehow King's dedication to humanity and his great achievements were not adequately presented.[30] He found it necessary to redraft many sections in order to bring out the full story of his family heritage and his "life's work in politics & reform."[31] King was a little more satisfied with the revised version; it gave the proper emphasis to his moral courage, his sincerity, his vision, and his ideal of public service.[32] The biography appeared in the summer of 1935 with Norman Rogers listed as the author; King's contribution to the volume was not mentioned.

The work on his biography drew King's attention to *Industry and Humanity*, which he had published in 1918. Rereading it convinced him that an abridgment would also be effective campaign material, showing as it would that he had always been a social reformer and that his ideas on the four partners to industry were still "a worth-while contribution to present day problems."[33] The last seventeen years, as he commented in his Introduction, had only confirmed "the soundness of the principles themselves, and the wisdom of their application."[34] King justified his literary activities as the preparation of campaign literature, but his own ego was clearly involved. He would not have devoted as much time and energy to publications concentrating on the achievements of the Liberal party.

Even more of King's time during the adjournment was devoted to Kingsmere. His property in the Gatineau Hills was more than a place to spend the summer. Laurier House was his residence but it still bore the name of his predecessor and had come to him as leader of the party, whereas Kingsmere was uniquely his; it was his refuge from the rest of the world and a tangible possession which partially met his need for security. More than thirty years before King had purchased a three-acre lot on the south shore of Kingsmere Lake. Since then he had extended his property to the south in a series of purchases and had spent almost thirty thousand dollars to acquire a five-hundred acre estate. He spent the summer months at Moorside, a spacious summer cottage overlooking a field that separated it from the wooded lakefront. In cooler seasons, in the spring and fall, King regularly came out to Kingsmere on weekends and, if the weather was good, might even come out for a picnic lunch during the week. He always regretted the last visit of the year and would return next spring as soon as the roads were clear.

Spring came late in 1935; snow fell at Kingsmere on the first of May. But King was eager to visit his property because he had undertaken major renovations of the building known as the Farm House, where the caretaker lived. His original intention had been to add a wing which could be heated, and so make it possible to spend weekends there at any time of the year. As so often with renovations, however, the plans became more ambitious. A basement had to be blasted out of the pre-Cambrian rock to provide for a furnace. A well had to be bored through the rock, a small greenhouse was added for bedding plants, and inside there were constant alterations and revisions, and much discussion with Joan Patteson about the furnishings. The work had been started in the fall of 1934 but there seemed to be no end to the details to be considered. At times he regretted ever having begun. And there was always the political risk—such a sizeable expenditure during the depression might be criticized.[35] For the moment, however, it occupied his time and reassured him that Kingsmere, more than ever, would meet his needs. As he explained to a friend: "I view it as insurance against fatigue and impaired health. I really need some place to come to at week-ends, and when I want to be absolutely free of interruptions."[36] It was an extravagant indulgence. Even after it was completed King spent his summers at Moorside and seldom stayed overnight at the Farm House.

His other indulgence at Kingsmere was the construction of ruins on a hill-top a few hundred yards south of Moorside. It began one day in May when King, returning from a visit to Kingsmere, saw an old Ottawa house being demolished. He decided on impulse that the bay window would make a marvellous ruin for his estate.[37] Once it had been dismantled, transported, and re-erected at Kingsmere, King was so taken by its beauty that he decided it should be integrated into a building—"something in the nature of a chapel or a library"[38]—a building worthy of the site, an edifice that would somehow combine the beauty of the Parthenon and of Westminster Abbey![39] The cost, at a time when the Farm House renovations were underway, was of some concern, but the political risk weighed even more heavily. The abbey, he decided, would have to wait. "Meanwhile," he convinced himself, "no one is likely to be critical of a ruin as an extravagance—and the public mind can be prepared for its completion later on."[40]

The ruins were never completed. There were some subsequent additions—including a fragment of the British House of Commons after it was damaged by a war-time bomb—and doorways and arches from other buildings were salvaged and erected around Moorside, but King's enthusiasm for construction at Kingsmere was a passing phase. Once back in office he had neither the time nor the need to indulge in such fancies. He soon forgot his bizarre plans and developed a great pride in his unfinished ruins.

99

But why did Mackenzie King think that a bay window on a Kingsmere hill-top would be a thing of beauty in the first place? King was not a man of cultivated tastes, and he preferred the old-fashioned and the familiar. He was shocked by modern styles in clothes and in art. Modern bathing suits, for example, seemed quite indecent; surely "a woman of refined feelings would find it impossible to exhibit her naked self to all sorts of men."[41] He reacted in much the same way to the "frightful" paintings of the Group of Seven;[42] his preference was the Venice of Canaletto or the romantic landscapes of Homer Watson. The scenery to which King responded was not the imposing Rockies or the untouched wilderness but the quiet countryside, with stone fences and hedgerows with paths where a man could walk and quote Wordsworth and feel he was communing with nature. He was a Victorian romantic, unsophisticated but sure of what he liked. Gothic ruins might be out of place in the Gatineau but for King they fitted into a countryside—an English countryside—which he equated with beauty.

III

For King, the interlude at Kingsmere had been a welcome breathing space. For Bennett, however, the adjournment had not been long enough. He returned from the Jubilee celebrations in mid-May, two days before the House reconvened, still not certain that his health would permit him to continue in politics. London doctors, he announced, had told him that his heart was sound but tired and had warned him not to undertake too much.[43] During the session, which continued until early July, he was frequently absent from the House and was so irritable that he openly bickered with his colleagues. On one notable occasion he even threatened from his seat in the House to dismiss R. J. Manion from the government.[44] It was not until late in the session that Bennett assured his followers that he would carry on. Even then he made it clear that he was yielding to a sense of duty rather than a feeling of renewed vigour; he was reported as having told caucus that he would "die in harness rather than quit now."[45]

It was generally agreed that Bennett stayed on because H. H. Stevens might have been chosen as his successor. Stevens had resigned from the government but he was still a Conservative, and although he had criticized the government he continued to imply that the party could be reformed. He was unacceptable to such right-wing Conservatives as C. H. Cahan but others believed he had "a very strong following throughout the country" and hoped for some compromise that would at least bring him back into the government.[46] The stumbling-block was Bennett who, according to one of his colleagues, was "so bitter towards Stevens that that beclouds every thought that comes to his head."[47]

The confrontation between Bennett and Stevens was provoked by the report of the Royal Commission on Price Spreads. Bennett in his New Deal broadcasts had promised legislation based on the commission's recommendations; and the commission had duly reported just before the April adjournment. The report was not an easy document to summarize because it had no coherent philosophy of social reform. At times it affirmed the virtues of free enterprise and saw untrammelled competition among a large number of firms as the ultimate safeguard for society. It proposed a federal Trade and Industry Commission which would restore competition by the rigorous administration of a strengthened Anti-Combines Act. Where large companies had established partial monopolies, this commission would intervene to prevent trade practices which threatened to eliminate competitors. The Royal Commission, however, was not convinced that competition could always be restored. Some monopolies seemed inevitable and in these cases the commission could only recommend that they should be regulated by government, either by fixing maximum prices or by taxing surplus profits.[48] At other times the report was less enthusiastic about competition. Primary producers, it argued, suffered from too much competition and it proposed co-operative marketing agencies similar to those established by the Natural Products Marketing Act to create what would be, in effect, producers' monopolies.[49] In yet another section the report suggested that, although competition was an ideal, the tendency in industry towards large-scale enterprises and monopolies was irreversible and recommended that employers should be organized into trade associations and employees into industrial trade unions, obviously influenced by the Roosevelt New Deal and the National Industrial Recovery Act.[50] In short, the report recommended restoring competition wherever possible but implied that the best that could be achieved in most sectors of the economy would be government-regulated monopolies. The Royal Commission also admitted that the constitution allocated most of the regulatory powers to the provincial governments. It brushed aside the constitutional problem by calmly asserting that federal action was necessary and some way must be found to allow federal intervention.[51]

Bennett was not prepared to go as far as the report proposed. The government introduced its Trade and Industry Commission bill early in June as an honest and sincere effort to carry out the commission's recommendations. The bill gave the Tariff Board the right to regulate commodity standards and the issue of new securities and to administer

101

the Combines Investigation Act. Some trade practices which had been condemned by the report were declared illegal by amendments to the Criminal Code. No attempt was made, however, to identify certain enterprises as monopolies and to regulate them as recommended in the report.[52] Nor was the government prepared to supervise the organization of industry into trade associations and to regulate industrial codes.[53] It was prepared to extend its definition of unfair trade practices and to enforce its regulations more effectively but there would be no drastic measures, either to restore free competition or to interfere with the normal trade practices of monopolies.

The government admitted that its legislation fell far short of the recommendations of the Royal Commission. In contrast to its stand on the Unemployment and Social Insurance Act, however, it now argued that it was limited by the constitution. It was beyond the powers of the federal government to regulate monopolies.[54] The government, according to Guthrie, had gone as far as it could. He even announced that it had gone too far. The government had resorted to amendments to the Criminal Code to restrict some trade practices because only by making them criminal offences could they come under federal jurisdiction. He went on to say that this was of doubtful validity—an extraordinary admission for a Minister of Justice—but he used this as an argument to show how determined the government was to carry out the recommendations of the commission.[55] Determined or not, the Trade and Industry Commission bill was an anti-climax after eighteen months of agitation over price spreads. The "corporations without souls" which the fearless Bennett had denounced in his New Deal broadcasts would still enjoy their "immemorial right of exploitation."[56]

Mackenzie King had recognized the importance of the Royal Commission on Price Spreads long before the legislation was introduced in the House. The public hearings of the Parliamentary Committee and then of the commission had, for many Canadians, linked reform with the regulation of corporations. King did not want the Liberal party to express any opinion on the recommendations of the Royal Commission when its report appeared; it would be wiser to wait until the government committed itself. His concern at one stage had been that the four Liberals on the commission might submit a minority report which would be interpreted as the party position in the election campaign.[57] Early in February he and some of his colleagues had met these four men and J. L. Ilsley, one of the commissioners, had outlined the probable recommendations. King had been much encouraged "to see how ready he & others were to accept all the advanced points of view."[58] If the Liberals could sign the report, the party could not be attacked for opposing reforms. E. J. Young of Weyburn was the only doubtful member, for his doctrinaire liberalism went beyond a hatred of tariffs to a rejection of any form of government intervention in economic activities. King was optimistic. "Ed Young said nothing," he had noted, "but I imagine he sees for the party's sake it is going to be necessary for him to join with others in making the report unanimous. If that is done, the last prop is out from under Bennett's structure—his hope has been to invite and encourage opposition."[59]

When the report appeared, it carried only three Liberal signatures. Even these three Liberals expressed two reservations. They proclaimed their preference for competition but fully accepted the desirability of national regulation of conditions of employment—provided that the federal government had the constitutional power to make regulations. Their other reservation was that the report did not sufficiently stress the importance of international trade in the Canadian economy; the best way to regulate monopolies would be to permit foreign competition by lowering tariffs.[60] Young, a man of principle, wrote a minority report which condemned all monopolies, belittled all government intervention, and saw lower tariffs and expanded markets as the only means of regulating the economy.[61] He was, however, a minority of one and his report could not be labelled the position of the Liberal party.

King at this stage did not know how the government would react to the report. But he was sure that any legislation would be more of an election promise than a genuine attempt at reform. It would be unwise for the Liberals to oppose the coming measures openly. King could not imagine that Bennett's legislation would go as far as Stevens wanted to go, and this was yet another reason for restraint. As he explained at the first caucus after the adjournment: "I pointed out the impression the disclosures before the Committee & Commission had made on the public mind for a year past, and said we would have to be guided in our action by what was proposed by the Govt., that it was better to let the Govt. and Stevens fight out the differences of view between them & keep out of it ourselves— being content largely with questioning the ultra vires of the legislation."[62] If Bennett and Stevens could be encouraged to fight each other, Bennett's claims to be a reformer would be completely undermined and the hypocrisy of the New Deal would be clear to all.[63]

This Machiavellian approach set the stage for one of the major confrontations of the session. Stevens had staked his political career on the work of the commission and was almost forced to protest when some of its recommendations were not adopted. The Liberals goaded him by frequent references to the wide gap between the report and the actual legislation. Stevens rose to the bait. In a biting speech he contrasted Bennett's ringing declarations in the New Deal broadcasts and the "wholly inadequate" measures which the government had produced.[64] Bennett replied in kind: "This country has a constitution," he pointed out with heavy sarcasm; "it is a federal union." To suggest that the constitution should be ignored was to encourage an "age of lawlessness," to take "the first step towards fascism." He even buttressed his arguments by quotations from none other than Stevens, in a forgotten speech delivered in 1923.[65] The breach between the two men might have been inevitable— one reporter quoted Bennett as saying of Stevens that "if that skunk has to be skinned I suppose I'll have to do the job"—but the Liberal tactics probably ensured maximum publicity for the split. King was delighted with the results; in his opinion Stevens had destroyed the effect of the government's legislation by his criticisms and Bennett had justified the Liberal position by his constitutional arguments. The Liberal party had emerged as the only winner.[67]

The only controversial measure still to be debated was the Grain Board bill. "The party has kept united," King noted with satisfaction after the debate on the Trade and Industry Commission, "and if we can remain so on the grain measure we will come before the country in splendid shape."[68] Agreement among the Liberals could not be taken for granted. Bennett had opted for a radical policy, a government monopoly of all grain marketing. Many western Liberals strongly supported this policy but most eastern Liberals found it totally unacceptable. King feared that in the debate this division would be exposed, with some Liberals supporting a government monopoly and others defending open market operations. He could only play for time and hope that the differences within the party could somehow be concealed.

The origins of the Grain bill went back to 1930 when the Conservative government had unwillingly become involved in wheat marketing. For years prairie farmers had been critical of the private grain dealers and the operations of the Winnipeg Grain Exchange. They argued that if one agency controlled all wheat sales, the wheat could be sold on world markets in a more orderly fashion and bring the producer higher and more stable prices. This had led to the organization of the voluntary Wheat Pools in the 1920s, which had marketed almost half of the prairie wheat crop each year through a Central Selling Agency. In 1930, however, the pools faced bankruptcy. The initial payment made to farmers when the grain was delivered became a serious overpayment when world wheat prices suddenly dropped. The banks which had advanced the money to the pools were threatened with crippling losses. Bennett, rather than run the risk of a collapse of the banking system, agreed to guarantee them against any losses. He then appointed John I. McFarland, a close friend and a widely respected grain dealer, as manager of the Central Selling Agency to dispose of its wheat holdings at the lowest possible loss to the government.[69]

What began as an emergency measure led step by step to an involvement of the government which neither Bennett nor McFarland had ever contemplated. The problem was that world wheat production exceeded world wheat consumption. European countries, which had been the major importers during the 1920s, had encouraged home production by tariffs and domestic subsidies. The world wheat surplus by the end of the decade had led to the sharp drop in prices. Importing countries had responded by raising tariffs and domestic subsidies even higher; in exporting countries the farmers had reacted to the lower prices by increasing their wheat acreage in an attempt to restore their income. Even the drought in North America had little effect on the world surplus. The price of wheat which had averaged well over a dollar a bushel in the 1920s had continued to fall until by 1932 it was less than forty cents a bushel, the lowest price since the industrial revolution. McFarland, with Bennett's consent, responded to the situation like an orthodox businessman. Because wheat prices were low in 1931 and selling the agency wheat would only depress them further, he held the wheat off the market. When the new crop was harvested the agency held some seventy-five million bushels and was still waiting for prices to rise.

The next step came in 1932 when McFarland and Bennett concluded that the price was artificially low. They blamed speculators for depressing the prices and again they adopted what seemed to them the logical response to this temporary aberration. Bennett authorized McFarland to buy futures to strengthen the market. Unfortunately prices remainded depressed. Even the succession of poor crops in Canada did not solve the problem; there was always some wheat harvested. For the next few years McFarland continued his market operations, buying futures to stabilize the price of wheat whenever the price seemed low, always hoping that somehow conditions would return to normal and that the wheat could be sold at a reasonable price. By 1935 the total wheat and wheat futures held by the agency exceeded two hundred million bushels—the entire Canadian surplus. The government had assumed a huge financial liability with no legislative authority and had acquired a monopoly of the marketing of Canada's major export by a series of *ad hoc* decisions.[70]

The Liberals had never drawn attention to this extraordinary situation. King might well describe the wheat problem as "by all means the largest question that Canada has to face. Even the railway problem pales into insignificance."[71] But although wheat policy was important and McFarland's almost clandestine operations could easily be criticized as an affront to parliamentary democracy, many Liberals pointed out to King that it would be dangerous to attack McFarland because he had supported the price of wheat and the farmers were grateful.[72] Bennett could even argue that McFarland had averted "stark, complete, absolute disaster beyond the ability of any man to see."[73] There was also the possibility that the government's gamble would pay off. The world wheat crop for 1935 was expected to be low and McFarland might be able to sell his wheat at a satisfactory price.[74] The Liberals had found it safer to keep quiet.

When the Grain Board bill was first introduced, it threatened to force the issue into the open and reveal the divisions within the Liberal party. Bennett's legislation would give statutory authorization to a government marketing agency. The bill, however, went even further than this. The Grain Board would purchase not only all the wheat but also all the other grain marketed in Canada. Bennett's decision to include all grains came as a surprise. There had been no pressure from producers for this drastic extension of government intervention. It was not untypical of Bennett to be dramatic when he finally decided to take action but in this case he may also have been persuaded that including all grains would increase the embarrassment of the Opposition. The Liberals would find it difficult to support such a measure but, if they opposed it, the Conservative claim to be the party of reform would be strengthened.

Mackenzie King was not eager to be embarrassed by the bill. A compulsory board seemed to him to contradict sound Liberal principles but to oppose the bill without offering any alternative would be politically disastrous. His first idea was to accept the measure as no more than a temporary expedient, necessary only to retrieve the situation into which the Conservatives had blundered.[75] Western Liberals, however, seemed to favour a permanent board, whereas "Lapointe and the eastern members will be very strongly against a Board having compulsory powers. In fact, most of Canada, other than the western provinces will be."[76] He was relieved to learn that some westerners, including Gardiner, Crerar, and Dafoe, were prepared to criticize the compulsory features of the bill. He was also impressed by Charles Dunning's analysis of the situation. Dunning was not in the House but he attended a caucus meeting where he argued "that we can no longer continue to think in terms of open market competition, owing to the action of other nations." His conclusion was that some form of state intervention had become inevitable.[77] King began to see hope for a compromise somewhere between the two extremes of an open market and a government monopoly.

The next step was to delay proceedings in the House until agreement had been reached in caucus. King suggested to his followers that the government be asked to refer the bill to a Special Committee. If it agreed, the Liberals would then vote for the bill on second reading without opposing it. King took personal credit for the acceptance of this proposal:

I took command of the situation in caucus before any discussion began . . . I stressed the importance of unity, above all else, and the impossibility of hoping to have eastern Canada support a policy of the Government's further participation in the wheat business. By adopting a quiet and firm attitude, and counselling those who spoke to avoid controversy, as much as possible, I was able to keep the caucus well in hand to get substantial agreement on our course.

If Bennett refused to refer the bill to a committee, King went on, the Liberals would have to state their position. He suggested that in that case Ralston would speak for the party and affirm "the Liberal attitude of regulation and control of business by the State, rather than participation in business." This had been its position on the central bank; the equivalent in this case would be "the State controlling the Winnipeg exchange, as well as other features of the grain business, to the extent that might be necessary."[78] This was so broad and so vague that caucus could hardly object.

Bennett was having problems of his own. When he introduced the bill for second reading he took advantage of the occasion to taunt the Liberals: "This is the test of their sincerity," he thundered, "and not the sneers as they sit in their seats nor the sneers they express as they talk among themselves. Let them speak up like men."[79] But Bennett had gone too far. The legislation might be embarrassing for the Liberals but it was also being bitterly criticized by the grain trade and even within the Conservative caucus there was strong opposition. He was forced to give way and agree to the appointment of a Special Committee to study the bill.

King had won the concession he had asked for but Bennett's partisan remarks could not be overlooked. Ralston therefore delivered a partisan reply. He congratulated Bennett on his "return to normalcy" as shown by "his truculence, his bombastic utterances and his general partisanship."[80] He then went on to criticize the compulsory features of the bill and to argue that a time of emergency was not an appropriate time to establish a permanent policy. King later summed up the Liberal position by explaining that the party would vote for second reading provided that "it is understood that the opposition is not thereby committed to any provisions of the

107

bill, beyond the establishment of a grain board, with such powers as may be agreed upon."[81] With these qualifications the Liberals had no difficulty in voting for the bill.

The Special Committee resolved the Liberal dilemma. Bennett chaired the committee with Ralston as the leading Liberal member. Witness after witness denounced the idea of a compulsory Grain Board. Even the representatives of the Wheat Pools, who had initially supported the bill, admitted in answer to Ralston's questioning that the essential objective was an adequate price for wheat and that the proposed Grain Board had broader powers than seemed necessary.[82] Bennett had gone too far; the hearings made it unlikely that even his followers would vote for the measure. The bill which he presented to the House after the committee hearings bore little resemblance to the original bill. It was now entitled the Wheat Board Bill; there would be no government marketing of other grains. Even the compulsory feature of the bill had gone. The Wheat Board would offer a minimum price to the producer, leaving farmers with the choice of selling their wheat to the board or to private grain dealers.

The final vote on the bill came at the end of the session. Nobody knew how wheat marketing would be affected by the revised measure. Everything would depend on the minimum price which the board would set. If it offered a price above the world market price, it would be offering a subsidy to the farmers and would handle the entire crop; if its price was below the world price it would get no new wheat and its only responsibility would be to dispose of the wheat the government already owned.* But at this point nobody wanted to prolong the debate. King and Ralston persuaded the Liberal caucus to allow the bill to pass without a division.[83]

The session ended on the fifth of July. It was a hot and humid Ottawa day and, as King noted in his diary, the members had little energy left and little interest in the ritual of prorogation:

There was no bitterness whatever in the day's proceedings. In fact, a sort of sadness seemed to pervade the Chamber. It was quite plain that the Tories recognized they were defeated, and that nothing could save them. The best evidence of this was given when, nothing was going on, I rose and suggested to MacNicol, who was in the Chair as Speaker, that the honourable members opposite who expected to be appointed to the Senate should rise. All of them burst into a hearty laugh; there was a sort of puzzled and shamefaced look on their faces. Quinn, of Halifax, came back with the retort that the members on our side, who expected to be taken into the Cabinet, should rise. The rejoinder

*The Wheat Board was appointed after the end of the session, with John I. McFarland as chairman. In September the board announced a price of 87½ cents, which was slightly above the open market price at the time.

108

made quite clear that the government side were expecting a new Cabinet to be formed from our side of the House.[81]

The members then quietly shook hands with friends from both sides of the House and left for their constituencies to begin the final phase of an election campaign which had started six months before. Mackenzie King packed the material he would need for his campaign speeches and left for the Gatineau. He paid a brief visit to the "Abbey ruin, which was beautiful in the moonlight" and then retired "in the quiet and the peace and solitude of my Kingsmere home." It was sobering to think of "the mighty tide of effort and of controversy" which the next two months would bring.[85]

CHAPTER SEVEN

KING OR CHAOS

ON THE FOURTEENTH OF OCTOBER 1935 the Canadian voters reacted to five years of depression and to five years of Conservative administration. R. B. Bennett, who claimed to have averted a worse economic disaster and to have preserved the social order, was decisively rejected. It was less clear what Canadians had voted for. No fewer than three new parties contested the election, each of them with its own solution to the depression. The fact that one voter out of every five voted for one of these parties shows how desperate many Canadians were and how willing they were to experiment with radical measures. The results also showed, however, that these new parties were regional rather than national parties.

Mackenzie King resisted the temptation to compete for votes by out-promising the other parties. He refused to go beyond the Liberal platform of 1933 and, instead of promising dramatic reforms, promised conciliation and co-operation. He appealed for national unity and a majority government, confident that most Canadians would not be taken in by visions of a brave new world. The results seemed to vindicate his strategy. The Liberal party won by a handsome majority and, although it received slightly less than half of the popular vote, it did receive a significant proportion of the votes in every province. In a country deeply divided by regional antagonisms this was a striking achievement. If the definition of a national party is a party with support from every major region in the country, Mackenzie King was the leader of the only national party in 1935.

I

In the election campaign Bennett was more than ever the dominant figure in the Conservative party. H. H. Stevens was gone and four other ministers resigned at the end of the session, finding refuge in the Senate or in other appointed positions.[1] Nor were there any prominent Conservatives at the provincial level; no province had a Conservative government or even an effective Conservative opposition. There were provincial elections in New Brunswick and Prince Edward Island in the summer of 1935. In both provinces Conservative governments were resoundingly defeated by the Liberal opposition. The only chance for the party was if Bennett could repeat his performance of 1930 and turn the tide by a stirring campaign. "Canada wants a fighter," ran the Conservative slogan; "Vote for Bennett." And Bennett responded to the challenge. He seemed to have recovered his health and he toured the country addressing surprisingly large audiences, shouting down the hecklers and dominating the restive crowds. His gloomy followers found renewed hope in the "magnificent impression" he was making and could even envisage a Conservative victory.[2]

But the reforming mood of the New Deal broadcasts could not be resuscitated, even though W. D. Herridge returned as a speech-writer. The session and probably the pressures from within the party had seen to that. Bennett no longer talked of abolishing the capitalist system if it could not be reformed; his government, he now claimed, had saved capitalism by adapting it to meet the needs of the time. He spoke of the phenomenal progress in the last two or three years. Canada, he boasted, had been saved from economic disaster and was on its way to full recovery; "it would have been impossible to do more, with the world dragging us back and dragging us down."[3] He knew there was more to be done and that the time had come for a bold assault on the problem of unemployment, but somehow his rhetoric seemed less convincing. His boast that "less than 500,000" Canadian were now unemployed[4] was certainly less inspiring than his solemn promise in 1930 to end unemployment or perish in the attempt. Nor did Bennett have enough new proposals to create the impression of a second New Deal. The compulsory retirement of all workers at the age of sixty to provide jobs for younger men[5] lacked the inspirational zeal of his earlier heralding of dramatic reforms. Only the attacks on the laissez-faire policies of the Liberals had the same virulence. According to Bennett, "even Mr. King's most ardent flatterers, among themselves in secret, gaze fearfully upon his incorrigible medievalism."[6]

If Bennett's zeal for reform had subsided, his zeal for law and order was once again in evidence. He had already seized an opportunity to show his firmness in July by his response to an organized protest of unemployed workers, known at the time as the "on-to-Ottawa trek." Since the beginning of the depression transient workers, known as "single, homeless and unemployed," had created special problems. Municipalities found it difficult enough to provide relief for their own unemployed residents and

111

had refused to support these migrants. The federal government had finally accepted full responsibility for them, moved by a desire to rehabilitate these victims of the depression and also by the fear of riots or even revolution if nothing was done. Work camps had been established in remote areas by the Department of National Defence and, since 1933, there had usually been about twenty thousand men benefitting from the food, shelter, work, and the twenty cents a day which these camps provided.[7] Discipline was often a serious problem and in June 1935 men from camps on the west coast had demanded full wages for their work and an end to military control. When the demonstrations were ineffective the men decided to go to Ottawa and had boarded eastbound freight trains. More men joined them on the way until they reached Regina, where Bennett had ordered the R.C.M.P. to halt the trek.

Bennett refused to make any concessions. He did allow eight of the leaders to come to Ottawa to present their demands but his reply was a prepared defence of the relief camps and a denunciation of the delegation as communist agitators.[8] The two thousand men, camped in the Exhibition buildings in Regina, were ordered to return to the relief camps and, to encourage obedience, the federal government cut off their relief supplies. Bennett was determined, as he informed J. G. Gardiner, "to maintain the fabric of our society and the institutions of our country against the illegal threats and demands of communists and their associates."[9]

He was provoked into further action when the men stayed on in Regina, supported by the charitable donations of local citizens. He decided to end this defiance by arresting the leaders of the trek. On Dominion Day, while most of the men were watching a ballgame at the Exhibition grounds, the police suddenly converged on a fund-raising rally in the city to seize the trekkers on the platform. A riot ensued in which one policeman was killed and scores of people were injured. The rest was anti-climax. The provincial authorities undertook to send the men back to their homes or to the relief camps of their choice and within a week the trek had disbanded.

Bennett's "iron heel" approach to the trek was part of the Conservative campaign to pose as the bulwark against impending revolution. The C.C.F. offered Bennett the most attractive target and he regularly fulminated against the horrors of socialism which, he explained, meant the confiscation of all private property and the serfdom of Russia. J. S. Woodsworth, he conceded, was a sympathetic and gentle man but unfortunately he did not understand "the sinister and ferocious and destructive force which he so benignly and unconsciously camouflages."[10] Bennett's most publicized reference to communism was his revelation that communists were plotting to kidnap him and set up a soviet dictatorship.[11] The Conservative campaign in Quebec relied almost exclusively on this anti-communist line although here the attack was against the Liberals who were "unconsciously aiding and abetting communism" by criticizing "our treatment of the Regina rebellion" and by insisting on the repeal of Section 98 of the Criminal Code.[12]

It was more difficult for the Conservatives to deal with the renegade H. H. Stevens. Stevens had waited until it was clear that Bennett would lead the Conservative party through the campaign and only in July, when his last chance for a return to the party was gone, did he announce the formation of the Reconstruction party. The great issue, he asserted, was that the control of the financial, industrial, and commercial institutions was being concentrated in the hands of the rapacious few; the solution was the economic reconstruction of Canadian society. He had no blueprint for the new society; it was enough for the moment to promise massive public works projects and housing schemes, special benefits for farmers, labourers, veterans, and young people, and to end unfair trade practices and unwarranted profits.[13] Stevens expected to win the support of dissident Conservatives but his former colleagues hesitated to attack him too forcefully. Bennett rarely referred to Stevens in his speeches except to describe his policies as demonstrably unsound and to deplore his attempt to divide the forces of progress.[14] It was wiser to ignore than to draw attention to a deserter.

Bennett's one hope at the beginning of the campaign to pose as a reformer had been the possibility of a trade agreement with the United States. He even hinted to the Americans that further delay on their part would force him to criticize their attitude openly during the campaign.[15] Canadian and American negotiators did meet late in August but the results were disappointing. The United States offered tariff concessions on lumber and cattle, which would be politically helpful in British Columbia and the west, but refused to include such items as codfish and potatoes which were of special concern in the Maritimes. Bennett was not prepared to grant the requested Canadian tariff reductions on manufactured items without further concessions from the United States.[16] He did reap what political benefits he could from the negotiations. He arranged for the publication of his note of the previous December to prove that he had taken the initiative and early in the campaign he talked optimistically of signing a treaty.[17] As the campaign progressed his position shifted; soon he was asking to be returned to office in order to complete the negotiations.[18] By the end of the campaign he had made a virtue of necessity and was explaining that he could have signed an agreement at any time but had resolutely refused to sacrifice the interests of Canadian producers.[19]

His restraint may have been justified but it did little to enhance the image of Bennett as the man of action.

If the Conservatives had been the only rival party, the Liberals would have had few worries. Even the existence of the C.C.F. seemed only a minor complication. Its strength was largely confined to western constituencies and even there it now seemed unlikely that many Canadians would support a socialist party. Stevens, however, was an unknown quantity. If promises could win an election, here was a force to be reckoned with. He had no national organization and no prominent colleagues but a total of 174 Reconstruction candidates were nominated, with representation in every province. Disturbing reports came in from Liberals in the field that Stevens rather than Bennett was the real threat, that he had seized the popular imagination, and that in general stores and barber shops, wherever men talked of politics, it was Stevens of whom they talked.[20] The conclusion of worried Liberals was that if they wanted to win they would have to face the challenge of the Reconstruction party.

In August another new party emerged to complicate the situation even further. In that month the Social Credit party swept Alberta in a provincial election. Federal politicians could argue that this astonishing event was a provincial affair. The United Farmers of Alberta had been in office for fifteen years and could not escape some of the blame for the depression. In 1935 the U.F.A. was also weakened by its identification with the C.C.F. and socialism in federal politics and by a scandal in the private life of the party leader. "Bible Bill" Aberhart, the Social Credit leader, was a force to be reckoned with in the province because through his Prophetic Bible Institute and his Sunday radio sermons he had established a huge radio following with active bible groups in communities throughout the province. His fundamentalist message, denouncing the evils of the modern materialistic world, with the promise of salvation through Jesus Christ, had gradually shifted in emphasis to a denunciation of the evils of economic exploitation with the promise of salvation through inflation, but it was still a gospel message with Aberhart as the evangelist. By 1935 the transition from a religious sect to a political movement was complete; Aberhart had emerged as a political leader and his bible groups had become the local Social Credit organization. The Social Credit theories of Major Douglas, a Scottish engineer, had been transmuted into a revivalist campaign for the redemption of the province.[21] After the sweeping victory in Alberta a full slate of federal Social Credit candidates had been nominated in Alberta and Saskatchewan, plus scattered candidates in British Columbia and Manitoba. Social Credit might not have the same appeal in a federal election but nobody could be sure what would happen.

To politicians in a federal election campaign, however, Aberhart's provincial victory had even more ominous implications. No other province could duplicate the political situation in Alberta and no other province had an Aberhart, but all provinces had been affected by the depression. If the people of Alberta were so desperate that they could reject the established parties and turn to a demagogue selling the nostrum of inflation, who could be sure that Canadians elsewhere would not be attracted by quack prescriptions for economic salvation? In a campaign which, according to one journalist, "undoubtedly set a new high in pre-election promising,"[22] what would happen to a party which did not offer its simple cure for the depression? Even a responsible leader might convince himself that it was his duty to compete in this auction if only to prevent the victory of a dangerous demagogue.

Mackenzie King remained calm and confident amid the confusion. When he began the campaign he had no intention of producing a new programme or announcing new policies. His theme would be that Bennett had almost destroyed national unity and that only the Liberal party could restore it. He would rely on the sound common sense of the electorate to see through the demagoguery of his opponents. Instead of offering magical nostrums the Liberal party would stress the necessity of co-operation, of working together in a common cause.

King was so sure of himself that for the month of July he isolated himself at Kingsmere, explaining to impatient Liberals that he had to prepare his campaign material.[23] His three radio broadcasts at the end of the month contained no surprises. Instead of disguising this or apologizing for it, King made it the central feature of his speeches. Bennett, he said, had made promises in 1930 and was still making them. They had meant nothing then and they meant nothing now. What was the good of promises if they were not kept? Bennett now claimed that he was no longer a reactionary Tory but what of his followers? He had never consulted his colleagues or his party. Would they support his policies if he were elected? The Liberal party, King argued, could be trusted. It had a platform which could be relied upon because it had been endorsed by caucus and by the National Liberal Federation. This platform was not the final word but it was "the complete consensus of agreement already secured." There would be no supplementary manifesto just to win the election.[24]

In his own way King also played on the emotions of his audience. He underlined the Liberal party's commitment to parliamentary government and democracy by elaborating on the frightening implications of Bennett's authoritarian approach. Bennett, he declared, was a one-man government in the pattern of European dictators. He had flouted Parliament by his blank cheque relief bills, he had used his executive power to raise tariffs, he had arbitrarily imprisoned citizens under Section 98. Even the federal public works projects had dangerous implications. Why was so much money being spent on drill halls and armouries? "It is to build up a great military force because all dictatorships demand force."[25] Election day would "see the end of the worst autocracy Canada had known."[26]

King concentrated his attacks on Bennett and the Conservatives and made only brief references to the new parties. The socialists under Woodsworth meant well but their solutions would lead to a rigid and authoritarian regime. King insisted that Stevens had to accept responsibility for the policies of the government while he was a member, and scornfully referred to him as the man who had deserted a doomed party, had named his own party, announced its policies, and was now looking for followers.[27] Even Aberhart's victory in Alberta did not provoke a Liberal challenge. Social Credit, King was sure, was only a temporary aberration and if the Liberals did not provoke hostility by attacking it, the electors of Alberta would support the federal party that could form a government.[28] There was no need for Social Credit to contest the federal election, he suggested on his western tour, because if it worked, every party in Canada would adopt Social Credit doctrines.[29]

King's major emphasis, however, was not on the short-comings of the other parties but on the Liberal party as the only one which could claim to be a national party. Recovery and reform would depend upon the co-operation of federal and provincial governments. Bennett had alienated provincial authorities by encroaching on their jurisdiction; a Liberal government would work in harmony with them. In 1935 this seemed more than campaign rhetoric because the Liberals were in office in eight of the nine provinces.* As King explained to Hepburn: "We cannot emphasize too strongly the degree to which Mr. Bennett's policies have served to handicap all governments, nor how much it will mean to the future of the federal and provincial governments alike to have the kind of co-operation between them which is only possible between governments that enjoy to the full each other's confidence and whose political views are also in accord."[30]

The possibility of federal and provincial collaboration was demonstrated in various ways. King was accompanied on the platform by the provincial Premier for his first campaign appearance in each province, with the exception of Alberta. Some Premiers participated more actively in the campaign: Angus L. Macdonald of Nova Scotia held meetings in Ontario

*Manitoba had a Liberal–Progressive coalition government under Bracken but in 1935 Bracken openly supported the federal Liberals.

116

as well as the Maritimes, and Hepburn toured all the provinces. King himself suggested what would be the most dramatic presentation of this form of national unity. One of the last Liberal election rallies was held in Maple Leaf Gardens in Toronto, with an audience of more than seventeen thousand people. Arrangements were made to begin this rally with brief radio addresses from the eight provincial Premiers, each speaking from his own province and each declaring his support for the federal Liberal party. King then pledged that his first step as Prime Minister would be to invite all the Premiers, including Aberhart, to a federal-provincial conference to devise measures for economic recovery. The technical achievement of a nation-wide broadcast, with speakers from coast to coast, assured wide publicity to an occasion which effectively symbolized the Liberal promise of government by consultation and co-operation.

King knew that co-operation, even with Liberal governments, would not always be easy. Some Liberal Premiers had political views that were not in accord with his. King still had grave misgivings about Pattullo in British Columbia, who earlier in the year had decided to build a bridge over the Fraser at great expense as a relief project and had passed the necessary legislation despite strong opposition.[31] Hepburn seemed even more erratic. In April 1935 the Ontario Premier had abruptly repudiated four Ontario Hydro contracts to buy power from Quebec power companies. King had said nothing in public but he feared that such irresponsible behaviour would undermine confidence in the Liberal party. Bennett's delay in calling the election, he noted at the time "is breeding increased discontent & radical tendencies that are positively dangerous. Hepburn's action in Ontario is unnecessarily extreme, and most unsettling from the point of view of confidence in governments—a bad precedent for the future."[32] During the campaign, however, the support even of these questionable Liberals was welcomed. For all their faults they did belong to the party, and party loyalty would surely help to keep them in line.

Relations with Hepburn during the election went beyond campaigning. The National Liberal Federation was little more than a federation of the provincial Liberal organizations, and the campaign largely depended on their co-operation. The men who raised funds for the party in provincial elections were expected to do the same in the federal election. Most of the campaign funds were collected in Montreal and Toronto, with some of the money from Montreal going to the Maritimes and funds from Toronto being used to supplement the budgets of the party in the western provinces. The Quebec organization had little connection with the national office. Under Senator Donat Raymond it collected funds, produced

117

its own literature, and ran its campaign almost independently and reported what it had done to Norman Lambert at the National Liberal Federation.[33] With the Ontario organization, however, the links were closer and there were some complications. Frank O'Connor, the president of Laura Secord Candy Shops, was the chief federal fund-raiser in Toronto, as he had been in the provincial election of 1934, and his close connection with Hepburn was a potential embarrassment. Hepburn might try to exploit the situation for his own advantage.

Mackenzie King had already heard disturbing rumours about Hepburn having used his influence to have his friends nominated as federal Liberal candidates.[34] When Norman Lambert told him in May that he was having some difficulties with Toronto and asked him to talk to Frank O'Connor, King was immediately on his guard. He had always insisted that the party leader should have nothing to do with party finances; this was "the sordid side of politics"[35] and the only way for the leader to be above suspicion was not to know who the contributors were. His experience in the 1930 election had only strengthened this conviction; as he told Lambert, "he had had a lesson from the Beauharnois affair."[36] On this occasion, however, his caution was reinforced by his suspicions of Hepburn. "I told Lambert," King recorded, that "I feared Hepburn's tactics in matters of the kind, and did not wish to be drawn in any way into a situation which could tie me up to him in matters of the kind."[37] King did go to Toronto later in May but was very circumspect: "Hepburn," he commented in his diary, "is certainly trying to build up a machine. O'Connor after a phone message with Hepburn pressed me to ask H. [Hepburn] to go on with public works etc. I told him H. knew what was best and I did not intend to interfere. H. is anxious I should get under obligation to him & his outfit."[38]

King might avoid making any explicit commitments but the relations between the federal party and the Ontario Liberal party remained ambivalent. Frank O'Connor did co-operate with Lambert and, technically at least, King was untainted by any detailed knowledge of party funds. There was no assurance, however, that Hepburn shared King's view of the situation. He might well feel that King owed him something and might expect something in return. Meanwhile, the necessary funds were collected and King had at least protected himself by avoiding any overt commitment.*

*Contributions came in slowly until late in the campaign. Eventually, however, some $600,000 was collected in Quebec for the national campaign, with $100,000 of this going to the Maritime provinces. Slightly over $550,000 was collected in Ontario for the national campaign with $100,000 going to English-language publicity and another $100,000 going to the western provinces. Granatstein, "Financing the Liberal Party," provides a relatively full account of this elusive topic.

Mackenzie King had begun the campaign with a firm view of campaign strategy. He was equally firm about his own responsibilities as party leader. He saw no need to exhaust himself in an arduous campaign; he was now sixty years old and insisted on limiting his activities. As he explained to one supporter:

I hope our men will realize that the more I talk and travel, the less clear and exact my judgement in all-important matters is likely to be. If any success I have had in the leadership of the party is due in any particular to my own part, I should put *facile princeps*, avoiding pitfalls through too much talking, and, above all other things, being careful to exercise wise judgement and caution with respect to decisions which are bound to be far-reaching in determining the course of action of the party either in the immediate present or later on.[39]

This was eminently sensible although he might have been less determined to spare himself if he had been less sure of victory.

His own itinerary reflected this husbanding of his energy. Most of his public meetings were held in Ontario, where the party hoped to make significant gains.[40] He made one trip to the Maritimes, making one speech in each of the Maritime provinces with two stops in Quebec on the way. Then there was a restful week at Kingsmere, followed by a two-week trip to the west coast, with two meetings in each of the four western provinces. He tried to avoid social events or diversions before his speeches, to give himself some time for preparation and rest. After a meeting he was prepared to shake hands with everybody and to spend some time with local party stalwarts.[41] He also had to find time to prepare radio broadcasts since this was the first federal election in which leaders could address a national audience directly. His campaign was physically demanding but the pace was certainly less hectic than that set by the leaders of the other parties.

As the campaign progressed many Liberals became apprehensive about King's strategy of stressing co-operation and avoiding specific commitments. The unpredictability of an election contested by five parties, with a record number of over nine hundred candidates, and an election in which so many promises were being made, convinced many of his followers that a more active and a more positive approach was needed. Western Liberals, for example, wanted more definite statements of the party's policy on wheat and would have liked some reference to the benefits of inflation.[42] King insisted that the policy already agreed upon should be defended but not modified, although he did persuade Charles Dunning to intervene actively in the campaign to explain the complexities of wheat marketing in a radio broadcast.[43] The tariff caused even more anxiety, especially in constituencies in central Canada with protected industries. King carefully explained publicly that a Liberal government would re-

119

move "the new excessive and arbitrary tariffs" imposed by the Tories but would do it gradually without injuring "any legitimate industry."[44] Even this cautious response provoked an outcry from prairie Liberals.[45] King was equally circumspect in private: "I could not begin to give undertakings with respect to individual industries," he told one worried candidate in Ontario. "That would be assuming an authority which belongs only to the party as a whole. Your own voice in parliament would be worth more to the industries of your constituency than anything I might say at this time."[46]

The growing pressure for a more dynamic—and more promising—campaign had no visible effect. Some of King's opponents were encouraged by his cautious approach. R. J. Manion, for example, sensed that public opinion was shifting back to the Conservatives. "Everybody says it," he told his son. "Everywhere it seems to be in the air. It is partly due to Bennett's excellent work but also partly due to the futility of King's attitude."[47] But King remained convinced that he could rely on the sound judgment of the electorate and the fundamental desire for co-operation. As he explained to Ernest Lapointe:

I find, from communications which I am receiving, that some of our friends in the West are getting a little panicky about not making promises enough with respect to unemployment and monetary reform, or being specific enough with regard to tariff reductions etc. Also that our friends in Ontario and some other parts, think I should drop the references to greater freedom of trade, and particularly, to a central bank which will be publicly controlled. All of which goes to show just how necessary and wise it is for us to hold to the course outlined in 1933 and approved both by caucus and the National Federation.[48]

King held firmly to this course through the entire campaign. The Liberal party, he reminded his audiences, had a record of social reform. It had introduced old-age pensions when in office and had supported the New Deal measures in opposition. Economic recovery, however, must precede reform. Social services had to be paid for and, until the economy had been restored, the country could not afford an ambitious programme of social legislation.[49] The first step was the expansion of trade. King had at first expected Bennett to announce a trade agreement with the United States "as his last trump card"[50] and he tried to anticipate him by drawing attention to the Liberal pledge to seek a reciprocity agreement.[51] Later in the campaign, when Bennett had failed to negotiate an agreement, King went farther and confidently assured his listeners that a Liberal government would be able to sign a treaty with the United States before the end of the year.[52] It was almost the only specific Liberal commitment during the campaign.

The pressure on King to be more definite had no effect on his strategy but on one occasion he did show some signs of strain. He expected conflicting advice from Liberal candidates and always tried to be conciliatory. He was less tolerant of Vincent Massey, President of the National Liberal Federation, who was still arguing for a more dynamic approach. Massey was in a vulnerable position because his ambition was to become Canadian High Commissioner in London, an appointment which only a Prime Minister could make, and King took advantage of the situation to give vent to his resentment. When Massey came aboard King's private car in Toronto to suggest the line to take for the last week of the campaign, King lashed out:

When he began telling me what to do etc. I let out at him very hard. Told him he had caused me more pain & concern than anyone or all else in the party besides, that I had never had my privacy invaded as he had, for years . . . it was always Rex must do this etc., also his talk about helping me & "the cause" was all nonsense, it was himself & London that alone kept him to the party, that I had to tell him, it was only in this way he could hope to get appointed. . . . It was a scathing review of his selfish actions including telling him frankly he had been quite wrong in his views on most things. He was quite crushed— perhaps I went too far but it was the "last straw." I told him when he was 60 he would come to see I was right—that I thought I knew something about political leadership or would not be where I have been for so long a time.[53]

It was a humiliating experience for Massey, all the more so because Nicol, King's valet, was present during the tirade. King could be charming and conciliatory but he could be very unpleasant with people who relied on his favours.

The Liberal campaign ended as it had begun, still stressing King's theme of national unity. In his words it was "not the fist of a pugilist that Canada needs but the hand of a physician."[54] The Liberal publicity committee, unable to persuade King to be more forthright as the campaign went on, had to concentrate on such slogans as "Only King can win. Give him a working majority." The most effective slogan, and the one which best summarized King's version of the central issue of the election, was "It's King or Chaos." It was not a promise of a brave new world; it was a claim that no other leader could restore harmony and co-operation.

The one issue that made King apprehensive was the possibility of a European war. Norman Lambert reported shortly after the Alberta election that King "says not worried about social credit. He is more concerned about Ethiopia."[55] In the summer of 1935 it was apparent that Italy's menacing attitude towards Ethiopia might lead to war. If the League of Nations imposed sanctions on Italy, Canada might be involved. King feared that the patriotic fervour which war might arouse would benefit the government in office. He protected himself as well as he could by criticizing Bennett for leaving Canada without a Parliament during this international crisis and by promising that a Liberal government would make no decision on foreign policy until Parliament had been reassembled.[56] Lapointe did express his personal opinion that nothing that happened in Ethiopia would be worth the life of a Canadian citizen[57] but the party had no official policy. Bennett was as evasive as King. His government "would not be embroiled in any foreign quarrels where the rights of Canadians are not involved" but he provided no definition of these rights.[58] Italy did invade Ethiopia early in October but neither King nor Bennett dwelt on the European crisis after the invasion. Canada would not be compelled to define its position until the League, or possibly Great Britain, had announced a policy. Ethiopia would be ignored until after October 14, and the election would be decided on domestic issues.

II

The election results amply justified Mackenzie King's strategy. One hundred and seventy-eight telegrams had to be sent out to successful Liberal candidates from Laurier House on election night. No party had ever before won such an overwhelming victory. The Liberals won twenty-five of the twenty-six seats in the Maritimes and sixty of the sixty-five in Quebec. Even in Ontario they carried fifty-six out of eighty-two—the largest Liberal representation in sixty years. Manitoba and Saskatchewan together returned thirty Liberals from thirty-six constituencies. Only in the far west were the results disappointing. One Liberal was elected out of seventeen ridings in Alberta and six from the sixteen in British Columbia.

For the other parties the results were depressing. The Social Credit party did elect fifteen in Alberta and two in adjoining constituencies in Saskatchewan. The C.C.F., however, with 119 candidates, had only elected seven, and all of them from constituencies west of Ontario. Stevens was now truly a one-man party; out of 174 candidates he would be the only Reconstruction member in the House. For the Conservatives it was a rout. Forty members were returned, twenty-five from Ontario, five from Quebec, five from British Columbia, one each from five other provinces and none from Nova Scotia or Prince Edward Island. Twelve of the eighteen Cabinet ministers, including all the French-Canadian Ministers, were defeated. It was the smallest Conservative contingent in the House of Commons since Confederation.

The popular vote tells a slightly different story. The Conservatives had clearly lost the confidence of many former supporters; the party which had received almost 50 per cent of the votes in 1930 received just under 30 per cent in 1935. Support for the Liberal party, however, did not increase significantly; even though half a million more voters cast ballots in 1935, the total Liberal vote only increased by two hundred thousand, and although it did receive almost 45 per cent of the popular vote, this was slightly below the percentage it had received in 1930. The party had received much the same proportion of votes among English Canadians in eastern Canada as it had in the previous election; an increase in support from French Canada had been balanced by reduced support in the western provinces. Many voters had shown no confidence in either Liberal or Conservative candidates; one out of every five had voted for parties which had not even existed five years before. The two-party system which had seemed almost re-established in 1930 was once more disrupted. If the choice was between King and chaos, more than half the voters had preferred chaos.[59]

The regional contrasts in the popular vote illustrate the deep divisions which had emerged in Canadian society. The interest in politics had been high; record crowds had turned out to hear the leaders and 75 per cent of the eligible voters had gone to the polls. Politics was seen as a major instrument of economic recovery or of social change. But this widespread interest in politics had produced very different responses across the country. The two-party system still existed in the Maritimes and in Quebec, with the Liberals gaining at the expense of the Conservatives, although even in these provinces almost one voter out of ten voted for a Reconstruction candidate. In Ontario the popular vote for the Liberals declined slightly, with a sharp drop in the Conservative vote balanced by almost one voter in five opting for the Reconstruction or C.C.F. party. In Manitoba and Saskatchewan the Reconstruction party was a negligible factor but the C.C.F. polled almost as many votes as the Conservatives. Albertans had a pattern of their own; almost half of them voted Social Credit and the rest divided their support among Liberals, Conservatives, and the C.C.F. The election results showed how deep the regional divisions had become.

The major factor was the disintegration of the Conservative party. The Conservatives were unlucky to have come into office at the beginning of the depression. A loss of popular support was to be expected, and the unequal incidence of the depression would account for regional variations in the response. But this is only a partial explanation. Economic factors alone cannot explain the extraordinary shift in the voting pattern, with so many traditionally Conservative voters changing their political allegiance. Canadians had not merely lost confidence in the government; they had decisively rejected it. For this, R. B. Bennett must accept some of the blame.

In many ways Bennett had reacted in a constructive way to the economic crisis. His tariff increases did give some aid to Canadian industries although they also penalized primary producers and so accentuated regional divisions. In other areas, however, his administration was less controversial. He established some important federal institutions, such as the Bank of Canada, the Wheat Board, and the Canadian Radio Broadcasting Commission. During his years in office the federal civil service attracted a nucleus of brilliant men, including Clifford Clark, Graham Towers, and Donald Gordon, who would remain key figures in the Canadian bureaucracy for the next decade. This was not a record to be ashamed of.

The most serious criticism of Bennett, however, is that he was a failure as a party leader. He never understood that the political party was a major instrument of national unity. He was a businessman who saw government as a business enterprise, responsible for the finances of the nation. He sometimes described his Cabinet as "the board of directors for the time being administering the affairs of this country"[60] and he obviously considered that as Prime Minister he was Chairman of the board. It was his duty to make decisions and accept responsibility for the results. He did not seek advice or delegate responsibilities to his colleagues; he announced the policies and expected his party to support him. With his style of leadership, his Cabinet Ministers were almost nonentities; none of them acquired the prestige which could establish them as effective spokesmen for their region. The unpopularity of the Conservative government, especially on the prairies and in Quebec, can be attributed at least in part to the obscurity of their Cabinet representatives, since Ministers from these regions had traditionally exercised a large degree of local authority. The impression that the Bennett government represented central Canada and, more specifically, the English-Canadian financial and commercial interests in central Canada, fostered a sense of alienation in the other regions.

Bennett also lost the confidence of many Canadians by his rhetorical exaggerations. He did respond to the needs of an industrial society to the extent that he accepted a greater responsibility in economic affairs than previous governments had done. But his sweeping promises, beginning in 1930 with his promise to end unemployment and culminating in 1935 with his New Deal broadcasts, had destroyed his credibility. Industrialists and financial leaders, traditionally Conservative in politics, had been disturbed by his talk of abolishing the system, but many Canadians saw only the contradiction between his rhetoric and the continuing depression. His authoritarian style and his hostile reaction to criticism gave the impression of an arrogant and insensitive leader, who made promises to stay in office but who had little sympathy for those who were suffering. His treatment of Stevens was consistent with this pattern. Stevens was a demagogue and many of his statements were irresponsible but he had evoked a popular response because he did appear to be the champion of the little man. Instead of using Stevens, instead of encouraging his investigations on price spreads while at the same time persuading him to qualify his public statements, Bennett chose to dismiss him and rejected any suggestions of reconciliation. As a result, the party was split and the Reconstruction party received the votes of many disillusioned Conservatives. In 1935 two of every three voters had rejected the Bennett government and many of them had opted for regional parties.

Mackenzie King, in contrast to Bennett, was always sensitive to regional diversity. When Liberals criticized the party line, King did not denounce them or read them out of the party; he saw them as spokesmen for Canadians who felt they had a legitimate grievance and he tried to accommodate them. By his emphasis on party unity he had at least avoided alienating any major region or group. He had not emerged as a popular leader—in a divided nation only regional leaders can win mass popularity—but he had survived as a national figure. Canadians had split their vote among five political parties but every region had shown some confidence in the Liberal party. In Alberta and British Columbia this party had been their second choice; in every other province it had been their first choice. In a country where regional divisions had become intense, this was a major political achievement. Mackenzie King had proved to be a very successful Leader of the Opposition. As his reward, he was once again Prime Minister.

CHAPTER EIGHT

THE REINS OF OFFICE

KING RETURNED TO OFFICE full of confidence. Economic conditions were improving and although unemployment was still high it was generally believed that the worst was over and that the business cycle was on the upswing. King also took it for granted that a Liberal administration could accelerate the economic recovery. Sound fiscal policies, by which he meant rigid economies, would restore the confidence of businessmen and encourage private investment. The other major contribution of the federal government would be the expansion of international trade. A strong Cabinet which took prompt action would soon restore the political as well as the economic health of the nation.

In the first few months after the election everything seemed to be going according to plan. Within a remarkably short time King had formed what was widely conceded to be a Cabinet of able men, had averted a potential crisis over the war in Ethiopia, had negotiated a satisfactory trade agreement with the United States, and had presided over an unusually harmonious federal-provincial conference. By the end of the year the impression of effective leadership and a dynamic government had been created. It was the honeymoon period for the new administration.

I

King's first step was to choose his colleagues. Much would depend on his choice because for King the Cabinet was of crucial importance. He relied on individual Ministers to present and defend the interests of the regions they represented and he relied on discussions in Cabinet to arrive at policies which would respect these interests. Shortly after Hepburn's victory in Ontario King had given him some advice on dealing with his Ministers. The advice had been wasted on Hepburn but it does summarize King's view of his relations with his colleagues:

My own experience has disclosed to me the wisdom of the collective mind and the collective will in public affairs. It is, I think, of the very essence of our British system of government. You will be wise to win as completely as you can the confidence of all your colleagues, and this can be done most effectively by giving them, to the exclusion of others, your own confidence, though, with respect to many thing·, there will be much which you will find it inadvisable to share even with them, but best to keep wholly to yourself. Don't forget what I said to you about having it understood that you would expect all major decisions to be discussed in advance with respect to appointments as well as policies. Adoption of this course will save you many pitfalls.[1]

Leadership, as King described it, did not mean presiding impartially over a Cabinet of equals. His colleagues were regional spokesmen and the Prime Minister had the final responsibility for identifying policies which balanced regional interests and so represented the national interest. But these policies emerged from the arguments between Ministers and would only be adopted when all Ministers accepted them. This form of leadership depended on forceful Ministers who could interpret and present the interests of their region effectively but who, at the same time, respected their colleagues and accepted the necessity of compromise. This form of collective responsibility would not work with a weak Cabinet or with a Cabinet dominated by one or two powerful individuals. It was King's initial responsibility to choose colleagues who could make the system work.

King, in theory at least, had a free choice. He had made no formal commitments to any individuals and was not even restricted to those Liberals who had been elected to the House of Commons. Inevitably his choice was limited by factors he could not ignore. Some individuals could not be overlooked because of their experience and their status within the party. It was also necessary to have representatives from the different regional and cultural groups even if it meant including some men of only moderate ability. But the final composition of the Cabinet shows how widely King ranged in his search for suitable Ministers; his eventual Cabinet included former colleagues, a few who had established their reputation during the years of opposition, some new members whose ability compensated for their lack of experience, and two men who were selected from outside of the House of Commons. It was also a mark of King's assurance and his authority within the party that he had chosen his colleagues, allocated the portfolios, and had his new government sworn into office only nine days after the election.

Ernest Lapointe was an automatic choice because Lapointe was indispensable. French Canadians were a major element in the Canadian spectrum and King realized that the success of his political leadership depended on an adequate weighing of their interests and aspirations when political decisions were made. But King also realized that he was not an expert on French Canada. He had few social contacts with French Canadians, his use of French was limited to reading prepared speeches with an English-Canadian accent, and, equally significant, he had no great admiration for their political or their religious traditions. His solution had been to create a unique structure within the party to ensure a French-Canadian input into all political decisions. At the beginning of his career as party leader he had decided that a Quebec lieutenant, the counterpart of a lieutenant from the Maritimes or the west, was not enough. He needed a French Canadian who would be his closest associate within the party, a man who would be consulted on every political issue.

King had not waited for this French-Canadian colleague to emerge. Back in 1921 Lomer Gouin, rather than Ernest Lapointe, had been the most prestigious French-Canadian Liberal. Gouin, however, had been a high-tariff Liberal, closely connected with Montreal business interests, whereas Lapointe was closer to King's definition of a Liberal. "As between Gouin and the big interests and Lapointe and the people," King had vowed in his diary in 1920, "my alliance is with the latter."[2] He had told Lapointe that he "regarded him as the real leader in Quebec" and had been careful to consult him even though Gouin was his most senior French-Canadian colleague. Within a few years a frustrated Gouin had resigned and Ernest Lapointe had been openly identified as King's Quebec lieutenant and his closest political associate.

Lapointe had amply justified King's choice. This tall, burly, and slow-moving man, with his simple tastes and old-fashioned virtues, had grown in stature both within the Liberal party and within French Canada. King had chosen him because he was a liberal by King's definition—he had sympathy for the under-privileged, a respect for individual liberties, and an overriding commitment to national unity. As a loyal Liberal he expressed his opinions frankly and openly to his leader but he also accepted his subordinate role and never questioned King's authority as his chief.

Lapointe's sterling qualities, however, do not in themselves explain his major role within the party. His prestige among his English-Canadian colleagues and in Quebec depended upon convincing evidence that he exercised political power. The evidence was there because King provided it. King always consulted him on major issues and weighed his opinions carefully. On issues of direct concern to French Canada he usually accepted Lapointe's advice. Lapointe was King's contact with French Canada and King relied on his judgment of the political situation in Quebec.

It is never easy to define an association in which the leader makes the decisions but the lieutenant exercises a palpable influence. King and Lapointe had fitted into complementary roles in which loyalty to the party, mutual trust, and an almost intuitive understanding of each other had established an unusually close political partnership. French Canada had continued to support the federal Liberal party in large part because, through this relationship, the interests and sentiments of French Canada were incorporated into the decision-making process.[3]

Lapointe's stature within the party was clearly reflected in the process of Cabinet formation in 1935.[4] Lapointe was the first colleague to whom King talked, and for the next week he was consulted on the candidates under consideration from all parts of the country and was often present when King talked to prospective Ministers. But if Lapointe was the senior colleague he was not co-Prime Minister. He had, for example, expressed a desire for the Department of External Affairs but when King said that the European crisis made it necessary for the Prime Minister to retain this portfolio, Lapointe raised no objections and accepted his old portfolio of Justice.

King's most important colleague, after Lapointe, would be the Minister of Finance. J. L. Ralston had been the Liberal financial critic during the years of opposition but he had decided to concentrate on his legal practice in Montreal and had not been a candidate in 1935. King and Lapointe tried to persuade him to return to politics but Ralston was adamant. Charles Dunning was King's second choice for the post. Dunning had been out of the House since his defeat in 1930 and had not contested a seat in 1935 but he still had political ambitions. He had stayed out of politics to achieve financial independence and was now financially secure. His experience in the pulp and paper and the milling industries and his contacts with the business world had reduced his political influence in western Canada but had broadened his political base and there is little doubt that he had ambitions to become Liberal leader in the future. He had paved the way by campaigning during the election. When the call came from Ottawa, Dunning accepted with alacrity.

King wanted Dunning as Minister of Finance because he represented fiscal conservatism. King knew that Dunning had been a potential rival for the party leadership in the mid-1920s and still had high ambitions but this did not disturb him. He felt sure of his own position within the party and, in any case, thought Dunning had put himself out of the running as his successor by his close association with the world of finance.[5] But Dunning had administrative ability and his presence in the government would reassure industrialists and manufacturers. Certainly his views on finance were orthodox. The depression, according to him, had been caused by reckless and irresponsible business practices; humanity, he had asserted in 1932, "is now doing penance in an economic sense for its infractions of the laws of sound economics."[6] There were no patent remedies or panaceas. Economic recovery, he was still insisting in 1935, was "essentially a rather slow process of bringing ourselves into harmony with natural economic law. . . . Quick economic miracles are quite impossible."[7] And recovery would have to precede reform. He had been afraid that both parties were "off on an orgy of expensive social reform without adequate regard to how it is to be paid for." He was not opposed to social reform, he insisted, but the first step was to establish "a sound economic base."[8] As Minister of Finance he intended to "stand for stability, non-interference with legitimate business, sanctity of governmental contracts and prevention of provincial raids upon the Federal Treasury."[9]

The other Cabinet choices were designed to provide a balance of regional interests within the government. King's first choice for a Maritime spokesman had been Angus L. Macdonald, the Premier of Nova Scotia, but when Macdonald decided to stay in provincial politics he had no hesitation in choosing J. L. Ilsley, taciturn but conscientious and honest, and a man who would defend Maritime interests with stubborn determination. Ilsley was given the portfolio of National Revenue. J. E. Michaud would represent New Brunswick with the portfolio of Fisheries, largely as a reward for his willingness to contest the Restigouche-Madawaska by-election in 1933. No member from Prince Edward Island seemed suitable but this omission was eventually corrected when a seat was found on the Island for Charles Dunning.

British Columbia would be represented by Ian Mackenzie who had served for a few months in the previous Liberal government and had been active as an opposition member; his reward was to become Minister of National Defence. There would be no Minister from Alberta as a salutary lesson to Alberta voters of the consequences of not voting Liberal. Manitoba posed a more difficult problem. T. A. Crerar was the senior Liberal from the province but both King and Lapointe felt that his political influence there was on the wane. No other candidate seemed satisfactory, however, and when J. W. Dafoe supported Crerar, his opinion carried the day. Crerar wanted the Railway portfolio but had to be satisfied with Mines and Resources.

The key Liberal in the west was J. G. Gardiner, the Premier of Saskatchewan. King had long admired Gardiner for his partisan loyalty and his ability as a political organizer and was determined to bring him into federal politics. He had even considered him a possible Minister of Finance if Dunning refused to return to politics.[10] Gardiner wanted to come to Ottawa but his long-standing rivalry with Dunning was a serious obstacle. King knew better than to avoid unpleasant topics; he "thought it advisable" to tell Gardiner immediately that if he came he would have to accept Dunning as a colleague. Gardiner was bitterly critical of his former Saskatchewan leader but may have been placated by King's assurance that Dunning would represent an eastern riding and that "so far as the west was concerned, the field would be left clear to himself."[11] Gardiner then caused some difficulty by demanding a more important portfolio than Agriculture or to have Agriculture expanded to include responsibility for wheat marketing, which came under Trade and Commerce. King consulted Lapointe and Dunning, only to find that Dunning was opposed to any extension of Agriculture into the area of international trade. King tactfully refused Gardiner's request but did assure him that the matter was not closed; "he could fight as hard as he wished" within Cabinet for the change if he came to Ottawa.[12] It was a great relief when Gardiner accepted on these terms.

Cabinet representation from Quebec also created some difficulties, although here it was Lapointe who made the suggestions with King raising objections. Lapointe wanted "Chubby" Power as his colleague from the Quebec region. He had earned this recognition by his activity in the House during the Bennett years and by his work as provincial organizer of the Liberal party. King conceded his virtues but insisted that he "was determined not to have men in the Cabinet who drank."[13] Lapointe pointed out Power's popularity among the members and his special qualifications as the only Irish Catholic of ministerial calibre. King finally agreed that he could not be excluded and, after telling Power of his reservations about his "particular weakness," appointed him to the portfolio of Pensions and National Health.

The Montreal region caused even more trouble. Lapointe assumed that Arthur Cardin and Fernand Rinfret would once again be in the government. Cardin was an outstanding campaigner, an able administrator, and an apparently obvious choice but King mistrusted him because of his connections with the Simard family, who had shipbuilding interests in Cardin's constituency. The Simards had invested in the Beauharnois Syndicate and even this tenuous link with the Beauharnois incident was enough to convince King that Cardin was an undesirable colleague. Rinfret seemed unsuitable because, despite his charm and his intelligence, he was lazy and ineffective in Cabinet discussions. King, in an uncharacteristic comment in his diary, deplored what he interpreted as Lapointe's desire to avoid unpleasant decisions but he had no alternative candidates

131

to propose and so Lapointe's choices were reluctantly accepted. There was still a minor crisis over Cardin. King talked to him and tentatively offered him the department of Secretary of State. He "did not seem to be very enthusiastic," King noted in his diary, so Cardin was told that the question could be discussed later in the day.[14] Cardin was certainly not enthusiastic; he took the next train back to Montreal and had to be persuaded to return. He insisted on a more important portfolio and King finally shifted somebody else in order to give him Public Works. Fernand Rinfret took Secretary of State without any objections.

The choice of the Ontario Ministers was complicated by the shadow of Mitchell Hepburn. There were already some indications that Hepburn intended to exert some influence within the Ontario wing of the federal party and a letter from Hepburn to King recommending Arthur Slaght for a Cabinet post re-enforced King's suspicions.[15] King immediately reminded Hepburn that he had refused to proffer any advice on Cabinet formation after Hepburn took office in Ontario and that even a hint of undue influence would be damaging to both governments.[16] The letter was tactful and conciliatory but the message was clear. The final composition of the Ontario representation in the Cabinet showed how independent King intended to be.

W. D. Euler was the only Ontario member from the previous Liberal administration who was almost automatically included. King had no great liking for Euler because of his protectionist leanings and his unyielding stubbornness in Cabinet discussions but he recognized his forthright honesty and his administrative ability. Euler was at first considered for Public Works but was finally given Trade and Commerce. King saw no other suitable candidates among the Ontario Liberals with previous experience in the House. Among the newcomers was Norman Rogers whom King had encouraged to enter politics; it seemed appropriate that his protégé should now go to the Department of Labour, which had been King's first portfolio. Another newcomer to the House was C. D. Howe, an engineer who had established his reputation as a builder of grain elevators and who, like Rogers, had contested and won a formerly Conservative constituency. King did not know Howe well but he seemed an ideal choice for the new Department of Transport, likely to be able to speak the language of railwaymen and to impose some efficiency on the patronage-ridden Harbours Boards. The fourth Minister from Ontario was no more than an interim appointment. J. C. Elliott had been a Cabinet Minister in the 1920s but King, when he first discussed Cabinet formation with Lapointe, had rejected Elliott as a man who brought little strength to the party and who had now reached "the garrulous stage."[17] King even took the unpleasant step of informing Elliott that he would have to give way to a younger man. But Elliott was safe and loyal, whereas the younger Ontario Liberals might have links with Hepburn. He was eventually offered and accepted Public Works; he then showed his loyalty by agreeing to become Post-master General when Cardin had to be placated. Hepburn's candidate, Arthur Slaght, was not considered even though Toronto had no representation in the Cabinet. King may have written a tactful letter to Hepburn but his choice of Ontario colleagues was a direct snub.

It had been a busy week. King had chosen his colleagues and allocated portfolios with the assurance of a man who knew the prerogatives of a Prime Minister. He had consulted only a few of the senior Ministers, and had avoided encounters or telephone calls from anyone who might be soliciting a Cabinet post or recommending a candidate. There had been a few necessary but unpleasant interviews with men who had some claim to recognition yet would not be included in the final list, but most of his time had been spent persuading prospective colleagues to take what he was offering. Decisions had been made quickly because delay would only increase the "pressure, lobbying etc." which he wished to avoid.[18] But if King had acted with despatch, he had not acted hastily. He had known what he intended to do and the final results were very close to the slate he had first outlined to Lapointe. It was a smaller Cabinet than its predecessor; by combining some portfolios and including only one Minister without portfolio—Raoul Dandurand would be government leader in the Senate—King had reduced the Cabinet from twenty-one to sixteen. It was also an able group, a combination of experience and promise, with strong representatives from each region. King had chosen the kind of Cabinet which was appropriate to his concept of political leadership.

There was no doubt, however, as to who was in control. Immediately after the swearing-in ceremony on October 23, the new Ministers returned to the House of Commons for their first Cabinet meeting. King arranged the seating, with Lapointe on his right and Dunning on his left. He also announced that there would be no smoking and no reading of newspapers during Cabinet meetings. He then outlined the first measures to be dealt with—the Ethiopian crisis, the trade agreement with the United States, and the Dominion-Provincial Conference. The next day was Thanksgiving and the new government had the day off. On the following day, however, the Ministers were to reassemble to discuss the international situation.[19] King did not intend to waste any time.

II

Before meeting the Cabinet again King had a session with O. D. Skelton, still the Under-Secretary for External Affairs. Skelton had been

King's personal choice for this post in the 1920s and the two men had established a close working relationship. Skelton had a phenomenal capacity for work, an uncomplaining willingness to devote his days and his nights to public service. He combined this with a remarkable talent for organizing material rapidly, for distinguishing between the significant and the trivial, and for producing memoranda or draft speeches at short notice which were models of both brevity and clarity. Skelton also had a clear perception of the subordinate role of a civil servant; he expressed his own opinions to his Minister with great frankness but he accepted his instructions loyally even when he disagreed with them.* In the past King had taken full advantage of his energy and ability. Skelton had been directly responsible for administering the Department of External Affairs but he had soon become the equivalent of the Prime Minister's Deputy Minister, involved in domestic as well as external matters. He had been the unofficial Secretary to the Cabinet, preparing the agenda and ensuring that decisions were implemented. He had also been a member of every major interdepartmental committee, the eyes and ears of the Prime Minister within the federal bureaucracy.

King always demanded loyalty and dedication from his subordinates and was often quick to find fault with them if their work was unsatisfactory or if their private life or their health interfered with their duty to him. Skelton was almost the only individual who measured up to his exacting standards. King knew how much he had depended on Skelton; one of his concerns at leaving office in 1930 had been the problem of losing his services. On that occasion, according to his diary, he had even told Skelton of his appreciation: "I wanted Skelton to be the last person with whom I wd. have a word on quitting the office. I told him I owed more to him than any other & that I cld. not express what our friendship & relationship meant. As ever he was modesty & humility itself. I regard him as the ablest man in the public service of Canada."[20]

The close collaboration with Skelton did not mean that the two men always agreed. The Under-Secretary had firm opinions of his own, one of which was a strong conviction that the British had to be carefully watched. He was not anti-British as some Canadian anglophiles claimed.[21] It was rather that he assumed that the policies of all governments were

---

*Skelton more than any other man shaped the Canadian public service in these years. He sought out bright young applicants and encouraged them in their career. His style became almost the trademark of the senior civil servants in Ottawa—the long hours of work, the shunning of publicity, and the loyalty to the Minister, whoever he might be. Even Skelton's memoranda, with their concise presentation of the problem followed by the policy alternatives, with the pros and cons of each, became the model for the next generation in the public service.

dictated by national self-interest and that the British government was no exception. When Englishmen talked of Commonwealth co-operation or appealed for Imperial solidarity he assumed that the rhetoric concealed a hard-headed attempt to exploit colonial loyalties for the benefit of Great Britain. He saved his scorn for Canadians who believed that British statesmen were somehow wiser and more righteous than the politicians of other countries and who took the British rhetoric seriously. He believed that Canada had its own national interests and that these did not always coincide with British interests.

Mackenzie King was less suspicious of British appeals for Commonwealth solidarity. He believed that the Commonwealth had a real existence, bound together by the invisible cords of heritage and tradition, and that British foreign policy, based on the traditions of liberty and justice, would generally reflect the common interests of all members of the Commonwealth. King knew that Skelton did not share his sentiments. As he had noted in his diary in 1929: "Skelton is at heart against the British Empire, which I am not. I believe in the larger whole, with complete independence of the parts united by cooperation in all common ends."[22] But King could work with men who disagreed with him. He saw Canadian autonomy as a prerequisite for the survival of the Commonwealth whereas Skelton saw it as an assertion of a separate Canadian identity but for King it was enough to know that Skelton could be relied on to defend this autonomy against any Imperial encroachments. In the decade of the 1920s, when the recognition of autonomy was the central issue in Canada's relations with Great Britain, differences between the two men had not complicated their relationship. King would have to be more careful if the central issue became the extent of Canada's support for British foreign policy.

For the moment, however, King was delighted once again to have Skelton as his Deputy-Minister. If it had been anybody else King might well have had misgivings about a man who had served R. B. Bennett for five years. But Skelton was punctiliously non-partisan. His loyalty was to the Prime Minister of the day and he had served Bennett as loyally as he had served King. Bennett, in fact, had come into office knowing of Skelton's Liberal sympathies and quite rightly suspecting that he had little liking for high tariffs or a closer Imperial connection; he had intended to replace him. Bennett, however, had come to appreciate Skelton's unrivalled knowledge of the Ottawa bureaucracy and of Canada's external relations and also his readiness to serve even a Tory Prime Minister. Skelton had stayed on and was soon re-established as the most influential civil servant in Ottawa. When the Liberals returned to office he continued to behave

135

with impeccable propriety. He did not contact King until the new government had been sworn in and King was officially Prime Minister. But Skelton did anticipate King's needs. His first note to King after the change of government helps to explain why two such different Prime Ministers found him an exemplary public servant. The note deserves to be quoted in full:

May I express my great pleasure in being able to work under you again? I enclose memos. on some points; I am afraid the Italo-Ethiopian sanctions question will require very early consideration and decision.[23]

Mackenzie King was equally businesslike. At his first meeting with Skelton, on October 25, he expressed his "great delight" at being associated with him once again and then immediately asked to be briefed on the Ethiopian situation.[24]

The problem was to determine Canada's commitments as a member of the League of Nations. Since the end of the First World War Canadian external relations had been largely restricted to Canada's relations with Great Britain and the United States. The issues at stake had seemed significant—it was important to define Canadian status within the Commonwealth and to deal with tariff questions—but the stark fear of national survival was absent. Diplomats could discuss and even disagree but nobody rattled the sabre. Canadians who read newspapers knew that other countries were less fortunate—or less civilized. They knew that there had been trouble in the Balkans and South America and that there was fighting in Manchuria. All this was deplorable but it seemed no more relevant than stories of remote floods or earthquakes. The invasion of Ethiopia, however, suddenly broadened Canadian horizons. There might be a major war and, if there was, Canada might be a participant.

Until 1935 membership in the League of Nations had been a symbol of Canada's enhanced status in the world but had not imposed any major obligations. Even the commitment to defend the territorial integrity of other members had been interpreted by Canadians to mean that the League might ask Canada to contribute to collective security but that only the Canadian Government could commit Canada to send troops.[25] The League was seen as an institution for preserving peace and Canadians, who took it for granted that disputes could be settled peacefully, had seen no hazards in League membership.

When Italy defied the League the Canadian Government was awakened from its unsuspecting slumber. As Bennett explained to the British Government early in September, Canadians were preoccupied with domestic issues although there was general agreement that Italy was the aggressor. His compatriots, Bennett continued, had never placed much confidence in sanctions but, on the other hand, "public opinion in Canada recognizes the importance of preserving the League from the loss of authority consequent on failure to carry out the undertakings of the Covenant, whether wisely made or not." The Canadian Government was therefore willing "if occasion arises, to discuss with other members of the League the question of the application of economic sanctions."[26] Bennett was not initiating such discussions, nor was he committing himself to imposing economic sanctions if other League members favoured the idea. As for military sanctions, his dispatch did not even express a willingness to discuss such a possibility. Canadian policy was still a pious hope for peace.

This hope was shattered early in October when Italian troops invaded Ethiopia. If the Assembly of the League declared Italy the aggressor the next step would be to discuss what action the League members should take. Bennett at first wanted Howard Ferguson, the Canadian delegate at Geneva, to abstain from voting on the issue of aggression. With the Canadian election only ten days away, it was "not considered advisable to anticipate in any way the action of the new Parliament."[27] Ferguson, however, explained that Anthony Eden and the other Dominions' representatives had agreed to vote and that this "would, of course, be without prejudice to our attitude towards any scheme of sanctions which might be later proposed."[28] Skelton still insisted that such a vote would implicitly commit Canada to apply sanctions later but Bennett overrode his scruples.[29] He authorized Ferguson to join in denouncing Italy as the aggressor.

The next question was what action League members should take. A large Co-ordinating Committee was to be formed with a smaller subcommittee, known as the Committee of Eighteen, to make recommendations. Should Canada serve on the Co-ordinating Committee? Bennett chose the path of least decision; the Canadian delegation was instructed not to volunteer but "should not refuse if requested to serve."[30] The delegation, however, not only volunteered for the Co-ordinating Committee but also accepted a place on the Committee of Eighteen. Nobody in Ottawa seems to have realized what had happened.[31] The government had no policy to suggest and doubtless assumed that, even on the Committee, Canada could play a passive role, at least until after the election. Ferguson did not share this reluctance to speak out. When the Committee of Eighteen met he called for prompt action: "Let them show the world that the League was no longer to be scoffed at, but that it means business," he pleaded.[32] Ferguson resigned after the election but W. A. Riddell, the Canadian Advisory Officer to the League, shared his views

137

on the need for positive action. In the absence of any instructions from Ottawa he took an active part in drafting the recommendations of the committee.

On October 25, when Skelton briefed King on the subject, the Committee of Eighteen had already proposed an embargo by all League members on imports from Italy and on the export to Italy of military equipment and certain products essential to military operations. Skelton warned King that these economic sanctions had grave implications. Italy might be provoked to retaliate and "the British were very alarmed as to the possibility of war."[33] To reject sanctions might undermine the efforts of the League to deter aggression; to enforce them might involve Canada in a war.

Mackenzie King, like most Canadians, had been unrealistic about the League. His own career had strengthened his faith that there was no disputes that reasonable men could not settle by discussion and compromise. The League, as he envisaged it, was a forum for discussion, at which disputing nations could present their case and where the pressure of world public opinion would help to make both sides more reasonable. He took it for granted that Canada did not need the League because Canada could always settle its international difficulties amicably. But Canada did have a responsibility to humanity to educate less reasonable nations by its own example and by adding its weight to the pressure of world opinion. On the night of the Italian invasion Canada's duty had seemed clear: "I confess," he wrote in his diary, "I feel it Canada's duty to stand four square behind the League of Nations. It is another fight of Force vs. Reason. The Brute vs. man. Dictatorship vs. Democracy."[34]

But this idealistic reaction was not a call to arms. The League which King supported was a league which represented justice and reason but it was also a league which relied on the moral force of public opinion. When he had spoken in the House on the Manchurian crisis in 1932 he had approved the League's declaration that Japan was the aggressor but he had also approved the decision to take no further action. "In international affairs, reason rather than force should prevail" but some men could only learn from experience that force would fail. In the meantime the League had educated world opinion and confined the conflict to the Orient. In a revealing analogy he had referred to the Industrial Disputes Investigation Act which, by investigation, could invoke the pressure of public opinion but which did not prevent strikes or lockouts if men insisted on being unreasonable. The League, like the Act, was intended to persuade but not to coerce.[35] King did not believe in "perilous policies for peace."[36] For him the League of Nations was an international forum for

138

discussion but it was not a military alliance against aggressors. He had ignored the inherent contradiction between this view of the League and the view that the League stood for collective security. The Ethiopian crisis forced him to clarify his thinking.

When King reported the situation to Cabinet that afternoon his colleagues readily agreed to impose the proposed economic sanctions. But King saw danger signals. As he commented in his diary:

It was interesting to see how clearly the division of feeling disclosed itself. Ilsley could scarcely wait to say how emphatic he thought we should be in the matter of declaring for sanctions. Rogers, and some of the others, were also quite strong on backing the League. Lapointe, Power and Cardin were all in the other direction. They felt the necessity of standing by the League, in view of our platform, from which there was no escape, but were anxious to say and do as little as possible. The entire council was against anything in the nature of military sanctions.[37]

A less cautious politician might have heaved a sigh of relief that a potential Cabinet crisis had been averted, but King was still worried. Economic sanctions might be only the first step and, if the League proposed more forceful measures in the future, the division within Cabinet might become more serious.

The problem was that the Ethiopian crisis had provoked quite different emotional responses among English and French Canadians. In each case the attitude towards Great Britain was a significant factor. Most English Canadians were favourably disposed towards the League but few had any deep commitment to the principle of collective security. But if they cared little for the territorial integrity of Ethiopia they did believe that the British Government was on the side of international justice. Their emphatic affirmative for economic sanctions was support for a policy which seemed both pro-League and pro-British. French Canadians, in contrast, were more inclined to have some sympathy for a Catholic Italy which had adopted the corporatist form of government approved by the Pope. Because they did not share their compatriots' confidence in British justice, they tended to see the debate at Geneva as a debate between Imperial rivals, with Britain attempting to frustrate Italy's ambitions in Africa to protect its own colonial Empire. What did it matter to Canada which European country ruled in Ethiopia? As one French-Canadian intellectual put it, why should Canadians fight "to rescue a certain tribe of negroes from the clutch of an imperial power?"[38]

King may not have understood why English and French Canadians reacted so differently but he recognized that there was a profound difference and he saw the danger. A discussion with Lapointe over the wording of the press release to announce the government's imposition of economic sanctions underlined the possibility of a major crisis. "As we went over the statement together," he recorded, "Lapointe said that, if the Government were to decide for military sanctions, he would resign at once. He also said that if we did not, and the question came to be one which we had to decide, he believed that Ilsley and one or two others would immediately resign." King went on to record his own reaction to this assessment:

In other words, if the question of military sanctions comes, we shall have the old war situation over again, with the party divided as it was at the time of conscription. My own feeling is that, if Canada carries out her part with respect to economic sanctions, we should not be expected to go further. . . . Our own domestic situation must be considered first, and what will serve to keep Canada united. To be obliged to go into war would force an issue that might become a battle between imperialism and independence. At all costs, this must, if at all possible, be avoided.[39]

The government's press release reflected this concern. It affirmed the "continued and firm adherence to the fundamental aims and ideals of the League of Nations" but defined these aims as "the adjustment of conflicting national aims" and not the reliance "upon force for the maintenance of peace." Canada would co-operate with other League members by enforcing the proposed economic sanctions but this was not a precedent for the future and did not imply "any commitment binding Canada to adopt military sanctions."[40] The statement, according to King, had "a little more in the way of caution and reservation than the majority of the cabinet would have liked" but he was prepared to err on the side of caution.[41]

The crisis King feared was almost provoked by the Canadian delegate at Geneva. Riddell had already gone beyond his instructions in the Committee of Eighteen and he continued to ignore orders from Ottawa to avoid taking any initiative. Four days after the press release, a summary of which had been cabled to Geneva, he introduced a resolution to add oil and some other items to the list of prohibited exports to Italy.[42] It was logical to ban these products if economic sanctions were to be effective. The resolution was no more than a rhetorical flourish, however, if the United States, the major exporter of oil to Italy, was not prepared to act; the United States was not a member of the League and Roosevelt had shown no intention of interfering with the sales of American oil companies. Riddell was acting on his own initiative, encouraged by the ap-

140

proval of the British delegates who were pleased to see Canada take the responsibility for a controversial proposal. Sir Samuel Hoare complimented Riddell for an intervention which he described as "both very effective and very well-timed."[43]

King did reprimand Riddell privately but there was no public repudiation because this would provoke a controversy in Canada which he hoped to avoid. He strongly objected to a resolution which might complicate Canada's relations with the United States and he was even more concerned about the domestic complications. There was still the possibility, however, that the Committee of Eighteen would promptly adopt the resolution. Instead of a Canadian proposal it would then be seen as a League proposal and the Canadian Government would be absolved from the responsibility of having taken the initiative. King instructed Riddell not to defend his resolution but after some hesitation he did authorize him to vote for it "if it meets with the approval [of] other members generally."[44]

Unfortunately for King the members of the committee were irresolute. France was afraid that Mussolini would retaliate and Great Britain was not prepared to act without the support of France. The debate at Geneva showed how weak the commitment to collective security really was; a month went by and the resolution was still being discussed. The continuing references in the press to "the Canadian proposal" were an embarrassment to a government which had no intention of taking any initiative.

Late in November, when Lapointe asked King if anything could be done, King decided that a public controversy was less risky than accepting the responsibility for a proposal which might lead to war.[45] He was holidaying in the United States with Skelton at the time, so Lapointe was authorized to announce to the press that Riddell had acted without instructions. The government, Lapointe explained, would consider any League proposal to extend economic sanctions but "it has not and does not propose to take the initiative in any such action."[46] The statement was intended to be no more than a repudiation of Riddell's initiative in the Committee of Eighteen but almost inevitably it was widely interpreted as a criticism of the proposal to extend economic sanctions. The French-Canadian press applauded, but many English Canadians were incensed.[47] Even some of King's colleagues thought the statement was "unfortunate in its phrasing."[48] King tried to placate the critics on his return to Ottawa by pointing out that the policy of the government had not changed; it would consider oil sanctions when the League officially asked it to.[49] His colleagues were mollified but some English Canadians still regretted that Canada was not providing leadership at the League.

King's "back-seat policy" was amply justified three days later by the startling announcement that Pierre Laval and Sir Samuel Hoare were prepared to concede Mussolini the territory his troops had seized in Ethiopia if he would stop there. As King commented in his diary, "it is a complete sacrifice of Ethiopia to Italy, as a means of ending war, evidently on the theory that it is better to sacrifice justice than risk a European conflagration."[50] If France and England were not prepared to support League sanctions at the risk of war, no initiative by the Canadian Government could have saved the League.

But this was not the lesson King drew from the Ethiopian crisis. He had learned that membership in the League could involve Canada in international crises and that Canadians might be deeply divided over the obligations which that membership entailed. As long as a significant number of Canadians believed that the League stood for collective security and the use of force against an aggressor, the League was a potential threat to national unity. For King national unity was more important than any international institution. He would never again refer to the League with unqualified platitudes and when the occasion arose he would try to limit the extent of Canada's possible commitments as a member.

III

The Ethiopian crisis had been forced on King's attention but on the trade agreement with the United States, King took the initiative. He had promised during the campaign to negotiate an agreement before the end of the year and when forming his Cabinet had told Dunning and Euler, the two Ministers most directly involved, that he intended to do the negotiating.[51] The day after taking office he had called on Norman Armour, the American Minister in Ottawa, to impress him with the need to reopen negotiations as quickly as possible and even offered to go to Washington if he thought it would help. Armour interpreted this as no more than an indication of King's strong interest; "it would," he reported, "seem well nigh impossible for Mr. King to absent himself from Canada" at this time.[52] He underestimated his man; within two weeks of taking office King was on his way to Washington.

The treaty was important to King in part for symbolic reasons. The last trade agreement between Canada and the United States had been the reciprocity treaty of 1854; since then both countries had relied on unilateral tariff changes to influence trade patterns. Any agreement would be a promising precedent for the future. King also shared the traditional liberal view that commercial contacts between nations fostered better international relations. "Economic nationalism," he had told Armour, "not only meant isolationism and trouble but created bitterness and poisoned good relations between countries."[53] King also saw expanded international trade as his government's chief weapon in its attack on the depression. During five years of opposition he had denounced Tory tariffs and argued that Liberal trade policies would foster economic recovery. His view of Canada's economic interests, his desire to foster good relations with the United States, and, above all, his campaign promise to negotiate a treaty account for his eagerness to reopen discussions immediately.

King also realised that any delay would be dangerous. Roosevelt would not be eager to sign a treaty in the spring, when Congress would be in session and Republican critics would have a public forum. By the summer of 1938 the presidential and congressional election campaigns would begin and Roosevelt would want to avoid having a trade agreement become a prominent election issue. As King commented on the eve of his departure for Washington: "Unless an agreement is reached within the next few days it will not be reached at all. Going to Washington at this moment seems the one and only chance. I am risking a great deal in the way of personal reputation, in taking the step, and also probably shall incur much hostility from several quarters, once an agreement is affected. To be courageous, however, is the only course at present. Now is the time to make at least a beginning."[54]

King knew he was taking a risk because by this time he had learned from Skelton and from a memorandum prepared within External Affairs by Norman Robertson that it would not be easy to negotiate a satisfactory agreement. During the talks, which had begun while Bennett was in office, the United States had insisted on the "most-favored-nation" treatment for its exports to Canada, which would involve lower tariff rates on some seven hundred items. In return the Canadians had asked for substantial tariff reductions on a number of items and discussion had centred on codfish, potatoes, milk and cream, cattle, and some categories of lumber. These items had not been chosen haphazardly; their inclusion would ensure that each of the major regions in Canada would derive some benefit from the agreement. The American negotiators, however, were reluctant to grant all of these concessions. King wanted a treaty but he was not eager to sign an agreement which benefitted some regions and not others. The popularity of the new government depended upon his success as a negotiator.

Norman Robertson's memorandum was a lucid analysis of the situation. The American negotiators, it pointed out, also had to take political factors into consideration. American cattlemen, for example, feared Canadian competition; a probable solution here was a quota on imports of

Canadian cattle, a quota large enough to satisfy Canadians but which would dispel any exaggerated American fears of unlimited imports. At one stage the American officials had been prepared to recommend acceptable concessions on all of the items except codfish. It was then, late in September, that Roosevelt had balked. Roosevelt feared the reaction in New England. As Robertson's memorandum explained: "The unwillingness to grant any reduction on potatoes reflects the Administration's nervousness about the political situation in New England and particularly in Maine, where a Democratic defeat in the pre-presidential elections next fall might have a serious influence on Roosevelt's prospects of re-election."[55] Robertson's conclusion was that satisfactory arrangements were unlikely on codfish, potatoes, and cream and that the American Government had made all the concessions it felt it could afford. King might have to decide "whether on balance these concessions represent an adequate consideration for granting the United States most-favored-nation treatment."[56] He would also have to face the fact that an agreement without codfish and potatoes would be very unpopular in the Maritimes.

King could not concern himself with all the complex details of quotas, categories, and tariff schedules. He relied on Skelton and the Canadian negotiators to brief him on the key points; his role would be to establish direct contact with the President and to reassure Roosevelt that he appreciated his political difficulties and could be trusted not to embarrass him unnecessarily.[57] King knew that State Department officials were sympathetic to Canadian demands and when he arrived in Washington on November 8 he began his visit by trying to enlist the support of Cordell Hull, the Secretary of State. King also knew that Hull believed with evangelical fervour that expanding international trade was the only hope for a world menaced by national animosities. Hull had the reputation of being a repetitive bore on this subject but King merely noted in his diary that he did outline his views "at some length." In return King "let him see wherein I was wholeheartedly at one with him in the point of view he represented." By lunchtime he was sure that "a very favourable relationship" had been established and he could even ask Hull how to present Canada's case most effectively to the President. King, for example, was attracted by the idea of announcing an agreement on Armistice Day. Canadian officials had told him that this was quite unrealistic, given the complex issues still to be settled, but King still asked Hull if he thought Roosevelt would respond favourably to the suggestion. Hull thought he would.[58]

The two men dined with the President at the White House that evening and then adjourned to the President's study to talk business. It was

144

an informal discussion in which Roosevelt was frankly political in his references to the coming elections and the regional interests which were opposed to specific concessions. King was startled on one occasion when the President regretted that no concession could be made on lumber because "Congress had tied his hands by the Excise Act." When King explained that he was under the impression that concessions on lumber had already been agreed on, both Roosevelt and Hull conceded that something might have been arranged of which they were not aware.[59] On the other items King made it clear that he knew of the political pressures to which Roosevelt was exposed and that he appreciated their importance. He knew enough about American politics to concede that Maine would object to competition from Maritime potatoes but could also remind Roosevelt that Virginia and other southern states would welcome lower tariffs on this item. He sensed, however, that the President was more willing to make concessions than he had been led to believe and that this was no time for "haggling or bargaining." He did not even refer to codfish, having been warned that Roosevelt was inflexible on this item. After a discussion of various concessions which might be politically feasible, they then turned to the possible timing of the agreement. All agreed that any delay would be fatal and King took this occasion to suggest an announcement on Armistice Day. Roosevelt, according to King's account, responded enthusiastically, and linked the suggestion to the speech he would have to make at Arlington cemetery on that day. A paragraph on the trade agreement and its contribution to international goodwill would be most appropriate.

King was justifiably pleased with his day's work. Roosevelt still wanted to talk to Henry Wallace, the Secretary of Agriculture, about potatoes and cattle but King already knew from his officials that Wallace was well disposed towards the proposals. The details and the final drafting would still take some time but an agreement was now assured—one which would be more satisfactory than the Canadian negotiators had expected.[60] King was also sure that he had established a friendly relationship with Roosevelt. He described him as "most informal, and in his manner of speaking and smiling very direct. I found it exceedingly easy to talk with him." He was also pleased by Roosevelt's suggestion that "it was great just to be able to pick up the telephone and talk to each other in just a few minutes. We must do that whenever occasion arises. I will always be glad to hear from you."[61] Cordell Hull later confirmed King's impression that all had gone well by telling him that he "had made a most favourable impression."[62]

King may have exaggerated his personal impact. Roosevelt usually impressed visiting dignitaries with his warmth and his friendliness and his treatment of King was not exceptional. King was, however, a North American with some knowledge of American politics and, like Roosevelt, a national leader in a federal state. It was probably more than political calculation or mere politeness when Roosevelt remarked that "we are speaking the same language, which makes it very pleasant to talk together."[63] The President also showed that he had special reasons for cultivating good relations with King. "He said to me," King recorded, "that he thought Canada and the United States understood each other better than the United States and Great Britain; that he believed I could help him in his relations with England; that Canada could be what has been described as an interpreter in dealing with some of the difficulties."[64] Roosevelt may not have thought of King as a personal friend but in international relations friendship is less important than self-interest. King had accomplished a good deal if he had won Roosevelt's confidence as a man who appreciated his political problems and who might be useful as a Commonwealth leader.

King decided to return to Ottawa as soon as the outlines of the final agreement were confirmed. He was sure his colleagues would be enthusiastic but, in keeping with the principle of collective responsibility, he wanted to have formal Cabinet approval. He also considered it desirable to be in Canada on Armistice Day and to have the preliminary announcement of the agreement made simultaneously from Washington and Ottawa on that day. There were still some minor complications with the final wording but these were amicably resolved.[65] By November 15 King was back in Washington for the ceremonial signing. He arrived to find Skelton and his officials exhausted but well satisfied. Skelton was still expected to draft some suitable remarks for King to use, while King rested for the occasion, but the ceremony went well and King retired that night "with a thankful albeit a tired heart."[66] The next day he and Skelton left Washington for a well-earned vacation in Georgia.

The reception of the agreement in Canada was all that King had hoped for. Liberal newspapers were jubilant and even Conservative newspapers were complimentary. There were isolated objections to some of the Canadian tariff concessions but in every region the applause outweighed the criticisms.[67] King had kept his election promise and had strengthened the impression of a government that could act promptly and effectively.

The reaction in the United States was more divided. Herbert Hoover was unkind enough to suggest that the "more abundant life" which Roosevelt had promised was apparently to be provided for Canadians.[68] The agreement also created controversy within the Roosevelt administration.

The New Dealers had been sharply divided, with economic nationalists competing with internationalists for the ear of the President. The treaty was interpreted as a victory for Cordell Hull's liberal trade policies. Raymond Moley, who had already broken with Roosevelt, denounced it bitterly and George Peek resigned in opposition to what he had described as Hull's policy of "unilateral economic disarmament."[69]

The division within the Roosevelt administration on trade policies illustrates a significant aspect of Canadian-American relations which King understood almost intuitively. From the perspective of the United States Canadian interests are not of direct concern. Most issues which affect Canada are seen primarily as domestic questions and the significant debate takes place between rival pressure groups within the country. Canadian contacts at many levels within the American administration—and within the private sector as well—are nonetheless so frequent that Canadian officials usually know where to find spokesmen for the policy which Canada prefers. During the Roosevelt administration the State Department had a good deal of influence and because it was more international in outlook it frequently fought for what Canadians saw as desirable policies. By close contacts and frank discussions with State Department officials, both in Washington and Ottawa, Canadians could feed them information and arguments while avoiding the formality or rigidity of international diplomacy. When formal negotiations were necessary, the State Department reciprocated by giving advice on tactics and by supporting their arguments. During the trade negotiations in 1935 King had clearly been wise to cultivate Cordell Hull as his ally.

A minor footnote to the treaty provides a further illustration of this relationship. Included in the agreement was a reduction of the United States tariff on Canadian whisky. Canadian distillers were in a favoured position because the end of prohibition had made it possible for even law-abiding American citizens to quench their thirst but it would be some years before American distillers would have properly aged whisky for sale. Henry Morgenthau, Jr, Secretary of the Treasury, had raised a last-minute objection to the treaty on the grounds that Canadian distillers had knowingly supplied vast quantities of liquor to American consumers during prohibition and, since the whisky had been smuggled in, the distillers had neglected to pay any tariffs or excise taxes. Morgenthau now insisted on collecting these taxes or, failing this, he threatened to ban Canadian liquor in the United States. It was an extraordinary request because only Canadian distillers were to be penalized in this way and also because, although the Treasury naturally had no reliable figures, its claims were in the range of one hundred million dollars. One possible explanation was that Treas-

147

ury was aiding American distillers who, as Skelton noted, "wish to have Canadian liquor excluded until their own newly-distilled product can be matured."[70]

The Canadian Government was never officially involved but Canadian officials did ask the State Department to intervene with Treasury on their behalf and Cordell Hull, when he found Morgenthau intransigent, appealed to Roosevelt to intervene.[71] The Treasury Department eventually modified its position and agreed to a negotiated settlement for a more modest three million dollars, although not before Hull again had to appeal to Roosevelt to order Morgenthau to accept this arrangement.[72] It was a minor incident, except perhaps for the Canadian distillers, but it does show how Canadian interests could benefit from friends at court.

IV

King had kept his promise to sign a trade agreement with the United States before the end of the year. He was just as determined to keep his other promise to arrange a Dominion-Provincial Conference—the invitations went out to the provincial Premiers even before he had officially assumed office. The Premiers all accepted and even William Aberhart, the unknown quantity, wired that he was "looking forward to cooperating with you and the Premiers of the other provinces in the progressive program you are planning."[73] The conference was delayed because Taschereau called a snap election in Quebec after the decisive Liberal victory in the federal election, but early in December the Premiers assembled in Ottawa. King confidently opened the proceedings by assuring them that the discussions would inaugurate "a new era of harmonious relations between the provinces and the Dominion."[74]

The conference seemed to justify his optimism. King himself set the tone; he promised that the federal government would not try to impose "a rigid, preconceived program of action" and would rely on "collective discussion and collective action."[75] Taschereau underlined the contrast to the previous conference, presided over by R. B. Bennett, "when we were given a lecture and told to go home."[76] Most federal-provincial conferences involve hard bargaining which belies the introductory platitudes but this conference was exceptional. Four days later the concluding speeches were still optimistically referring to the benefits of harmony and co-operation. The conference did not adopt any dramatic new policies—it was a conference and not a legislative body—but it did accept a number of recommendations which the respective governments would consider. The emphasis was on continuing consultation and co-operation; effective action would take time but the conference was a promising beginning.

The Premiers concentrated on financial questions for obvious reasons. The depression had disrupted the traditional balance between revenues and expenditures at all levels of government. Municipal governments, with the primary responsibility for welfare, could not balance their budgets because their revenues from property taxes were inadequate and they had difficulty borrowing money. A delegation to the conference representing the mayors of Canadian cities pleaded their case. "Their story," King noted in his diary, "was one of virtual bankrupty of the municipalities already, and actual bankruptcy if they have to continue to raise money for relief purposes."[77] The provincial governments were not much better off. They had to accept responsibility for relief payments when municipalities could do no more, but they too found their revenues declining as their expenditures increased. The western provinces were already such poor credit risks that they could not borrow money because investors would not buy their bonds.

The federal government also had its problems. Under Bennett it had reluctantly come to the aid of the provinces and had spent almost two hundred million dollars on relief.[78] The total debt of the federal government, including the railway deficits, was now three billion dollars, an increase of almost one billion dollars since 1930. There would be no end to these financial difficulties until economic conditions improved, until Canadians and foreigners could buy Canadian goods, and more Canadians could be employed producing these goods. Only then could taxes yield higher revenues and the expenditures on welfare be reduced.

The Premiers, however, could not concentrate on the objective of economic recovery because their more immediate concern was to avert bankruptcy. As political leaders they could not give their full attention to long-range solutions when the electorate would pass judgment on their administrations within a few years; as provincial leaders they were most concerned with special problems within their jurisdiction and of regional inequalities and disparities. It must also be remembered that in 1935 few people believed that governments could stimulate economic recovery by spending money and by going even deeper into debt.* Almost inevitably each Premier concentrated on measures which would improve the finan-

---

*J. M. Keynes, *General Theory of Interest, Money and Banking*, only appeared in 1936. He had already expressed some of his radical views on the correlation between investment and the level of economic activity but even among economists there were few converts. The Canadian Premiers who favoured inflationary policies, such as Aberhart and Pattullo, did not rely on Keynesian arguments.

cial position of his government. From his perspective the federal government could ease his problems. The federal government could levy indirect as well as direct taxes and so had more flexible sources of revenue than provincial governments which could only impose direct taxes. It could also borrow money more easily. If the federal government would take over some areas of provincial responsibility or would transfer some of its sources of revenue to provincial governments, his financial problem would be eased.

Mackenzie King was prepared to discuss some changes in the financial structure of the existing federal system but not the changes which the provincial Premiers wanted. He too was primarily concerned with his own budgetary problems. He was orthodox on fiscal policies, believing that governments should balance revenues and expenditures, and he was also orthodox on constitutional policies, believing that each level of government should be responsible for its own policies and for collecting the money to implement them. He was appalled, as the head of the federal government, at a system in which he could not control federal expenditures because he was obliged to provide grants or loans to provincial governments which could not manage their own affairs. His objective was something closer to the classical concept of federalism, in which each level of government would operate independently in separate water-tight compartments. He was ready to modify the existing financial relations between the federal and provincial governments only if the changes would give him fuller control over the finances of his own government and improve the possibilities of a balanced federal budget. He was not prepared to take on new responsibilities or surrender revenues just to ease the financial difficulties of provincial administrations.

This underlying contradiction between provincial and federal hopes did not become apparent at the conference because neither King nor the provincial Premiers wanted a confrontation. The conference inevitably gave a high priority to the costs of unemployment relief but the committee which dealt with this topic restricted its discussion to modest objectives. Instead of discussing ways of reducing the number of unemployed, it concentrated on establishing a more uniform and more efficient administration of unemployment relief. Norman Rogers guided it to the conclusion that all relief recipients should be registered and classified; the techniques of the social scientist, including questionnaires and punch cards, were expected to eliminate wastefulness and duplication in relief payments. The committee recommended a federal Commission on Unemployment to supervise the expenditure of all federal relief funds.

The provincial Premiers accepted this federal proposal because it was combined with the promise that the federal government would spend more money for relief. Bennett had seemed both niggardly and arbitrary in his aid to the provinces for unemployment. The new administration seemed more generous. It agreed to accept full responsibility for the relief of individuals who could be classified as permanently unemployable. It also offered an immediate and substantial increase in federal grants to the provinces for relief. Mackenzie King, in his closing address, conceded that municipalities and provinces could no longer cope with relief costs and that the federal government must accept more financial responsibility. But there were some strings attached to this offer. The larger grant was possible, he explained, because the Premiers had also agreed to the supervision of relief expenditures by a federal commission. "Without this added precaution," he warned, "we would not feel secure in making any additional outlay."[79] He obviously assumed that this extension of federal control would eventually reduce waste and extravagance. The provincial Premiers paid little attention to this caveat. Their immediate problem was to get more money and they welcomed the federal promise of an immediate increase in its grants for unemployment relief.

Another committee discussed the possibility of constitutional amendments. The Bennett New Deal legislation was seen as an encroachment on provincial jurisdiction and one of the first steps of the new government had been to refer this legislation to the Supreme Court. The court would at least rule on the existing constitutional powers of the federal government. King was not averse to the extension of federal authority to regulate wages, working conditions, and combines and had supported the Bennett legislation to that extent. But although King was ready to raise the question of constitutional amendment and, in part because of the influence of Norman Rogers, wanted a flexible amendment procedure which would not require the unanimous consent of all provinces for every change,[80] he did not have any specific amendments to propose. He preferred to concentrate on the preliminary step of establishing formal amendment procedures.

The conference seemed to bring the possibility of agreement on amendment procedures much closer. At the Dominion Provincial Conference of 1927 Taschereau had opposed any discussion of how to amend the British North America Act.[81] Now, however, he warmly supported the proposal that Canada should have the power to amend its own constitution and even conceded that some amendments were needed.[82] The conference finally agreed that federal and provincial officials should immediately begin discussions on amendment procedures. It seemed probable that, when agreement had been reached on procedures, constitutional amendments would follow.

King was less optimistic than many observers. He suspected that Taschereau was no more enthusiastic about changing the constitution than he had been in 1927 but that the centralizing trend of Privy Council decisions had modified his attitude towards amendment procedures. Formal procedures might protect provincial rights.[83] In any case, Taschereau no longer spoke with the same authority. He had won the provincial election but his majority had almost disappeared and the collaboration between a dissident group of young Liberals and the provincial Conservatives under Maurice Duplessis probably meant his early retirement. Ernest Lapointe and C. G. Power were still in touch with the dissident Liberals and hoped to negotiate some arrangements which would bring them back into the provincial party, and it was clear that Taschereau's resignation was a necessary part of any reconciliation. Even King was involved in some of the discussions to reunite the provincial Liberal party.[84] No progress on amendment procedures was likely until the political situation in Quebec had stabilized.

Another committee of the Dominion-Provincial Conference dealt more directly with financial relations between federal and provincial governments. Charles Dunning raised the possibility of transferring certain tax fields to the provinces. He also explained that he might be prepared to back provincial bond issues by a federal guarantee, which would make it easier for provinces to borrow money and reduce the interest rates they would have to pay. He did not go into details but he did link this to a Loan Council which would involve some federal supervision of provincial finances along the pattern of the Australian Loan Council. Provinces which could still borrow money probably attached little importance to the proposal; provinces which had difficulty in selling their bonds could not afford to object. The conference expressed interest in the idea of a Loan Council and decided that provincial treasurers would meet with the Minister of Finance to continue the discussion. Again the impression was created that a major step had been taken.

The delegates to the conference were well pleased with the results. King's concluding statement was a modest but optimistic appraisal: "As a result of meeting here, we shall all, as respects the problems which confront us, go forward into the new year with a truer sense of proportion, and a deeper sense of responsibility and, I believe, with more hope and belief in their ultimate satisfactory solution."[85] Provincial Premiers had been promised larger federal grants for relief. The conference had agreed on the need to establish procedures for amending the constitution, and had agreed to discuss a Loan Council. It seemed that a major revision of the federal system had begun and that the co-operation which King had promised the electors had already produced results.

CHAPTER NINE

THE LIBERAL RESPONSE TO
THE DEPRESSION

THE HONEYMOON WAS SOON OVER. In 1936 Mackenzie King would learn that even with a Liberal government in office at Ottawa the depression was still there, shading every aspect of Canadian life in sombre gray. King still believed that the expansion of international trade would restore prosperity, but there was little he could do if other countries insisted on maintaining their tariff barriers. The trade agreement with the United States was a beginning but by itself was little more than a gesture. Within Canada he relied on the co-operation of the provincial governments to improve administrative procedures for relief and to reduce federal expenditures until the crisis had passed. He would soon be disappointed; the provincial Premiers proved to be regrettably unco-operative.

For this Mackenzie King was at least partly to blame. Five years of depression had challenged many of the traditional assumptions about politics as well as economics but his own views had undergone little change. He still assumed that economic recovery depended ultimately on private enterprise and that governments could only play a secondary role. King had already had some experience with an economic depression, having come into office in 1921 during the post-war recession. In the years that followed his government had deliberately adhered to a policy of rigid economy, resisting pressures to spend more money, gradually bringing the federal budget into balance, and, as conditions improved, lowering federal taxes to encourage private investment. The wisdom of this approach seemed to have been confirmed by the results; the post-war depression had ended and had been followed by years of unparalleled prosperity. If his government once again followed this pattern he assumed that the costs of production in the private sector would go down and private investment would again be stimulated. Economic recovery might be slow but it would be sure, and King had four years to prove that he was right.

Mackenzie King was also unprepared for any dramatic expansion of federal activities because in 1936 he had not yet realized that his tradi-

153

tional view of federalism, in which each level of government operated independently in its own sphere, was now outmoded. Canada had become an industrialized country with an integrated economy which showed no respect for provincial boundaries. The federal constitution might give provincial governments the responsibility for relief but when the economy of an entire region could be shattered by industrial unemployment or by falling prices, provincial governments could not fulfil their constitutional obligations.

Most Canadians had been slow to recognize how vulnerable they had become to economic forces beyond local control. Five years of depression, however, had undermined some of their traditional assumptions. The rugged individualism of an agricultural society had been eroded by the gradual realization that even responsible and hard-working men could not protect themselves from disaster. This had led to a significant shift in what was expected of governments. Canadians now looked to government to provide a larger degree of economic security because they as individuals were no longer masters of their own fate.

The federal government would be the most directly affected by this changing attitude towards the responsibilities of governments. The impact of the depression varied from one region to another and only Ottawa could tax the less affected regions in order to aid the depressed areas. The constitution was also important because only the federal government could levy both direct and indirect taxes. Fifteen years earlier the depression had been less severe; provincial governments had managed by levying higher direct taxes and by borrowing money, and the federal government had been able to put its own financial house in order within the existing federal structure. By 1936, however, the severity of the economic crisis and the growing conviction that governments could and should provide positive remedies meant that King's restricted view of federal objectives was no longer adequate. It was not enough to balance the federal budget and then lower federal taxes. If private enterprise could not stimulate economic recovery the federal government would be expected to take more positive action.

Mackenzie King might have been more responsive to these changes if he had been more balanced in his judgment of R. B. Bennett. Bennett had been inconsistent but he had sensed the increasing reliance on governments and had responded by promising to do something. The results had not been impressive but Bennett had established public agencies and extended government economic activities. Even the abortive New Deal had at least reflected the need for an expanded federal role. He had promised too much and had been defeated but he had encouraged Canadians to look to Ottawa for economic solutions and this attitude was one of the legacies of his administration. King had interpreted the promises as irresponsible demogoguery, the new government activities as encroaching dictatorship, and the New Deal as unconstitutional. His scorn for Bennett and all his works had blinded him to the new expectations which Bennett had encouraged.

King therefore had limited objectives in 1936. He was a federal politician and his immediate concern was to improve the financial position of the federal government. He felt no pressure to introduce more positive measures because the answer to the financial problems of the federal government seemed so obvious. Unemployment and farm relief were the major cause of federal deficits. Provincial governments had the primary responsibility for relief expenditures. If they could be persuaded to administer relief more efficiently—which meant more economically—or to pay a higher proportion of the total relief costs, federal expenditures would be reduced and the federal budget balanced. King would eventually learn that federal retrenchment and a reliance on private enterprise were not enough. His first lesson would come from the provincial governments. Even Liberal Premiers would refuse to co-operate when King tried to balance the federal budget by shifting more of the relief costs on to them.

I

Mackenzie King did not rest on his laurels after the Dominion-Provincial Conference. The December increase in federal relief grants had been an interim policy, intended to help provincial governments through the winter months, but it had been linked in King's mind with his plan for a National Employment Commission which would establish a more efficient relief administration. The conference had also agreed to discuss procedures for establishing a Loan Council and for amending the British North America Act to increase provincial revenues. The federal government followed up each of these lines of attack in 1936 and by midsummer its financial policies had become much more explicit. Its relations with provincial governments had also become much more strained.

Mackenzie King had special reasons for his interest in unemployment policies. He had an almost paternal feeling for Norman Rogers and was delighted with the Minister of Labour's masterful presentation of the unemployment situation.[1] As Rogers explained to the House of Commons in March, there were still 1,300,000 Canadians receiving relief, a total which included heads of families and their dependents. This was a decrease of some 200,000 since 1933 but, as he drily remarked, "it would be an abuse of the language to say that it was a substantial or, indeed, a very encouraging decrease."[2] Rogers would also be directly responsible for the National Employment Commission, and King believed that the commission would dramatically reduce relief costs. He saw it as a major step towards balancing the federal budget.

The commission was to have two functions. It was to bring some order into the administration of relief, collecting data and advising the Minister on how best to co-operate with provincial and private agencies to eliminate duplication and extravagance. Its other function was to recommend programmes and projects which would provide employment.[3] The Chairman of the new commission, Arthur B. Purvis, was a prominent industrialist who combined executive ability with liberal views on labour questions.[4] It was, however, no more than an advisory commission. How could King expect it to have a significant impact on federal relief costs?

King had convinced himself that Bennett's grants-in-aid to the provincial governments had encouraged extravagance and waste. He could not avoid continuing federal grants for the time being; "the principle of contributing grants is, without doubt, a vicious one," he commented in his diary, "but apparently there would be riots, and possibly much suffering if the grants in aid were not forthcoming."[5] Provincial governments, however, had almost certainly been reckless with relief funds because they were spending federal money. He was also shocked at the irresponsible attitude of people like J. S. Woodsworth and Agnes Macphail who could argue that people had an inalienable right to be provided "with food, clothing, comfort, etc. at the expense of the State" without any corresponding obligation to work. He could only conclude that they were "developing from sincere radicals into clap-trap politicians of the cheapest variety."[6] His obsession with protecting the federal treasury convinced him that the commission, by its supervision of relief administration, would eliminate "obvious abuses, rackets, overlapping and the like" and save the federal government vast sums.[7] In April, when the bill received royal assent, he noted:

During the day I had the satisfaction at 5 minutes to 6 to hear the deputy Governor-General give his assent to the Canada-U.S. Trade Agreement, and to the Ntl. Employment Commission—both policies I had advocated and both measures for which in the main I was almost wholly responsible. . . . I knew by these measures I had on the one hand helped to bring millions of dollars in work and wages to homes, in reduced costs of living to families all over Canada, and while helping to provide work, save the Treasury and thereby the taxpayers many million of dollars as well, if one takes account of the means to restore control by Parl't expenditures etc. I felt it was worth all this strain and stress of public life.[8]

Even if the commission achieved all that King hoped, the federal government could not wait patiently for the results. Financial disaster seemed too imminent. In mid-March Charles Dunning warned his colleagues that the deficit for the fiscal year would be close to one hundred and twenty-five million dollars.[9] Two weeks later it appeared that even the awesome estimate of fifty million dollars for the federal share of direct relief was too low. For King, as for Dunning, this was the road to bankruptcy. As he commented in his diary early in April:

In stating last night that the additional outlay for relief and employment would come to some 50 millions, I find that I was 25 millions short of what it will really come to. This is an appalling sum on top of all the regular expenditures of government, together with a loss of 40 millions or more on the Ntl. Rlwys. The truth is, that not only municipalities and provinces are tending towards bankruptcy, many of them are already bankrupt, but that the Dominion itself will be in the same category if the wasteful practices which have become accepted in the last two years are continued.[10]

One immediate step was to reduce the federal proportion of provincial relief costs. The 15 per cent increase in federal aid in December seemed a regrettable mistake. The chastened Cabinet agreed to a 25 per cent reduction now that winter was over, although a lenient King did yield to Rogers' plea and allowed this reduction to be spread over two months.[11] The provincial governments showed no gratitude for this concession. The Ontario government reacted by promptly reducing its grants to municipalities and blaming the federal government.[12] To all provincial administrations, however, the message must have seemed clear. King's much vaunted federal co-operation, which had promised such substantial benefits in December, had now become almost indistinguishable from Bennett's authoritarian approach.

Some provincial governments had already learned to be sceptical about federal offers of co-operation. Dunning had met with the provincial treasurers in January to discuss the Loan Council proposal and the possibility of allowing provincial governments to levy some indirect taxes. At this meeting there had been unanimous agreement on both items and in May a resolution was introduced in the House of Commons to amend the British North America Act along these lines.[13] During the interval, however, some provinces had had second thoughts. A Loan Council might help them to borrow money but the possible encroachment by the council on provincial autonomy made them uneasy.

The Loan Council had an obvious advantage for those provincial governments which were considered poor credit risks and which could only borrow money at high rates of interest if they could borrow at all. Under the Loan Council plan they would be able to borrow money more cheaply because the federal government would guarantee the payment of both interest and principal. The federal government, however, could not be expected to endorse provincial loans without taking some precautions. The council, which would include the federal Minister of Finance and the Provincial Treasurer, would have to authorize every loan. But under what conditions would the council give its approval? Nothing was stated explicitly but it must have been obvious that federal approval would be more than a mere formality. Dunning was not likely to endorse a provincial loan if he felt that the provincial government could exercise more rigid economies or could levy higher taxes. The agreement of all provincial Treasurers in January is only explicable if it is assumed that those who did not expect to need federal guarantees for their bond issues had no objections and those who needed federal assistance were either too desperate or too eager to weigh the costs.

"Duff" Pattullo of British Columbia was the first Premier to ask embarrassing questions. Pattullo had a direct interest in the Loan Council scheme because he believed governments should provide employment during a depression by spending money on public works. He had no sophisticated theories to justify his attitude; his readiness to provide "work and wages" owed more to the booster mentality of British Columbia than to the ideas of John Maynard Keynes.[14] For two years Pattullo had found Ottawa unco-operative. Bennett had insisted that British Columbia would have to budget for a reduced deficit and would have to set up a sinking fund for the repayment of its debt before the federal government would lend it any money. Pattullo had finally decided to finance his own relief projects; one of his major undertakings was the construction of a four-million dollar bridge across the Fraser River. The change of government at Ottawa held out the hope that the federal government would now help British Columbia find the money for its relief works.

Pattullo was ready to accept a Loan Council if he could have some assurance that British Columbia loans would be approved. Dunning, however, would make no promises. Pattullo appealed to King in a series of interviews, letters, and telegrams, but King was no more explicit than his Minister of Finance.[15] King was tactful but non-committal. In private he was much less restrained. A passage in his diary after an interview with Pattullo shows how shocked he was at the Premier's cavalier attitude towards public funds: "He entertains absurd ideas about the extent to which public monies should be spent at this time, and the extent to which the province should be permitted to borrow from the Dominion, and spend, without any control over expenditures or security to the Dominion for monies advanced."[16]Pattulo was never informed directly that the federal government did not intend to guarantee loans for his provincial projects but after a few months he could read between the lines. He decided to meet the province's maturing obligations and to borrow more money without the benefit of federal assistance and so avoid the constraints of the Loan Council scheme.

William Aberhart seemed to have no option. An Alberta debenture issue of some three million dollars would fall due on April 1, 1936 and the government had no money and little chance of borrowing the money except from the federal government. In March Charles Cockroft, the provincial Treasurer, requested a federal loan.[17] King persuaded his colleagues to insist that Alberta must first agree to a Loan Council:

We had a long discussion of Dunning's Bill re financial Councils in relation to the amendment of the B.N.A. Act for purpose of helping the provinces but protecting Canadian Treasury and credit. I spoke in favour of keeping the proposed amendment on the order paper, but not advancing it till provinces agreed absolutely to our so doing. Meanwhile, if they apply for loans, they should be refused further advances even if it means their defaulting. Council as a whole were strongly of this view, except Gardiner and to a lesser degree Crerar, who do not like the Financial Council control. It seems to me we have to face in Canada the possible default of provinces and municipalities and might as well do so sooner rather than later. Lapointe and I agree however we would never press a B.N.A. Act amendment without provinces wholly in accord—that is the view of Council.[18]

Provincial approval of a Loan Council would thus be completely voluntary—except that there would be no federal loans unless it was approved.

Aberhart refused to accept this ultimatum. Cockroft had raised no objections to a Loan Council in his meeting with Dunning and the other provincial Treasurers,[19] but Aberhart now saw the danger of federal control over Social Credit financial policies. He asked for the loan first and for discussions of the Loan Council later.[20] King had formed a favourable impression of Aberhart at the Dominion-Provincial Conference in December. The Alberta Premier had been the outsider at the conference as the only non-Liberal present, and King had made a point of being gracious to him. Aberhart had responded warmly and King had concluded that he was a simple but friendly person, a little out of his depth in politics but "really a Liberal and would make a first-class leader if guided aright."[21] When Aberhart refused federal guidance, however, King quickly revised

159

his opinion. The Social Credit Premier, he commented in his diary, "has been preaching the second coming of Christ in 1943. His own reign is rapidly coming to a close."[22] To yield to Aberhart would only encourage Pattullo and other Premiers. After a good deal of soul-searching it was decided to hold firm and to allow Alberta to default if necessary.[23]

On April 1st the province of Alberta did default, making only a token interest payment on the provincial debentures which matured that day. It was the first occasion on which a provincial government had failed to meet its obligations. Aberhart naturally blamed the federal government but King was reassured by public reaction. The Canadian press showed little sympathy for the Social Credit arguments and in England most newspapers supported Dunning's efforts to protect the federal treasury.[24] By the end of the year Alberta had defaulted on yet another maturing loan and had arbitrarily reduced interest rates on all provincial bonds by one-half. Aberhart had made his point. He was not going to accept the federal tutelage which a Loan Council involved.

King and Dunning were reluctant to admit defeat. Dunning suggested a slightly modified scheme early in May but neither Pattullo nor Aberhart found it any more attractive.[25] Premier Patterson of Saskatchewan was prepared to accept a Loan Council; he was more orthodox than Aberhart on the obligations of governments to pay their debts and his province was in even more serious financial difficulty. Graham Towers of the Bank of Canada feared that default on a Saskatchewan issue in May, following so closely on Alberta's default, could lead to a series of municipal repudiations and a major threat to Canada's credit rating abroad. Dunning and King agreed that the Bank of Canada should finance the maturing obligations on the understanding that Saskatchewan would come under the Loan Council scheme when it became law.[26] It was now obvious that most provinces would have nothing to do with the scheme and King was already regretting "the effort even indirectly to 'control' the provinces in any of their acts."[27]

The provincial premiers had no objection to the proposed amendment to the B.N.A. Act, which would allow them to levy certain indirect taxes. The existing constitution restricted the provinces to direct taxes so the proposed amendment really involved a transfer of some tax sources from the federal to the provincial level.* The Premiers naturally welcomed the proposal. As Ernest Lapointe told the House of Commons when introducing the resolution, the provinces had approved the amendment and

---

*Direct taxes are those collected directly from the consumer; indirect taxes are paid by a purchaser who is expected to recover this expense by reselling the goods at a higher price.

their only criticism was that they would have liked even broader taxing powers.[28]

The opposition came from the Conservative benches. Provincial governments, according to Bennett, already had taxing powers "sufficiently broad and comprehensive for every purpose that can now reasonably be conceived": provinces should bear their own burdens and face the unpleasantness of paying for their own extravagance.[29] The resolution was adopted by the House but faced even stronger criticism in the Senate, where the Conservative party had a majority.

By this time Mackenzie King had decided that it was all a mistake. He was already dubious about forcing loan councils on reluctant provincial governments and he now found that he really agreed with the Opposition that it would be unwise to surrender any federal tax resources. He chided himself in his diary for not having "watched this legislation more closely," and was "immensely relieved" when it appeared that the Senate would reject the amendments.[30] The Senate was co-operative. It voted down the resolution; the two amendments, which even the government now believed were ill-prepared and ill-advised, ended there.

Mackenzie King had blundered because he had thought only of protecting the federal treasury and had paid too little attention to the financial predicament of the provincial governments. The two amendments had not been designed to reform federal-provincial financial relations but only to reduce the amount of federal aid to the provinces. Indeed, the two proposals were contradictory when viewed from the perspective of reforming the federal system. The Loan Council scheme would have extended federal control over provincial finances whereas the tax transfer would have had the opposite effect by making provincial administrations less dependent on federal aid. There was no clear pattern because King did not yet see that the fundamental problem was the financing of all government activities in Canada and that the financial problems of the federal government could not be resolved separately. The abortive Loan Council scheme had angered Pattullo and Aberhart and made future co-operation more difficult without accomplishing anything. King, however, drew no positive lesson from this experience. At the end of the session in June he could even include among his achievements the "problem of debt and taxation squarely faced."[31]

The efforts to establish formal procedures for amending the constitution also came to nothing. The B.N.A. Act could only be modified under existing procedures by a joint resolution of the House of Commons and the Senate, requesting the British Parliament for a specific amendment. Lapointe, and King to a lesser extent, had long seen this as a theoretical

161

infringement on Canadian autonomy. There was little objection to eliminating the formal approval of the British Parliament but provincial governments could not be expected to give the federal Parliament the right to alter the constitution unilaterally and so some new procedures were required which would protect provincial as well as federal jurisdictions. The Dominion-Provincial Conference had suggested a committee to discuss the problem and in February 1936 Lapointe had met with the provincial Attorneys-General. Their report was an impressive document. It recommended the unanimous consent of all legislatures on certain sensitive sections of the constitution, such as the educational guarantees for religious minorities. It recognized, however, that an insistence on unanimity for all amendments could inhibit any constitutional changes. In the area of social legislation the committee proposed that amendments would only require the consent of the federal Parliament and a two-thirds majority of the provincial legislatures.* The fact that the provinces did not insist on the absolute power to veto any amendment shows how industrialization and the impact of the depression had undermined the traditional support for provincial autonomy.[32]

The proposed procedures were never adopted. New Brunswick had opposed any change in amendment procedures at the Dominion-Provincial Conference and had not participated in the committee discussions. The federal government refused to take any further steps until New Brunswick relented. But King made no effort to force the issue. He still saw no urgent need for a major constitutional revision and so he gave formal amendment procedures a low priority. The report of the committee was filed away and forgotten.

King's major objective was still the balancing of the federal budget. The Loan Council was only one aspect of this plan; major reductions in all federal expenditures would be necessary and might be sufficient to eliminate the deficit. Both King and Dunning conceded that the budget could not be balanced in the government's first year in office but they were determined to get off to a good start. Dunning's estimates for the exceptional expenditures over the next year included twenty-six millions for direct relief grants to the provinces, almost sixty millions for public works projects, and forty millions for the Canadian National Railway deficit.[33] Dunning's plan was to increase federal revenues by twenty-five millions and to accept a deficit of one hundred million for this year. It would at least be a significant improvement over the deficit of one hundred and sixty million for the fiscal year just ending.

---

*There was a proviso that the consenting legislatures should represent at least 55 per cent of the total population, this ensuring that either Ontario or Quebec would have to be included in the majority.

Dunning had to face some opposition within the Cabinet. There was agreement on the objective of a balanced budget but T. A. Crerar argued that there were other ways in which this could be achieved. He was convinced that a half-million dollar reduction in the taxes on mining would stimulate economic activity in this sector, would reduce unemployment, increase railway revenues, and, in the long run, would increase federal revenues.[34] Crerar was reflecting his special interest as Minister of Mines but his arguments had broader implications. He was proposing a different approach, a policy of tax reductions as a stimulus to economic recovery, even if it meant a larger federal deficit in the short run. Neither King nor Dunning were impressed. They wanted to balance the budget as quickly as possible and were not prepared to reduce federal revenues. It was agreed that new mines would be given a three-year tax exemption but that was the only concession.

The Cabinet also spent some time arguing about the tariff. The trade agreement with the United States accounted for the major tariff reductions but King was determined to include some additional reductions if only to prove that the new government was true to its liberal principles. It was decided to lower the tariff on farm implements, which would be consistent with the aim of lowering the costs of production. Euler prolonged the discussions by repeatedly demanding increased protection for furniture; many of the furniture companies in his constituency had ceased operations. King was annoyed by Euler's offensive manner but when his other colleagues opposed any increase, he expressed great satisfaction with the frank and open discussion, the "fearlessness and honesty of Cabinet— prepared to oppose colleagues for principle, even knowing them to be vitally interested. Dunning kept temper well even under extreme provocation."[35] King's pattern of collective decision-making was becoming established.

Dunning's budget, when it was presented to the House early in May, was consistent with the assumption that recovery depended upon private enterprise and that the government could only encourage private enterprise by putting its own financial affairs in order. "The declared purpose of the government," Dunning explained, was "to end in the shortest practicable time the era of recurring deficits." The sales tax was to be increased from 6 to 8 per cent for an additional revenue of some twenty-three millions and corporation income tax was increased to provide six millions more. To raise taxes any higher, Dunning argued, would involve a degree of deflation that would be intolerable; to do less would weaken the confidence of businessmen and investors.[36] The budget was neatly summed up by one Liberal who told Dunning that "It is lucid, it is bold, it is comprehensive, it is illuminating, and God pity us, it is depressing."[37]

The budget was depressing but even the opposition parties did not question the necessity of eliminating the federal deficit. Bennett thought that the higher sales tax was intolerable but in a gesture to encourage a government which was at least fiscally responsible he refrained from moving an amendment.[38] The C.C.F. also objected to the new sales tax but they too conceded the need for more revenue; their proposal was a higher income tax.[39] Only the Social Credit members ignored the problem; they used their time to advocate their inflationary nostrum.[40] The dogma of a balanced budget was still unchallenged. King himself deplored the tax increases, which would increase the costs of production, but tax reductions would have to wait.[41] For him the 1936 budget was only a beginning. "From this year on," he wrote in his diary, "we should be able to materially reduce both taxation and debt, as we did after coming into office in 1921."[42]

II

The session, which lasted from the beginning of February until the end of June, was also preoccupied with a good deal of business carried over from the years of opposition. The Liberals had adopted a platform in 1933 and King was determined to show that his party kept its promises. Since then the party had also criticized some of Bennett's legislation and again it was important to prove that the new government was responsible and trustworthy. King intended to underline the contrast with the previous administration which, in his view at least, had lost the confidence of the public by making promises which it could not keep.

One of the explicit promises had been the repeal of Section 98 of the Criminal Code. The Liberal party had long been opposed to making it a crime merely to advocate the use of force "to bring about any governmental, industrial or economic change," and after the imprisonment of Tim Buck and other communists under Section 98 its repeal had been included in the party platform. Lapointe, in introducing the amendment to the Criminal Code, took the precaution of stating his horror of communism, but affirmed his faith in British justice as the surest safeguard against revolution. If there were overt acts of violence against the government, the laws against sedition were sufficient.[43] Bennett still had misgivings "in these days of uncertainty and unrest"[44] but even he was not adamant, and Section 98 was quietly eliminated.

The promise to amend the Bank of Canada Act was more controversial. Mackenzie King had no criticism of Graham Towers or of the policies of the newly constituted bank but the Liberals had argued vehemently in favour of government control over the central bank and King was not prepared to let this sleeping dog alone. Dunning showed some reluctance to open the question again but King insisted that Liberal promises had to be kept and that a majority of the directors would have to be government appointments.[45] Some western Liberals, however, were still convinced that majority control was not enough and argued vehemently in caucus for full government ownership, even threatening to vote against the proposed amendment.

King seized this occasion to outline his views on the role of the backbenchers. He would not discipline the Liberals who broke party lines in the House, he explained, because this was not his way. He did, however, object strongly to members airing their opposition to party policies in public; he "gave the freest latitude for discussion in caucus, but in the H. of C. I expect the party to act as one." Caucus adjourned "with loud and sustained applause."[46]

When the debate on the amendment came early in June, the danger of a party split was lessened because the Speaker ruled on a technicality that a C.C.F. motion for government ownership was out-of-order.[47] The legislation also stated, however, that the Bank of Canada notes would be bilingual and Bennett solemnly stated his conviction that the decision to print notes which used both French and English would destroy the fabric of the nation: "Each one in his own conscience," he warned, "must answer whether or not in a community that is overwhelmingly British, the circulation of notes of that kind is not fraught with the gravest danger to harmony between races in other parts of Canada."[48] King entered the debate to defend the rights of French Canadians to full citizenship and to defend English Canadians against the charges of intolerance and bigotry.[49] He noted with pride in his diary, and perhaps also with relief, that every Liberal had voted for this clause of the bill: "This I think was a real achievement, having regard to the size of the party and what one knows of the efforts to defeat Liberal candidates in Saskatchewan and elsewhere in previous elections on the bilingual issue."[50] When the final vote came the next day the party remained united; no Liberal opposed the measure.

The new government also amended Bennett's railway legislation. C. D. Howe, as the new Minister of Transport, explained that the Liberals were as committed as their predecessors to reducing unnecessary expenditures but argued that the administration of the government railway by a Board of Trustees had proved confusing and inefficient. His amendment replaced the three trustees by a Board of Directors, which would be concerned with policy but would leave administrative detail to the president of the railway.[51] Bennett had a different interpretation of the legislation. He saw a government eager to appoint Liberals to replace the trustees appointed by a Conservative government; the new structure had more to do with patronage than with efficiency.[52]

Howe was probably justified in his criticism of the existing structure, in which the lines of authority were far from clear. It was also unfair to accuse him of partisan motives because three months later, when he submitted his nominations to Cabinet for the new Board of Directors, there was no evidence of patronage. King was shocked to find that "Howe had a Board picked largely from Montreal & Hamilton—a few tories—no representative from the entire west & not representative in other ways."[53] He expressed special concern about the lack of western representation, since railway policy was of major importance to that region, but he may also have been surprised that Howe had included some Conservatives. The neophyte Minister was instructed to start over again and produce a list which was more representative.

Howe might lack political sensitivity but another bill which he introduced showed his courage and his concern for efficient administration. There were seven separate federal Harbour Boards in Canada, each one responsible for large expenditures and each one, it was generally agreed, was riddled with patronage and probably grosser forms of corruption. Howe's solution was to consolidate them by a National Harbours Board, which would be less susceptible to local pressures and could exercise a closer supervision of all expenditures.[54] This time even Bennett approved. He candidly admitted that he himself had favoured this reform but had not dared to override the regional protests.[55] By the end of the session King had developed considerable respect for Howe's energy and his administrative ability. He had less confidence in his political judgment and noted that Howe was "inclined to go much too far in committing the administration"[56] but had no qualms about his own ability to keep his new Minister in check.

Mackenzie King had no reservations about Norman Rogers, the other inexperienced colleague. Rogers, in addition to the legislation on the National Employment Commission, had been able to close down the relief camps which had caused so much bitterness. These camps had been transferred from the jurisdiction of National Defence to the Department of Labour. Rogers had subsequently negotiated with the railways to undertake maintenance projects which had been postponed because of the depression. Under the agreement the two railways hired all the single, homeless, and unemployed in the camps at the going wage and the government then reimbursed them for the wages the men received. By midsummer the camps were empty. King was delighted with Rogers' success, "his great honesty of mind, as well as sound judgement."[57] He was reminded of his own experiences as a young Cabinet minister and of Laurier's interest in him, and already he saw Rogers as a possible "Party Leader & P.M."[58]

The new government also had to deal with the Wheat Board. When Bennett had named the board in the summer of 1935 it already owned some two hundred million bushels of wheat. Early that fall the Conservative government had established a price of 87½ cents a bushel, which was above the open market price, and so the board had also acquired the bulk of the 1935 wheat crop. The Liberals reluctantly accepted the board; they had little choice until the wheat was sold. From the beginning, however, the Wheat Board was seen as a temporary expedient. The Liberal government was convinced that the existence of the huge Canadian surplus was depressing world prices. Its policy was to sell the surplus as quickly as possible and then to end this government intervention in wheat marketing. "The aim," in King's words, "should be to get away from unnecessary regulation as much and as soon as possible."[59]

John I. McFarland, the Chairman of the Wheat Board, did not agree with this policy. He was convinced that world prices were artificially low and that Canadian wheat should be held until prices rose. The government was determined to have its way. McFarland was asked to resign and when he refused he was abruptly dismissed in December by order-in-council. J. R. Murray, the new Chairman, was a Winnipeg Liberal with wide experience in the grain business who had supported the Liberal policy of disposing of the Wheat Board holdings.

J. G. Gardiner became the principal defender for the new policy in the House. He had not managed to have the Wheat Board transferred to his department; instead a Cabinet committee including Euler, Dunning, Crerar, and Gardiner was asked to supervise wheat marketing. Gardiner, however, was aggressive and, as the leading prairie Liberal, wheat was his major concern. In March he clashed directly with Bennett, ridiculing McFarland's stabilization policies and provoking a furious rejoinder.[60] King obviously enjoyed the confrontation. "Bennett," he recorded in his diary, "more or less lost his head throughout the discussion. Gardiner went for him in splendid fashion."[61]

The government was fortunate in its timing. Poor crops in other parts of the world allowed the Wheat Board to increase its sales without depressing world prices.* By August 1936, when the new crop had to be

*It is estimated that the Wheat Board finally lost about twelve million dollars on the 1935 crop but made a profit of almost nine million dollars on McFarland's earlier stabilization purchases. D. A. McGibbon, *The Canadian Grain Trade*, p. 77; V. C. Fowke, *The National Policy and the Wheat Economy*, p. 267.

considered, the open market price was higher than the Wheat Board price. King was convinced that this was the time for the board to end its purchases; "It was clear to me," he wrote in his diary, "if we do not get out of the price-fixing now, we shall never be able to." He was disappointed that Dunning disagreed—he seemed to King to be "heading into the regulation attitude"—but encouraged that Gardiner was more willing to take the risk.[62] At King's suggestion the Cabinet eventually adopted a compromise. The Wheat Board would maintain 87½ cents as a floor price but it would not accept any wheat unless the open market price fell below 90 cents. Since the price remained above that level the Wheat Board made no purchases and could concentrate on disposing of its carryover from the previous years.

Gardiner's performance in the House and in Cabinet impressed King. It was reassuring that the Minister of Agriculture shared his conviction that wheat marketing was best left to private enterprise. King also knew that Gardiner, unlike Howe, could be trusted to weigh the political aspects of every question even at the risk of being partisan. Gardiner's rivalry with Dunning did him no harm. In comparing the two after the August discussion over the Wheat Board King concluded that "Gardiner is the more honourable & [has] better judgement & courage."[63]

The session ended on June 23rd. King savoured the occasion on which he, the grandson of an alleged rebel, took the salute on Parliament Hill on the King's birthday. But most of all he took pride in what he saw as an extraordinarily successful beginning to his term of office. The Cabinet, he believed, was equal or superior to any other Cabinet in Canadian history. Caucus, unprecedented in size and containing wide ranges of opinion on most topics, had remainded united "without the loss of a single Member on any of the divisions during the session. . . . I do not suppose this performance will ever be equalled again." He even boasted to Vincent Massey that more significant legislation had been passed than "by any previous Parliament in its several sessions combined" and that the Liberal party had fulfilled "more of the promises and pledges given to the electorate than has been the case, I believe, with respect to any Party in Canada or, indeed, in any country."[64]

Mackenzie King was exaggerating the achievements of the session. He had done nothing to resolve the fundamental problems of regional disparity and the economic depression. The Loan Council scheme had failed and he had nothing to offer the struggling provincial administrations except Bennett's policy of giving as little aid as possible. But there was some justification for his pride. He had effectively imposed his leadership on an able Cabinet and an active caucus, and the legislation, while it offered little that was new or innovative, did promise competent administration. Even Bennett might have conceded this much. His secretary described the session at one stage as "dull beyond words" and had commented "even our head man, who is head and shoulders above any of them, finds difficulty in sustaining his interest."[65] This at least suggests that the session had gone well for the government. Oppositions are prone to be bored by governments which offer little opportunity for criticism.

CHAPTER TEN

CANADA AND THE EUROPEAN VORTEX

MACKENZIE KING had given most of his attention to domestic issues during the session of 1936 but international events could not be completely ignored. At Geneva the Committee of Eighteen had continued to discuss Riddell's resolution to extend economic sanctions against Italy while in Ethiopia Italian troops had continued to advance. Then, in March, Hitler had provoked an international crisis by sending troops into the German Rhineland in open defiance of the Versailles Treaty and the Locarno Pact. In July, shortly after the session ended, civil war broke out in Spain. The vision of a peace-keeping League was shattered; the question now was whether wars could be limited or whether all Europe would be involved.

King was not an isolationist. He knew that events in Europe would affect Canada and he believed that under some circumstances Canadian interests might seem so directly involved that participation in a European war could not be avoided. In 1936, however, it seemed unlikely that all Canadians would interpret Canadian interests in the same way; French and English Canadians had reacted differently to the Ethiopian invasion and their sympathies in the Spanish civil war were also divided. If participation seemed to hinge on the question of being at Britain's side the two cultural groups might also disagree. Since it seemed probable that any decision to go to war would endanger national unity, King's first instinct was to avoid any situation which might oblige the government to make such a decision.

Canada belonged to two institutions which might draw it into the European vortex—the League of Nations and the British Commonwealth. There was no question of withdrawing from either the League or the Commonwealth but in 1936 King did try to limit the obligations which membership entailed. He left for Europe in mid-September and at Geneva, Paris, and London urged policies which he hoped would avert a major European war or which would at least make it possible for Canadians not to intervene. His trip, however, left him with a feeling of

170

profound uneasiness. A European war was possible and even probable and if Britain was drawn in, Canada would not be able to stay on the sidelines. The abdication crisis, remote as it was from other events in Europe, was for King an illustration of how intimately Canada was associated with Great Britain. By the end of the year he had decided that the risk of war could not be ignored and that Canada would have to increase its defence expenditures.

I

During the session of 1936 King had deliberately tried to avoid any discussion of the government's foreign policy. His argument was that Canada was too remote and too insignificant to influence events or to provide leadership for Europe and that irresponsible suggestions would only complicate the delicate negotiations of the major European powers. King's policy was open to criticism because it could mean that Canadians would stand idly by while their fate was being decided in the chancelleries of Europe. For the moment, however, King believed that no more forthright position was possible. Any policy of intervention or, on the other hand, any affirmation of Canadian neutrality would provoke a bitter debate and make eventual agreement more difficult. Until a consensus seemed possible, he preferred to avoid public controversy.

The German reoccupation of the Rhineland in March made King more cautious than ever. Canadians showed only a fleeting interest in Hitler's provocative move. The reaction of the English-language press was moderately favourable; the World War was over and after eighteen years Germany could hardly be blamed for asserting its right to occupy its own territory. Even in French Canada, where there was more sympathy for France, there were no clarion calls for Canadian intervention.[1] King himself was ambivalent. His first reaction was that "Germany having breathing space anew may help to bring about a situation that will break down other barriers."[2] A few days later, however, when France insisted that the Locarno Pact must be respected, King thought Britain would have to support France. "It seems to me," he commented in his diary, "that Britain has no alternative, unless she does the opposite of what she did in the Great War; Germany has treated her treaties as 'scraps of paper.'"[3] But King's main concern was not the rights or wrongs of the Rhineland occupation. He was worried about divisions at home if Britain and France went to war.

There would be no domestic crisis if France and Britain accepted the occupation quietly. King did what he could to encourage the British

Government to be conciliatory. It was the Canadian Government's "earnest hope," he cabled ten days after the occupation, that a peaceful settlement could be negotiated; to encourage concessions the despatch went on to point out that Canada had not signed the Locarno Pact and therefore did not consider herself automatically committed to apply any economic sanctions the League might propose.[4] But King also knew that this was only a technicality. As he commented in his diary: "If League decided to support France as I believe the Council will, I feel Canada will have to support the League to the extent of sanctions, as imposed against Italy, but with the same limitations, namely economic sanctions only and not military as well."[5]

In public, however, it seemed wiser to avoid even a hint of taking sides. Any suggestion that Canada favoured accepting the *fait accompli* would make it more difficult to win support for sanctions against Germany if they became necessary. When J. S. Woodsworth protested that the House of Commons had no indication of the government's attitude, King tried to make a virtue of his reticence:

In a word the attitude of the government is to do nothing itself and if possible to prevent anything occurring which will precipitate one additional factor into the all important discussions which are now taking place in Europe. I believe that Canada's first duty to the league and to the British empire, with respect to all the great issues that come up, is, if possible, to keep this country united. I believe that can be more effectively accomplished at this stage if we wait until we are a little more fully informed than we are at the moment, with respect to all the considerations of which we should have knowledge before attempting to pronounce too definitely upon the position which we are taking or shall take with regard to European affairs.[5]

King was very pleased with this reply, not because he had evaded the question but because he felt that he had answered it very directly. "In the course of the reply," he confided in his diary, "I used an expression which I question if the House or the country will catch the significance of, but which some day will serve to indicate the Liberal policy with respect to Imperial and Foreign affairs. It was that we believed our duty was to keep Canada united and avoid controversies or discussions liable to create trouble abroad."[7] Mackenzie King realized more clearly than many of his contemporaries that foreign policy was an aspect of domestic policy and that the government's attitude to events in the Rhineland must be largely determined by the situation at home. His discreet silence in public reflected his conviction that Canadians would not be ready to agree on any commitment, either to intervene or to affirm their neutrality. Much to King's relief, the crisis was averted because France and England were not prepared to face the consequences of asking the League to apply sanctions.

Economic sanctions against Italy, however, continued to complicate European diplomacy. The abortive Hoare-Laval proposal had shown that France and England were not prepared to fight to preserve the territorial integrity of Ethiopia and the Rhineland crisis made French intervention even more unlikely. By June, after Italian troops had occupied Addis Ababa, the existing economic sanctions had failed and the discussions of the Committee of Eighteen on extending the sanctions to include oil and other items had obviously become irrelevant. Neville Chamberlain, eager to restore the balance of power in Europe by placating Italy, drew the logical conclusion and denounced the continuation of sanctions as "the very midsummer of madness."[8]

Mackenzie King fully agreed. He had been prepared to support the extension of economic sanctions if the League recommended it, and had instructed Riddell to concur in this extension in the Committee of Eighteen if Britain and France supported the motion.[9] But this was not because King thought Canadians favoured sanctions. He believed that they would disagree if the debate focussed on whether Canada should extend sanctions against Italy. If it became the official policy of the League, however, the issue would be whether Canada should support the League and on this he thought Canadians would agree. Until the League decided King would do nothing. "It is sometimes well to allow sleeping dogs lie," he wrote to a friend. "This, I believe, is especially true when they happen to be the dogs of war."[10] Chamberlain's statement ensured that that sleeping dog would never have to be wakened. King felt that his policy was now fully vindicated; he had avoided a divisive debate over sanctions by waiting.[11] Cautious to the end, he still kept silent. Canada had not initiated the policy of sanctions and it would not initiate its reversal. Only after the British Government had formally announced that it would ask the League Assembly to end economic sanctions did King announce his support for this policy.

In mid-June, when the Ethiopian incident had come to its inglorious end, King finally decided it was safe to deliver a major speech to the House on foreign affairs. It was a lucid justification of Canadian policy at Geneva, a policy of supporting every decision adopted by the League of Nations. But what of the future? Here King was much less explicit. He pointed out that collective security depended upon a League to which all major nations belonged and a League in which all members were committed to the use of force—"collective bluffing cannot bring collective security." The present

League did not meet these conditions. At the moment it was primarily a league of European nations with little interest in disputes remote from Europe's shores. Under these circumstances Canada could not accept binding commitments to apply economic or military sanctions. But, like Christianity, "the league has failed but the league is not a failure." It was an indispensable agency where "the statesmen of great countries are forced to come in the open and defend in public, before a world forum, the policies of their government." The League was still the embodiment of "the conscience of mankind" and Canada needed and must support it.[12]

The speech had the desired effect. It gave a few interested members the opportunity "to give speeches which had been carefully prepared," King noted,[13] but it did not provoke any controversy. Woodsworth deplored King's failure to enunciate the fundamental principles on which Canadian foreign policy was based but even he had no criticism of the government's "concrete actions."[14] Bennett gave his unqualified approval. He congratulated King on his statement and argued that it was unfair to suggest "that any Prime Minister in these days could outline a foreign policy for the country; it cannot be done."[15] That ended the discussion for the session. When one member congratulated King on the last day for having prevented a debate on foreign policy, he took it as a compliment.[16] A constructive foreign policy was a policy which did not endanger national unity, and avoiding public controversy was part of that policy.

II

King knew it was not enough to avoid debate. As an ideal the League might represent the conscience of mankind but in its present imperfect form it might still recommend that its members go to war. The Ethiopian and the Rhineland crises had forced King to recognize the risk of League membership. "It is becoming apparent to all," he commented in his diary in March 1936, "that Europe is becoming a maelstrom of strife, and that we are being drawn into a situation that is none of our creation by membership in the League of Nations."[17] The next crisis might find Canada forced to approve or reject a League policy of military sanctions and, whatever the government's decision might be, the country might be bitterly divided. In the summer of 1936 King decided that the risk was too great. He would have to prevent this by limiting Canada's commitment to the League.

King was "so concerned about the League matters generally and Canada's relation to the League in particular" that he headed the Canadian delegation to the League Assembly in September.[18] At Geneva he bluntly rejected the principle of collective security. The League, he told the Assembly, had tried sanctions and had failed. Any attempt to strengthen its coercive power would only weaken it. Some nations had rejected military sanctions from the beginning—a pointed reference to the United States— and "every vacant seat in this Assembly is a broken link in the chain of collective security." As for Canada: "there is general concurrence in the view, which has been expressed by leaders of all political parties since the beginning of the League, that automatic commitments to the application of force is not a practical policy." Any decision for Canada to participate in a war would be made in Ottawa and not in Geneva.

King insisted that this did not mean that Canada was withdrawing from the League. Instead, he wished "to reaffirm her adherence to the fundamental principles of the Covenant." All Canadians favoured international co-operation to preserve world peace and for this the machinery of the League was essential: "if the League did not exist, some such world organization would have to be invented." For the moment, however, the League should "emphasize the task of mediation and conciliation rather than punishment." If in this way the League could re-establish goodwill and confidence among European nations it would be able to build on that foundation and "fulfil its mission to mankind."[19]

Mackenzie King was well satisfied with his speech. He doubted "whether a more unqualified speech has been made at any time, at any place, than that made here in Geneva."[20] He was also sure that most Canadians would agree with the opinions he had expressed; "There is no doubt," he told the Governor General, "that what I have said represents the general opinion of Canada."[21] The available evidence suggests that King was right. French-Canadian newspapers expressed unqualified approval. Some English-Canadian Conservative newspapers regretted that King had not suggested the Commonwealth as an alternative to the League but with one exception the English-Canadian press agreed with King that membership in the League did not and should not involve any automatic commitment to military intervention. Only J. W. Dafoe argued that collective security was the fundamental principle of the League and that, by rejecting this, King had repudiated the League.[22] Even Dafoe, however, conceded in private that the League was already doomed and that King could not have saved the institution.[23] In effect, Dafoe was advocating a quixotic defence of a moribund League. King, who was a political leader and not an editorial writer, preferred to describe the League as it was in the hope that most Canadians would then forgo the temptation to tilt at windmills.

III

Mackenzie King was pleased with his speech at Geneva but did not delude himself into thinking that he had thereby saved Canada from European entanglements. Any incident might lead to hostilities in Europe and the ideological divisions within European countries made it almost certain that the war would spread. Early in September he had commented that "Anything might happen at any time—I fear revolution in France. The real danger is Fascism vs. Communism, Capital vs. Labour—class warfare in all the European countries, & who will say not also in America. The world is in a terrible state."[24] His visit to Europe did not change his mind. In his more optimistic moments he hoped that war was not imminent —on the day of his Geneva speech he recorded his belief "that war will come eventually between Germany and Russia, but that may be some time yet."[25] At other times, however, he was less sanguine. Later in the year, for example, he commented that he would "be surprised if this decade does not miss a European war, I should think it might come in 1938."[26] He did not expect his lecture to the League Assembly on the need for international goodwill to bring peace to a Europe which seemed intent on a confrontation.[27]

Four days in Paris after the Geneva visit did nothing to ease his mind. He had the usual distractions of a visiting dignitary, including a visit to the site of the Vimy memorial and an evening at the opera to hear the French-Canadian tenor, Raoul Jobin, in "Romeo and Juliet," but he was much more interested in his conversations with members of the French Government. King was prepared to believe that Léon Blum's Popular Front was "a liberal administration, a sort of fabian socialist type believing in government ownership of utilities etc."[28] More significant for King, however, was the evidence of France's deep fear of Germany. Both Blum and Delbos, the Foreign Minister, made this point forcefully: "They are . . . afraid of Germany, not so much because of her power and strength as because of the uncertainty of her actions; because of her having a dictator at the head of affairs. And a dictator who is a very uncertain type of man. He might do anything at any time, something that he has not contemplated a day or two before. This I believe is the truth of the situation."[29]

He left Paris with the impression that fascist intervention in Spain made the European situation more volatile, and that the French saw their alliance with Russia as "essential to keep Germany in her place."[30] He found the discussions of French foreign policy so engrossing that on his last day he had only two hours for the inevitable visit to the Louvre before leaving for London.

France's attitude was important for what it revealed about the European situation but King was not primarily concerned with Europe. A European war would be a disaster for Europeans but Canadian participation was not inevitable. The crucial question was whether Great Britain would be involved. Membership in the League was not seen as an automatic commitment to collective security, but Canada was also a member of the British Commonwealth and many Canadians took this association more seriously. The only European crisis which would threaten Canadian unity would be a war in which Britain was a belligerent. Some Canadians would then insist on being at Britain's side while others, who resented any response which smelled of colonialism, might still oppose participation. The country—and the Liberal party—might be divided. There was no thought of withdrawing from the Commonwealth. For King the surest way to avoid a political crisis at home was to have Great Britain keep out of a European war.

King was not satisfied with a pious hope. He had had long discussions with British officials at Geneva and there were more meetings in London. King took advantage of these opportunities to warn that Canadian participation in a British war could not be taken for granted. As he explained to Malcolm MacDonald, the Secretary of State for Dominion Affairs:

What might be done would be a matter of sentiment and would all depend upon the circumstances at the time, that I could conceive cases where the Dominion might feel it needed to assist in some way out of a situation which might develop and because of sentiment, but certainly no agreement could be made to that end beforehand, and it is not something on which reliance could be put. That a British war with Europe might mean the break up of the Empire; that the great difficulty would be to keep Canada united in any such situation. I pointed out that growth of nationalistic feeling in Quebec and the feeling that many had of sympathy with the United States' point of view, that as a North American continent, we should not be drawn into the Old World situation.[31]

Any attempt to force a decision now would deepen existing divisions; any future decision to participate would depend on how future events influenced Canadian attitudes.

It was reassuring to find that British politicians were as eager to avoid war as he was. Anthony Eden at Geneva, Neville Chamberlain in London, and Stanley Baldwin at Chequers all told him the same story; they were working for peace and that war was possible but not inevitable. King explained that "Canada's wish in the whole situation was that Great Britain would keep out of any European war altogether."[32] The British politicians apparently shared his sentiments. Eden saw the Franco-Russian alliance as a regrettable complication; "if that were out of the way, France could be given greater securities by Britain" and Germany would not likely run the risk of a war in western Europe against both France and Britain.[33] Chamberlain also expressed misgivings about Russia, a "mischief maker in all parts of the world."[34] King drew the logical inference that Great Britain would not intervene in a war between Russia and Germany if France could be persuaded to remain neutral. But King also learned that Britain had commitments in Europe which seemed essential to its own security—it was committed to defending the sovereignty of Belgium and Holland and to keeping the Mediterranean open.[35] Thus, if a European war broke out, there was a possibility that Britain—and so Canada—would not be involved but there could be no assurance of British neutrality.

The European situation, critical as it was, was not the only topic discussed in London. Every conversation seemed to turn eventually to the private life of Edward VIII. Edward had been a romantic and popular figure as Prince of Wales but what Lord Tweedsmuir once referred to as "his bachelor habits" had caused some uneasiness even after his succession to the throne in January 1936.[36] When King reached London he was exposed to constant gossip about Edward's private life and, more particularly, about his infatuation with an American by the name of Mrs Simpson. The Monarch, so he was told, had regularly visited this woman's suite at Claridge's, had bought her a house in Hyde Park, and had missed official engagements to be with her.[37] Gossip about the private life, even of a king, would have been no more than gossip except that by October the affair threatened to provoke a constitutional crisis. Mrs Simpson had filed for her second divorce and Stanley Baldwin feared that Edward's intentions were honourable. As he told King, "he would not mind if the King kept her at Belvedere, or anywhere but not flaunt her on the public." Marriage was another matter. The respect for middle-class morality would then conflict with the tradition of allegiance to the monarchy and nobody could be sure of the outcome. Baldwin believed marriage would mean that Edward would have to go but, as he told King, the political implications were frightening.[38]

Baldwin and Alexander Hardinge, the King's secretary, both raised the subject with King because they hoped he would be helpful. The British press had voluntarily ignored Mrs Simpson but the American press was less reticent and American publications were circulating in Canada. Could King tell Edward that the Canadian people were deeply disturbed by his liaison with Mrs Simpson? King was not very co-operative. He wanted no responsibility in such a delicate matter; his excuse was that he had left Canada before there had been any publicity about the affair and that he therefore knew nothing about the reaction there.[39]

When King saw Edward neither of them made any reference to Mrs Simpson. Edward expressed great interest in the value of Canadian railway stocks, in the eccentricities of Hepburn and Aberhart, and expressed his personal concern about Russia, but he said nothing of his personal affairs. King was equally reticent. He did tell Edward of the exalted place "which he held in the hearts of the Canadian people," and stressed the importance of the Crown to the Empire. When Edward demurred, King "repeated [that] it is within your power to save civilization itself and you can do it by following your own true instinct in the matter."[40] If this was advice it was not very pointed. Edward may not have seen any connection between these comments and his private life; if he did, he was left to guess where King thought his true instinct should lead him.

Geoffrey Dawson of *The Times* made a point of going to a party given by Vincent Massey that evening, hoping to hear that King had warned Edward of the risks he was taking. He was disappointed to learn, "that he had done nothing of the kind—had, indeed if anything, made matters worse by discoursing on the King's popularity in the Dominions."[41] Mackenzie King had a different reaction. It was enough that he, the boy from Berlin and the grandson of a rebel, had had an audience with His Majesty and had, as King believed, left a good impression. King's companion in the taxi from the theatre to the Massey reception had been Ingrid Bergman, "a famous young movie star," but even she had made no impression on a man who had just talked with the King.

IV

Mackenzie King reached Ottawa early in November, pleased with the results of his European visit. He had exerted whatever influence he had to keep the League and Great Britain out of any European war and had made it clear that, if there was a war, Canada had no formal commitment to participate. Short of a declaration of neutrality, he had gone as far as he could to ensure that external events would not pull Canada into the maelstrom against its will. But if King was satisfied with what he had accomplished, he also realized that Canadian unity might still be endangered. Canadians might be able to take a detached view of events on the Rhine, in Madrid, or even at Geneva but London was closer to home. There were no formal commitments but there were ties which could not be ignored. If war came, the Canadian Government would have no obligation to participate but public pressure at home might leave it no choice.

179

King returned from Europe convinced that this possibility could not be ignored.

The state of Canada's armed forces was directly related to this problem. If Canada did become a belligerent it would need forces that were equipped and trained; the government would be held responsible if the country was unprepared. In 1936, however, it was painfully obvious that Canadian forces were inadequate for any purpose. The Bennett government had reduced annual defence expenditures to some thirteen million dollars and although this sum had been increased in 1935 and again in 1936 to almost twenty millions, the defence budget had not permitted the purchase of new equipment and had restricted training to little more than parade-square drill.[42] Canada was in no position to defend her own territory, much less aid possible allies in a war. Coastal defence guns, dating back to the First World War, were rarely fired because a few more rounds would wear them out; field guns were obsolete and little ammunition was available; there was not one modern anti-aircraft gun in the country. Canada had no tanks, no armoured cars, no tractors for field artillery. Some of the Canadian destroyers were no longer seaworthy, and the twenty-five service aircraft in Canada were useless except for training purposes.[43] If the possibility of a war could not be ignored, massive expenditures were needed for equipment and training.

Increased defence expenditures, however, might provoke a domestic crisis which would be as dangerous to the government as being unprepared if war came. King and his colleagues, committed to a balanced budget, were reluctant to increase any expenditures. They were even more reluctant to allocate money for defence measures at a time when they were insisting that no additional funds could be found for relief. And how could the expenditures be justified? What enemy threatened Canadian security? Invasion from the United States was unthinkable—and defence against a hostile United States would be impossible anyway. Canada was shielded from any other invader by the British Navy and the Monroe doctrine. If Canada needed no defence, military expenditures might be interpreted as preparations for an offensive war, as evidence that the government, in spite of its public declarations to the contrary, was secretly committed to a policy of fighting at Britain's side. The political results of preparing for a war might be as disastrous as doing nothing. It was tempting to wait and to hope that Canada would never have to decide to fight.

Mackenzie King would have preferred to wait. Even before his trip to Europe, however, the problem of defence expenditures had beome urgent. The Baldwin government, after a period of indecision if not outright hypocrisy, had committed itself to rearmament[44] and, as early as the

spring of 1936, had privately inquired of the Dominions "what, if anything, they could or would do" to assist.[45] Some British politicians had
spoken openly about assurances of help from the Empire. One one occasion King had publicly contradicted one such statement.[46] He had not
objected to the idea of co-operation; "What is most regrettable," he wrote
in his diary, "is the fact that these statements have to be made at the most
critical moment and at the very time when, if other people would not make
false representations, a united front could be observed without anything
being said."[47] Australia and New Zealand, however, apprehensive of the
Japanese in the Far East and less inhibited by internal divisions, had increased their defence expenditures as a contribution to Imperial defence.[48]
A decision by the Canadian government to increase expenditures might
be interpreted as an Imperial commitment but a decision not to increase
them might be interpreted as a rejection of the Empire. The problem was
not only to decide what to do about Canada's military forces but also to
avoid alienating those on the one hand who were suspicious of the British
connection and those on the other side who had strong Imperial sympathies. The situation, as O. D. Skelton drily pointed out in March, "emphasized the advisability of early consideration of Canada's defence policy
before the discussion is complicated by developments in Europe or proposals from London."[49]

King had decided, even before leaving for Europe, that the government would have to do something. In August he and his senior colleagues
had met with the Chiefs of Staff to hear a review of the situation. "The
impression left on my mind," King recorded, "was one of the complete
inadequacy of everything in the way of defence."[50] King had seen, however, that this almost total neglect of Canada's military establishment
might now make it possible to increase defence expenditures without provoking a political crisis. Funds could be specifically allocated to the defence of Canadian territory, thus reassuring those who feared direct contributions to Great Britain and at the same time placating the critics who
said that Canada was doing nothing.

King had immediately proposed this solution to the full Cabinet, relying heavily on the interview with the Chiefs of Staff: "[I] gave my own
view that we would be failing in our responsibility if we did not immediately begin to strengthen the country's coast defences—especially on the
side of Naval and Air defence. . . . I said in Council . . . with the world
situation what it is, I should deserve to be shot did I not press for immediate action & should a war come on with nothing accomplished meanwhile."

His ministers were not prepared to challenge this paramount duty directly but nobody was enthusiastic. Lapointe, loyal as always, supported King but insisted that no money should be spent for Canadian forces to be sent abroad. C. G. Power questioned whether the Chiefs of Staff could be trusted. Dandurand thought that the protection of the United States was enough. Charles Dunning protested that Canada could not afford any increased expenditures. Nevertheless, "Council generally accepted the view we must take action at once & next step to get a practical scheme for consideration."[51]

Two weeks later, in September, the Chiefs of Staff had submitted a proposal. They defined the primary role of the Canadian forces as the defence of Canada and, as a secondary responsibility, the co-operation with other Empire forces in an overseas war. They did not provide a breakdown of the respective costs of these roles; their proposal to cover both responsibilities was a five-year plan involving two hundred million dollars, with the cost for the first year amounting to approximately sixty-five millions.[52] This came as a shock to a government which that year was spending only twenty millions on defence and which had a total annual expenditure of less than five hundred millions. "All the French members, except Lapointe," King noted, were "pretty well content to leave matters as they are." Even Ilsley, from Nova Scotia, "saw little or no need for safeguarding Atlantic coasts" and other English-Canadian Ministers were reluctant to increase the estimates. J. G. Gardiner was the only strong advocate, apart from Ian Mackenzie, the Minister of National Defence, and he, according to King, "made a first class presentation of the need of protecting Canada's commerce with Britain through the St. Lawrence." King stressed the obligation "to our country to protect it in a mad world" and argued that it would be humiliating for Canada to "accept protection from Britain without sharing in the costs, or to rely on the United States without being willing to at least protect our neutrality."[53] King had then left for Geneva with no decision made and with his colleagues still reeling from the shock.

King was disturbed by the reluctance of some of his colleagues to admit even the necessity of improving Canada's coastal defences because he saw a need for going further and actually preparing for the possibility of supporting Britain in a European war. His conversations in London, however, had suggested a way of achieving this goal without a Cabinet split. Baldwin had stressed the importance of air-power in any future war: "He thought," King recorded, "that we should give attention mostly to air force; while Canada might be the last country to be attacked, the air force would be the most helpful of any in case of attack, and training of men for the air and plenty of equipment was the essential of modern warfare. He did not seem to think the navy was the thing to be concerned about, nor did he speak at all of the army."[54] Expenditures on the army, as King knew, would immediately be interpreted in some circles as preparing an expeditionary force for Europe and naval expenditures would be seen as a contribution to the British Navy, but an expanded air force could be justified as necessary for the defence of Canada. And yet if Canada did find itself fighting at Britain's side, an air force would be the most useful contribution Canada could make to the common cause.

When King returned to Canada in November defence expenditure was one of the first items on the Cabinet's agenda. King was much encouraged by a talk with Power, who at first argued that increased defence expenditures might "cost us the entire province" of Quebec, but who, when King suggested the major emphasis should be on the air force, had conceded that, "if carefully handled, this might be possible."[55] King does not appear to have explained to Power or to any other Minister that the air force might also be used abroad if there was a European war. In Cabinet he stressed that Canada needed "some protection overhead, against the new inventions of the day in a world that had become increasingly one and full of madness."[56] His major argument was that Canada must do something: "That if Canada were independent, she would have an enormous cost to meet in the way of defence, and that unless we were ready to do something, we might get the support neither of Britain nor of the United States except at a price which we might deeply regret."[57]

A decision was finally reached in December after what King described as "a very hard session of the Cabinet." Over the protests of Charles Dunning it was agreed that the budgetary deficit would only be reduced by twenty-five millions over the next year and this made it possible "to allow Mackenzie some 15 millions to work out a defence policy."[58] This increase would mean a total defence expenditure for 1937 of thirty-five millions, far short of the Chiefs of Staff proposal for sixty-five millions but nonetheless a positive response to the threat of a possible European war.

v

Late in November another issue had arisen which to King seemed even more significant than the defence estimates. On November 27 Sir Francis Floud, the British High Commissioner, called to say that he had received an important message which he would deliver in person the next day. King commented to a sceptical Skelton that this would be about the King.[59] He was right. When Sir Francis arrived, he had a letter from Baldwin informing the Dominion Prime Ministers that Edward VIII intended to marry Mrs Simpson and asking them for their opinions on whether Mrs Simpson should become Queen, or the King's wife with no title, or whether the King should abdicate.[60] Mackenzie King was sure there was only one satisfactory solution. As he told Floud, he "saw no other course than voluntary abdication if the King were to retain his self-respect & respect in the eyes of his people."[61]

Mackenzie King was nonetheless very conscious of Edward's popularity and of the possibility that any hint of an ultimatum would provoke a popular sympathy for the King which could endanger governments and even disrupt the Commonwealth. He warned Baldwin privately of the importance of not appearing to force the decision on Edward; the abdication must be voluntary.[62] King also tried to protect his own position. It seemed important to establish in advance that the Canadian Government was not to blame in case a political crisis developed in Britain. In spite of the misgivings of Lapointe and Skelton, King insisted on issuing a press release a few days later to affirm that no "proceeding or course of action in Great Britain has been at the instance or upon the insistence of the Dominions, and of Canada in particular."[63] A few days later King shifted his ground slightly; to give advice would be dangerous but he might also be blamed if he did nothing. He decided to appeal directly to the King to follow the narrow path of duty and, by implication, to give up Mrs Simpson. His message was so cautiously worded, however, that it was almost incomprehensible: "There is no doubt in our minds," it read, "that a recognition by Your Majesty of what as King is owing by you to the Throne and to Your Majesty's subjects in all parts of the British Commonwealth should, regardless of whatever the personal sacrifice may be, be permitted to outweigh all other considerations."[64]

Edward was unmoved by this and by other more direct reminders of his duty. The alternative of abdication, however, would require a British statute to alter the succession to the throne. By the Statute of Westminster this legislation would have to affirm that it had been officially requested by the Dominions. King still feared a wave of popular sympathy for Edward and was determined to avoid any impression that he was responsible for the decision. His fears led to a number of Cabinet discussions and a series of telegrams and telephone conversations with officials in London and other Dominion capitals over the precise wording of the legislation. It was finally agreed that the Act would state that Canada had "requested and assented" but that this would be qualified by the phrase "in accordance with section 4 of the Statute of Westminster."[65] Many who were involved in these discussions must have doubted whether all this fuss was necessary and must have concluded that King was making a mountain out of a mole hill. King himself had no doubts. He believed that many Canadians had deep emotional attachments to the Crown and where emotions were involved no details were unimportant.

Mackenzie King took the abdication crisis so seriously that he was not prepared to delegate any responsibility to his colleagues or his officials. He discussed the despatches with them but he had little confidence in their judgment if they disagreed with him. "I felt," he commented on one occasion, "regardless of the judgement of all the Cabinet combined, in some things I know absolutely what is best and necessary to do."[66] His colleagues shared his opinion that the abdication must appear to be voluntary and that there must be no suggestion of official advice from the Canadian government but they seemed to be less impressed with the gravity of the situation and less fearful that an apparently innocuous phrase might be misinterpreted. King, however, insisted on consulting them and having their tacit consent for every step. Even when King was determined to have his way he respected the principle of collective responsibility.

On December 10, when Edward announced his "irrevocable determination to renounce the Throne," there was no political crisis in England or Canada. In retrospect King still believed that the fate of the Empire had been at stake and that he had helped to save both Crown and Commonwealth.[67] There is little evidence to suggest that there had been any danger of a crisis in Canada. There had been some newspaper criticism of King's refusal to comment on the situation in the weeks preceding Edward's announcement but after the abdication there was general approval of his dignified conduct.[68] King may well have exaggerated the dangers and exaggerated his part in resolving what he considered "the most important historic incident in this country"[69] but his fault, if fault there was, had been to err on the side of caution. King would not have admitted that a politician could ever be too cautious.

The year 1936 had been, King recorded, "eventful to a degree I had never anticipated." It had been a good year for him—God had surely guided and guarded him. The next year might well be even more eventful but King saw no prospect of improved international relations; 1937 might "ere its close, become a year of universal terror": "The most I imagine can be hoped for is the saving at least of a part of the world from all but annihilation of a multitude of men. One naturally hopes and believes that it will be one's own land and the democracies which will be spared the conflict; if, however, they are, that will be a miracle indeed."[70] Even King's caution and God's help might not be enough to keep Canada out of the war.

CHAPTER ELEVEN

PORTENTS OF DISUNITY

IN THE EARLY MONTHS OF 1937 Mackenzie King could have found many reasons for complacency. The international scene was relatively calm and, in Canada, there were convincing signs that the depression was lifting and that economic recovery was well under way. The political situation also favoured the Liberals. The Conservative party had never recovered from its disastrous defeat in the last election and was marking time until R. B. Bennett either resigned or exerted some authority as leader; the C.C.F. and Social Credit parties remained regional protest parties, weakened by internal divisions. And King managed to keep his followers united on most major issues in spite of the overwhelming Liberal majority and the temptations to resist party discipline. The parliamentary session of 1937 was unusually brief, with the House meeting in mid-January and proroguing early in April; the increase in the defence estimates proved to be the only controversial issue. The Liberal government seemed to have the situation under control.

Mackenzie King, however, was deeply worried. The House of Commons might be following his baton but he could still hear discordant notes coming from off-stage, from the provincial capitals. The problem was that the House did not reflect the tensions within the country. In spite of the signs of economic recovery there was widespread discontent and disaffection and Canadians seemed somehow less willing or less able to accept reasonable solutions. Because the federal political parties provided no outlet for the grievances a new pattern was emerging in which the provincial governments were becoming the major critics of the federal administration. King commented on this regional pattern at the first meeting of caucus in the new session: "I then spoke," he recorded, "of the necessity of national unity and the disintegration that was taking place in Canada on the part of the Provinces, Alberta becoming isolated, and Manitoba and Saskatchewan emphasizing sectional interests through financial embarrassment, Quebec talking of separation, New Brunswick

186

of itself as a Province of the United Kingdom etc."[1] By the end of the session the list of dissident provinces would be expanded, with Ontario under Mitchell Hepburn as the most striking illustration of national fragmentation.

O. D. Skelton was, if anything, more depressed by this pattern than King. Skelton, usually the epitomy of the unruffled and pragmatic civil servant, told King in April that he saw only impending disaster if the federal government could not re-establish its authority:

Some early and definite action by the Canadian Government to take control of the chaos that is developing throughout the Dominion seems vital. The disintegration of Canada is proceeding fast. Extreme assertions of provincial power, tendencies in several provinces of the Governments to adopt an arbitrary and semi-Fascist attitude, the increasing distrust of the East on the part of the Western provinces, the bitterness and recklessness developing from the continued unemployment in spite of the spotty prosperity that has come to some sections of the population; these and many other manifestations of unrest make the situation in Canada today the most disturbing in my recollection.[2]

King and Skelton were deeply disturbed because they both believed that the federal government had done all that was possible to restore prosperity. The growing regional bitterness seemed to them to be unjustified and almost irrational. What could be done to preserve national unity when, in Skelton's words, "good administration and sane policy on the part of the Federal Government is not enough"? Mackenzie King was equally at a loss for a remedy to the malaise. He could continue to be reasonable and conciliatory and could appeal to the provincial leaders to be patient but none of them seemed to be listening. Small wonder that he felt tired and depressed.

I

In more normal times King would have been delighted with the federal budget for 1937 because it seemed to provide convincing evidence that the Canadian economy was responding to sound and orthodox fiscal policies. Charles Dunning pointed with pride in his budget speech in February to the marked improvement over the past year and argued that most of the economic indicators showed that the worst of the depression was over. Even farm revenue had increased; farm production was down because of the drought on the prairies in 1936 but higher prices for farm products had more than compensated for the decline in production. The construction industry was still depressed and unemployment was still high but, as Dunning explained, there was certain to be improvement in these areas as the economic recovery gained momentum. His survey of the past year led him to the optimistic conclusion "that since 1929 no New Year has dawned with brighter promise for Canada."[3] He even considered it necessary to sound a warning about the dangers of irresponsible optimism and excessive speculation.

This economic recovery could also be seen in the improved financial position of the government. Relief expenditures were still high because of the continuing unemployment and the government railway again had a large deficit, largely because of the reduced crops on the prairies. Government revenues had increased, however, because the greater economic activity had produced higher tax returns. A year before Dunning had forecast a deficit of one hundred million dollars; he could now report an actual deficit of less than ninety millions. He modestly admitted that Canada had benefitted from economic recovery abroad but also gave the government some credit: by rigidly controlling its expenditures the federal government had facilitated the recovery in the private sector.

For Charles Dunning and for Mackenzie King this analysis led to a logical conclusion. If the government maintained its policy of retrenchment, economic conditions would continue to improve. Government revenues presented no difficulties; even without any increase in the rates of taxation Dunning estimated that revenues would increase by some thirty millions. It was logical to assume that relief expenditures and the railway deficit would decline. If other expenditures could be held down the government would come close to its objective of a balanced budget.

This confident forecast, however, concealed an emerging dissatisfaction within the government. Both King and Dunning had been surprised and even shocked to discover that some of their colleagues were less than enthusiastic. The other Ministers still paid lip-service to the idea of a balanced budget but most of them had submitted increased estimates for their own departments. The pattern was familiar—ministers usually wanted more money—but this time they had been more intransigent than usual, insisting on the special needs or the special opportunities for government action within their area of responsibility. After two years of holding the line the Ministers were responding to the pressures for more positive government measures. The prolonged discussion on departmental estimates had shown that many Ministers favoured a more interventionist role for the government even if it meant an unbalanced budget.

King had shown no sympathy for this attitude. He still believed that a balanced budget was the major instrument of economic recovery and he could only conclude that his colleagues had become so accustomed to government deficits that their moral fibre had been weakened: "The truth is," he commented, "the Ministers have lost all sense of responsibility to the tax-payer, and are thinking only of making a showing in their particular fields, with public monies. All have got into the habit of yielding to pressure, and particularly with unemployment, doing the thing that is likely to help some Province."[4] It was all very disillusioning but for King his duty was clear. He had challenged the proposed increases in departmental estimates item by item and although it had been distasteful and unpleasant he found some satisfaction in the results. He calculated that in three days of acrimonious debate he had managed "to save the public treasury between five and seven millions of dollars" by reducing the estimates.[5]

Dunning made no reference to these difficulties in his budget speech late in February. He proudly announced a reduction of some twenty millions in the estimated expenditures for the coming year—the expected decrease in relief costs and the railway deficit would more than balance the estimated increase of ten millions in ordinary expenditures. This reduction in expenditures combined with the expected increase in revenues would mean a probable deficit of only thirty-five million dollars. Dunning took some pride in this achievement but made it clear that he hoped to do even better in the future. "If we can attain this objective in 1937–38, I am confident that it should not be beyond our powers to wipe out the deficit altogether during the following year and begin the period when progress can be made in liquidating the accumulated deficits which have been funded during the depression. This is the goal which we must steadily keep in sight."[6]

The budget debate in the House of Commons did nothing to shake Dunning's or King's confidence in their orthodox fiscal policy. R. B. Bennett's amendment did regret "that the government has failed to take effective measures to deal with the problem of employment,"[7] but this could be interpreted as a political manoeuvre, since this was the same budget amendment which the Liberals had moved when they were in opposition. Bennett, in his speech, implicitly criticized the government for doing too much rather than too little. He deplored the magnitude of the proposed deficit and went on to deplore the high level of taxation: "It is my firm conviction," he declared, "that any effort to raise from the Canadian people by taxation any substantial sum in excess of $400,000,000 is to put upon them a strain which they cannot bear."[8] If taxes were too high and the deficit too large, Bennett presumably favoured an even more rigid policy of government retrenchment.

The C.C.F. and Social Credit members were less committed to fiscal

189

orthodoxy but even they did not directly challenge the goal of a balanced budget. They merely criticized the government for not doing more without discussing how to pay for the expanded services or, in the case of the Social Credit members, by arguing that the printing press could solve this problem.

The debate did show, however, that federal policies, successful as they might have been in reducing the deficit, had done little to reduce regional divisions. One Conservative backbencher from Ontario bluntly argued that central Canada was being exploited by an improvident west: "How long," he asked, "are Ontario and Quebec going to remain a pair of placid milch cows to be stripped dry to pay the bills of provincial governments over whose expenditures they have no control?"[9] Western members were quick to reply that these two milch cows had grown fat from a tariff which had poured western wealth to the industrial centres of the east.[10] Sound fiscal administration had not eliminated regional animosities.

The other major debate of the session came on defence expenditures, which were to be increased from twenty millions in 1936 to thirty-six millions in 1937. King knew that there would be strong opposition within the caucus on this measure even though his Cabinet colleagues had already been convinced. He "thought it best to anticipate discussion" so he had opened the proceedings of the first Liberal caucus of the session by a one-hour appeal for party unity on this issue. He admitted that he had no liking for a policy of rearmament but nor did he like what was happening in Europe. The government must accept the necessity of some defence expenditures while rejecting the other extreme of a commitment to Imperial defence: "the defence of our shores and the preservation of our neutrality—these are the two cardinal principles of our policy." When some western Liberals still expressed their misgivings, King pointed out that Bennett and Arthur Meighen were already criticizing the government for not spending enough on defence. A surprisingly docile caucus raised no further objections.[11]

This apparent agreement was short-lived. In the Canada of 1937 there was deep-rooted opposition to militarism in any form; in the House the C.C.F. appealed to this popular sentiment by denouncing the policy of spending more money on armaments. Other Canadians, however, favoured increased defence expenditures as a contribution to Imperial defence, an attitude reinforced by the major increases in the British defence budget and the criticism by Churchill and others that even this was not enough. In the Canadian defence debate, however, this viewpoint was not presented; the Conservatives kept strangely silent. The result was that the Liberal party was placed in the invidious position of being the only

party to support rearmament. Some Liberals who shared the popular aversion to defence expenditures found this so embarrassing that they insisted on expressing their personal sentiments even if it meant disagreeing publicly with government policy.

The opposition to rearmament had many roots. The idealism of the First World War—the war to end wars—had been dissipated by the obvious failure of the war to establish a lasting peace and by the revisionist criticisms of the Treaty of Versailles, which argued that the victors had despoiled the vanquished. Nor was it easy to be enthusiastic about defence expenditures in a world where the major confrontation seemed to be between fascism and communism. Many Canadians were tempted to isolate themselves from foreign disputes and to focus attention on the pressing domestic problems created by the depression. Geography supplied a powerful argument for this isolationist sentiment. Even if expenditures were really for defence and not for participation in foreign wars, on what grounds could they be justified? Against what enemy was Canada defending itself? The United States was no threat and there was no danger of invasion from abroad. The government, as one critic commented acidly, seemed to think "that Canada is in the Balkans instead of North America."[12] If Canada was in no danger of attack what purpose lay behind the increased defence estimates, Was the government already secretly committed to participation in a European war? Even if there was no commitment, a Canada that was prepared for war ran the risk of being drawn step by step into a European holocaust. In the Canada of 1937 to advocate rearmament seemed almost to favour war.

One illustration of this fear of rearmament was the deep hostility to the munitions industry. In the United States armament manufacturers had been accused of encouraging wars and had been blamed for bringing the United States into the First World War. Books with such titles as *Merchants of Death* and *Iron, Blood and Profits* had popularized this view of their evil machinations.[13] A Senate Committee under Gerald Nye had put its official stamp on this interpretation in 1934 and had warned that while peace-loving Americans talked of neutrality, unscrupulous arms manufacturers and international bankers were already filling foreign orders for munitions and establishing vested interests which might once more push the United States into war. The committee had concluded that the most effective safeguard was to eliminate the possibility of profits by prohibiting the export of munitions to any country at war. Popular sentiment was so strong that even President Roosevelt's objections had been over-ruled by Congress and the Neutrality Act of 1935 had made this embargo mandatory as soon as war was declared.

The fear that a munitions industry would increase the risk of being involved in war was not confined to the United States. Mackenzie King himself, as long ago as 1928, had flatly refused to have two new destroyers for the Canadian Navy built in a Canadian shipyard, arguing that he would "never permit my name to be associated with planting a canker of the kind in the side of our young nation."[14] In 1935 he still believed that nations must "above all else, expose what lies at the base of the hideous traffic in the paraphernalia of war."[15] King had eased his own conscience by the argument that the increased defence expenditures would not require the construction of large munitions plants[16] but other Canadians were less easily reassured. He did suggest to Ian Mackenzie, the Minister of National Defence, that legislation to control profits on munitions would make the estimates "more palatable" but a committee which studied the proposal could not suggest any effective regulations.[17] Mackenzie King could only offer the House the unconvincing assurance that the government would do everything possible to safeguard the public interest.[18]

This conspiratorial view of munitions makers shows how fearful many North Americans were of being involved in some foreign war against their will. Canadians, however, had an even more compelling reason to fear involvement. Canada was a member of the British Commonwealth. Did the defence appropriations imply a commitment to Great Britain to stand at Britain's side in case of war? The C.C.F. critics of the defence estimates stressed this possibility. Even before the estimates were tabled J. S. Woodsworth had moved that "in the event of war Canada should remain strictly neutral regardless of who the belligerents may be." His party, he explained, believed that all wars were capitalist wars, the inevitable result of economic competition and class conflicts. And Woodsworth underlined the point that British wars were no exception; the British government was as capitalistic and as imperialistic as any other great power.[19] During the defence debate the C.C.F. spokesmen were even more forthright. They quoted recent statements of British politicians to the effect that Britain could rely on the co-operation of the Commonwealth. It was surely more than a coincidence that the Canadian Government had followed up these statements by announcing increases in its defence expenditures. The obvious inference was that the Canadian Government was secretly committed to military support for Great Britain.[20]

The most remarkable feature of the debate on the defence estimates was that no speaker in the House spoke in favour of Commonwealth co-operation. Arthur Meighen, in the Senate, did argue that the defence of Canadian territory was not enough, that Britain was Canada's first line of defence, and that Canada could best defend itself by fighting at Britain's side.[21] Bennett certainly shared this view and he might have been expected to make at least some reference to Commonwealth obligations. He and his followers, however, maintained an unexpected silence; not one Conservative member participated in the defence debate.

Bennett did not find it easy to justify his silence. Earlier in the session he had lamely argued that "the foreign policy of this country is so obvious that it does not require much discussion"[22] and had followed this up later in the session by the equally surprising statement that "the government was best able to determine what was desirable in the public interest with respect to defence."[23] It was a tacit admission that increased defence expenditures were unpopular and that rather than support them the path of political wisdom was to say nothing. Abstention also offered a tactical advantage. It was no secret that many Liberals were unhappy about the increased estimates. Opposition speeches in favour of a Commonwealth defence policy would make it easier for the dissident Liberals to support the government's more limited Canadian defence policy; silence might force the Liberal divisions into the open.

Bennett's tactics did embarrass the government. King had welcomed the C.C.F. motion opposing the increase in the estimates because it went on to suggest that the money would be better spent on social security for Canadians. This could easily be interpreted as advocating socialism and even Liberals who regretted spending more money on defence could use this argument to justify voting against the amendment. When the opposition was confined to a criticism of the increased expenditures, however, many Liberals felt impelled to announce that they too had serious misgivings. As J. T. Thorson of Manitoba explained, "it would be a mistake to let it be assumed either in Canada or elsewhere that the Liberal party is united on the question for such is not the case."[24]

The most notable effect of the Conservative silence was the active participation of French-Canadian Liberals in the debate. French-Canadian backbenchers did not often feel the need to express their personal views on major government measures and were usually content to allow the French-Canadian Ministers to speak for them on national issues.[25] On this occasion, however, the issue roused apprehensions in French Canada which the Quebec members could not ignore. "French Canada," King noted, "thinks there is some conspiracy to have Canada drawn into Imperial wars."[26] With no Conservative arguments to counterbalance the C.C.F. criticisms the debate threatened to identify the Liberal party with this conspiracy. Sixteen French-Canadian Liberals felt compelled to explain their personal point of view. Most of them stressed that the defence expenditures were for the defence of Canada only, in order to justify their support for the revised estimates, and went on to express confidence in their party leaders. Four of them, however, said bluntly that they were opposed to any increase in the defence estimates.[27]

Mackenzie King deplored this public exposure of the division within the party. He and Lapointe defended the government's policy in caucus once again and appealed to the members to end "the kind of thing which has been going on in the past two days."[28] Then, late in February, on the last day of the debate King himself addressed the House. He did his best to reassure those who feared any Imperial commitments: "There will be no participation by Canada in a war overseas," he declared, "except by the consent of our own parliament." The proposed expenditures were necessary for the defence of Canada: "what we are doing we are doing for Canada alone." But King, eager as he was to reassure the party dissidents, would not commit himself to a policy of armed neutrality. The defence of Canada could also be seen as a contribution to the defence of the Commonwealth and "towards the defence of all those countries that may some day necessarily associate themselves together for the purpose of preserving their liberties and freedom against an aggressor."[29] It was a precarious balancing act but King would certainly have agreed with the comment of one observer that it was also "statesmanship honestly striving for national unity."[30]

The vote on the C.C.F. amendment came almost as an anticlimax. Even the Liberals who had criticized the estimates closed ranks and voted with the government; they might regret the policy but they still had confidence in the party leaders. The Conservatives too voted solidly against the amendment.* King was tremendously relieved: "I confess," he recorded, "I felt a feeling of genuine pride when I saw that large following standing as one on what threatened to be the most dangerous of all divisions of the session. One thing is certain, the right course has been steered, just enough has been done and not too much. We have kept the unity of the party, and the unity of the country which, after all, is the important thing."[31] But he also knew that the fundamental differences had not been resolved. The defence estimates had passed but the country and even the party were still far from a consensus on defence policy.

II

Mackenzie King found the session more tiring than usual. Under other circumstances he might have been encouraged by the passing of the bud-

*The final vote was 191 against and 17 for the amendment. Three Social Credit members voted with the C.C.F. *Can. H. of C. Debates*, Feb. 19, 1937, p. 1073.

get and the defence estimates but in 1937 he did not have his usual optimism and resilience. He complained about his colleagues, who expected him to make all the decisions and who, when King talked of taking a holiday, "were most unresponsive and seemed distressed at the thought of my not being in Council."[32] The feeling of being overworked and the constant strain of meeting Cabinet and caucus, however, were nothing new. What was new was that western Canada seemed to have become more radical and that even western Liberals no longer seemed prepared to defend national policies or liberal principles. King found himself forced to temporize, to give way to pressures, to make concessions which were inconsistent with his views of sound administration but which seemed necessary to prevent an even more serious western revolt. What did the future hold when even western Canada, so long a fortress of Liberalism, seemed to favour a confrontation with eastern Canada?

Western unrest focussed on the problem of debt. Aberhart had dealt with the provincial debt by defauting on some bond issues and by arbitrarily reducing the interest rate on all provincial bonds. Western farmers, however, were in worse financial difficulties than their provincial governments. Most of them had mortgages on their land but crop failures and low wheat prices meant accumulating arrears of both principal and interest. The depreciated value of farm land meant that in many cases farmers now owed more than their farm was worth. They found themselves going deeper and deeper into debt with no hope of escape. Even if conditions improved any money they received would go to banks and mortgage companies.

There had been some legislation to reduce mortgages. The Farmers' Creditors Arrangement Act, passed by the Bennett government in 1934, had established tribunals which could scale down mortgage debts when a farmer could not meet his payments. The underlying principle of this and similar provincial measures was that the size of the debt should be determined by the debtor's capacity to pay.[33] Many businessmen found even this too radical. Meighen, who had supported the legislation in 1934, concluded a few years later that it encouraged farmers to evade their financial obligations and deprived lenders of their legitimate income: "The law which I supported," he wrote, "is just as wrong as it can be. It has contributed, along with other laws, to the disintegration of debtor morale all through this Dominion. The disintegration of debtor morale means the decay of society, the undermining of civilization."[34]

Westerners were more inclined to believe that banks and mortgage companies, most of them with their headquarters in eastern Canada, were undermining their civilization. Even scaling down mortgages on the basis of the farmers' capacity to pay gave them little relief; they still owed all

195

their savings and their earnings. Aberhart had provided a more attractive solution for Alberta farmers in 1936 with his Reduction and Settlement of Land Debts Act. This legislation retroactively cancelled all the interest owed on mortgages on Alberta farms since 1932; if farmers had already made interest payments that amount was to be deducted from the principal.[35] Even farmers who could afford to pay benefitted from this moratorium. Nor was there any doubt that the majority of Albertans warmly approved of this legislation.[36] As one Liberal explained to King, any federal intervention to protect the rights of the mortgage companies "would undoubtedly precipitate a Provincial Election and Mr. Aberhart would go back stronger than ever."[37]

Mackenzie King had little sympathy for this arbitrary repudiation of debts. He did not react as violently as the *Financial Post* which saw it as "an unprecedented attack on private capital" and had labelled the legislation as communist;[38] he was inclined to put at least some of the blame on the mortgage companies which had refused to lower their interest rates voluntarily.[39] His primary concern, however, was the divisive effect on east-west relations. And yet there seemed no way in which the federal government could intervene. Any federal challenge to Aberhart would only consolidate his popular support. What was needed was some Alberta village Hampden or a William Lyon Mackenzie to rally "the yeomanry of the province" and to win Albertans back to sound liberal principles.[40] In the meantime King could only watch events in Alberta with despair.

But King could not ignore the possibility that the revolt might spread to the other two prairie provinces. If the Liberal governments in Saskatchewan and Manitoba did not follow Aberhart's example they might well be replaced by provincial governments that would. As one observer wrote:

The possibility of Social Credit arising in other Western Provinces . . . is something that every Canadian must consider very carefully. The people of the West are in an angry mood, and they are particularly offended at the Banking and other financial interests. Notwithstanding all the concessions, and all the fairness that has been displayed by individual organizations, there is a deep-rooted feeling that the financial interests have been unduly harsh and, in fact, are in large part responsible for the depression itself. In other words, the people in large numbers are determined to give the financial institutions a trimming.[41]

In an effort to bolster up the provincial Liberal administrations J. G. Gardiner had brought the mortgage companies and the Saskatchewan government together in 1936, and had persuaded the companies to cancel two years of mortgage interest in the drought areas, with the provincial government cancelling tax arrears and relief indebtedness for the same period. The federal contribution to this settlement was the cancellation of some seventeen millions for relief debts. In Manitoba the municipalities had been reluctant to cancel their tax arrears but the mortgage companies did cancel some interest payments and the federal government had cancelled its relief loans.[42] Gardiner could argue that the agreement, by including tax arrears, was more helpful to the farmers than Aberhart's legislation.[43] The federal government, however, had used its assets to help keep the Liberal governments in office.

Mackenzie King faced a more difficult decision when it became clear that the governments of Saskatchewan and Manitoba were bankrupt. In Saskatchewan the provincial revenues were less than the combined costs of relief and the interest payments on its provincial debt. Farm relief in Manitoba was less burdensome but relief in metropolitan Winnipeg was so costly that the Manitoba government was almost as badly off.[44] Should the federal government lend them the money to keep them solvent? It had already refused a loan to Alberta in March 1936. If it reversed its policy now what would become of its hopes of putting its own financial house in order and balancing its budget?

The government had discussed the problem at length in mid-December 1936: "The Cabinet," King recorded, "was practically united in opposition to more loans as simply sending good money after bad money, continuing the error made by Bennett. Dunning seemed to think Canadian credit would suffer if two provinces defaulted. Others, including myself, were of the opinion that Canada's credit would be strengthened by its being seen through the world that we were ceasing to bolster up impossible positions."[45] Charles Dunning, who had shown so little sympathy for provincial administrations a year before, had now shifted his ground because as Minister of Finance one of his major responsibilities in 1937 would be the refunding of more than three hundred million dollars of federal bonds. He hoped to sell the new issues at 3 per cent instead of the 5 per cent or higher on the maturing issues, for an annual saving of some six million dollars,[46] but much depended on the credit rating of the federal government at the time. He preferred not to have provincial governments defaulting while he was refunding the federal debt. Graham Towers, the Governor of the Bank of Canada, supported him; provincial loans of two million dollars might "tide over the situation," he suggested to King, and ensure a low rate of interest on the federal bond issues.[47]

Mackenzie King was still reluctant. The pressure from his financial advisers was reinforced by the pressure from western Liberals who still feared a shift to Social Credit if the provincial Liberal governments got no federal support. King knew that to yield would be an admission that his approach to financial relations with the provinces had failed. The federal government would once again be lending money to cover provincial deficits without any effective control over provincial finances. And yet to hold firm might deepen the division between east and west. He finally gave way in January 1937, after a series of discussions with his colleagues:

> The Cabinet was fairly evenly divided on the matter of allowing Saskatchewan and Manitoba to go into default. . . . I felt it would be too great a risk at this time when we have vast refunding operations on war debt account, and when the world is in the disturbed condition it is, and when unrest in Canada might assume alarming proportions at any time. Also I think it would be unfortunate to have repudiation become general throughout the West, and there is no saying where it might end . . . This has been the most difficult decision which I have had to make this year. It was clearly up to me and I took the step which I believe was wisest, everything considered.[48]

Mackenzie King was right in thinking that the decision was of major significance. He knew that the special subsidy to Saskatchewan and Manitoba was only a stop-gap measure and not a solution to the problem of federal-provincial financial relations. But he also recognized that the decision was a tacit admission that the attempt to restore order to federal finances by insulating the federal budget from the financial problems of the provinces had failed. Dunning's proposed Loan Councils had proved unacceptable and now the alternative of allowing provincial governments to default had been rejected. King had not yet faced the full implications of these developments. His primary objective was still to balance the federal budget and he was reluctant to admit that the financial plight of the provincial governments was also a federal problem. Gradually, however, he was being forced to realize that his government could not isolate itself from the problems of provincial administrations.

Dunning was less flexible than King. He was prepared to lend money to Manitoba and Saskatchewan until his refunding operations were completed but he still believed that in the long run provincial governments could balance their own budgets. In December 1936 he had convoked a meeting with the provincial Premiers to discuss financial problems. His proposed agenda had reflected his conviction that waste and extravagance were to blame for many of the financial difficulties of governments and that administrative efficiency was the solution.[49] The Premiers at the three-day conference virtuously approved of co-operation and efficiency but they also asked for more money.[50] As an exasperated Dunning later reported to the House of Commons: "There was only one approach to problem after problem; 'Will the dominion give the province this, that or the other in a financial way?' or, 'Will the dominion yield up to the provinces this, that or the other source of revenue which it now enjoys?' "[51] Until Dunning admitted that provincial deficits could not be blamed on extravagance and that federal finances could not be isolated from provincial finances, his advice to King would be of little help.

Gardiner had a simple answer. He suggested an increase in the annual federal subsidies to the prairie provinces. The federal government had increased its subsidies to the Maritime provinces in 1927 and Gardiner had argued then and still argued that another three million dollars per year to the prairie provinces was justified.[52] King knew, however, that this was politically unacceptable. Other provinces also had financial problems and would resent any special concession to the prairies. Dufferin Pattullo, for example, had already demanded "better terms" for British Columbia and had protested bitterly at King's procrastination.[53]

Provincial finances were only one side of the coin. Provincial revenues could hardly be discussed without referring to provincial responsibilities and this in turn would raise the broader issue of the distribution of powers between federal and provincial governments. Bennett had raised this question in the House in January by arguing that the present constitution had become unworkable and by proposing a constitutional convention to change it.[54] There was little support for the idea of a constitutional convention but there was general agreement in the House that the constitution needed to be amended.[55] Then, later in January, the Judicial Committee of the Privy Council published its judgments on Bennett's New Deal legislation. The Natural Products Marketing Act, the Employment and Social Insurance Act, and all the labour legislation were declared *ultra vires*. King could take some satisfaction from the fact that he had been right and Bennett had been wrong about the constitutionality of the New Deal but even he realized that the Privy Council decisions would make it more difficult for the federal government to initiate social reforms in the future.[56] M. J. Coldwell, speaking for the more ardent reformers, went farther and argued that they created "something of a national emergency in relation to the whole question of social and economic legislation."[57]

King had already been considering a Royal Commission on federal-provincial financial relations. He knew a commission would be interpreted as an evasion of responsibility but it would have the advantage of taking the question out of the political arena for a year or so and of educating Canadians on the constitutional problems. He had been encouraged when the prairie and Maritime Premiers had favoured the idea in December, during their meeting with Dunning, and when Quebec had expressed no objections.[58] Pattullo had objected because he wanted a special commission for British Columbia and feared that a wider study would delay the "better terms" he expected.[59] Ernest Lapointe had also been dubious because he feared that Duplessis would greet it as yet further proof that the federal government had no respect for provincial autonomy. The grant to Saskatchewan and Manitoba, however, was the deciding factor for King. When in mid-February a Bank of Canada study confirmed that the two provinces could not avoid repudiation without federal assistance, King recorded that Cabinet "decided, inside of half an hour, that we would have a Royal Commission investigate financial relations of the Provinces and assist Manitoba and Saskatchewan pending the report."[60]

King announced the decision to the House of Commons the same afternoon. At this stage he knew that the financial relations between the federal and provincial governments were of crucial importance but he saw the commission as no more than a preliminary step in what would be a prolonged process. He thought of it as a fact-finding body which would organize the data on government revenues and expenditures and suggest how these might be redistributed to allow each level of government to balance its own budget independently. He foresaw that the real difficulties would begin after the commission had reported and the various governments would have to be persuaded to agree on the necessary constitutional amendments.[61] He recognized, however, that the terms of reference for the commission would have to be very broad just to assemble the data.[62] But King was finding the pressures of the session so exhausting that he postponed the detailed consideration of the mandate and the personnel of the commission until after the House had prorogued.

III

In the spring of 1937 the alienation of western Canada, serious as it was, received less attention because of a new threat to national unity. Mitchell Hepburn, the ebullient and erratic Premier of Ontario, was in political trouble and blamed the federal government for many of his difficulties. It was not surprising that some federal policies were resented at Queen's Park—every provincial government had some grievances. Hepburn, however, seemed to be looking for trouble. For King this was doubly disturbing. A confrontation with Ontario, the most populous province, would be a threat to national unity; a confrontation with the Liberal leader in Ontario would shatter the unity of the Liberal party. King recognized the need for caution and circumspection.

Ontario had been less affected by the depression than western Canada. Ontario farmers had suffered from the drastic decline in the prices of farm products but rainfall had been close to normal and they still had feed for their poultry and livestock. There was unemployment in the industrial cities but many factories were still operating, even if on a reduced scale. In northern Ontario the pulp and paper industry was recovering from the disastrous price-cutting of a few years before and the mining industry was actually enjoying a period of major expansion.[63] It was easy for Hepburn to believe that if Ontario was left to its own resources it could cope with the depression and even prosper. It was tempting to be critical of a federal government which took money from Ontario taxpayers and used it to subsidize western Canada.

King found it difficult to deal with Hepburn because the Ontario Premier seemed so unpredictable. He might at any time interpret a disagreement with the federal government as a personal insult and retaliate with little heed for the consequences. In the spring of 1936, for example, he, like the other provincial Premiers, had resented the federal decision to reduce the relief grants to the provinces. Hepburn, however, had reacted petulantly. He had boycotted the annual meeting of the National Liberal Federation that year and had informed Norman Lambert, the National Secretary, that in future the Ontario Liberal party would have nothing to do with the federal party. "It will be our intention," he wrote, "and I make this very clear, to keep our organization separate and apart from yours."[64] Lambert was naturally very disturbed; the federal Liberal party was really a federation of provincial organizations and Ontario was not only the largest province but also the major source of party funds. Mackenzie King, however, refused to intervene.[65] He knew how damaging the split in the party could be but did not believe that a direct appeal to Hepburn would have any effect.[66] It seemed wiser to ignore this provocative gesture.

In the spring of 1937 the question of the St. Lawrence waterway threatened to complicate relations even further. Hepburn was still deeply embroiled in his dispute with the Quebec power companies. He had repudiated the power contracts but his provincial legislation was being challenged in the courts. Even more embarrassing was a report from Ontario Hydro early in 1937 that the increasing demand for power in Ontario could soon lead to a serious power shortage.[67] The ideal solution from Hepburn's point of view would be to increase power generated at Niagara. It would be possible to increase the flow at Niagara by damming rivers flowing into James Bay and diverting the water south into the Great Lakes, a project known as the Ogoki and Long Lac diversion. The existing Hydro installations could then generate the additional power

Ontario would need without having to rely on Quebec power. The only problem was that the United States would have to agree that Ontario would be entitled to all the power resulting from the additional flow at Niagara. Franklin Roosevelt had not been enthusiastic when the question had been raised in 1936. He wanted a St. Lawrence waterway and had insisted that any changes in the international agreement at Niagara would have to be linked to this larger project.[68] Hepburn, however, was not interested in a seaway which would produce far more power than Ontario could use. If King could not persuade Roosevelt to change his mind, Hepburn might well blame him for Ontario's power problems.

This issue was raised in February 1937 when Roosevelt invited King to come to Washington and suggested that the St. Lawrence waterway should be one item on the agenda.[69] King was flattered by the invitation and he also saw it as an opportunity to escape from Ottawa during the session and take a holiday. But there must be no risk of provoking Hepburn. Skelton had already told American officials that Ontario Hydro experts now estimated that the province would need the power from the St. Lawrence waterway within a decade but he had also warned them that Hepburn had not yet been convinced that the waterway was necessary; even if he decided in favour of the project it would be more from a "desire to be independent of Beauharnois than a statesmanlike desire to meet expected power shortage."[70] As a further precaution Mackenzie King made a special trip to Toronto to see Hepburn before going to Washington.

King was very careful to explain to Hepburn that the federal government "was not specially interested in the St. Lawrence waterway; that our only interest was one that had come to us from Roosevelt's desire to have the matter considered and the Ontario government's desire to have it considered." It was a great relief to hear Hepburn say that he wanted no discussion of the waterway for the moment. He agreed that some arrangement with the United States would be necessary either on the Long Lac diversion or the seaway but nothing could be done until the dispute over the Quebec power contracts was resolved. He also confided that he was planning an early election which was yet another reason for delay. King assured him that there would be no discussions with Washington until Ontario was ready.[71]

Hepburn was surprisingly cordial during King's visit. He introduced King to his wife and his two adopted children, suggested that King take a seat on the floor of the legislature, and invited photographers into his office to publicize the meeting of the two Liberal leaders. King was careful not to disrupt the friendly atmosphere. There were no references to party organization or federal financial policies; when Hepburn boasted that his budget would show "a surplus of several millions and afford reduction of taxation," King complimented him and resisted the temptation to point out that the surplus was made possible by the federal relief grants. Hepburn seemed pleased that King had come and King could hope that the visit would help to improve their relations.[72]

When King arrived in Washington early in March Franklin Roosevelt created no difficulties over the seaway. King frankly explained that he intended to do nothing without the co-operation of Ontario and outlined Hepburn's reasons for postponing any discussions. Roosevelt assured King that he understood the situation. Even from his point of view there was no urgency. Congress already had all the legislation it could handle and it would be better to leave the treaty over until the next session.[73]

IV

The visit to Washington nonetheless required a concentration which the exhausted King found difficult to maintain. It was no secret that the American Government hoped to negotiate a trade agreement with Great Britain and the timing of Roosevelt's invitation, before King's departure for the coronation and the Imperial Conference, left little doubt that Washington hoped to persuade King to use his influence in London to facilitate the negotiations. King strongly favoured closer trade relations between Britain and the United States but he had to be circumspect. An Anglo-American trade agreement might depend on reducing the Imperial preference for some Canadian exports to Britain and King was not prepared to promise concessions without careful consideration.

A preliminary interview with Cordell Hull caused him no embarrassment because the Secretary of State never got beyond generalities about the need to lower the barriers to international trade and "the question of negotiations with Great Britain," to King's great relief, "was never so much as mentioned." Indeed, at the end of the interview, according to King: "Mr. Hull apologized for having done all the talking and keeping me listening for over an hour. This happily was what I could most have wished as it did not draw me into commitments of any kind, or, for that matter, into any expression of opinion."[74] Hull's record of the interview, however, makes it clear that he expected King to get the message. "Knowing that he was going to London, where he had considerable influence with the British government," Hull wrote, "I made an earnest plea with him which I felt might have some effect in the United Kingdom."[75]

Roosevelt gave King more opportunity to express his opinions. The President had invited King to spend the night at the White House and the two men chatted from five o'clock until midnight and then met again briefly after breakfast the next morning. Again, however, the discussion was very general. They talked about the abdication, the Neutrality Laws, and Roosevelt's decision to enlarge the Supreme Court. Much of their time was devoted to the European situation, with Roosevelt speculating about sponsoring an international conference and with King trying to outline the advantages of a permanent international body—a league of all nations —to discuss social and economic problems. King was so enthused by the idea and so encouraged by Roosevelt's apparent interest that he later sent him an outline of the proposal.[76]

The White House visit ended with King feeling that he had handled the situation very well. He had encouraged closer American ties with Europe and with Britain without promising anything more than moral support. Roosevelt and Hull were probably equally pleased. Hull was sure "that Mackenzie King would faithfully interpret to the British government what I had said."[77] Roosevelt had more tangible evidence of this; King in his note to the President spoke of promoting fuller understanding between the United States and Great Britain by presenting "a North American background" at the Imperial Conference.[78]

King stayed on in the United States for a two-week holiday even though the House was still in session. He felt desperately tired and quite unprepared to face the political problems at home. He was worried enough about his condition to see his doctor in Baltimore, where he complained of lack of energy and fatigue, but was told that, apart from having put on some of the weight he had lost two years before, he was "in the best possible physical condition" for a man of sixty-two.[79] He regretted his initial decision to go to New York because this meant meeting people and being sociable but when he moved to a Virginia resort he found it depressing to be alone. He came back to Ottawa "in a very unsettled and still depressed state" and not at all encouraged by the "wintry, raw, cold March weather."[80] His only consolation was that he would have felt even worse if he had not taken a holiday.

V

There would be no rest in Ottawa. During his visit to the United States King had heard a great deal of talk of John L. Lewis and the militant Congress of Industrial Organizations. Lewis and some other labour leaders had concluded that the traditional craft unions were outmoded in an industrial society and advocated the organization of workers by industry rather than by craft. The arguments were often couched in the rhetoric of the class struggle but the industrial unions in 1937 went beyond rhetoric. The United Auto Workers had defied the law as well as defying General Motors with their occupation of the Flint plant in a sit-down strike. Nor did this trade-union militancy stop at the Canadian border. There were sit-down strikes in small factories in Sarnia and Kitchener early in March and the United Auto Workers had been signing up workers and now claimed the right to negotiate the contract at the General Motors plant in Oshawa.

Mackenzie King, who considered himself a friend of organized labour, was repelled by the radical rhetoric and shocked by the illegal tactics of the C.I.O. Lewis, he suspected, was "aiming at political control as well as industrial control by the workers of America."[81] He foresaw trouble in Canada too. "An emissary of Lewis is at Oshawa to foment trouble there," he commented in his diary on March 23rd, two days after his return to Ottawa. "Canada's only salvation in this matter is to compel respect for law & do it promptly."[82] To make the government's position clear he arranged for a question in the House the next day which gave Ernest Lapointe, as Minister of Justice, the opportunity to announce that sit-down strikes were illegal in Canada and would not be tolerated.[83] But King was careful not to criticize the C.I.O. directly. He recognized the right of workers to join the union of their choice, even if the choice seemed to him to be regrettable, and the right of the union to call a strike as long as it kept within the law. King had not forgotten that the law protected workers as well as employers.

Mitchell Hepburn had also announced that sit-down strikes were illegal. But Hepburn did not stop there. Unlike King he showed little respect for the legal rights of the workers. Even before a strike had been called he announced his opposition to the C.I.O. and denounced "the professional agitators from the United States" who were trying to introduce the serpent of industrial unrest into the peaceful garden of Ontario.[84] When the Oshawa workers went on strike early in April it made no difference to Hepburn that there was no violence and that the General Motors plant had not been occupied. He announced that "the time for a showdown" had come.[85]

Hepburn's attitude can be explained in part by his background. His roots were in rural rather than industrial Ontario; he had little understanding of the importance of collective bargaining for workers and little sympathy for urban wage-earners who seemed well paid for eight hours of work. But this does not account for the violence of his reaction. Hepburn, by 1937, had developed political and personal commitments which convinced him that industrial unionism was a destructive force.

Hepburn saw northern development as the instrument of economic recovery for the province. Ontario Premiers, Conservative and Liberal, had long encouraged the exploitation of the province's natural resources; the party in office issued leases or sold the mineral rights to entrepreneurs who in turn created jobs and might even contribute to the party's campaign fund. In the case of Hepburn this political partnership was strengthened by his personal friendship with the lumbermen and mining magnates of Ontario. He had never been at ease with the established businessmen and professionals of the province but he enjoyed the company of the flamboyant and wealthy entrepreneurs of the new frontier. Men like George McCullagh, Sir James Dunn, and J. L. Timmins became his companions as well as his political associates[86] and strengthened his belief that what was good for northern development was good for the province.

Industrial unionism seemed a threat to northern development because the C.I.O. was active in the mining as well as in the automobile industry. If the Oshawa strike succeeded it would not be long before C.I.O. organizers would disrupt industrial relations in northern Ontario. Mackenzie King, watching developments apprehensively from Ottawa, understood the situation only too clearly. "The truth of the matter," he commented in his diary, "is that he [Hepburn] is in the hands of McCullagh of the Globe, and the Globe and McCullagh, in the hands of financial mining interests that want to crush the C.I.O. and their organization in Ontario."[87]

Hepburn's strategy was to transform an industrial dispute at Oshawa into a crusade against destructive alien forces, doubly damnable because they were being brought to Ontario by agitators who were both Americans and communists. He recruited four hundred special constables—known as Hepburn's Hussars—for the violence that never came. Men who questioned his actions were promptly denounced as C.I.O. sympathizers; he assembled reporters in his office one morning to hear him dictating a letter to his colleagues David Croll and Arthur Roebuck, demanding their resignation because they were not supporting him in his "fight against the forces of John L. Lewis and of Communism." He also imposed himself as a conciliator during the strike but refused to meet the union negotiators because they were American citizens; he even broke off discussions with the Canadian union representatives at one stage because they were in contact with the United Auto Workers' headquarters in Detroit.[88]

Hepburn had to be satisfied with an equivocal victory. The strike, which lasted sixteen days, ended on April 23rd. The new contract conceded higher wages but it did not formally recognize any affiliation with the United Auto Workers. The workers might think of their union as a U.A.W. local but technically, at least, Hepburn had kept the C.I.O. out of Canada. Politically, however, the results were more conclusive. Hepburn's emotional crusade against foreign agitators and communists won widespread popular support in Ontario. His stand was applauded by businessmen, newspapers, priests, and Protestant clergymen, and even by some labour leaders. The Conservatives in Ontario were split by the controversy. George Drew, the provincial organizer, had advocated a coalition with Hepburn to fight the common enemy of communism and had resigned when his advice was rejected. Earl Rowe, the provincial leader, had not supported Hepburn but neither had he supported industrial unionism. Hepburn's position in Ontario seemed unassailable.[89]

Mackenzie King had watched these developments with a sense of impending disaster. He was horrified at "the deliberate attempt to identify the Ontario government's action in the Oshawa strike with an effort to suppress Communism" and saw Hepburn as a threat to liberalism and to democracy in Ontario. He had expressed his fears in his diary in mid-April:

In this he [Hepburn] has gone out of his way to raise a great issue in this country, the fearful possibilities of which no one can foresee. . . . The situation as he has brought it into being has all the elements in it that are to be found in the present appalling situation in Spain. Hepburn has become a Fascist leader and has sought to have labour, in its struggle against organized capital, put into the position of being under Communist direction and control. Action of the kind is little short of criminal.[90]

King had never been tempted to support Hepburn in his attacks on the C.I.O. because he held firm to his conviction that labour had legitimate rights and that the principles of collective bargaining should be respected. He had no sympathy for what he saw as the political ambitions of John L. Lewis but this was balanced by his misgivings about the political influence of the mining magnates in Ontario. And King had what Hepburn and many others lacked; he had confidence in the common sense and moderation of Canadian workers. He did not believe in a communist menace. A few weeks after the strike had ended he expressed his personal views during an interview with King George:

He [King George] asked me about Canada, as to whether we had many 'Reds' in our country. I told him that there were not many, that in some of the cities there were groups; that the Catholic Church was very much afraid of Communism, and that I thought many of the politicians, for political reasons were exploiting ideas of Communism to a greater extent than was advisable. I then said that I thought that one of the real dangers today was that of identifying Labour with Communism and Capital with Fascism, and making the struggle between Labour and Capitalism, one between these two ideologies.[91]

King could not control Hepburn but he did at least avoid becoming identified with Hepburn's crusade. "If the Oshawa strikers remain quiet, as I believe they will," he told his colleagues, "the whole thing will react as a boomerang against the Globe and Hepburn." There was still the possibility of a crisis in which he might be forced to intervene but until then "the thing to do was to keep out of the trouble altogether."[92] He tried to be tactful and conciliatory in his relations with Hepburn but he insisted on respecting the legal rights of the workers.

Mitchell Hepburn had created difficulties by demanding federal co-operation. Even before the strike began he had asked the federal government to deport the U.A.W. organizers and was outraged when T. A. Crerar, as Minister of Immigration, had explained that nothing could be done "unless they encourage in Canada any illegal activities."[93] When the strike began Hepburn immediately asked for a detachment of Mounted Police to maintain law and order. King acceded reluctantly but made sure that the commander of the detachment was warned to hold his men discreetly in reserve.[94] A few days later Hepburn asked for more Mounted Police. Lapointe felt that the government was obliged to accede to any such request from provincial authorities but King "told him I thought it would be a great mistake to do so," and arranged for a telegram to be sent to Hepburn explaining that the federal Cabinet would have to discuss the request before any decision could be made.[95] That same day Hepburn took umbrage at the announcement by Norman Rogers, Minister of Labour, that the conciliation services of his department were available if the disputing parties in the strike were interested. Hepburn, who had taken charge of the strike negotiations, was furious. His telegram to King described Rogers' offer as "unwarranted interference" and even "treachery" and concluded that "this action is quite in common with the treatment that this government has received from most of your ministers and in my opinion constitutes an overt act."[96] King tried to placate the irate Hepburn by assuring him that Rogers had no intention of intervening unless both parties requested his services as a conciliator,[97] but King's tact had its limits. He was convinced that a second detachment of Mounted Police would be interpreted as support for Hepburn against the strikers and persuaded his colleagues to refuse the request, justifying the refusal to Hepburn by explaining that the R.C.M.P. had no men to spare.[98]

This refusal was the last straw for Hepburn. He drafted a scathing reply which explained that "in view of the vacillating attitude taken by your Government . . . we have decided to depend no longer on Federal aid"[99] and, in a typical gesture, gave a copy to the press before the message reached Ottawa. King learned the contents of the telegram from a journalist while on his way to Cabinet meeting. He immediately saw this as an opportunity to extricate the federal forces completely: "I said nothing," he recorded, "but felt immensely relieved, and pleased at this circumstance. When in Council, I dealt at once with the strike situation and we all agreed that as soon as Hepburn's wire was received Lapointe should reply stating that the police would be immediately withdrawn. The wire came in about four and this course was taken."[100]

Hepburn did not overlook personal differences. He was convinced that he had won a decisive political victory by his settlement of the strike but he would not forgive King for having refused to join in his crusade. Early in June, six weeks after the strike ended he took the opportunity of a banquet at the Royal York hotel to express his feelings publicly. He was going to make a serious statement, he announced, "one that will probably make a headline. I am a Reformer. But I am not a Mackenzie King Liberal any longer. I will tell the world that and I hope he hears me."[101] The news travelled quickly. By then King was in London at the Imperial Conference but he got the message the next day. He commented in his diary that Hepburn would eventually destroy himself but that he would cause a lot of trouble in the process.[102] It was a remarkably calm reaction to the news that the Liberal leader of the most populous province in Canada was now in open revolt against the federal Liberal leader.

CHAPTER TWELVE

A FORAY INTO EUROPEAN DIPLOMACY

MACKENZIE KING left for Europe late in April 1937 almost with a sense of relief. He was leaving his most urgent problems behind and he promised himself that on his return he would devote his full attention to the regional divisions in Canada and to the divisions within the Liberal party itself.[1] Almost unconsciously, however, he saw the coronation and the Imperial Conference as a temporary escape from the frustrations of domestic politics. For ten weeks he would be able to escape from the stress of the bickering within the Cabinet and the provocation of irresponsible provincial Premiers and could concentrate on the less controversial issues of foreign and Commonwealth policies.

King found this an attractive prospect because at least in external affairs he felt he knew what the policy of his government should be. In domestic affairs the objective of national unity was not easily translated into specific policies but in foreign affairs it seemed much simpler; national unity depended on the rejection of any military alliance or even the hint of any commitment to give military aid in case of war. He knew that he would face strong pressures in London to support a common Imperial foreign policy and to co-operate in Imperial defence production, but he also knew that he held the trump cards. Nobody in London would openly challenge the principle of Dominion autonomy and so nobody could force him to make any commitments. Even the embarrassment of appearing to be obstructive would be tempered by the fact that he had just increased Canada's defence expenditures. He could always point out that he had already gone as far as the political situation in Canada would allow.

Mackenzie King also had other reasons for seeing his European visit as a welcome interlude. He enjoyed the larger stage of international diplomacy, of associating with the powerful and famous, of participating in historic events and feeling that he was making a contribution to historic decisions. The coronation might be little more than a mediaeval pageant but King enjoyed his place of honour as Prime Minister of the senior

210

Dominion, and his satisfaction was enhanced by the conviction that he had played some part in placing King George VI on the throne. And in 1937 this public prominence gave King an even deeper personal satisfaction because it was the anniversary of the rebellion in Upper Canada. A hundred years ago his grandfather had been proclaimed a rebel by Queen Victoria. His own role at the coronation was both a justification of his grandfather's struggle for responsible government and a recognition of his own contribution to the cause: "the fulfilment by one generation of the labours of those who preceded it."[2]

I

Mackenzie King was not a pleasant travelling companion. The seven-day voyage on the *Empress of Australia* late in April 1937 was marred by the loss of a despatch-box. It did not matter that the box contained only stationery and London addresses; it was "all part of the lack of efficient organization" of his staff according to King and he was righteously indignant. Journalists sent back light-hearted accounts of Cabinet ministers and secretaries wandering around the ship with harried looks and of rumours about attractive young ladies who were really secret agents of unnamed foreign powers, but King was not amused.[3] He was nervous because he always felt that others were judging him and he wanted to make a good personal impression, especially in England. The lost despatch-box gave him an excuse to relieve his tension by reminding his companions of their incompetence.

Mackenzie King spent seven weeks in London. The coronation itself was an impressive ceremony. King not unnaturally enjoyed the procession from Buckingham Palace to Westminster Abbey and especially the cheers that went up as his carriage, followed by a detachment of Mounted Police, passed the crowds along the route.[4] As a Canadian and as an elected politician he was critical of the precedence given to the titled aristocracy in the coronation ceremony—he would have preferred more awareness of the importance of those commoners who, as Prime Ministers, more adequately represented the people of the Commonwealth—but for him, as for many others, the coronation was nonetheless a very moving ceremony, focussing attention on the diffident monarch with the impediment in his speech who had been called unexpectedly to the throne and who already seemed to be restoring stability and dignity to an institution which only a few months before had been shaken by scandal.[5]

Two days after the coronation the Commonwealth Prime Ministers met to discuss the future of the Commonwealth. In 1937, with the League

211

of Nations discredited and with war in Asia and the possibility of war in Europe, the most important topics on the agenda were inevitably foreign policy and defence. Earlier conferences had established the autonomous status of the Dominions; the issue now was whether these freely-associated nations could plan together for their collective security. To what extent could they agree on a common foreign policy and to what extent could they co-operate for their mutual defence?

Mackenzie King would have the major responsibility for presenting the Canadian position. The Canadian delegation was a large one—it included Ernest Lapointe, Charles Dunning, Ian Mackenzie, and T. A. Crerar, as well as O. D. Skelton and a number of other civil servants—but they were largely involved in special committees on the more peripheral questions of trade and tariffs. The delegation was already agreed on Canada's position on foreign policy and defence; the problem was to ensure that the final wording of the conference report was consistent with this position. King consulted his colleagues regularly on the successive drafts of this report but it was up to him, during the meetings of the Prime Ministers, to explain what Canada would or would not agree to and to insist on changes in the draft when they seemed necessary.

The preliminary documents, circulated before the conference, had shown that the Canadian position would not be popular. The British Government obviously hoped that the Commonwealth would present a common front on foreign policy and would co-operate on Commonwealth defence measures. Australia and New Zealand, conscious of their isolation and fearful of Japanese aggression in the Pacific, had unequivocally supported proposals for Imperial co-operation. Hertzog of South Africa would oppose any formal commitments but he would not play a prominent role, inhibited as he was by the criticisms of South Africa's mandate over the former German colonies in southern Africa. King would not be able to play the role of conciliator as he had at the 1926 conference. This time he would have to reject the demands of Britain and the other Dominions if he wished to avoid commitments that would create difficulties at home.

King's opening statement at the first private session of the Prime Ministers was a lengthy argument against any form of collective security within the Commonwealth. Canada, he explained, was always a difficult country to govern and "the strains and stresses of economic depression and unemployment are today making that task doubly difficult." At this very moment the federal union was being challenged by provincial leaders who were trying "to stretch old powers and assert new ones, to demand federal aid and reject federal control." Any controversy over foreign policy would only exacerbate the existing divisions in Canada. The League of Nations

212

posed no problem, King went on, because the majority of Canadians, whatever their cultural or regional ties, were opposed to a League based on the principle of collective security. The Commonwealth, however, was a different matter.

Many Canadians, King explained, would favour participation "in a conflict in which Britain's interests were seriously at stake":

There would be the strong pull of kinship, the pride in common traditions, the desire to save democratic institutions, the admiration for the stability, the fairness, the independence that characterize English public life, the feeling that a world in which Britain was weakened would be a more chaotic and dangerous world to live in. The influence of trade interests, of campaigns by a part of the press, the legal anomalies of abstention, the appeal of war to adventurous spirits, would make in the same direction.

But this was only one side of the picture:

On the other hand, opposition to participation in war, any war, is growing. It is not believed that Canada itself is in any danger. It is felt that the burdens left by our participation in the last war are largely responsible for present financial difficulties. There is outspoken rejection of the theory that whenever and wherever conflict arises in Europe, Canada can be expected to send armed forces overseas to help solve the quarrels of continental countries about which Canadians know little and which, they feel, know and care less about Canada's difficulties—and particularly if a powerful country like the United States assumes no similar obligations."

King's conclusion was a warning to the other Prime Ministers. They would have to recognize that Canadian participation could not be taken for granted if the rest of the Commonwealth was at war: "Much would depend upon the circumstances of the hour, both abroad and at home—upon the measure of conviction as to the unavoidability of the struggle and the seriousness of the outlook, and upon the measure of unity that has been attained in Canada." To force the issue at this stage, to commit Canada to collective action before the threat to Canadian security was recognized, would only exaggerate the existing divisions and might make future co-operation impossible: "Certain it is that any attempt to reach a decision, or take steps involving a decision, in advance would precipitate a controversy that might destroy national unity without serving any Commonwealth interest, and that the decision given on an abstract issue in advance might be quite different from the decision taken in a concrete situation if war arose."[6]

King's statement of the Canadian position set the stage for the subsequent discussions on foreign policy and defence. Lyons of Australia and

Savage of New Zealand bluntly disagreed. They argued forcefully that if the Commonwealth meant anything, its leaders must be prepared to agree on broad policies and co-operate on defence measures. King constantly assured them that he was as anxious as they were to strengthen the Commonwealth but he was adamant that there would be no commitments which might create controversy and disunity at home. As a last resort he always fell back on the principle of Dominion autonomy; Canadian policy would be decided by the Canadian Government and if other Commonwealth leaders insisted on resolutions favouring a common foreign policy or a common defence policy for the Commonwealth he would have to insist that the final report also include Canada's objections to those resolutions.

Neville Chamberlain who succeeded Stanley Baldwin as British Prime Minister during the conference, emerged as the conciliator. King had associated him with the centralizing Imperial policies of his father, Joseph Chamberlain,[7] but for Neville Chamberlain an open breach within the Commonwealth was unthinkable. When King was intransigent it was often Chamberlain who suggested the anodyne wording which would satisfy him: "Everyone," he said on one occasion, "must recognize the force of what Mackenzie King had said. There was no use making agreements here in London, if they are to cause difficulties in other parts of the Empire. He felt that the Conference would have to be guided by Mackenzie King on the Canadian aspect."[8]

King took full advantage of the situation. At his request the proposed "resolutions" on foreign policy became a "statement" on foreign policy. The initial assertion that the policies of the Dominions would be conducted "in accordance with the principles of the Covenant of the League of Nations" led to a sharp exchange between King, who objected that this might be interpreted as supporting the principle of collective security, and Savage of New Zealand, who refused any further weakening of the statement on League support. Chamberlain adjourned the discussion at this point and eventually placated King by amending the phrase to "desiring to base their policies on the aims and ideals of the League." Savage had to be satisfied with a footnote which explained that this did not prevent some Dominions from advocating more positive support for the League.

King also objected strongly to the reference in the first draft to co-operation "with one another with a view to the preservation of the vital interests of the British Commonwealth." When he pointed out that this might be interpreted as a Canadian undertaking to defend the Suez Canal, Chamberlain produced a revision which referred to "the cause of peace" and the intention of the Dominions "to consult and co-operate with one another in this vital interest and all other matters of common concern."[9] After a week of such revisions King was satisfied. He was sure there was nothing in the final statement which would provoke any controversy at home.

The discussions on Imperial defence followed the same pattern as the discussions on foreign policy. If the British government was to plan for possible wars it naturally needed to know what assistance the Dominions would provide. A review of defence planning by the Imperial Chiefs of Staff, circulated among the Dominions before the conference, even went so far as to discuss the possibility of war against Germany or Japan and to suggest the possible contribution of the respective Dominions in each case. As Skelton commented scathingly in a memorandum which King had read at a Cabinet meeting, the Chiefs of Staff took it for granted that all parts of the Empire would participate in these wars and, even more presumptuously, assumed that Canada would supply armed forces as well as munitions and food.[10] In London, however, it was again left to the Australian and New Zealand delegations to present the arguments for "a coordinated system of defence for the Commonwealth."[11]

The Canadian delegation reiterated its policy of no commitments. Ian Mackenzie in a statement approved by his colleagues stated bluntly that Canada would not share in plans for Imperial defence. Canadians, he told the other delegates, supported a policy of national defence but any further increases in defence expenditures or any Imperial commitments would only create dissension. The government would not support a centralized Imperial defence scheme; "the best contribution that Canadians could make either to Canada or the Commonwealth was to keep Canada united."[12]

The members of the other delegations, however, found it difficult to believe that Canadian unity precluded any references to co-operation. They might concede that any formal commitment of the Canadian armed forces was out of the question but surely membership in the Commonwealth had some meaning? If Canada could not even participate in the planning for the production of munitions and food, Canadian autonomy seemed almost indistinguishable from Canadian isolationism. The other Commonwealth leaders needed to know if Canada could be counted on to co-operate because Great Britain would need an assured source of wheat if war came; its defence production, which was already putting a heavy strain on its industrial capacity, might be seriously disrupted by bombing raids, and Canada, more than any other Dominion, was in a position to supply Britain's war-time needs. It had the physical capacity and the technological sophistication to produce munitions of high quality and the trade route from Canada was less vulnerable. The American neutrality legislation made Canadian supplies even more crucial. It would be difficult to plan for Commonwealth production of food and munitions if Canadian production could not be counted on; it would be impossible to make any plans at all if King would not say whether Canada would or would not co-operate.

Mackenzie King pointed out that any participation in planning for defence production meant a commitment to supply munitions and food if war came. How could he persuade Canadians that the Canadian Parliament would decide on the issue of participation if he now agreed on an integrated scheme of Commonwealth defence production? Ian Mackenzie, the Canadian member of the conference sub-committee on the topic, would only accept a report which stated that there had been helpful discussions on Imperial co-operation. Even this was too explicit for King. When the sub-committee report came up for discussion he insisted on substituting the even blander comment that there had been a useful exchange of information.[13]

After the preliminary discussions the British delegation prepared a draft of the conference report on defence. Although it did refer explicitly to the sacred principle of Dominion autonomy, King was still not satisfied; he objected to subsequent references to common interests and to co-operation. The Australian and New Zealand delegates protested that to delete any approval of joint action was almost a denial that the Commonwealth existed but King would not give way. If there had to be references to co-operation he insisted on such qualifying phrases as "by certain members of the Commonwealth" or "by the Governments concerned" which would exclude Canada. On one occasion even Chamberlain showed some impatience and drily commented that he found it hard to believe that "the whole of Canada would take exception" to a phrase to which King was objecting.[14] It was embarrassing to insist but King was adamant. Again Neville Chamberlain played the role of conciliator and frequently suggested a rewording which removed the slightest hint of Canadian responsibility for Commonwealth defence.[15]

Mackenzie King's fear of anything which might be interpreted as a commitment went beyond the phrasing of the conference report. The British Army had decided in 1936 to adopt the Bren machine-gun as an infantry weapon and the British Government was prepared to place an order for Bren guns in Canada. The Canadian Army had also adopted the Bren and was looking for a Canadian manufacturer to supply its requirements. Mackenzie had already explained to King that the cost per gun would be high because the manufacturer would have to recover his investment in machine tools. A joint contract including the British and Canadian requirements would significantly reduce the cost per gun.[16] King had no objection to the British Government negotiating a contract directly with a Canadian manufacturer[17] but he shied away from the political risks of a contract negotiated jointly by the British and Canadian governments. British officials could point out that the advantage of lower costs would be lost if two contracts were negotiated independently but King was afraid that a single contract would be seen by some Canadians as proof that Canada was secretly committed to some scheme for Commonwealth defence production. On the other hand, to refuse to co-operate on the Bren gun contract when the advantages to Canada were so obvious would be tantamount to saying that Canada would never co-operate with other parts of the Commonwealth. Rather than choose between the alternatives of co-operating or not co-operating, King refused to make any decision at this stage of the Bren gun contract.

It would be wrong, however, to conclude that King was entirely obstructive. He was determined to avoid any suggestion of military or defence commitments because of the political risks involved but he was eager to participate in any other form of Commonwealth co-operation which might lessen the likelihood of British involvement in a European war. He actively encouraged a Commonwealth policy of trying to ease European tensions by international negotiations. This policy, commonly referred to as appeasement, had the great advantage for King that it held out the hope of peace in Europe without risking divisive political controversies at home. Canada might have to make some concessions if foreign grievances were to be appeased but the sacrifices would not involve any serious threat to Canadian unity.

King had come to London committed to a special form of appeasement. "Enduring peace," he asserted in his opening remarks at the conference, "cannot be achieved without economic appeasement."[18] He contended that the English-speaking countries had a unique opportunity because they could appease the economic grievances of other countries by lowering their own tariff barriers and thus encouraging the expansion of international trade. The logical first step, according to King, would be a trade agreement between Great Britain and the United States; the economic recovery of these two powers would then facilitate subsequent trade agreements with Europe and undermine the economic nationalism which threatened European peace. Even if this economic appeasement of Europe failed, the closer economic ties between Britain and the United States would strengthen Anglo-American friendship and erode American isolation. Here was a constructive policy, consistent with Canadian unity,

217

which King could therefore advocate during the conference and in private conversations in London.[19]

King associated Neville Chamberlain with the Ottawa Agreements and the restrictive policy of a Commonwealth trading bloc; he was therefore pleasantly surprised to hear him support the idea of an Anglo-American trade agreement. Chamberlain's comments on trade matters at the conference, according to King, "went to the heart of the possibility of war and the extent to which relations between America and Britain might help to save, not only the day, but the World." He recognized that Chamberlain might have ulterior motives—his speech was "all part of an appeal to have the Dominions yield up some of the privileged positions they have in the British market"—but for the moment any possible Canadian trade concessions paled into insignificance before the prospect of world peace: "Personally," he recorded in his diary, "I feel that even a defeat of my own administration at Ottawa, were it inevitable, but at the same time might be the means of saving a European war or a world disaster, is not a consideration which should be permitted to weigh for a moment in making that sacrifice. No sacrifice can be too great which can save a war; next to that, promote enduring friendship between the English speaking peoples."[20]

King had referred directly to economic appeasement but he had no objections to appeasement in wider terms. To him it meant resolving conflicts by peaceful negotiations rather than by military force. Appeasement would later be denounced as an irresponsible policy of trying to placate aggressors by yielding to their demands but King in 1937 still assumed that European powers would negotiate in good faith and that legitimate grievances could be appeased.

The other Commonwealth leaders shared his sentiments. In the words of the final report of the conference, the alternative to "international appeasement" was "the division, real or apparent, of the world into opposing groups." The Commonwealth leaders therefore opted for appeasement, with the logical corollary "that differences of political creed should be no obstacle to friendly relations between Governments and countries";[21] to argue that relations with communist or fascist powers could not be friendly would be to admit the inevitability of war. The phrase, which appeared in the original draft statement, seemed so uncontroversial that it was included in each successive version without provoking any comment.

Mackenzie King had every reason to be pleased with the results of the conference. He had come determined to avoid any suggestion that Canada was in any way committed to a policy of collective security, either through the League or the Commonwealth, and to avoid even a hint of participation in Commonwealth defence planning. The wording of the conference report was convincing proof that he had succeeded. On the more positive side, the report did speak of international co-operation and conciliation and had included a willingness to consider the reduction of tariffs and other trade barriers.

One critical observer compared the pious hopes and vague generalizations of the conference to those of "a dinner of the Royal Antediluvian Order of Buffaloes,"[22] but for King the platitudes concealed the significance of a conference in which he had forestalled political dangers at home and had left the way open for constructive measures. His had been a difficult mission, he wrote to a friend, "but its results were so much better than I had ever anticipated they could be."[23] The most convincing evidence of King's success can be found in the reaction of two very different men. Maxime Raymond, who had led the French-Canadian Liberal opposition to the increased defence expenditures earlier in the year, was now reassured that there were no secret commitments to the Commonwealth; in the following session he congratulated the Canadian delegation and declared that the report of the conference had dispelled "the apprehensions raised by the increased appropriations of last year."[24] Neville Chamberlain, on the other hand, was convinced that his conciliatory tactics had won King's confidence and told his colleagues that "the personal relations established should prove of incalculable value in the future."[25] From King's point of view an Imperial Conference which reassured French-Canadian nationalists without alienating the advocates of Commonwealth unity was a major triumph.

II

The Imperial Conference, significant as it was, did not absorb all of King's time in London. There was a constant round of social functions, of teas and formal dinners and weekends at country estates, where sophisticated men and women shifted easily from discussing affairs of state to comments on art and music, usually seasoned with a great deal of political gossip. Mackenzie King always found this a stimulating experience. He was now a senior Commonwealth statesman and knew most of the leading politicians and members of the British aristocracy and, although at times he might decry the snobbery and the idle gossip, he was flattered to be included in this society.

At the same time these social occasions were an ordeal for King because as an outsider and a colonial he was always worried about the impression

219

he was creating. He worried about the simplest details of social intercourse. Which invitations should he accept and, once he had arrived at a social function, when should he leave? Had he overstayed his allotted time in an interview with King George? Would a personal thank-you note after a visit with the King and Queen be presumptuous? And always there was the pressure of time. In addition to preparing for the conference meetings he had to write gracious notes and send gifts to his hosts of the day before, keep up his personal correspondence with friends and colleagues at home, as well as maintain a detailed record of his activities in his diary.

His greatest trial was having to speak in public. As Prime Minister of the senior Dominion he was often expected to reply to toasts or to produce an after-dinner speech. These were significant occasions for King because he believed that one of the measures of a statesman was his ability as an orator and here in London King wished to impress his peers. He was sure that his opinions and his sentiments were worthy but he had less confidence in his ability to express them with felicity. Rather than rely on an impromptu delivery, he preferred to prepare a text in advance, complete with literary allusions and carefully phrased metaphors. But since it was not good form to read a text, King's technique was to remember the sequence of his speech and to memorize the actual wording of the dramatic phrases and the peroration. Always there was the nagging worry that he would forget some passages or stumble in his delivery and so fail to measure up to the test of a statesman.

On this visit the social function which created the greatest strain was the banquet on Empire Day, the 24th of May. King had agreed to reply to the toast to the Empire, a familiar topic for him, but because this was London and because the thousand guests would include all the leading dignitaries of the Commonwealth, he found it an awesome occasion. "How little others can begin to imagine what carrying responsibility of the kind means to the individual who has that particular burden placed upon him," he complained in his diary.[26] The first draft of the ten-minute talk seemed quite inadequate and for a week King took time from his other activities to put his view of the Empire in suitable form. The theme posed no problem—he would stress the unity based on the high moral purpose which all parts of the Empire shared and would also remind his listeners that this unity could only be preserved by respecting local autonomy. The phrasing was more difficult because it would have to be worthy of the occasion and of the speaker. King did not enjoy the dinner obliged as he was to make conversation with the ladies seated beside him while he tried "to keep my mind sufficiently quiet to run over, in thought, the outline of the speech just before getting up to speak." The speech went well but as usual King was dissatisfied with his performance. "I had the material," he told himself, "and with rest and peace of mind, could have made, on that audience, an unforgettable impression."[27] There would have been less strain if King had been more intent on his material and less concerned with the personal impression he was making on his audience.

Informal discussions in London were not as exhausting for King because he could concentrate on the substance without excessive concern for the impression he was creating. One of the topics discussed was the proposed Anglo-American trade agreement. Chamberlain and King had agreed on the potential diplomatic significance of such an agreement during the conference but talks between British and Canadian officials were less harmonious. The United States wanted lower tariff barriers for its exports to Great Britain but the British tariff on items such as apples and lumber could not be lowered because the Ottawa Agreements had guaranteed Canada a fixed margin of preference. An Anglo-American trade agreement would only be possible if Canada surrendered some of its advantages in the British market. King was prepared to co-operate but he expected some concessions in return. The British officials spoke vaguely of showing "a most sympathetic attitude" towards any future requests by Canada for tariff changes or suggested that the United States might give sympathetic consideration to Canadian requests for American tariff reductions,[28] but this was not enough. Mackenzie King might talk altruistically about the sacrifices Canada should make to promote Anglo-American friendship but he was not prepared to sacrifice the interests of Annapolis apple-growers and British Columbian lumbermen for nothing more than vague promises of sympathetic consideration. Canada, he asserted, would not surrender its preferences without some compensation.[29] What this compensation should be would depend on the specific terms of the Anglo-American agreement. The only conclusion reached in London was that Canadian interests were so intimately involved that Canadian negotiators would have to participate directly when Anglo-American negotiations began.[30]

King felt that his informal discussions with the British Government on foreign policy were more fruitful. Peace in Europe was obviously desirable but even a war in Europe would not be disastrous if Britain could remain on the sidelines. King was prepared to believe that Germany could not be restrained for long but he also believed that German ambitions could be satisfied by expansion in eastern Europe. From this it was logical to assume that Germany would welcome peaceful relations with western Europe and would make any reasonable agreement with Britain which would leave her free to pursue expansion.[31] But would Britain be equally reasonable? King found Anthony Eden's attitude encouraging. At one of the conference sessions on foreign policy, he noted:

I asked specifically if what Eden had said did not mean England's attitude to be neither encouragement of German expansion on one hand, or in opposing resistance to that expansion on the other, but simply that of an interested spectator with the emphasis on the word "interested" as realizing that unwise action by Germany or indeed by any other countries concerned, might ignite the spark which would set Europe aflame; that Eden stated was the position. He was quite emphatic about England having no obligations growing out of the Franco-Soviet pact; also as to the unlikelihood as to any probable action by any countries concerned under the Pact.[32]

Chamberlain was equally encouraging. He was prepared to concede that Germany had legitimate economic interests in eastern Europe and that Britain "could not afford to stand in Germany's way of natural development if it could proceed by peaceful means which, he thought, was possible." He warned that a critical situation might develop if England showed her indifference and Hitler then recklessly relied on force in eastern European countries, but King found his attitude "very sound and sympathetic, anything but bellicose."[33] German and British interests might still conflict and there were "immense problems and uncertainties still to be dealt with," but at least the British government clearly hoped to avoid a confrontation.[34] Neville Chamberlain in turn must have been reassured by King's private explanation of the Canadian position: "I made clear to the British Ministers that in Canada we could not and would not consider anything in the nature of an Expeditionary Force or make appropriations beyond our own security . . . I stated, however, that if it became evident that Germany or any other country was guilty of aggression, I thought the voluntary feeling in Canada would assert itself in a strong way, and that it would be difficult to hold back those who would be prepared to see that aggression was stayed."[35] The British Government might regret that King's interpretation of the political situation at home obliged him to avoid any open commitments but for British leaders, who could not imagine going to war unless provoked by an aggressor, this was almost an assurance that if war came Canada would be at Britain's side.

Mackenzie King was also prepared to explain the Canadian position to other European leaders. Ribbentrop, the German Ambassador to London, spoke confidently to King of the possibility of Anglo-German friendship and suggested that King should visit Hitler to form his own impressions.[36] King was fascinated by the possibility of playing a major role in fostering

Anglo-German understanding and was encouraged by both Chamberlain and Eden, who assured him that a frank statement of the Canadian position "would help more than all the despatches in the world to preserve the peace in Europe."[37] King left for Germany convinced that he was undertaking a diplomatic mission of major significance.

The formal interview with Adolf Hitler lasted for over an hour. King carefully noted his appearance and manner:

His face is much more prepossessing than his pictures would give the impression of. It is not that of a fiery, over-strained nature, but of a calm, passive man, deeply and thoughtfully in earnest. His skin was smooth; his face did not present lines of fatigue or weariness; his eyes impressed me most of all. There was a liquid quality about them which indicate keen perception and profound sympathy. He looked most direct at me in our talks together at the time save when he was speaking at length on any one subject; he then sat quite composed, and spoke straight ahead, not hesitating for a word, perfectly frankly, looking down occasionally toward the translator and occasionally toward myself.

Hitler's words were as reassuring as his manner. He talked of the rights of Germany, of the injustice of the Treaty of Versailles, and of the dangers of communism, but he also emphasized the horrors of war and the peaceful aspirations of the German people. King got the impression of a mystic, a man dedicated to the welfare of his countrymen who "feels himself to be a deliverer of his people from tyranny." In short, he saw Hitler as an intense nationalist, resentful of the wrongs against Germany, but not a reckless or irrational man who would heedlessly provoke a war with Britain.

King's own remarks at the interview could not have had much impact. He assured Hitler that England wanted peace and that Chamberlain had a broad outlook. He tried to explain that Canada was an independent country, pointing out the significance of the fact that he was not accompanied by the British Ambassador, but went on to affirm that, if the freedom of any part of the Commonwealth was threatened by an aggressor, all the Dominions would rally to its defence. Hitler replied that he could understand this but there is no evidence to suggest that he gave it the same significance as King. He could not be expected to understand the policy of Britain or of Canada until the meaning they gave to freedom or aggression became clear. What was for King an important diplomatic exchange was for Hitler probably no more than a brief audience with a minor visiting dignitary.[38]

Even for King, however, his conversations in London seemed more significant than his conversations in Berlin. He was now convinced that Chamberlain could be trusted to work for peace and that even German expansion in eastern Europe might not bring Britain into a European conflict.[39] His confidence is illustrated by an incident in Paris on his way home. At the opening of the Canadian Pavilion at the Paris Exposition he declared that freedom was the essence of the Commonwealth and that all parts of the Commonwealth would rally together if that freedom was imperilled. The speech was accurately reported in Canada.[40] In England, however, he was quoted as saying that any threat to England would bring Canada to her side; presumably English reporters saw no distinction between a threat to freedom and a threat to Britain.[41] King did not issue a denial, even after British politicians cited this misinterpretation of his remarks with warm approval. He knew this version would be appreciated in Britain and thought it might be helpful in the international situation; confident that Chamberlain could be trusted, King was prepared to risk some criticism at home.[42] His correction was delayed until the next session of Parliament.[43]

King was back in Ottawa in early July. He was well satisfied with his two months in Europe and the break from the continuous pressures of domestic politics had done him good. After the tense atmosphere of the European capitals, Canada seemed "a smiling land, a land of hope and promise,"[44] and the reports of a devastating drought in western Canada were less depressing when seen in this perspective. Even the international situation now seemed less menacing; there might be fighting in eastern Europe but at least Neville Chamberlain was a man of peace. King's advice to Chamberlain, in a letter sent to a friend in London later that year, was a clear statement of his own views on European affairs: "When you are talking with him [Chamberlain] tell him at all costs to keep the Empire out of war. If other people want to fight, and are determined to do so, do not let us be drawn in because of some future possibilities. If the British Empire can be kept out of war, it will be able to take care of itself whatever the situations are with which it may be confronted in the future. If drawn into war, I firmly believe disruptive forces will begin to operate which will be beyond the control of all concerned."[45]

CHAPTER THIRTEEN

THE PROVINCIAL CHALLENGE TO
NATIONAL UNITY

THE TWO MONTHS IN EUROPE had been as good as a holiday for Mackenzie King. He would never face domestic controversies with serenity or eagerness; politics was a solemn responsibility and even he recognized regretfully that he could not "be light-hearted or seem to get much enjoyment out of it."[1] But at least he was no longer tired and depressed, and he had regained his usual confidence that conflicts could somehow be resolved. His confidence would be severely tested over the next few months; the Canada to which he returned in July 1937 was in serious difficulties.

The economic indicators in the spring of the year had all confirmed that Canada was recovering from the depression. In western Canada, however, the spring and summer of 1937 were the driest on record and by July it was obvious that over most of the prairies there would be no crops harvested and no fodder for the livestock. Relief measures and railway deficits would disrupt King's cherished plans for a balanced budget. More serious still, the disastrous conditions in the west, coming at a time when the end of the depression had seemed in sight, would almost certainly amplify the political protests from a region that was already bitter and disillusioned. And yet increased federal aid to the west would have serious repercussions in central Canada where Hepburn and Duplessis were already denouncing the financial burden on Ontario and Quebec. In the next few months federal policies would be directly challenged by provincial leaders.

I

The first serious challenge came from Alberta. King had long ago recovered from the initial shock of William Aberhart's election. Aberhart had somehow swayed the voters of Alberta with his promise of economic salvation but common sense and reason would eventually triumph even there. Common sense to King meant cautious administration and economic retrenchment; either Aberhart would forget his Social Credit theories or else his government would soon be discredited. In either case the path of wisdom for the federal government was to try to avoid any confrontation. Social Credit was Alberta's problem and King did not intend to interfere.

Two years of Social Credit government in Alberta had done nothing to modify King's detachment. On the two occasions that he had met Aberhart in Ottawa he had found him a likeable gentleman, possibly out of his depth in politics but certainly not radical or eccentric. Aberhart had at times been regrettably stubborn and strong-willed—he had rejected Dunning's proposal for a Loan Council in 1936, preferring to default on Alberta's bonds, and he had passed discriminatory debt legislation which the courts had subsequently rejected—but in both incidents King believed that the federal government had been conciliatory but firm and the Liberal party had benefitted from these tactics.

Aberhart ended this period of tentative jousting in a special session in September 1937. In part he was doubtless driven to more radical measures by the crop failure that year but the actual measures he introduced were also a response to a threat to his leadership from within his own party. Aberhart had warned the Alberta electors in 1935 not to expect miracles and that it would be eighteen months before the results of his Social Credit measures could be assessed.[2] The provincial session of 1936 had disillusioned many Social Crediters, however, because no significant steps had been taken to hasten the coming of the millennium. In England, even the official publication of Major Douglas, the founder of Social Credit, had been sharply critical; in July 1936 it had sarcastically commented that "back east they thought the Social Credit gun was loaded. It now turns out to be a pop gun with a cork in it. Every now and again the Premier shoots it off, and his followers, hearing the noise, still believe he is a very bold man."[3] Aberhart had ignored the criticism. In the spring session of 1937 there had still been no outline of Social Credit legislation and the financial measures, with higher taxes and reduced expenditures, had been explicitly aimed at a balanced budget.[4] This was the last straw for some of his followers, who denounced the budget as a complete denial of Social Credit and demanded that it be withdrawn.

For the next month Aberhart's fate was in the balance. A majority of the caucus supported the insurgents and the Premier's resignation seemed inevitable. Aberhart, however, proved to be an adroit politician. He substituted an interim supply measure for the budget and appointed a Social Credit Board of five members, with one of the insurgents as Chairman, to plan a Social Credit programme and to appoint a commission of experts to put it into effect. He then adjourned the session. For the next few weeks Aberhart used his Sunday radio broadcasts to appeal for public support. The response was unmistakeable; in the words of one insurgent, his constituents "almost tore the hide off me when I took the stump against him."[5] The revolt had been crushed when the legislature reassembled in June. The members of the Social Credit caucus had been asked to pledge their support to the government in its efforts to carry out "the will of the people in Alberta." Six members who refused had been disbarred from the caucus.[6] Aberhart was once more in control of his party.

It was less clear who was in control of government policy. The Social Credit Board had contacted Major Douglas in England who sent out two experts to prepare legislation to introduce Social Credit in Alberta. The experts had drafted three bills. The principal bill would require all bank employees in the province to be licensed; no licence would be issued until each employee had signed an undertaking not to interfere with "the property and civil rights of Alberta citizens." Since one of the cardinal tenets of Social Credit was that credit was a civil right, the obvious implication was that licensed bankers would be obliged to lend money on terms which reflected the popular will. To ensure that the bankers would respect their obligations this bill also authorized the Social Credit Board to set up citizens' committees to supervise local bank operations; bankers who did not co-operate would lose their licence. The other two bills were designed to prevent the courts from interfering; one denied unlicensed bankers any recourse to the courts and the other ruled out any attempt to challenge the validity of these acts in a court of law.[7]

Aberhart's personal reaction to these proposals is not clear. His faith in Social Credit seems beyond question but until 1937 he had shown no sense of urgency about introducing Social Credit legislation. His Attorney-General, John Hugill, also informed him that the proposed legislation was unconstitutional. Politically, however, Aberhart had much to gain and little to lose by accepting the recommendations of the experts. His critics within the party would be silenced and if the legislation was subsequently nullified by the federal government or the courts he would not be to blame. Whatever his motives, Aberhart made up his mind quickly. In September he called the provincial legislature into special session and introduced the three proposed bills without any modification of the wording. The Attorney-General resigned but the bills were quickly passed by the legislature.[8]

The federal government found this legislation embarrassing. The two Acts which denied recourse to the courts were clearly invalid and the courts could be relied on to deal with them. The licensing legislation, entitled the Credit of Alberta Regulation Act, was certainly an infringement on the federal jurisdiction over banking and again the courts would presumably rule that it was *ultra vires*. Reliance on the courts to annul this legislation, however, had one serious disadvantage. At least a year would elapse before a judicial decision could be expected and in the meantime the banking system in Alberta would be in chaos. One alternative was to disallow the legislation.

The federal government's power of disallowance was absolute in law; the federal government could veto any provincial law without giving any explanation and the veto could not be appealed. Disallowance, however, while it had no constitutional limitations, could have undesirable political effects. If the legislation was popular the government at Ottawa ran the risk of losing seats in the province at the next federal election. Federal Ministers of Justice had usually preferred to leave it to the courts to nullify laws which were *ultra vires* and to leave it to the provincial electorate to deal with governments which passed laws which were unjust.[9]

Mackenzie King and Ernest Lapointe certainly shared this preference. Their instinct was to rely on negotiation and compromise to avoid a confrontation; a resort to the arbitrary power of disallowance would be an admission that the normal political procedures had failed. Some provincial statutes had been disallowed during King's first administration but the federal power had not been used since 1924.[10] As Lapointe had explained in 1936, when justifying his refusal to disallow another controversial provincial statute, the law might be both invalid and unjust but these were not adequate reasons for federal intervention. He was reluctant to interfere unless there was a direct and deliberate "invasion of federal jurisdiction or federal policy or federal power."[11]

The Social Credit legislation in the special September session clearly encroached on federal jurisdiction over banking. Even so, King's first reaction was to avoid resorting to disallowance. The legislation was "unquestionably *ultra vires* but it is by no means certain that for us to disallow it would help matters in the long run" because Aberhart would probably react by calling and winning a provincial election on the issue of provincial rights.[12] King concluded that in this case, however, the political risks of disallowance were outweighed by the risks of doing nothing. The legislation was a direct and deliberate defiance of federal jurisdiction and was also a threat to federally chartered banks. To ignore the challenge would be to surrender federal authority over national institutions. King therefore decided that the legislation must be disallowed. This was a political decision but once it was made King typically justified it by invoking moral principles. His diary entry for the next day stressed the shocking disregard for civil liberties: "It was perfectly clear to me that the Dominion could not afford to allow any legislation to close the courts to its citizens . . . this was going back prior to the days of the Magna Carta; that above all else we should prefer freedom and liberty—also not permit the federal jurisdiction to be invaded."[13] Lapointe fully agreed that the challenge to federal authority could not be ignored.[14]

King still hoped to avoid disallowance. He quickly sent a telegram to Aberhart to inform him that disallowance was being considered and suggested that a preferable alternative would be to refer the legislation to the Supreme Court before it came into force.[15] Aberhart's response ended any hope of avoiding a confrontation. His lengthy telegram was an extraordinary outpouring of demagoguery and Social Credit jargon: "This government," ran one typical sentence, "unanimously and wholeheartedly upholds Confederation and would deeply regret the results if tension among a debt ridden and poverty stricken people were increased by faintest suspicion that federal government would side with plutocratic bankers alien to province against democratic Albertans earnestly seeking their economic freedom." The telegram went on to defy "financial tyranny to reveal itself," and insisted on the right to "monetize the credit of Alberta" and to implement "the clearly expressed will of the people."[16] Aberhart obviously wanted a confrontation. His telegram was addressed to King but the message was directed to the citizens of Alberta.

Mackenzie King's immediate reaction was almost as incoherent and emotional as Aberhart's telegram. He wrote in his diary that the issue was now crystal clear: "whether the will of the people as a whole—the Nation of Canada—shall be destroyed by the will of the minority—a single province (albeit a majority in a province), whether the Provincial legislatures are to usurp the Constitution of the law, and over-ride the law of the land." He would have to face the issue squarely and save the nation.[17] But King, unlike Aberhart, did not give vent to his emotions in his formal correspondence. He believed that the Canadian public would be more impressed by reasoned arguments than by an impassioned outburst, and so his reply to Aberhart merely affirmed his respect for the constitution and expressed his regret that Aberhart's unwillingness to compromise left him no alternative but to disallow the legislation.[18] He knew that his arguments were "a little over the heads of the average readers" but he was sure that in the long run good form would reap more political rewards than invective and that eventually "the meaning will become clear in discussion and in the press."[19]

King had good reason to rely on the press. When the federal government announced its disallowance of the three statutes there were headlines and editorials in almost all Canadian newspapers and, whether the newspaper was Liberal, Conservative, or independent, the federal action was applauded. Even the press in Alberta was no exception; editors insisted that Aberhart was wrong and that the federal government had no alternative but to disallow the legislation.[20] Aberhart might insist that he was fighting for the rights of THE PEOPLE in Alberta—the two words were often capitalized in his letters[21]—but by his definition the newspapermen in his province were now against the people.

Aberhart reacted by defying the federal government. In October he reconvened the provincial legislature for a second special session. It was easy for the federal government to ignore his absurd resolution, which declared that the federal power of disallowance "no longer exists," and his equally absurd refusal to have a proclamation of the disallowances printed in the provincial *Gazette*.* Even the passage of a slightly modified Credit of Alberta Regulation Act posed no great problem. The modification, such as the substitution of the phrase "credit institution" for the word "bank," were intended to weaken the constitutional arguments against the bill,[22] but this was so obviously a subterfuge that the federal government could hardly avoid disallowing the new Act. Aberhart, however, also introduced new legislation which was much more controversial. A Bank Taxation bill was designed to punish the banks for their opposition by imposing a special levy on their paid-up capital and reserve funds. Aberhart also singled out the newspapers for special attention. Convinced as he was of the justice of his cause, he could only conclude that their opposition was further evidence of the machinations of international bankers. His solution was the Accurate News and Information bill which would require every newspaper in Alberta to divulge its source for any news item on request and to publish every official government statement in full.[23]

Mackenzie King had no misgivings about vetoing this new legislation. Some of the western Ministers were hesitant but King knew that to back down at this stage would be a major political blunder. It would not be necessary, however, to disallow the legislation. The Lieutenant-Governor could reserve the bills for the consideration of the federal government and if the latter did not give its explicit approval within a year the bills would not become law. This was less dramatic and therefore politically preferable to disallowance and so the Lieutenant-Governor was authorized to reserve the bills.[24]

Aberhart's reaction to the reservation of his measures came as a pleasant surprise. Instead of a violent outburst with rhetorical flourishes about the will of the people and paranoic references to plutocracy, the Alberta

---

*The full absurdity of this minor incident is recorded in the correspondence between the Lieutenant-Governor of Alberta and the Secretary of State. The proclamation was eventually published in a special issue of the Canada *Gazette*.

Premier "respectfully submitted" that the federal powers of disallowance and of reservation should be tested by a reference to the Supreme Court. He would not even object to a referral of the Press bill although he did argue that the Credit Regulation and Bank Taxation bills should be approved and that their validity could then be tested before the courts in the normal way.[25]

This olive-branch posed some difficulties for the federal government. King and Lapointe welcomed the proposal to refer the questions of disallowance and reservation to the Supreme Court because they were certain that the federal power would be sustained. They were prepared to insist that the reservation of the Credit Regulation and the Bank Taxation bills should remain in effect while the courts ruled on their validity but were sure that this would not have serious political consequences even if Aberhart continued to object. The Press bill was a different matter. King was determined to block this legislation but there was no assurance that it was unconstitutional and a reference to the Supreme Court might produce a decision that it was valid. It would be safer to disallow the Press bill immediately rather than risk the political embarrassment of having to disallow it after the courts had established that it was *intra vires*. Lapointe, however, was very reluctant to disallow the bill solely on the grounds that the legislation was unjust.[26] King finally gave way and in November the Supreme Court was formally requested to rule on the validity of the three provincial bills and to define the constitutional limitations on the federal powers of disallowance and reservation. For the next few months at least the confrontation with Alberta had been taken out of politics while lawyers and judges argued about the limits of federal and provincial jurisdictions.

II

The truce with Alberta was especially welcome because by November the federal government was being openly attacked by the Premiers of Quebec and Ontario. King did not expect co-operation from Maurice Duplessis, whom he had always considered a political opponent, but by 1937 Duplessis had shown unexpected political talents. By exploiting the issues of communism and provincial rights he had put the Quebec Liberals on the defensive. Mitchell Hepburn, however, was a Liberal and a confrontation with Hepburn, whatever the outcome, would divide the Liberal party in Ontario. By the end of the year the political situation had become even more menacing because Duplessis and Hepburn had joined forces with the avowed intention of defeating the Liberal government at

Ottawa. A clash with Alberta was serious enough but a confrontation with the two largest provinces in Canada would be an irretrievable disaster.

King could do little more than observe political events in Quebec. Duplessis had quickly consolidated his position as party leader after the Union Nationale's sweeping victory in the provincial election of 1936. What had been a coalition of Conservatives and dissident Liberals was soon a united party, with the leading figures in the Action Libérale Nationale either relegated to minor portfolios or out of politics entirely and with Duplessis as the unchallenged *chef*. King, who had taken it for granted that the Union Nationale would be a Conservative party in all but name, tried to draw what comfort he could from the situation: "On the whole," he told himself, "I am not sorry to have a Conservative government in power in Quebec. It is easier to govern at Ottawa with the provinces *contra*. Also it will help us in dealing with the other provinces, and in meeting constitutional questions etc."[27] But King was only trying to make the best of a bad situation. Taschereau had been an embarrassment at times, especially on constitutional issues, but at least he had helped to elect Liberal candidates in federal elections. The ideal for King would have been a genuinely Liberal government in Quebec—a government, in other words, which agreed with his version of national unity. He believed that in Quebec, as in the rest of Canada, the majority of citizens were liberal-minded and would support liberal policies if the issues were effectively presented. His problem was that he could not intervene directly. Leadership was needed but it would have to come from a French Canadian.

Ernest Lapointe did not seem equal to the task. He was deeply depressed by events in Quebec but believed that for the moment nothing could be done. It was not only that the provincial Liberal party was in disarray and that Duplessis was in office. Lapointe also saw an illiberal clerical nationalism sweeping the province. He was convinced that any Liberal counter-attack, any appeal based on liberalism and national unity, would be futile until these emotional forces were spent. He felt so helpless that even his health was affected and he talked of resigning rather than having to face another federal election.[28]

Under these circumstances even minor incidents took on a major significance for Lapointe. Late in 1936, for example, a request from four Spanish Loyalists for permission to visit Canada on a speaking tour put him at odds with his colleagues. King and the English-Canadian Ministers favoured granting the request, arguing that the liberal principle of freedom of speech must be upheld. King himself expressed this view forcibly in his diary: "I would rather go out of office and out of life itself, if need be, fighting to maintain the liberties we have and which have been bought so dearly, than to be a party to losing them through fear and prejudice however strong." But Lapointe did not agree. He too believed in freedom of speech but he also believed that French Canada would place a different interpretation on this decision. Duplessis and Cardinal Villeneuve had already denounced a previous Loyalist rally in Montreal and that meeting had broken up in a riot. If the federal government now permitted these Loyalist speakers to come it would be interpreted as approval of their position and support for their communist ideas. "He seemed to think," noted King, "that if they were allowed to come into Canada at all, it might only lead to the secession of the province of Quebec from the rest of Canada."

King thought that Lapointe's fears were exaggerated but Lapointe did have the support of the other French-Canadian Ministers. He finally agreed to a compromise by which the Loyalists would be admitted to Canada but "told plainly that if they came near Quebec and caused disturbances they would be immediately deported." King knew this was a contradiction of his liberal principles but he was not prepared to override the political judgment of his French-Canadian colleagues. He could only reflect with regret that Lapointe, liberal though he was, seemed to have lost the will to fight: "Lapointe's fear of the Cardinal and Duplessis amounts to absolute terror. No one can convince me that if he, himself, and a few others would begin to expound the doctrines of Liberalism to the younger generation of Quebec, it would not take long to free them from clerical or political intolerance."[29]

King did not understand Lapointe's feeling of helplessness because he did not understand what was happening in Quebec. French Canadians had always had a feeling of insecurity, the feeling that as a minority their survival was menaced. Survival had always seemed to depend on unity in the face of external threats to their distinctive identity; alien ideas or radical views were suspect because they were a threat to this unity and might leave French Canada more vulnerable to external forces. The depression had added a new dimension to this insecurity. In other parts of the world the apparent failure of free enterprise and democratic government had led to the spread of socialist ideas, and even to revolution and civil war. The fear of internal divisions, always present in Quebec, had been intensified. The wave of clericalism and nationalism which so disturbed Lapointe was the conservative reaction of a society which saw social change as a threat to its survival.

This reaction was based on a concept of French-Canadian identity which had a long history. To be French Canadian was to be a French-speaking Roman Catholic, but the definition of cultural identity went

233

much farther. The cultural values which distinguished French Canada from the English-speaking Protestants were seen as the values of a rural community, with the parish as the centre of family and social relations, in contrast to the urban and materialistic values of the rest of North America. This emphasis on rural values was already outmoded in a Quebec which had become industrialized and where most French Canadians now lived in urban communities, but the image of French Canada as a rural society still survived.

The emotional response of French Canada to the depression was strongly influenced by this image. There was no place for the urban worker in this idealized version of French-Canadian society; no influential French Canadians had become spokesmen for the working class and there was little awareness of the problems of an urban proletariat. Some priests had organized Catholic trade unions but they had been more concerned with the pernicious influence of the alien and materialistic international unions than with the workers' claims for higher wages or better working conditions. Even the political parties continued to emphasize rural problems rather than industrial relations; the 1934 platform of the young reformers in the Action Libérale Nationale had begun with agricultural reforms and had not even mentioned collective bargaining. Industrial workers might be French-speaking and Roman Catholic but their problems seemed peripheral and almost unrelated to the question of French-Canadian survival.

The result was that most responsible or respectable French Canadians had no interest in and no sympathy for left-wing views. If workers acted as a group and demanded special rights they would only create divisions within French-Canadian society and endanger its survival. Strikes and protests were seen as a reflection of alien materialism and the class struggle. There were no fine distinctions; workers' rallies, militant trade unionism, and socialism all seemed equally subversive. Urban or industrial unrest, however moderate in form, was seen as a menace to the traditional values of French Canada.

In this context it was almost inevitable that any working-class movement would be blamed on revolutionary agitators and associated with the heretical and pernicious doctrine of communism.* The fear of communism during the depression was not confined to Quebec—Mitchell

---

*André Laurendeau, a young French-Canadian intellectual at the time, has described his shock when he discovered that in France many prominent Roman Catholics actually expounded left-wing views and supported left-wing movements. See *La crise de la conscription*, p. 11, translated by Philip Stratford in *André Laurendeau: Witness for Quebec*, p. 4.

Hepburn had successfully exploited the communist menace in Ontario during the Oshawa strike—but in French Canada the strength of rural values and the official denunciation of communism by the Roman Catholic church intensified this fear. Communism seemed to be the antithesis of everything which French Canada stood for and the label was easily attached to anything which appeared to challenge the accepted version of French-Canadian identity.

Duplessis put the Quebec Liberals on the defensive by establishing himself as the leader in the struggle against this subversive doctrine. His hostility to communism was certainly sincere but he also knew that a dramatic confrontation with this evil would bring political benefits. He needed a positive measure which would identify him as the unrelenting foe of communism and the defender of French Canada and which would distinguish him from the moderate and compromising Liberals. In 1937 he found the ideal measure in the Padlock Law.

The Act Respecting Communist Propaganda, to use its official title, was a badly drafted law but it was remarkably effective as a political document. The act made it illegal to use a house "to propagate communism or bolshevism by any means whatsoever." If Duplessis, as Attorney-General, believed that the law had been broken, he could order the house locked up for a period of up to one year. The owner of the house could reoccupy the premises only if he could convince a judge that the law had not been broken or that the house would not be used again for this illegal purpose. Police officers, again on the instructions of the Attorney-General, could also confiscate and destroy any documents "propagating or tending to propagate communism or bolshevism." But how were communism and bolshevism to be defined? The act did not say. The Attorney-General could establish his own definition and could impose the legal penalties without the usual safeguard of a public hearing. Duplessis openly defended this omission in the legislature on the grounds that "any definition would prevent the application of the law." His own definition can be deduced from his revealing comment that "communism can be felt."[30] To many Quebec citizens, for whom any working-class propaganda seemed subversive, Duplessis was only stating the obvious. Those who feared communism would sleep more soundly knowing that Maurice Duplessis was alert to the danger and had the power to act.

The Padlock Law was a serious embarrassment to the Quebec Liberals. To oppose it would be interpreted as defending the rights of communists. But Duplessis went even farther. The legislation was necessary, he argued, because the federal government had refused to keep out communist immigrants or to ban the entry of communist newspapers. Instead of taking positive action, the Liberals had encouraged communists by repealing Section 98 of the Criminal Code. The Padlock Law, according to Duplessis, was needed because the Liberal government at Ottawa had failed to do its duty.[31]

Lapointe found himself in an agonizing dilemma. As a French Canadian and a Roman Catholic he found communism repugnant "on moral, religious and sociological grounds." As a Liberal, however, he abhorred arbitrary measures of repression and was convinced that the best defence against subversion was to eliminate economic grievances. On this basis he believed the federal government was doing more than the Union Nationale to fight communism.[32] It was infuriating to be accused by Duplessis of tolerating and even abetting this alien and atheistic doctrine.[33] But even if Duplessis did not have the answer to communism he did have the political advantage. The supporters of Duplessis' crusade even included some of Lapointe's own followers.* Lapointe saw no way in which he could challenge Duplessis openly without strengthening the latter's hold on the province and encouraging the dangerous polarization between fascism and communism.

The Padlock Law became even more embarrassing to Lapointe after the disallowance of the Alberta legislation. Canadian spokesmen for civil liberties had promptly denounced the Padlock Law as unjust and probably invalid and had petitioned the Minister of Justice to disallow it. If the federal government was prepared to protect the bankers in Alberta how could it refuse to protect the citizens of Quebec? Lapointe knew that many of his English-Canadian colleagues favoured disallowance but he was not prepared to face the outrage in French Canada which this would surely provoke. The power of disallowance could be invoked at any time within a year of the passage of a provincial law and Lapointe preferred to delay as long as possible before making up his mind. There would be no decision by the federal government on the Padlock Law until the summer of 1938.

III

Hepburn was potentially a more disruptive figure than Duplessis because he was a Liberal. Hepburn, however, had been remarkably restrained at least in public during the summer of 1937; after his announcement in

---

*Jean-Francois Pouliot, the Liberal M.P. for Temiscouata, wanted the federal government to co-operate with Duplessis and Cardinal Villeneuve in this war against evil. One of his suggestions was that the R.C.M.P. should investigate such socialists as Frank Scott and Eugene Forsey because of their subversive ideas. Jean-Francois Pouliot to W.L.M.K., Feb. 11, 1938.

June that he was not a Mackenzie King Liberal there were no further tirades against Ottawa. It was not that he had changed his mind. King received a number of letters or reports from supporters to whom Hepburn had outlined his lengthening list of grievances against the federal government.[34] But the provincial Premier was planning a provincial election even though he had been in office for only three years. He intended to take advantage of his popularity following the Oshawa strike and to be safely back in office before the issue of waterpower became embarrassing. Hepburn might be impetuous and erratic but he was not so foolhardy as to attack the federal Liberals openly during an election campaign.

Mackenzie King did not intend to force the issue. On his return to Canada in July he had refused to make any comments on Hepburn's provocative remarks. The announcement of a September provincial election in Ontario, however, did create some difficulties for the Ontario Liberals in the House of Commons. Would they be disloyal to King if they campaigned for Hepburn? King gave no advice; "it is for each member of the party to decide for himself who he wishes to support in the provincial campaign."[35] Some Liberals did not find it an easy decision to make but in the end all the Ontario Ministers took some part in the election; even Norman Rogers, who was harshly critical of Hepburn, supported the local Liberal candidate in his Kingston constituency. Two other Ministers, J. G. Gardiner and Ian Mackenzie, also campaigned in Ontario and Mackenzie even appeared with Hepburn at one political rally. King himself at first announced that it was his "usual practice to refrain from taking any part in the campaign"[36] but this aloofness was interpreted by some Liberals as opposition to Hepburn. At the last minute King did announce to the press that he hoped Hepburn would be re-elected:[37] "I felt it unwise to leave this until after tomorrow's results and let it be said that I had allowed the Tories to capitalize on my feelings against Hepburn," he confided to his diary. "Should he lose I would be blamed for it, should he win I would get no thanks for any part taken in the campaign and emphasis would be placed for all time on not having helped."[38] The Liberal party was not united but it did close ranks for the election.

The campaign, however, raised questions about the loyalty of King's colleagues. Rogers was furious about a report that Gardiner had expressed approval of Hepburn's stand on the Oshawa strike at one political rally and he threatened to resign if the federal government did not issue a statement which affirmed its support for collective bargaining. King convinced him that any such statement during the campaign would be misconstrued, and Rogers was mollified by Gardiner's assurance that he had been misquoted,[39] but the possibility that some federal Ministers were sympathetic to Hepburn could not be ignored. King analysed the situation with remarkable objectivity. He expected his colleagues to plan for the future and to prepare for his own eventual retirement; with Hepburn in the ascendant in Ontario it was natural for some of them to look to him as a future ally. But would any of his Ministers go farther? Would they try to replace King before he was ready to go? King, in the privacy of his diary, did not rule out this possibility:

Rogers thinks Gardiner is ruthless, very ambitious and would be disloyal to win his own ends. I doubt that. I believe, however, that Mackenzie and Power are Hepburn men and Gardiner is listening in, to be as far as he can "on all sides"—but I believe he is loyal to me. If there is treachery I shall certainly go out to meet it, but will be cautious and take the right moment. Meanwhile I have no reason to think that any of my colleagues are in a conspiracy. . . . I have written all this just because there is smoke, which the last moment of an election has helped to break out a bit into flame. My belief is it will die down once the provincial contest is over.[40]

If any of King's colleagues were looking to the future, the results of the Ontario election would encourage them to think of Hepburn as the rising star. Hepburn had created a popular issue out of the Oshawa strike and by calling a snap election he had taken full advantage of the split within the Conservative opposition. The Liberals almost duplicated their sweeping victory of 1934 and Mitchell Hepburn, now more than ever the dominant figure in the provincial party, was back in office for another term. King found some encouragement in the defeat of the Tories and the even more decisive setback for the C.C.F., but he knew that the results could also be interpreted as a victory for the Hepburn wing of the party. The election results would increase the dangers of a split between the federal and provincial Liberals in the province. For the time being, however, King could do no more than resolve to be on his guard, to avoid any provocation, and to trust in the loyalty of his colleagues.[41]

It was not easy to avoid provocation even on minor issues because King did not always know what the erratic Hepburn wanted. Even the appointment of a Lieutenant-Governor could be complicated. The term of the incumbent, H. A. Bruce, would expire in November 1937, but Bruce was apparently on good terms with Hepburn and King concluded that the least controversial step would be to extend his term, provided that Hepburn was agreeable.[42] Hepburn, however, wrote to King early in October to explain that he intended to close Chorley Park, the official residence of the Lieutenant-Governor; since Bruce was not willing to stay on under these conditions, Hepburn suggested that Duncan Marshall, the defeated

Minister of Agriculture, should replace him.[43] King thought Marshall with "his aggressive way of speaking and rough manners" was a singularly inappropriate choice for a position of dignity and social prominence but he was prepared to make the appointment.[44] To his surprise, Hepburn then sent a message by way of a Liberal M.P. to ask that his letter be ignored and to say that he would really prefer to have Bruce stay on at Chorley Park for two more years and have Marshall in the Senate.[45] King was still willing to co-operate but before any announcement could be made Hepburn changed his mind again and told King in mid-October that Government House was to be closed within a week.[46]

King was in Toronto a few days later and called on Hepburn to clear up the confusion. Both men seem to have been on their best behaviour and King found Hepburn so cordial that he even made a casual reference to the Ontario Premier's denial that he was a Mackenzie King Liberal. Hepburn reiterated his grievances against some of King's colleagues but apologized for having brought King's name into the discussion. King let the matter pass but in his diary he noted with some bitterness that his photograph was no longer on Hepburn's desk and that Hepburn did not accompany him to the door when he left the Premier's office. On the question of the Lieutenant-Governor Hepburn affirmed that Government House would be closed and King agreed to appoint Marshall when Bruce resigned.[47] King was no sooner back in Ottawa than he learned that Hepburn had changed his mind again and had agreed to let Bruce stay on in Chorley Park.[48] Three weeks later the mercurial Premier reversed himself once more. This time the decision seemed final; Mrs Bruce learned through a servant that the government would not clean the chimneys or replace electric light bulbs at Chorley Park![49] By this time King had also changed his mind. He decided to name Albert Mathews, a prominent Toronto broker with the appropriate political and social qualifications, as Lieutenant-Governor, with Marshall going to the Senate. Hepburn protested vigorously but finally agreed.[50] Mathews' appointment was quickly announced and a few weeks later Duncan Marshall became a Senator. It was a comic-opera performance but it showed how volatile and unpredictable Mitchell Hepburn could be.

King could try to humour Hepburn on matters of federal patronage but he could not so easily modify federal policies to placate the Ontario Premier. Even before the gates of Chorley Park were closed Hepburn was demanding a favour that King was not prepared to concede. Hepburn's dispute with the Quebec power companies was not yet resolved. His legislation to cancel the power contracts had been overturned by the courts and the Ontario Appeal Court had upheld this decision just before

239

the provincial election. The Ontario Government had immediately appealed this ruling but Hepburn knew that there was little chance of success; this had been one reason for calling an election before the case could be heard.[51] Shortly after the election he began negotiations with the Beauharnois company to settle out of court. He now faced the humiliation of admitting that the "power barons" had won but he could at least save face if, when announcing that Ontario would import Quebec power, he could at the same time announce an agreement to export power from Ontario to the United States. The only obstacle was the federal policy dating back to 1907 and reaffirmed in the 1920s of prohibiting the export of power. Hepburn now asked the federal government to make an exception by allowing Ontario Hydro to export 120,000 horsepower to the state of New York.[52]

King did not intend to modify the federal position. By refusing to export power Canada would attract industries which relied on cheap electricity. In any case the federal government, which only a few months before had declined permission to Beauharnois to export power directly from Quebec,[53] could hardly reverse its stand now. King knew that Hepburn would be furious and was so upset by the impending confrontation that his "nerves seemed to be all on edge." He did not even feel equal to participating in the Cabinet discussion on Hepburn's request, although his absence made no difference. His colleagues knew what his opinion was and the decision to reject the application was almost unanimous.[54]

Hepburn refused to take no for an answer. He telephoned King the next day and demanded to appear before a special meeting of the federal Cabinet. King did not relish the idea but "was determined, however, not to have him say that we had refused even to hear him."[55] A meeting was arranged even though King had to postpone his departure from Ottawa for a holiday. When Hepburn arrived he refused to listen to any arguments about the long-standing policy against export; he wanted to talk business and not play with mere words. If he could not export power he could not agree to import power from Quebec and that would mean that Ontario would probably have to pay heavy damages to the power companies. Taxes and Hydro rates would go up, and it would all be the fault of the federal government. When King reviewed the federal position Hepburn shouted that he was wasting his time and, according to King's record of the meeting, "he became quite heated and required a little cooling down by one or two of the Ministers." He repeatedly threatened to fight Ottawa on the issue and warned that the people and the provincial Liberals would support him. After three-quarters of an hour, Hepburn

240

asked for an immediate answer and retired to his hotel room at the Chateau Laurier to await the decision.

King was disappointed to discover, in the Cabinet discussion that followed, that some of his colleagues were intimidated by Hepburn's threats. He finally brought the discussion to an end by pointing out that nobody had supported Hepburn, that those who were equivocal were largely concerned with the political risks of a refusal, and those who were opposed were firmly decided. He then delivered a lecture on the need to respect the courts and Parliament and his belief that what "was right in itself was best in the end politically!" "I then said," he recorded in his diary, "that I proposed to say to Hepburn that Council had considered the matter very carefully, but that we could not agree to grant the application he had made. I asked if there was any exception on the part of anyone to my saying this. All were silent."

King then went in person to the Chateau Laurier to deliver the unwelcome message. His rather lame explanation that Cabinet could not overrule the expressed will of Parliament could not have been convincing to Hepburn, who had never been sensitive to procedural restraints. Even King's suggestion that something might still be done when Parliament met was brushed aside as an evasion. Hepburn insisted that King was "forcing the issue" and that "he would have to fight." The two men shook hands as King left but it was only a formality. King was sure that Hepburn "is of such a nature or character that in order to destroy me he would be quite prepared to destroy the Party and, no doubt, we shall find intrigue continuously from now on." He could only console himself that he had right on his side and that if he had to take the platform against Hepburn, he would also have the people on his side.[56] It was small comfort for a man who knew that even if Hepburn lost, King and the Liberal party had nothing to win by an open breach.

One ironical aspect of this dispute is that Ontario actually required the Quebec power for its own needs. The demand for power in Ontario had been steadily increasing and Ontario Hydro officials already knew that the province was facing a power shortage. Hepburn had been aware of this before the provincial election although he had bluntly denied any danger of a shortage during the campaign.[57] His request to export power was a face-saving political tactic which bore no relation to the provincial power requirements. But Hepburn was not inhibited by inconsistency. Now that King had turned down his request he lashed out in another direction. Why had King refused to co-operate? Hepburn had an unexpected explanation. Franklin Roosevelt, he announced to the press, wanted a power shortage in the United States in order to maintain support for the St. Lawrence waterway and Mackenzie King was aiding the President by blocking the export of Ontario power. "Mr. King," he declared, "is taking a made-in-Washington policy and is trying to force it on Ontario."[58] He assured incredulous reporters that he had copies of the correspondence between Ottawa and Washington which outlined this conspiracy, although "Mr. King, with his usual cunning, has marked these formal state communications regarding the St. Lawrence waterway as confidential." Two days later he overcame his respect for confidentiality and released the correspondence.*

Hepburn had gone too far. Even the *Globe and Mail* pointed out that "the plain fact is that the correspondence fails to substantiate Mr. Hepburn's wild charges."[59] King was pained but not surprised that the Premier of Ontario had shown himself to be both dishonest and uncouth.[60] He at least intended to maintain the proper standards of decorum. His press release next day merely pointed out that the correspondence clearly showed that the federal government had only acted as an intermediary between Queen's Park and Washington. He did take the liberty of releasing a letter from the Provincial Secretary in Hepburn's government warmly thanking King for his efforts in Washington on behalf of the province and which, as King pointedly remarked, "significantly enough, appears to have been omitted from the correspondence given to the press by Mr. Hepburn this morning."[61] King would never be uncouth but he too could wield a knife.

IV

By December 1937 Maurice Duplessis and Mitchell Hepburn had gone beyond their separate confrontations with the federal government and had announced an open alliance against Ottawa. The two men had much in common. Both of them were encouraging the exploitation of natural resources but were opposed to the militant trade unionism which accompanied industrialization and resented what they saw as federal tolerance of alien agitators. Both of them had supported applications for the export of power only to have the proposals blocked by Ottawa. Their major grievance, however, was the federal aid to the drought-stricken prairies and the conviction that central Canada was paying for this federal generosity.

*Hepburn did ask King to release the "official documents very improperly marked confidential" (M. F. Hepburn to W.L.M.K., Dec. 19, 1937) and King, after consulting the American Minister in Ottawa, had decided to table the correspondence when the House met (Diary, Dec. 19, 20, 1937) but Hepburn had not waited for a reply.

But the Hepburn-Duplessis alliance was based on more than common political interests. Both were convivial and uninhibited men, scornful of respectable conventions, who revelled in the game of politics and enjoyed the personal exercise of power. The two men became friends and when they met their roisterous parties had the added spice of political scheming.[62] And for both of them the obvious enemy was Mackenzie King, the leader of the federal government and also the sanctimonious and hypocritical compromiser who epitomized for them the old-fashioned respectability which they despised. It seemed natural and logical for them to join forces. Given their temperaments, however, it was also natural for them to exaggerate their power and to overreach themselves. They underestimated the sentiment of national unity even among the citizens of central Canada, and they also underestimated the political talents of Mackenzie King.

King was an inviting target because he still had no positive proposals for the reform of a federal system that seemed to be breaking down. He had reluctantly agreed to give financial aid to bankrupt provinces, had refused to join in any crusade against industrial unionism or communism, and had defended the existing constitutional prerogatives of the federal government, even invoking the power of disallowance, but he had not tried to initiate any fundamental changes in the constitution. Even the rejection of the Bennett New Deal legislation by the Privy Council had not prodded him into action.

One exception was his proposal to the provincial governments in November 1937 of a constitutional amendment which would give the federal government the power to introduce unemployment insurance. King did not expect any opposition but even on this issue he was still circumspect. What would he do if one of the provinces refused its consent? King would only say that "it would be desirable that there be unanimous approval."[63] Six provincial Premiers, including Hepburn, did agree to the amendment but Duplessis, Aberhart, and Dysart of New Brunswick were more cautious; they wanted to see the proposed legislation first.[64] King did not try to force the issue. As he explained to the House of Commons in January 1938, "cooperation would facilitate the early introduction of the legislation" and he was waiting for co-operation.[65] Since the federal government was volunteering to take on a financial responsibility which would relieve provincial governments of some of their relief costs in the future, King believed that he could afford to wait.

The other federal initiative was the appointment of the Royal Commission on Dominion-Provincial Relations. King had announced the decision to have a royal commission in February,[66] but serious discussion of

243

the personnel and terms of reference was postponed until after his return from Europe. He had thought of Stanley Baldwin as a possible Chairman but when Baldwin showed no interest[67] King and his colleagues decided not to go outside the country.[68] There was no dearth of candidates for the chairmanship—both Bennett and Dunning showed considerable interest[69]—but King proposed N. W. Rowell, now Chief Justice of the Ontario Appeal Court, with J. W. Dafoe from Winnipeg and Thibaudeau Rinfret of the Supreme Court of Canada as his colleagues. The three men were Liberals but they were senior statesmen whose recommendations would carry weight in the regions they represented. King also knew that Rowell and Dafoe could be trusted to reject radical solutions and to show respect for the financial stability of the federal government. His first suggestion was to limit the commission to three members—he apparently assumed that if central Canada and the west could agree the rest of the country would follow[70]—but after further consideration it was decided to add R. A. Mackay, a political scientist from Dalhousie, and H. F. Angus, an economist from the University of British Columbia. These two younger men were considered politically reliable—Mackay had published a complimentary article on the political ideas of William Lyon Mackenzie and Angus had been a critic of Major Douglas' ideas on Social Credit—but King saw their nomination as a concession to regional sentiment. They would profit from the experience but to King "the real Commission was Rowell, Dafoe & Rinfret."[71]

The personnel and the terms of reference were finally announced in mid-August. The terms of reference were deliberately broad but the fine hand of Mackenzie King was visible to the discerning eye. "Economic and social developments since 1867" had led to an unforeseen extension of government responsibilities. The emphasis, however, was not on a fundamental analysis of the role of government in Canadian society but on a reallocation of existing revenues and expenditures so that both provincial and federal governments would be financially independent. Among other benefits, this would help to keep "the burden of public expenditures . . . to a minimum."[72] The commission might recommend the transfer of responsibilities to the federal government or federal sources of revenue to the provinces but the objective was to end federal aid to bankrupt provinces. King still believed that classical federalism would leave the federal government free to manage its own affairs—and balance its own budget.

The timing of the announcement helps to explain the generally favourable reaction. Royal Commissions are often seen as a means of evading or delaying government action. On this occasion, however, the announcement came a few days after Aberhart's first attempt to regulate banking in Alberta and just before the federal disallowance of his legislation. Most Canadians were prepared to admit that there was a crisis in federal-provincial relations and welcomed the decision to seek the advice of prominent men outside active politics. Editorial comment was almost unanimously favourable.[73] Even the *Canadian Forum*, usually critical of federal inactivity, was so impressed by the members of the commission that it could "hardly resist the temptation to conclude that, when Mr. King appointed them, he really intended something to be done about dominion-provincial relations."[74] Some federal politicians were less tolerant. Bennett had a long memory and denounced both Rowell and Dafoe as "violent partisans."[75] Woodsworth was less virulent but he did object to "an exhaustive study of things we already know."[76]

King could expect criticism from the Opposition but the reaction of the provincial Premiers would be more significant. King did not anticipate any co-operation from Maurice Duplessis. The Quebec Premier was almost certain to add the commission to his list of federal encroachments on provincial autonomy and could appeal to the deep-rooted suspicions of French Canadians who identified both Rowell and Dafoe with conscription.[77] But Duplessis bided his time. William Aberhart was less restrained. He had just learned of the federal decision to disallow his banking legislation and interpreted the terms of reference and the nomination of Dafoe and Angus, both arch-foes of Social Credit, as further evidence that the federal government was the willing tool of international bankers. It was his duty, he told King, to resist "the dangerous and undesirable possibilities for centralizing federal control and weakening the sovereignty of THE PEOPLE."[78] Hepburn's reaction, however, was more reassuring. He expressed his satisfaction with the members of the commission and promised that his government would "cooperate in every possible way."[79]

Hepburn's unwonted restraint was short-lived. The changeable Premier, encouraged by his election victory and angered by King's refusal to permit the export of power, soon found an occasion to reverse his position. In December 1937 he linked the commission with western demands for more federal aid and announced to the press that he and Duplessis would resist. "We are going to form an economic alliance with Quebec," he declared. "The demands from the western provinces seem to indicate that Ontario and Quebec will have to stand together on representations to the Commission."[80] Duplessis promptly confirmed this alliance and made it clear that for the two provincial Premiers Ottawa was the real enemy.[81]

V

Mackenzie King was not surprised. When he had announced the commission he had expected opposition, "with all the demagogues working together to overthrow the federal administration—possibly Hepburn, Duplessis & Aberhart—not forgetting Pattullo should we encounter difficulties."[82] The open defiance of the federal government came almost as a relief. Now that Hepburn and Duplessis had declared their narrow regionalism, his role as the defender of national unity would be more easily appreciated. It was "just as well to have these two incipient dictators out in the open. The public will soon discover who is protecting their interests and freedom. . . . We will win in a 'united Canada' cry."[83]

The reaction of the other provincial Premiers provided some confirmation for this analysis. Maritime leaders denounced the idea of an eastern bloc. Western leaders were even more outspoken. Aberhart protested that "The East should keep its hands out of our pockets,"[84] and Pattullo told King that British Columbia was "getting pretty tired of eastern domination and that there would be trouble if Hepburn and Duplessis propose to appeal to the prejudices of the people of their provinces."[85] The Premiers of Quebec and Ontario, by talking of an alliance against the rest of Canada, had gone too far.

Two by-elections late in the year strengthened King's conviction that Canadians would respond positively to an appeal for national unity. In British Columbia the Liberals won a by-election in Victoria, a riding which had been held by the Conservatives for thirty years. This was all the more encouraging because Pattullo was still bitter at King's refusal to help finance the Fraser River bridge and the victory was achieved with little help from the provincial Liberal organization.[86] Lotbinière in Quebec had always been a Liberal riding but the by-election there was significant because the Liberal candidate was opposed by a fiery independent who campaigned on a platform of provincial autonomy and international neutrality.[87] The election of the Liberal with a large majority suggested that even French Canadians could accept King's version of unity.

These promising political portents had one serious hazard. Mackenzie King was lulled into a false sense of security. It was wearing to be constantly on guard in his relations with the provincial Premiers but his conviction that the majority of Canadians would support him made it easier to be calm and firm in the face of provincial attacks. But Aberhart, Duplessis, and Hepburn were more than irresponsible demagogues. They were reacting, at least in part, to the devastating drought on the prairies and the recession of 1937. King, conscious of his tactical advantage and confident that he could win the next federal election, was too inclined to see the recession as no more than a temporary economic setback for which his government could not be held responsible. Eventually the rains would fall and prosperity would return. He therefore underestimated the disillusionment of many Canadians whose expectations of economic recovery had been dashed and who were now more inclined than ever to look to governments for remedial action. He still did not realize that regional frustrations were too profound to be resolved by political tactics.

King's unwillingness to consider new federal initiatives is illustrated by an unpublicized incident late in the year. In December 1937 Mrs Mary Sutherland, a member of the National Employment Commission, told him that the commission was now drafting its final report and would be recommending that the federal government should take over the full costs of unemployment relief. King was shocked. Such a recommendation would receive widespread support but it would also make it difficult to balance the federal budget. He immediately told Norman Rogers that the commission would have to revise its report. Rogers defended the recommendation, arguing that it was a logical extension of a national unemployment insurance scheme, but King paid no attention. He insisted that Rogers see Purvis, the Chairman of the commission, and tell him that the proposal was unacceptable.[88]

There was a bitter discussion when the Cabinet met next morning. Rogers again defended the recommendation and also protested that the commission had already agreed on its report and that he could not interfere. King showed no respect for the traditional independence of Royal Commissions when he thought the survival of his government was at stake. "I pointed out," he recorded, "that a Commission is an arm of Government, and should not be used to destroy the body that created it." Gardiner finally suggested a way out of this dilemma. The proposed recommendation had financial implications; perhaps the National Employment Commission could be persuaded to refer the problem to the Rowell Commission which was now studying federal-provincial financial relations. Rogers was given the unpleasant task of asking Purvis to amend his commission's report.[89]

Purvis was naturally reluctant to submit to political pressure but King insisted that Rogers must force the issue. This was a political question, according to King, and the government had a duty to impose its will; he wrote off Purvis as a man "bred in industry, and promoted because of ruthless attitudes of mind, and reliance on force, rather than any helpful cooperation."[90] King finally had his way. When the commissioners met again in January 1938 they still insisted that the report should express

247

their opinion that "a unified and coordinated system of nationally-administered Unemployment Insurance, Unemployment Aid and Employment Service" was needed, but instead of a formal recommendation to this effect they referred the problem to the Rowell Commission.[91] King was even more pleased by Mrs Sutherland's minority report which criticized the modern trend towards centralization and defended the local administration of relief.[92]

King had rejected the proposed extension of federal jurisdiction because he felt no political imperative to take on new federal responsibilities. He could not be swayed by Rogers' arguments whatever their logic; his answer was that politics was the art of the possible and that he, as an experienced politician, knew what was possible. King knew that William Mackintosh, an economist from Queen's University, had been an influential member of the commission and he explained to Rogers, himself a former Queen's professor, that intellectuals might be right in theory but still wrong in practice: "Rogers spoke of being logical, etc. and I pointed out that in politics one had to do as one at sea with a sailing ship; not try to go straight ahead, but reach one's course, having regard for prevailing winds. That it was the academic mind which saw only its theory and objective, and the logic, but left the human factor out of consideration which occasioned so much failure in public affairs."[93] King's confidence in his own judgment was not affected even when he learned that O. D. Skelton and Clifford Clark, the Deputy-Minister of Finance, favoured the recommendation. He merely noted that these two men were also from Queen's: "This . . . caused me to see the whole picture in one minute which was that these men, all of whom are Queen's University, Department of Economics, have come together, and have been working jointly to seek to bring about a change in constitutional relations which will lead to a centralization of powers and away from the present order of things."[94] Until Mackenzie King became conscious of political danger he would rely on his assessment of the "prevailing winds" and would resist any change from "the present order of things."

CHAPTER FOURTEEN

THE RELUCTANT ASSERTION OF FEDERAL LEADERSHIP

MACKENZIE KING expected a relatively uneventful session in 1938. The Conservative Opposition had been weak and almost leaderless since the last election and could be expected to avoid any controversial issues until after its leadership convention in July. The trade negotiations with Great Britain and the United States would be difficult but King was confident that the results would be satisfactory. Some of the provincial Premiers would likely be troublesome but King had no plans for any federal initiatives which might provoke a confrontation. The emphasis was to be on sound administration and a low political profile.

King was wrong because he had underestimated the significance of the economic recession. His policy of retrenchment and his plans for a balanced budget would be challenged, not by his political opponents but by some of his own colleagues who had come to the conclusion that the federal government should increase its expenditures even if it meant a large federal deficit. There was no public debate but within the Cabinet there were prolonged and heated discussions. The budget of 1938, when it was finally presented in the House, represented a major shift in federal policy. Instead of economizing, the government had turned to federal expenditures to stimulate economic recovery. Mackenzie King had responded reluctantly and regretfully to the pressure of his colleagues—but he had responded. Although few people recognized its significance at the time, the budget of 1938 marked a new and very different approach to fiscal policy.

In the months that followed the session there was also a perceptible change in King's relations with the provincial Premiers. He took a firmer line with Pattullo and Aberhart in western Canada. There was no confrontation in Quebec over the Padlock Law but in Ontario Hepburn finally went too far and by the end of the year King had found a suitable occasion to challenge the provincial Liberal leader. What had promised to be an uneventful year turned out to be a turning-point in federal policy and in federal politics.

I

When the session began, late in January 1938, Mackenzie King had still not questioned his orthodox view of fiscal policy. He believed that economic recovery depended upon private enterprise and that governments could encourage this recovery by reducing expenditures and by reducing the burden of taxation; he still adhered to the policy of fiscal responsibility which had restored prosperity in the 1920s. In November 1937 he had made a direct appeal to his colleagues "to see that we get our budget balanced and expenditures curtailed with taxes reduced. In other words to parallel the picture of our previous administration." He was disturbed to note that, apart from Dunning, none of his colleagues responded with enthusiasm to his appeal for retrenchment but he was determined to have his way. When some Ministers talked of increasing their departmental estimates he deplored this evidence of the erosion of fiscal responsibility and accused them of yielding to "the socialistic and other trends of the times" instead of holding firmly to their duty as trustees of the public purse.[1] His own fiscal orthodoxy was unaffected by these trends because it was firmly based on his conviction that at the next election the majority of voters would show their approval of a government which had balanced its budget.

The recession of 1937 was a serious setback to his plans only because it would now take longer to bring the federal budget into balance. Charles Dunning outlined the financial picture to the Cabinet in January 1938. There would probably be a deficit of twenty-five million dollars by the end of the fiscal year, mainly because the prairie drought had increased the railway deficit and the costs of agricultural relief. If the budget was to be balanced in the following year he would not be able to introduce any tax reductions except for the tariff changes which would be part of the trade agreement being negotiated in Washington; the emphasis would have to be on reduced expenditures. Mackenzie King supported his Minister of Finance: "I made a strong plea for a balanced budget for next year at all costs," he recorded in his diary, "pointing out that it would, in all probability, be the last year's record before a general election, and that it was all important that we should have a surplus and some reduction of taxation before going to the country. Moreover the danger of a temporary recession made it more imperative that we should economize as much as possible."[2] He followed this up by a letter to each Minister asking them individually to reduce the estimates of their departmental expenditures.[3]

Most of the Ministers accepted King's assessment of the political situation and agreed with the necessity of limiting expenditures. C. D. Howe expressed the views of the majority when he assured King of his "entire agreement as to the desirability of balancing the budget and if possible making a start at reducing taxation," and went on to promise his full co-operation.[4] Some Ministers did stress the difficulty of reducing the estimates of their own departments but even they promised to do their best.[5] Only T. A. Crerar, the Minister of Mines and Resources, questioned King's fiscal policy. Crerar did not use the Keynesian argument that any increased government expenditures would stimulate economic activity during a recession; he agreed that "unnecessary expenditures" should be eliminated. His argument was that the budget could not be balanced by retrenchment. Most of the federal expenditures were fixed costs—interest payments, railway deficits, defence requirements, and re-lief payments were unavoidable—and so a balanced budget depended on increased revenues. Since higher rates of taxation were out of the question the only answer was to stimulate economic activity and thus increase the revenue from existing taxes. By spending money for the discovery and development of new mines, for example, government revenues would eventually be increased. Crerar was advocating direct assistance to private enterprise rather than the indirect assistance of reduced taxation.[6] King thanked him for "the care and thought" he had given to the problem[7] but he was not convinced, probably because Crerar's scheme would not pro-duce the desired results before the next election. By the end of January, however, the apparent consensus of his other colleagues had produced disappointing results. Most of the Ministers submitted estimates for their departments which were higher than the year before. A committee of Cabinet, under strong pressure from King and Dunning, did reduce these submissions by some twelve million dollars but, even so, the main estimates when they were tabled in the House early in February still showed an increase over the year before of almost ten million dollars. And this had not been easy. "At times," according to King, "the discussion was quite heated with Ministers seeking to defend expenditures of their Departments."[8] He deplored the intransigence of his colleagues but consoled himself that he and Dunning had done as much as could be done.[9]

The next two months brought strong pressure on the government to do something more. The rest of Canada was feeling the effects of the western crop failure in 1937; by the spring of 1938 the seriousness of the recession could not be ignored. The government was attacked in the

House for doing "practically nothing."[10] Government backbenchers were also becoming restive and, as one Manitoba Liberal reported, "there is a rumble which may develop into a roar in the very near future if something is not done in a spectacular way."[11] By the end of March there were disturbing reports from British Columbia of high unemployment figures and of a militant attitude among the unemployed, exacerbated by Pattullo's efforts to reduce provincial aid to municipalities.[12] Dunning still insisted that a balanced budget was the best way to win public confidence but King began to have second thoughts.

His first step away from fiscal responsibility came early in April when he decided that some public works projects were necessary to provide employment and named a Cabinet committee to prepare "a broad programme of national development." The cost of the programme was not specified but the membership of the committee was significant. Norman Rogers was chairman and all the other members were Ministers who had resisted cuts in their own estimates in January. Dunning was not on the committee. King, however, would still not admit that the appointment of this committee was anything more than a pragmatic response to a temporary crisis. He noted in his diary:

In politics one has to continually deal with situations as they are in the light of conditions as they develop from time to time. The world situation has headed the countries more and more in the direction of the extension of State authority and enterprise, and I am afraid Canada will not be able to resist the pressure of the tide. The most we can do is to hope to go only sufficiently far with it as to prevent the power of Government passing to those who would go much farther, and holding the situation where it can be remedied most quickly in the future, should conditions improve.[14]

King was prepared to yield to pressure but he still intended to act with restraint. Even Franklin Roosevelt's dramatic response in mid-April to the recession in the United States did not impress him. Roosevelt had sharply reduced expenditures on relief and public works in 1937, encouraged by signs of economic recovery. The economic downturn late in the year left him completely at a loss. By March 1938 the stockmarket was plummetting and four million Americans were out of work. There were demands for federal action but Roosevelt had been reluctant to admit that only government spending could keep the economy afloat; he conceded privately that he was just "treading water" and waiting to see what would happen.[15] But Roosevelt did not believe in half-measures. By mid-April he could wait no longer and in a radio address he called on Congress to provide more than a billion dollars for emergency relief projects. Mackenzie King, relaxing at Kingsmere while the House was recessed, had listened to the President's broadcast with strong reservations; he was sure that Roosevelt had "gone too far."[16]

When the House reassembled late in April King still foresaw no major financial problem. He was even encouraged by the reports of his colleagues on the political situation across the country. There was "increased poverty" in British Columbia and Duplessis and Hepburn were still creating political difficulties but there was the prospect of good crops on the prairies and there were no problems in the Maritimes; the reports, according to King, "on the whole were remarkably good."[17] Even the first Liberal caucus was restrained. Western Liberals raised the usual questions about the tariff but King noted with considerable satisfaction that there "was scarcely any mention of unemployment."[18] Emergency expenditures might still be kept to a minimum: "I feel," he recorded, "we must try to come as near getting our budget balanced as possible before an election. It will be a hard fight to prevent these extra expenditures but I will stand with Dunning in trying to reach the point where we can reduce taxation."[19]

The Cabinet discussion on what was now called "the conservation and development programme" began in earnest a few days later. Dunning was prepared to accept the usual supplementary estimates to cover the railway deficit of forty-two millions for 1937 and six or seven millions for items not included in the main estimates, plus another twenty-five millions for the emergency. The Cabinet committee chaired by Norman Rogers had gone beyond a cautious response to a temporary emergency. It proposed projects totalling more than seventy-five million dollars. King was startled by the committee's recommendations and even more startled to learn that many of his colleagues favoured this reckless extravagance. He recorded, almost with disbelief, that "it was the most trying day we have had in Cabinet since the beginning of the year. With the exception of Dunning and myself, all other members seemed to be intent upon large and, in some respects, wasteful expenditures at the present time."[20]

The differences were even more profound than King realized. He still assumed that the objective was to keep the federal deficit to as small a figure as the political situation would permit. Rogers, in contrast, had modified his views on fiscal policy and now saw positive economic benefits in federal deficits. King, who believed that Rogers shared his liberal ideals, was quite unprepared for him of all people to be arguing for fiscal irresponsibility.

Rogers' views had evolved slowly. His liberalism, like King's, was shaped by a sense of moral responsibility for the underprivileged; social services such as old-age pensions and unemployment insurance seemed to him a legitimate responsibility for government in an industrial society. He had been more inclined than King to assign the federal government a major social role but had always conceded that the federal government must be fiscally responsible. Economic recovery had therefore seemed a necessary preliminary to social reform.[21] His experience as Minister of Labour may have made him more acutely aware of the tragedy of unemployment and more frustrated by the restraints of fiscal orthodoxy but until 1938 he had assumed, like King, that economic recovery would be achieved by encouraging private investment. Now, however, he had changed his mind. Instead of defending federal expenditures on humanitarian or on political grounds, as a regrettable but necessary response to an emergency, he argued that spending more money was a constructive response to the depression.

Rogers' ideas seem to have come from the maligned National Employment Commission. The final report of the commission, tabled in April 1938, had included some fairly obvious recommendations. It had argued, for example, that direct relief was wasteful and government funds would be better spent on public-works projects. It had also underlined the economic importance of the construction industry and the tourist trade and had suggested a youth-training scheme. The commissioners had stressed the need for a nationally co-ordinated employment programme; it was this concern which had convinced them that the federal government should take over the full responsibility for unemployment relief.[22] The significance of the report, however, was less in its recommendations than in the arguments it used to justify its proposals. It recognized what most Canadians only dimly sensed—that Canada had become an industrialized country and that industrialization led to economic instability. The depression was a result of this industrialization: "though crop failures and other disasters may intensify the distress arising from depression, unemployment of labour, capital and resources is of its essence."[23] If depressions, like periods of frenetic economic expansion, were part of an industrial cycle, the solution was to regulate the employment of labour and capital so as to minimize economic fluctuations. The answer, according to the commission, was to regulate the level of investment. Private investment tended to increase in times of prosperity and decline during depressions and thus exaggerate the cyclical pattern. The total investment, however, was the sum of private and public investment. Governments could therefore moderate the cyclical swings by "a policy under which public expenditures might be expanded and contracted to offset fluctuations in private expenditures."[24]

The commission did not claim to have a magic cure for the depression. It admitted that Canada was dependent on international trade and could not insulate itself from economic conditions elsewhere in the world. Nor did it recommend massive government intervention; its specific recommendations were modest and almost tentative. The underlying theory, however, was a radical contradiction of orthodox fiscal policy. Governments in the past had tried to balance the cost of the services they provided with the revenue they collected; politicians weighed the popularity of expanded services against the unpopularity of collecting more taxes. The commission was proposing a completely different approach. The government, instead of being concerned with paying for the services it provided, was to concern itself with the total expenditures, public and private, which would maintain a stable economy. The budget would become the balance wheel of the national economy instead of the balance sheet of the government. John Maynard Keynes had come to Canada.

Norman Rogers was a ready convert to this Keynesian approach because he had always favoured a major social role for the federal government but had been frustrated by the need to balance the budget. The report of the National Employment Commission now provided him with a theoretical justification for federal action. He became the spokesman for the new approach within the Cabinet and, as King noted, "showed a great deal of impatience at any suggestion of seeking to have the budget even approximately balancing."[25] Convinced that federal initiative was now both necessary and feasible he even threatened to resign "in the event of not having his stand upheld."[26]

Mackenzie King had reacted differently to the report of the National Employment Commission. He had been appalled at the suggestion that the federal government should take over full responsibility for unemployment relief because he did not want to increase federal obligations. He dismissed the other recommendations of the commission as irrelevant until the federal government had the necessary surplus funds. He ignored the arguments for a Keynesian fiscal policy because he lacked Rogers' sense of urgency to do something. King, dominated as always by his political perspective, saw no need for his government to consider a radical fiscal innovation. He belittled the report as an "academic treatise" and was sorry he had ever appointed the commission now that it threatened to complicate his life.[27]

King might pay little attention to the report of a Royal Commission but he did react to divisions within the Cabinet. Rogers had talked of resigning if the government did not increase its expenditures. Charles Dunning, who was not converted by Keynesian arguments, was equally adamant that such expenditures would be wasteful and irresponsible and that it was his duty to keep the deficit to a minimum. If his colleagues over-ruled him, he threatened to resign.[28] King might not be impressed by academic arguments but he did see the political danger of a Cabinet split. He was not so much concerned with deciding which fiscal policy was right as with trying to find a compromise which both of them would accept. The alternative, as he told his colleagues, was a split in the party "which would affect its future."[29]

King's warning may have had some effect. Some of the Ministers had sided with Rogers, not because they were convinced by Keynesian argu-ments but because they saw the opportunity of increasing the estimates of their own departments.* Many of them now conceded that not all the increases were necessary and it was agreed that Dunning would meet with Rogers' committee to prepare a new set of estimates. By May 30, after almost three weeks of discussions, the full Cabinet finally agreed on a revised estimate of expenditures for the year.

The new estimates, which included the railway deficit, the increased departmental estimates, and the national recovery programme, came to a total of one hundred million dollars and brought the total estimated expenses for the year to almost five hundred and twenty-five millions. The recovery programme, which Dunning had first tried to limit to twenty-five millions and for which Rogers' committee had proposed seventy-five millions, had finally been set at fifty million dollars.† It was a compromise but it was still 10 per cent of the total budget. King's response to the con-frontation with the Cabinet had significantly modified the government's fiscal policy.

In addition to the revised estimates two complementary measures were introduced to stimulate the construction industry. The Municipal Im-provements Assistance Act authorized the federal government to lend up to thirty million dollars to municipalities at a low rate of interest for the construction or improvement of municipal works. The National Housing Act, which replaced the Dominion Housing Act passed by Bennett in 1935, encouraged house construction by increasing federal guarantees for first mortgages from 80 to 90 per cent on low-cost housing.[30] Mackenzie King was dubious about federal involvement in housing but he accepted

---

*King was especially critical of Howe, Ilsley, Power, and Gardiner who had agreed earlier to the need for a balanced budget but were now asking for large supplementary estimates.

†Almost half of this amount was to be spent on roads, including access to mines and tourist highways, to harbours, canals, and airports but significant sums were included for water storage on prairie farms and for youth-training projects connected with forest conservation. *Can. H. of C. Debates*, May 20, 1938, pp. 3093–6.

this measure because some incentive to the housing industry seemed necessary and because the social emphasis on low-cost housing made it more acceptable.[31]

The final addition to this economic recovery programme appeared in the budget. Both King and Dunning still believed that tariff reductions would stimulate economic activity by reducing the costs of production. Tariff changes in 1938, however, were linked to the trade negotiations with Great Britain and the United States. The budget had been delayed in the hope that these negotiations could be completed and the new tariff schedules included in the budget but by June the government could wait no longer. It would have to introduce a budget with no tariff reductions. King was worried about what he described as a "featureless budget"[32] and for psychological reasons he urged Dunning to include some tax reduction. His suggestion was to reduce the sales tax from 8 to 6 per cent as a further stimulus to construction.[33] Dunning agreed that some tax concession was desirable and eventually decided to remove the sales tax entirely from building materials.

The recovery programme of 1938 marks a significant extension of federal economic intervention. King still thought of it as a response to a temporary emergency, a regrettable aberration from the principle of fiscal responsibility. But the reluctant agreement to increase federal expenditures during a recession was a tacit acceptance of the Keynesian policy of contra-cyclical budgetting, of the idea that federal expenditures should compensate for a low level of private investment. For King it had been a response to a political problem but the confrontation between Dunning and Rogers had been based on contradictory views of fiscal policy. To avert a political crisis King had accepted a new and radical approach to economic policy. The federal responsibility for the level of economic activity, once conceded, would never be revoked.

The radical implications of the budget were largely overlooked at the time. Some Liberals objected but they did not challenge the Keynesian fiscal policy directly. Some of Dunning's colleagues were surprised to learn that even with the increased estimates the Minister of Finance still expected to have a deficit of only twenty-three millions; it confirmed their suspicions that Dunning had been exaggerating the financial difficulties of the government.[34] The sharpest criticism, however, came from the western Liberals who regarded freer trade as the cornerstone of Liberal fiscal policy and who saw nothing Liberal in a budget which included no tariff reductions. They argued in caucus that the government had shifted its policy from "one of unilateral lowering of tariffs to one of solely bargaining" and openly accused Dunning "of becoming Conservative, and yielding to St. James Street as against his old principles when living in the west." Dunning defended himself "in an almost passionate way" but the criticism was so intense that it seemed likely some Liberals would vote against the budget. Mackenzie King did his best to placate the dissidents. He argued that any unilateral tariff reductions would make trade negotiations impossible but assured caucus that if the negotiations failed the next budget would include tariff changes.[35]

Dunning was obviously affected by the accusation that he had sold out to St. James Street. He told King in the House that afternoon that his heart was bothering him. A few minutes later he collapsed. King was surprisingly unsympathetic; "I had the feeling myself," he commented, "that a good deal of his trouble was emotional and fatigue, and that while his heart no doubt was slightly affected, that the matter would not prove serious." Indeed, King saw Dunning's illness as almost providential: "My own feeling is that having secured a victim to satisfy their emotional strain, some of the Western members will now come a little more to their senses and, in the end, we shall probably do better on the division than we otherwise would have done."[36] Most of the western Liberals did come to their senses, either as a result of King's appeal or Dunning's collapse, and when the vote came only one Liberal went against the budget.[37] For King it was a very satisfactory conclusion to a very trying session.[38]

II

King was also pleased because this was the last session with R. B. Bennett as Leader of the Opposition. He had never liked Bennett, with his wealth, his self-righteous bombast, and his Tory principles. His dislike had been intensified by Bennett's victory in 1930; King attributed this to demagoguery and had seen Bennett as little better than a usurper, occupying the place that really belonged to him. Bennett's personal attacks during the Beauharnois investigation had embittered King even further and had strengthened his desire to humiliate his rival. Even Bennett's unprecedented defeat in 1935 was not enough; King looked forward to the day when the Conservative party would reject him.

King usually managed to conceal his feelings—he believed that politicians should behave with dignity and propriety—but he could not always resist the temptation to remind Bennett that he had been defeated. During the 1938 session, with the Conservative leadership convention scheduled for July, King found the temptation almost irresistible. When Bennett's retirement was announced in March King paid a tribute to his devotion to public affairs and expressed sympathy for his poor health because, as he commented in his diary, "it was the right thing to do."[39] When Bennett's sister, Mildred Herridge, died in May, King provided the government railway car to bring the body to Ottawa and went to the station to see Bennett off. Again it was the right thing to do but the gesture also gave King the satisfaction of feeling that it must have been galling for Bennett to have to endure such kindness from a man who had so decisively defeated him.[40]

By the end of the session, however, some cracks appeared in this veneer of propriety. Bennett was partly to blame. He was a proud man who knew he had worked unremittingly for five years, and who believed that he had sacrificed his health to save his country, only to find that his efforts were unappreciated and unrewarded. It was all the more galling to have lost to King, with his unctuous manner and his unprincipled lust for power. The death of his sister had also been a deep personal tragedy for Bennett because Mildred had been his confidante and his hostess at social functions until her marriage to W. D. Herridge, and her death intensified his loneliness. It was not surprising, therefore, that he became more than usually partisan late in the session. On one occasion in June when Liberal backbenchers were heckling him Bennett reacted by criticizing Mackenzie King for his absence from the House.[41] A few days later he accused Norman Rogers of personal patronage in his administration of relief and when a Liberal retaliated by producing correspondence which linked federal expenditures on roads with the Conservative election campaign in 1935, Bennett lashed out at King, the man who pretended to be so honourable but who encouraged his followers to be so despicable.[42]

Mackenzie King was outraged. In the House he launched into a bitter diatribe against a man who in two elections had tried to win political power by demagoguery. 'In all Canadian history there has never been an exposure of corruption and corrupt political methods so disgraceful." When Bennett interrupted with "Beauharnois! Beauharnois," King reminded him that for all his talk of Beauharnois in the last election Bennett had come back "with his party emasculated, well-nigh annihilated" and that his record would "follow him to the end of his days."[43] It was a petty and untypical outburst but King had no regrets. Bennett would go out of politics "discredited as he deserves to go."[44]

King quickly recovered his self-control but Bennett found it more difficult to hide his feelings. He came back to the topic of alleged patronage on two subsequent occasions but King kept out of the debate.[45] On the last day of the session King even drew the attention of the House to the fact that this might be Bennett's last appearance as Leader of the Opposition and, although he gave no eulogy, he did refrain from making any barbed comments. Bennett was unmollified. He expressed his "grateful appreciation of the observations of the Prime Minister" but went on to tell King that he would "never forget your kindness at times or your cruelty at others."[46] A few minutes later the House prorogued. In his last words in the House Bennett had not been able to conceal the accumulated bitterness of ten years of political rivalry. Mackenzie King had also been unable to hide his dislike for Bennett. He had shown more respect for the outward forms of political propriety but he had shown no magnanimity for a defeated opponent.

Early in July, a few days after the session ended, Conservative delegates assembled in Ottawa to choose a new leader. The convention, far more than the petty wrangling in the House, revealed how decisively King had won out in his political rivalry with Bennett. The Conservative party had been unlucky to be in office during the depression but the divisions within the party, which no appeals to partisan loyalty could conceal, were also a reflection on Bennett's ten years as leader. In 1938, as the proceedings of the convention made clear, the party could not agree on any of the current major issues, domestic or international. Most party conventions have to be satisfied with anodyne or platitudinous resolutions but there is usually some consensus, some agreement on the broad lines of party policy. The Conservative party, however, could agree on almost nothing.

The issues raised by Bennett's New Deal were still unresolved. Some Conservatives had never accepted the extension of federal intervention in economic affairs and the defeat in 1935 had strengthened their opposition; others still hoped to identify the party with economic reform and to lessen the apparent influence of big business and high finance within the party. The result was that most economic issues were passed over in silence. The problem of industrial unionism which had so divided the Conservatives in Ontario was never mentioned; the convention could only approve the platitude that labour "should not be regarded merely as a commodity." On the question of provincial autonomy the delegates were so divided that the organizers could only agree not to have the subject discussed.[47]

Even more glaring was Bennett's failure to win the confidence of French Canadians. The Conservative gains in Quebec in 1930 had never been consolidated. Bennett had not given his French-Canadian colleagues any authority or prestige within his government and had ignored their advice on such sensitive issues as bilingual currency and French-Canadian representation in the public service.[48] The situation had not improved since 1935. The party had disappeared at the provincial level with the formation of the Union Nationale and its weakness at the federal level is illustrated by its failure even to contest by-elections in French-Canadian constituencies.[49] For this Bennett was at least partly to blame. His Quebec colleagues were convinced that he had written off French Canada as irrelevant.[50]

The convention did nothing to reassure the minority. Arthur Meighen, with Bennett's approval, tried to make Imperial loyalty the rallying cry and in his keynote address he spoke passionately of Canada's duty to the Empire.[51] The French Canadians interpreted this as an open attack on them. They were not even mollified by the final, rather innocuous resolution which pledged the party to maintain the integrity of "our country and of the British Commonwealth of Nations." When the majority voted for this resolution they "sat silent, almost sullen, in their seats."[52]

The major responsibility of the delegates, however, was to choose a new leader. Here too the deep divisions within the party were apparent. There was no French-Canadian candidate. R. J. Manion, as a Roman Catholic with a French-Canadian wife and with no strong commitment to the Empire, had the support of the French-Canadian delegates. Manion, however, was not the choice of either Meighen or Bennett, both of whom found him too reserved on Imperial relations, too critical of business and financial institutions, and generally too mediocre to be entrusted with the leadership of the party. The problem was to agree on an alternative. One indication of the weakness of the party was that no other candidate showed strength or popularity. Many delegates vainly hoped that Meighen or Bennett would save the day by becoming a candidate. At the last minute the opponents of Manion tried to rally behind Murdoch MacPherson of Saskatchewan but by then it was too late. Manion was elected on the second ballot.[53]

Mackenzie King followed the convention proceedings with considerable satisfaction. Manion had a "bitter tongue" and would say "very nasty things at times," but at least he had "a generous side to his nature and was originally a Liberal."[54] More important to King than his personality, however, was the fact that he did not have the confidence of the leading Conservatives or of the businessmen who traditionally supported the party. The Conservative party was in disarray and King saw little likelihood that Manion could do anything about it: "On every side in the ranks of the Tories, confusion has become worse than confounded, as a result of holding a Convention. This also they have to thank Bennett for. It looks to me as though unless our own people make some grievous mistakes through division in their own ranks, either the Federal Party over questions of policy, or what would be worse, the continuous friction between Hepburn and others, Liberalism should be able to retain power in Canada for some years to come."[55]

III

In a minor way, Mackenzie King's outlook in 1938 was also affected by changes in his own office staff. When King had returned to office in 1935 he had soon discovered that the ad hoc arrangements of his previous administration were no longer adequate. The role of the federal government had expanded and inevitably the responsibilities of the Prime Minister had also increased. O. D. Skelton, who had once acted almost as King's Deputy Minister in all areas, now found that external affairs absorbed most of his time. Skelton could still be relied on to brief King and to prepare drafts of speeches or press releases on international developments at short notice but for domestic affairs he was no longer available and there was nobody to take his place. Within a few months of taking office King was bitterly complaining about "the utter impossibility of seeking, with my inadequate staff, ever to overtake what already has accumulated in the way of arrears, to say nothing of additional demands which are becoming terrifying in their proportions."[56]

Mackenzie King's domestic needs were adequately taken care of by an imposing number of servants at Laurier House. His staff there consisted of a butler, a cook, and usually two maids. He was also provided with a chauffeur and a confidential messenger, John Nicol, who served primarily as a valet. King had a resident caretaker at Kingsmere and, during the summer, in addition to some of the servants from Laurier House, he employed a fluctuating number of gardeners and workmen on his estate. He sometimes found his responsibilities as an employer a burden; he worried because his butler drank too much and did not always polish the silver, or because one of the maids seemed impertinent and sometimes stayed out on a date until midnight.[57] These were relatively minor problems, however, and on the whole King's household met his personal needs without complicating his life. The major problem was the organization of the Prime Minister's office.

King's official establishment consisted of a Private Secretary, H. R. L. Henry, an Assistant Private Secretary, E. A. Pickering, both of whom had been with him in opposition, together with a junior secretary and a number of clerks, stenographers, and messengers. There was provision for a Principal Secretary but King kept looking for the perfect secretary and so for three years this position went unfilled. Meanwhile he supplemented his meagre secretariat by borrowing staff from other departments. Edouard Handy had come from the Franchise Office and was eventually added to the Prime Minister's establishment. He became King's personal stenographer and by 1938 he had proved to be so discreet that King was dictating his diary to him instead of writing it out laboriously in longhand. Walter Turnbull was borrowed from the Post Office department for undefined duties and was soon dealing ably with the series of visitors who wanted to see the Prime Minister. Hugh Keenleyside and Norman Robertson were seconded in succession from External Affairs, although in the case of Robertson both he and Skelton had agreed with reluctance and Skelton was determined to get him back.

The problem of organizing King's staff, however, was more than a question of increasing the establishment. King was a difficult man to work for. In theory his office was in the East Block on Parliament Hill, but he had two offices in the House of Commons—a large office he rarely used and a small office behind the Chamber where he withdrew when his presence in the House did not seem necessary. When the House was not in session or on days when there was no Cabinet meeting he worked at Laurier House or even at Kingsmere and members of his staff were expected to accommodate themselves to his convenience. Any attempt to impose some organization was also frustrated because King was seldom punctual and kept no regular office hours. Nor did he have much respect for office procedures; he was always impelled by a sense of urgency, whatever his concern of the moment, and expected everybody to be at his beck and call. The confusion extended even to the stenographers and clerks who had to work evenings and weekends if King needed them; the fact that they were often not classified as civil servants and had no job security gave them little choice.[58] Until 1938 there was some justification for King's frequent complaints that his office was understaffed and badly organized but he himself was partly to blame.

A major improvement occurred almost fortuitously late in 1937 when J. W. Pickersgill, a junior officer in the Department of External Affairs, was assigned to the Prime Minister's office to replace Norman Robertson. Pickersgill adapted himself with surprising ease because he enjoyed the work and had no objection to the irregular hours or the inconsiderate demands of his employer. King, never reluctant to impose on his staff, took full advantage of Pickersgill's capacity for work, and soon acquired a high respect for his ability and judgment. In July 1938, when Pickering resigned, King turned to Pickersgill to prepare memoranda and drafts of speeches on a wide range of topics.[59]

Another change would come in October 1938 when Arnold Heeney became Principal Secretary. In theory this was to be a non-political post, modelled on the position of Sir Maurice Hankey, the Secretary to the Cabinet in England, but, as Heeney later learned, he and King would not always agree on what his official duties were.[60] Heeney, however, did bring a semblance of order into the administration of the Prime Minister's office, although no structure could ever impose a routine on King or adapt easily to the alternation between periods of procrastination and spurts of feverish activity. For King the significant improvement was the presence of Pickersgill, still temporarily seconded from External Affairs, still a probationary third secretary, but more and more the individual on whom King could rely for the day-to-day preparation for meetings and conferences, for speeches, or for the debates in the House of Commons.

IV

By the summer of 1938 King could find some encouragement in the political developments in western Canada. Duff Pattullo in British Columbia had continued to be an embarrassment, with his proposals for massive public works to provide work and wages for the unemployed and with his insistence that the federal government should help to finance the projects. His most recent project had been a highway to Alaska. British Columbians had talked of an Alaska highway for years but the costs had always seemed prohibitive. By 1937, however, Roosevelt was worried about the possibility of war with Japan and saw the highway as an inland link to Alaska. The impulsive Pattullo, who cared little for protocol, talked to Roosevelt in the fall of 1937 and made a special trip to Washington in the spring of 1938. He then informed King triumphantly that Roosevelt was prepared to lend up to fifteen million dollars for the highway.[61] King was not impressed with this generous offer. The United States would certainly insist on an explicit guarantee that it could use the road in the event of war with Japan even if Canada was neutral. King commented that this "would be, as Lapointe phrased it, a matter of financial invasion or, as I termed it, financial penetration."[62] Pattullo interpreted this concern for Canadian sovereignty as yet another of King's evasions but the only concessions he got from Ottawa were a meeting with the federal Cabinet to present his case and the appointment of a commission to consider the proposal.[63] The commission deliberately procrastinated and Pattullo's venture into international relations was tactfully ignored.[64]

By May 1938, however, Pattullo was less inclined to challenge the federal government because of his difficulties with the unemployed in Vancouver. He had always maintained that the federal government should be responsible for the relief of migrants from other provinces. To force the issue he had abruptly reduced the provincial contribution to unemployment relief in the spring of 1938 and had insisted that the only aid for those from outside the province should be free transportation to their homes. Some of the unemployed had reacted by occupying the Vancouver Post Office and the Art Gallery. Pattullo insisted that the men were a federal responsibility and that he would do nothing for them. The federal government refused to intervene. Rogers reminded the House of the federal recovery programme which was intended to create jobs in all parts of the country but he refused to make special concessions to British Columbia.[65] In the meantime, however, the unemployed were trespassing on government property. Euler, as acting Postmaster-General, admitted that the occupation of the Post Office could not continue indefinitely but assured the House at the end of May that so far there had been no interference with the postal operations.[66] Three weeks later, after increasing pressure from Vancouver and from the Opposition, the federal government reluctantly decided to evict the men.

The R.C.M.P. did drive the men out of the Post Office but only with the aid of tear gas and batons, and the unemployed retaliated by smashing windows in downtown Vancouver.[67] King had agreed to the eviction but, as a liberal, he was embarrassed by this resort to force. When Lapointe, as Minister of Justice, tried to justify the eviction in the House King commented that he "dealt with the police side of the matter not too effectively. Like myself he finds it very difficult to speak on matters of this kind.[68] But the government was lucky. Nobody was killed in the riot and the unemployed blamed Pattullo rather than the federal government for their plight. The situation remained tense in British Columbia, with the unemployed marching on Victoria in protest, but by mid-July the men had dispersed and King could even claim that the federal recovery programme had helped to ease the situation.[69] In any case, Pattullo's political difficulties in British Columbia would make him less inclined to challenge the federal government in the future.

The political situation on the prairies also provided some tense moments for King in 1938 but there too the position of the federal government showed marked improvement. In March 1938 the Supreme Court had published its opinions on the federal powers of disallowance and reservation and on the three Alberta bills which had been reserved by the Lieutenant-Governor. The judgments had favoured the federal position on all counts. The court had confirmed federal power to disallow or reserve any provincial legislation and had also declared that the reserved bills were *ultra vires*. It had rejected the Press bill on a technicality but at least the bill had been rejected.[70] King was naturally relieved. "It should let the electorate see," he commented, "that Aberhart has been wasting time and money of the Province in legislation that has been of no value whatever."[71] Even Aberhart seems to have conceded that the legislation was invalid. The Alberta Government did appeal the judgments of the Supreme Court but when the appeals came before the Judicial Committee of the Privy Council it only submitted arguments on the Bank Taxation bill. When the committee upheld the Supreme Court decision Aberhart went no further. He made no attempt to introduce yet another modified version of the legislation; the attempt to implement Social Credit theories had ended.

King's enthusiasm, however, was restrained because Aberhart was already threatening the federal jurisdiction on another front. His earlier legislation to cancel all interest on farm mortgages since 1932 had been blocked by the courts in 1937. He now introduced legislation to establish a one-year moratorium on all debts, to prohibit foreclosures on private homes, and to prevent any legal action to collect debts contracted before July 1936. In addition, there was to be a provincial tax levied on the principal of any mortgages held by non-residents of the province.[72] In sum, provincial debtors were to be protected regardless of their ability to pay; creditors would bear the loss with no compensation and would be taxed if they lived outside of Alberta. Financial institutions immediately appealed to the federal government to disallow this "legalized theft," pleading the cause of investment companies, with the usual reference to the defenceless widows and orphans who would also suffer.[73]

The legislation had political as well as financial implications. Aberhart hoped to extend the Social Credit party beyond its Alberta beachhead and these measures were designed to win support for Social Credit candidates in the Saskatchewan provincial election in June 1938. When the Alberta legislature adjourned in May he and some of his colleagues moved across the border and took an active and much publicized part in the election. The federal Liberals rallied behind the Patterson government, with J. G. Gardiner directing the campaign. More significantly, eastern Conservatives feared that the charisma of Aberhart and the popularity of his legislation would produce a second Social Credit government in the west and, in the face of "a real menace which otherwise may overwhelm the country," they forsook the provincial Conservative party and gave their financial support to the Liberals.[74]

The election results ended the Social Credit threat. Only two Social Credit candidates were elected and the Liberals were returned with a stable majority. Aberhart could proclaim that his crusade was only beginning but the Saskatchewan election marked his last effort to carry his gospel beyond the Alberta boundaries. King's press release was a partisan exaggeration of this "triumph of Liberal principles and policies" but there was at least some truth in his conclusion that the Liberal victory "would do more to steady the whole of Canada than anything that has happened since our general election."[75]

King had resisted all the pressures to disallow the Alberta debt legislation during the Saskatchewan election. He was already convinced that it would have to be disallowed to prevent "a collapse of some of the big Insurance and Trust companies, with very serious results to the whole financial structure of Canada"[76] but he was obviously not sure that prairie farmers would find this argument convincing. In June, with the election safely over, he was ready to act.[77] Lapointe expressed some reluctance but eventually agreed to disallow the statutes which restricted foreclosures and taxed the mortgage holders.[78] Aberhart, as was to be expected, attributed this to "the thumb-screws applied by the financial barons" but his reaction was surprisingly subdued.[79] He made no effort to reintroduce similar legislation at the next session.

Lapointe's hesitation had more to do with the political situation in Quebec than in Alberta. Almost a year had elapsed since the passage of the Padlock Law and in that time it had been invoked against a number of left-wing organizations and individuals.[80] The pressure for its disallowance had continued and if the federal government did not act soon its power to disallow would lapse. The long delay had not resolved Lapointe's dilemma; the federal disallowance of Alberta legislation only made it more difficult to ignore the Duplessis legislation. Woodsworth had already pointed out that the federal government had been quick to use its power to protect financial institutions but seemed less interested in protecting civil liberties. Social Credit members from Alberta had also commented on the apparent bias of the federal government although they attributed it to regional rather than class discrimination.[81] But although the disallowance of the nefarious Padlock Law might be seen as a tardy affirmation of Liberal principles or as proof of regional impartiality, Lapointe was also sure that it would be politically disastrous for the Liberal party in Quebec.

Lapointe finally submitted his recommendation to the Cabinet in July 1938. His reluctant conclusion was that the government should take no action. He defended his recommendation with constitutional arguments —he conceded that the law was unjust but this in itself did not justify disallowance; the Padlock Law, unlike the Alberta statutes, was not a direct invasion of federal jurisdiction and did not directly affect citizens in other provinces. But these were only arguments. Lapointe's decision was really based on his analysis of the political situation in Quebec.[82]

Mackenzie King did not understand the deep-rooted fear of communism in Quebec. He still believed that French Canadians would respond to an appeal to their liberal sentiments and could be persuaded that the Padlock

Law should be disallowed. If Lapointe could not be persuaded to make such an appeal, however, King could not insist. To override Lapointe's judgment would be a contradiction of his form of political leadership. If the Liberal party was to remain a national party he had to respect the views of his French-Canadian colleagues. King's confidence in Lapointe's liberalism remained unshaken. When Lapointe nonetheless insisted that an illiberal law should not be disallowed, King could raise objections but in the end he had to acquiesce.

King and his English-Canadian colleagues accepted Lapointe's recommendation with reluctance: "All," according to King, "would have preferred a reference to the Supreme Court as to the constitutionality of the Act, and I think all would have been prepared to disallow it had it not been that it was clear that Lapointe would not go that far. . . . In the circumstances we were prepared to accept what really should not, in the name of liberalism, be tolerated for one moment." King could convince himself that national unity—"the test by which we should meet all these things"—justified the decision but even he found it a sad commentary on the state of the nation when national unity meant that liberal principles had to be compromised.[83]

Mackenzie King's major concern in 1938, however, was not western Canada or Quebec but Ontario where Mitchell Hepburn continued to attack the federal government. Hepburn had alienated many voters outside of the province by his criticism of federal aid to less favoured regions and he had disturbed many of his own supporters by his feud with the federal Liberals and his alliance with Duplessis. Some aspiring peacemakers within the party had gone to talk to him but the Ontario Premier, probably encouraged by these visits, had bluntly replied that he would make no concessions; either King and some of his colleagues must go or the Ontario Liberal organization would be used to defeat the federal government in the next election.[84]

King was now convinced that Hepburn must go if the Liberal party in Ontario was to survive but he still hoped to avoid the risks of an open confrontation. He would defend the policies of his government but there would be no counter-attacks. As he explained to his colleagues early in May: "My own view, strongly asserted, was that we should not allow matters to come to an open breach; to absolutely refuse to let the party get divided until the moment of an election, working quietly meanwhile to get our own position strengthened. My feeling is that Hepburn will destroy himself ultimately by being at outs on so many sides."[85]

Hepburn was less patient and less calculating. He interpreted King's restraint as further evidence of weakness or cowardice and could not resist the temptation to goad him even more. When the Royal Commission on Dominion-Provincial Relations held its hearings in Toronto in May, Hepburn ignored his earlier promise to co-operate and appeared in person to denounce the commission as a devious attempt to exploit Ontario, with the probable result that "many millions would have to be taken out of the already half-emptied pockets of the people of this province."[86] A few months later he announced that Ontario would have nothing more to do with the commission.[87] During the summer and fall of 1938 he rarely spoke in public without including some caustic comment on federal relief policy, its "asinine" wheat policy, or its deliberate attempts to make Ontario "the milch cow for the rest of the country."[88] He now asserted that "Mackenzie King never did like Ontario" and that his own support for the federal party in 1935 was "a mistake I will never be able to live down."[89]

Hepburn was so intent on his attacks on the federal government that he sometimes ignored the interests of his province. He had threatened to fight the federal prohibition of the export of power but the issue was settled in March 1938 when Roosevelt, influenced by the advocates of public power in the United States, announced that he would not authorize any import of electricity from Ontario.[90] Hepburn, however, knew that Ontario, far from having a surplus, would soon be needing new sources of power. The St. Lawrence waterway could meet the province's future needs and this became a distinct possibility in May when the United States submitted a new proposal for the waterway. The proposed terms were financially attractive because Canada would receive credit for the money already spent on the Welland Canal[91] and the federal government in turn was willing to offer Ontario what it considered to be generous financial assistance for the province's share of the construction costs.[92] When the federal government asked for the provincial government's reaction, however, Hepburn did not even bother to reply.

Roosevelt raised the issue publicly in August when he visited Canada for the dedication of the Ivy Lea bridge across the St. Lawrence. With a frankness which surprised some of his Canadian listeners, he extolled the benefits of the seaway: "All that is needed," he went on, "is cooperative exercise of technical skill by joint use of the imagination and the vision which we know both our countries have. Can anyone doubt, when this is done, the interests of both countries will be greatly advanced?"[93] Skelton reacted to the speech with the typical caution of a federal public servant; he described it as "a forthright performance but unfortunately timed."[94]

King still refused to get involved in the controversy. "Our only desire," he told the press, "is to reach an amicable settlement with the provincial governments as well as with the United States."[95]

Mitchell Hepburn was less restrained. He had deliberately boycotted the ceremonies at the Ivy Lea bridge but he could not resist using the occasion for yet another attack on King. In a letter which he released to the press he challenged King to explain the federal policy on the St. Lawrence waterway—if he had one—and went on to declare that "Irrespective of any propaganda or squeeze play that might be concocted by you, you may rest assured that this government will resist any effort to force us to expend public funds in such an unwarranted manner or to foist upon the people of Ontario an additional burden of debt and taxation."[96] Hepburn's outburst was both rude and irresponsible because a few days later the Chairman of Ontario Hydro frankly admitted to American officials that Ontario would need the power which the seaway project would provide and even expressed the hope that King would ignore Hepburn's opposition.[97] King was certainly not prepared to intervene in a provincial matter to protect Ontario from the consequences of Hepburn's policy; in his reply to Hepburn's letter he merely suggested a joint study of the technical problems by federal and provincial officials. Hepburn's blunt response was that he was not interested in a conference.[98]

Mackenzie King could ignore Hepburn's verbal excesses, confident that most Canadians would approve of his own dignified restraint. But Hepburn's political activity behind the scenes was more disturbing. He was attempting to retain control of all donations to the Liberal party in Ontario and was reported to be using his influence with Duplessis to prevent corporations in Quebec from making contributions to the federal party.[99] He was also threatening to intervene more directly by actually campaigning against King. A federal by-election in Waterloo South in mid-November showed that this was more than a bluff. The riding had returned a Conservative by a narrow margin in 1935 but the Liberals now hoped to win the seat. The provincial Liberals, however, took no part in the campaign and, probably because of their abstention, the Conservative candidate won by a large majority. King's conclusion was that the federal government might be defeated at the next election unless "the situation in Ontario was remedied in the interval."[100]

Hepburn drew the same conclusion from the result of the by-election. Gardiner told King a few days later of his extraordinary interview with Hepburn in which the provincial Premier had threatened to repeat Waterloo South "in almost all the constituencies of Ontario at the next federal election" unless King resigned. Hepburn also offered to support Gardiner if he succeeded to the leadership.[101] King had Gardiner repeat this conversation at a Cabinet meeting early in December and then announced that "it was clear that Hepburn was a traitor, false to myself, false to the Government, and that the time had come when I should openly denounce him."[102]

Hepburn had finally gone too far, even for King, but King was still careful to set the stage for his counter-attack. As he explained to his colleagues early in December: "I thought from the point of view of strategy, that it was better that I should not appear to be defending myself or taking to heart what was being said against myself, but that it might be preferable I thought for the Ministers themselves to say something which would bring forth a protest from Hepburn at which time I could then follow the matter up, and would not be put in the position of appearing to defend myself."[103] The appropriate occasion was quickly found. The federal Liberals in Port Arthur were to hold their nominating convention within a few days and Hepburn had already threatened to run his own candidate against C. D. Howe. Howe and Norman Rogers both addressed the convention and used the occasion to denounce Hepburn's apparent ambition to have a government at Ottawa "which would be largely dependent on and largely controlled by the provincial governments at Toronto and Quebec."[104] Hepburn could not resist the bait. He called a press conference to denounce King and the federal government once again and on this occasion he even talked of voting for Bob Manion—"at least he's human."[105] It was a typical Hepburn remark, colourful and caustic but not calculated to please those Ontario Grits who might find it difficult to choose between the provincial and federal Liberal leaders but who would never condone betraying the party by voting for a Tory.

Mackenzie King, also true to form, carefully avoided showing any personal animosity. In his press release he explained that he had watched events in silence, hoping to avoid a confrontation. He had been prepared to overlook personal and partisan considerations but the issue now "has become one involving the standards which are to prevail in the public life of Canada, in the relations between the provinces and the Dominion, and the whole question of national unity."[106] As King described it the conflict had nothing to do with the rivalry of the two Liberal leaders in Ontario; he was defending public morality and championing the cause of national unity.

Mitchell Hepburn was no match for Mackenzie King in this form of political warfare. King knew that he held the trump card—that Hepburn had violated the canons of party loyalty by his threat to work for the Conservatives. Over the next few days King took the initiative. When

271

Euler asked him what the federal Liberals from Ontario should do, King avoided a direct reply but he did say "that if he discovered a viper gnawing in his breast he would know, I think, what to do with it." This was not to be interpreted as advice, King went on. He could only decide what his own position was; his supporters would have to follow the dictates of their own conscience.[107]

The federal members from Ontario read between the lines and concluded that they must now choose between King and Hepburn. A special caucus was hurriedly assembled which included all the Liberal Members of Parliament, the Senators, and the defeated Liberal candidates from Ontario. King did not attend. A resolution was introduced declaring complete confidence in King's leadership and pledging full support for him in the future. The resolution was passed unanimously, was signed by every member present, and was subsequently signed by almost all of those who had not attended.[108] It was not surprising that an assembly of federal Liberals should affirm their confidence in their leader on the eve of a federal campaign but the unanimous support for King was a striking affirmation that Mitchell Hepburn had been defeated. He could no longer claim that he had any influence over the federal Liberals in Ontario. King had not been able to avoid a confrontation but he had carefully chosen the time and the issue and he had won decisively. Hepburn could still cause trouble but, in federal politics at least, the Ontario Liberals had declared that they were Mackenzie King Liberals.

CHAPTER FIFTEEN

ON THE EDGE OF THE VORTEX

FOREIGN AFFAIRS had been almost ignored during the session of 1938. The international situation had been far from calm: the Japanese invasion of China had begun in July 1937 and, in Europe, Germany had marched into Austria in March and, in the months that followed, had threatened to intervene in Czechoslovakia on behalf of the Sudeten Germans. Mackenzie King, however, had deliberately tried to avoid any discussion of these menacing developments because he saw no possibility of influencing events abroad and no possibility of a consensus at home. As he wrote in his diary in March, "the least that is said means the least stirring up in the Commons and the Press and in the minds of the people."[1] The leaders of the Opposition parties co-operated. They were no more eager than King to initiate a debate on Canadian foreign policy because, like King, they were not prepared to take sides for or against German expansion. A forthright stand would imply a commitment to participation or to neutrality if European powers declared war and either alternative was politically unacceptable. It seemed wiser to keep silent.

Events in 1938, however, forced the government to move closer to a decision. It was not enough to insist that Parliament would decide. War was a possibility and Canada had to prepare for war. But how could it prepare without co-operating with the rest of the Commonwealth? To co-operate would imply a military alliance and participation in a Commonwealth war; to refuse to co-operate would suggest the probability of Canadian neutrality. In 1938 the British Government raised the issue by proposing a joint contract for the manufacture of Bren guns in Canada and by asking for permission to train British pilots in Canada. King procrastinated, reluctant to say yes or no, but by the end of the year he had acceded to both requests. The final terms were hedged with safeguards but the shift towards Commonwealth defence planning was evident.

The Canadian Government's policy on international trade was more positive. Negotiations for a three-way trade agreement between the United

273

Kingdom, the United States, and Canada had begun in the fall of 1937. King strongly favoured such an agreement and hoped it would be a major step towards the lowering of all international tariff barriers. The negotiations, however, had proved to be far more difficult that he had anticipated and it had not been possible to include the expected tariff reductions in the budget of 1938. The discussions at Washington continued through the summer of 1938 and the final agreements were not signed until November.

The most significant event of the year, however, was the Munich crisis in September. The Canadian Government took no part in the negotiations but Munich was nonetheless a turning-point in King's foreign policy. In Europe Munich was the last major attempt to appease Hitler but for King it had a different significance. During the Munich crisis he finally admitted to himself that his hopes for British neutrality in a European war were no more than wishful thinking. Munich was thus a personal crisis for King because for the first time he faced the unpalatable fact that a war in Europe would be a British war. He took it for granted that Canada would therefore be involved but he also feared that the Liberal party and the country would be divided. For three years King had refused to admit to himself that this was possible and had tried to convince himself that somehow he would be saved from the fateful decision of going to war. Munich brought the realization that the unthinkable had become probable.

I

Mackenzie King had returned from Europe in 1937 with the reassuring conviction that Neville Chamberlain was a man of peace and would do all he could to keep Britain out of war.[2] He found further confirmation of this in February 1938 when Anthony Eden resigned as Foreign Secretary in protest against Chamberlain's efforts to restore friendly relations with Italy. King could describe Eden as "a splendid man" but he fully approved of Chamberlain's policy.[3] Hitler's intervention in Austria in March had worried him because even Chamberlain's good intentions might not be enough to keep Britain out. King's first reaction to Hitler's threats had been that war in eastern Europe was inevitable and that Russia would become involved; "the problem," according to King, "will be whether Britain and France can, in some way, stay out. I wish with all my heart that the French–Russian alliance was at an end."[4] It was a great relief when Austria submitted. "Only the wisdom of not attempting to meet force with force but yielding to an overpowering force has saved war between Austria and Germany today," he commented in his diary.[5]

274

Over the next few weeks King welcomed any evidence that peace in Europe was still possible. Hitler had arbitrarily invaded Austria but King saw some extenuating circumstances. Dolfuss, after all, had been a dictator who had suppressed the Labour party in Austria, and the Nazi party, for all its faults, "stands in part for Labour."[6] The almost unanimous support for the *Anschluss* in the Austrian plebiscite in April gave further reassurance that there was some justification for Hitler's actions; the results had doubtless been influenced by propaganda and fear but the sweeping affirmative vote surely indicated general approval. And, regardless of the fate of Austria, "anything is better than war. . . . I am not without belief that having attained the results that have thus far been achieved, Europe may still escape war."[7]

Subsequent events did not justify his optimism. The Austrian coup had left Czechoslovakia in a vulnerable position and over the next month Hitler belligerently championed the cause of its Sudeten Germans. King could still tell himself that Hitler was dedicated to social reforms in Germany but he had to find some explanation for his aggressive behaviour. Was the war machine on which he had relied now out of control? "I waver at times in my feeling about the European situation," he admitted, "but still stake my belief in Hitler's word that the people themselves do not want war and that he, himself, has primarily the interests of the people at heart."[8] The frontier incidents in May were discouraging but at least Britain was "doing all she can to bring Czechoslovakia to her senses."[9] King could not admit that Hitler had deliberately provoked the crisis because that would mean that appeasement was impossible and that a war which would involve Britain was almost inevitable.

Then came the announcement on May 24 that negotiations between Germany and Czechoslovakia had broken off and that both countries were mobilizing. King was revising a speech on foreign affairs when he heard the news; he went to Parliament Hill that afternoon believing that there would be war in eastern Europe and that Britain—and Canada—would be drawn in. He saw no hope for national unity when that happened. As he recorded in his diary: "I wondered whether I would have the strength to continue at the head of the Government or whether the Government would last any time, as it was certain that Canada would immediately become a divided Dominion."[10]

King saw no escape from disaster. In the House of Commons that afternoon he could only plead with Canadians to avoid any premature commitments and to wait on events. They could not be indifferent to the European crisis but they must keep a sense of proportion. Their own domestic problems were challenging enough; they were "unlikely to have any surplus of statesmanship or good fortune to bestow elsewhere."[11] He admitted that the crucial question was to what extent the British connection involved Canada in European affairs but he offered no answer. One by one he eliminated the various possibilities. It was obvious that Canada should not automatically support Britain regardless of the consequences. Automatic neutrality was equally unacceptable; it would be "an unwise encouragement to potential aggressors" and, in any case, British policies might well merit support. But there was no middle way. Canada could not control the situation by influencing British policies because "a policy is not adopted at one stroke; it is the sum of many actions," and consultation before every action was impossible. All that remained, King argued, was for Canadians to decide their policy "when and if the emergency arises, in the light of all the circumstances at the time."

Mackenzie King frankly admitted that this policy "was not wholly satisfactory, not free from difficulties, not a completely logical position." The basic problem was that Canadians had not yet reached a consensus on Canada's relations with the Commonwealth in time of war. A more forthright policy, either for participation or neutrality, would divide the country. Under the circumstances the policy he had outlined was the only hope of maintaining national unity: "To force an issue like this on the country would bring out deep and in some cases fundamental differences of opinion, would lead to a further strain on the unity of a country already strained by economic depression and its aftermath. To invite this risk on a hypothetical question would be as great a disservice to Canada as any government could render."[12]

What of recent events in Europe? The Canadian Government, King explained, had expressed no opinion and offered no advice to the British Government. Nor would he presume that it was his duty or within his power to solve the problems of Europe. Only by implication, when he spoke of the British efforts to preserve peace, did he give any hint of his personal preference for a policy of appeasement.

Ernest Lapointe, who spoke later that evening, made it clear that he shared King's views. His own definition of the aim of Canadian foreign policy—"to keep Canada out of war; to keep Canada at peace"—gave no hint of what Canada would do if Britain went to war. Lapointe went farther than King, however, in his praise of British policies. Great Britain, he affirmed, had saved the world from war during the Ethiopian crisis and he believed it would save the world again by resolving the Sudeten crisis.[13]

Mackenzie King's speech introduced the only formal debate on Canadian foreign policy during the session but, apart from Lapointe, only

R. B. Bennett and J. S. Woodsworth spoke. Significantly, neither of them directly challenged the government's policy and they both prefaced their qualified reservations by explaining that they were only expressing their personal views and not the official policy of their party.[14] Bennett argued that King was wrong in rejecting consultation and co-operation with Great Britain. It was not only possible but necessary; if any part of the Commonwealth was at war Canada was liable to attack. The only logical alternative was to secede from the Empire. But even Bennett conceded that the Canadian Parliament should decide the extent of Canadian participation and that the government should make no commitments in advance.[15] Woodsworth disagreed with Bennett's view of the Commonwealth and thought he was more in sympathy with King's position. He could not be sure, however, because he was still puzzled as to what the government's foreign policy was. He himself was against war and his only wish was that Canada would lead the world back to peace through conciliation.[16]

Mackenzie King's policy may not have been satisfactory or completely logical but in the session of 1938 no political party was prepared to suggest an alternative. J. H. Blackmore, the leader of the Social Credit party, did not even participate in the debate; his position was defined earlier in the session when he described himself as "an ardent advocate of collective security" but plaintively admitted that he did not know with whom to collect.[17] The government's position evoked no flag-waving enthusiasm but nor did it provoke any clear opposition in the House. The silence on all sides was a tacit admission that Canadians saw no choice but to wait on events.

The debate on the defence estimates for 1938 revealed a similar concensus; nobody advocated significant changes in defence expenditures. The estimates presented by the government were down by some two million dollars from the year before. Additional funds were allocated to west-coast defences and two new destroyers were to be purchased because the war in China had caused uneasiness in British Columbia but other expenditures were reduced, largely because of the delays in the delivery of some equipment ordered from Great Britain.[18] This time some Conservatives did participate in the debate; they doubted whether defence preparations were adequate but they strongly approved of the expenditures for defence. The C.C.F. members repeated their misgivings about possible commitments to Commonwealth defence and four French-Canadian Liberals again reiterated their objections to high defence appropriations. In 1938, however, there was no Opposition amendment and the tenor of the debate was neatly summarized by the entry in King's diary: "There

277

appeared to be general acceptance of the Government's proposal," he wrote; "much less opposition in Quebec than last year, though still one or two men holding out blindly against the necessity of any Defence measures, and a tendency on the part of some of the Tories to go farther."[19] Mackenzie King's conclusion was that his foreign policy and his defence expenditures had successfully balanced the contradictions in Canadian attitudes.

II

Mackenzie King was unduly complacent. He had effectively blunted criticism by raising and maintaining a higher level of defence expenditures while at the same time insisting that the money was to be spent for the defence of Canada. This political compromise, however, left one critical aspect of defence policy unresolved. To what extent did the defence of Canada depend on Great Britain? Effective planning was almost impossible until the government decided its answer to this question. If Canada was to rely on Commonwealth forces and had reciprocal obligations to other members of the Commonwealth, this would determine her defence requirements. If, for example, Britain was Canada's first line of defence, it was not enough to plan for the defence of Canadian territory. The decision on participation could be postponed but preparations for possible involvement could not wait until the outbreak of war. During the summer of 1938 the British Government forced King to face this problem by asking whether the Canadian Government would supply Bren guns for the British Army and whether it would allow British pilots to be trained in Canada.

King found these requests embarrassing. He believed that Canadian and British interests were closely linked and that co-ordinated defence planning was logical because war-time co-operation was almost inevitable. He still believed, however, that it was politically imperative to avoid any appearance of a binding commitment to be at Britain's side. He had to rely on his political judgment to decide which forms of peace-time co-operation would be acceptable to most Canadians and which might be interpreted as commitments to a military alliance. His first reaction to both British proposals was to avoid any involvement by the Canadian Government. His procrastination frustrated the British Government but, more importantly, it provoked strong criticism in Canada because some Canadians interpreted it as a policy of isolation. By the end of the year King had cautiously but unmistakeably shifted towards closer co-operation with Great Britain in defence planning.

The possibility of manufacturing Bren guns in Canada had been discussed at the Imperial Conference of 1937.[20] At that time the British had suggested that the Canadian Government negotiate a contract with a Canadian manufacturer to produce Bren guns for both the Canadian and British armies. The advantages to Canada were obvious; jobs would be created and the Canadian Army would be equipped with Brens at a significantly lower cost. In 1937, however, King had been too apprehensive about the political risks of such collaboration and had postponed any decision. By January 1938 the British Government was losing patience and insisted that if there was any further delay it would have to make other arrangements.[21]

The Canadian Government, faced with the possibility of losing the British order, made up its mind quickly. It immediately began negotiations with James Hahn, a Toronto manufacturer. Hahn was an obvious choice because he had been asking for the contract for two years, had acquired the idle John Inglis plant, and had already been to England to study production problems and costs.[22] The alternative of producing the Brens in a government arsenal was never seriously considered because of high capital costs. The terms were settled by March; twelve thousand Bren guns were to be manufactured, five thousand for Great Britain and seven thousand for Canada, at a price based on the costs of production plus 10 per cent, with carefully specified regulations on costs and standards of quality. The only unusual aspect of the agreement was that two contracts were signed—one with each government—even though in each case the cost per gun depended upon the existence of the other contract.[23] The Canadian Government was still trying to avoid any appearance of Anglo-Canadian co-operation in defence production.

The Bren gun contracts became a controversial issue in September 1938 when George Drew published a magazine article entitled "Canada's Armament Mystery." The article probably attracted some attention because it appeared during the Czechoslovakian crisis. Drew, however, played on the North American fears of munitions makers by criticizing the decision to have the Bren guns manufactured by a private company. "For good or evil," he warned, "the stage is now set for the private manufacture of primary implements of war." Drew also tried to rouse other emotions by implying that the contract was a form of party patronage. One of Hahn's partners was the brother of a Liberal Member of Parliament. Was this the explanation for the cost plus 10 per cent contract?[24]

Mackenzie King reacted quickly and effectively. Within a week he had a Conservative appointment to the Supreme Court as a Royal Commissioner to investigate the Bren gun contract and had insisted that he be given all the relevant documents for his investigation.[25] Even Drew, in his appearance before the commissioner, conceded that King had responded "with the most commendable promptness" and had shown "the utmost fairness in assuring a full disclosure of everything connected with the contract."[26] In his report, submitted late in December, the commissioner exonerated the government by stating that there was no evidence of any corruption or misconduct by either politicians or civil servants.[27] He did recommend the establishment of a Defence Purchasing Board to eliminate any suspicion of profiteering in the future and King, determined to avoid any criticism, announced the appointment of the board at the opening of the 1939 session. The Opposition was also given every opportunity to debate the contract and the report.[28] His precautions defused the issue. The contracts, which might have linked the government in the popular mind with munitions manufacturers and political scandal, were only debated for three days in the House and were then all but forgotten.[29]

Two men emerged from the Bren gun controversy with diminished reputations. One was George Drew, who had hinted at devious political activities but could produce no evidence when the contracts were investigated. He had blundered because he had gone too far. Drew might have made an effective case against the government for its procrastination. For almost two years it had known that the Canadian Army needed Bren guns and that the British Government was interested in a joint contract with a Canadian manufacturer. The decision had been postponed because King had feared the political risk of co-operating with Great Britain and when the decision was finally made it had been too late to ask for tenders. Drew, by hinting at corruption, had missed the opportunity to draw attention to two years of equivocation.

The other loser was Ian Mackenzie, the Minister of National Defence. Mackenzie had proved to be surprisingly ill-informed about the details of the contract during the investigation and he also reacted badly to the criticism. Instead of defending his department in the House, he lashed out at "the sustained campaign of political calumny" and implied that the disruption of the morale of "the great Department of National Defence" was the work of fascists and communists.[30] King already knew that Mackenzie was drinking heavily and, after this performance, concluded that his usefulness in the government was gone: "I question now," he wrote in his diary, "if he has not aroused an antagonism which will pursue him relentlessly and possibly down him in the end. I feel extremely sorry for him but if he is undone, it has been his own undoing from the kind of habits that have been contracted through associations that are not too good. There was a time when I really believed that he might succeed to the leadership of the Party but that time has disappeared."[31]

The Bren gun contracts had threatened to become a political crisis but for King the British proposals for the training of air-force pilots in Canada caused more concern. Again it was a matter of political judgment: to what extent could Canada co-operate without convincing some Canadians that it meant a commitment to war-time co-operation? King found it difficult to make up his mind. The British Government was also partly to blame, however. In its eagerness to involve Canada in Commonwealth defence planning it sometimes ignored King's warnings and tried to win his approval of schemes which he had already rejected as politically unacceptable.

The first proposal went back to September 1936. The British Government had decided to expand its air force, which meant establishing training bases and training more pilots. Would the Canadian Government allow the Royal Air Force to establish training schools in Canada?[32] The Canadian Government decided that it would be "inadvisable to have Canadian territory used by the British government" for this purpose[33] and there the matter rested until May 13, 1938 when Sir Francis Floud, the British High Commissioner, again asked if the British Government could construct bases and train pilots in Canada. King reminded him of the fate of the earlier proposal and bluntly explained that it was still out of the question; "that any step of the kind would be certain to create suspicion, and arouse criticism on the score that an effort was being made to create Imperial forces, and to bring about a condition whereby Canada would be committed to participation in a European war."[34] A wiser man would have understood that King meant what he said. Sir Francis, however, returned that same afternoon with J. G. Weir, a British official who was on a mission to North America, to discuss aircraft production. Weir again raised the possibility of R.A.F. training bases and King tartly reiterated that they were political unacceptable.[35]

King's irritation grew to indignation in mid-June when Arthur Meighen posed questions in the Senate which showed that he knew the details of this meeting. Sir Francis Floud had assured King that neither he nor Weir would breathe a word of it but somebody had talked to the Opposition. Senator Dandurand tried to avoid any discussion by denying that there had been any formal requests or proposals, a deception which only showed that the government feared political repercussions if the details became known.[36] On July 1, 1938, the last day of the session, R. B. Bennett raised the issue again, with an emotional attack on the government's refusal to stand by the Empire: "Who," he asked, "would deny to the old partner who established us, the right in this country to create those centres which she may not have at home, to preserve her life and the life of every man who enjoys freedom and liberty under the protecting aegis of that flag."[37]

Mackenzie King had first interrupted Bennett to deny that there had been anything more than exploratory talks but as Bennett's Imperial rhetoric continued he decided, in his own words, "to launch out into a clear statement of full sovereign self-government."[38] He was, he told the House, completely opposed to "a military station to be put down in Canada, owned, maintained and operated by the imperial government for imperial purposes" and if the Opposition disagreed he would be happy to fight an election on this issue.[39]

It was all very well to oppose anything which could be construed as colonial subservience but this did not resolve the question of co-operating with Great Britain. Bennett's attack forced King to make a concession. As he noted in his diary, "the Whip behind me said, when I spoke again, to sound the loyal note,"[40] and a few minutes later the note was sounded. He would not consider British defence establishments in Canada, he repeated, but if the British wanted to, they would be allowed to have their pilots trained in Canada in Canadian training schools.[41] King had gone farther than he had intended to when the debate began and had announced a new policy without consulting his colleagues, but he had no serious qualms. Canadian autonomy would be preserved and at the same time the criticisms of Canadian imperialists would be forestalled.[42]

The air-training scheme was still far from settled. King's colleagues were "solidly behind" his proposal, as he had expected, and were quite prepared to increase the defence estimates for new training schools. The British Government also expressed its interest and sent Group Captain J. M. Robb to Ottawa to discuss the details. Unfortunately Robb had a different scheme in mind. He assumed that the pilots to be trained would be Canadians who would then join the R.A.F. The officials in the Department of National Defence saw no objection to this and a scheme was drawn up for providing facilities for the training of three hundred Canadian pilots.[43] Early in August, however, when Mackenzie presented the scheme to Cabinet, Mackenzie King expressed strong objections. Some of his English-Canadian colleagues saw no problem at first but when King pointed out "the political implications and the danger that this step might seem a commitment of war" all were agreed that Robb's proposal was unacceptable.[44]

King could only conclude that Robb and the Defence Department officials had forgotten about the political situation and were operating on the assumption that Canada would inevitably be involved if war came.[45] He was probably being too kind in his interpretation. The British Government was naturally disturbed by the possibility that Canada might remain neutral and was, in the words of a senior British official at this time, interested in reducing "the aloofness of that Dominion from Imperial defence and its disassociation from the problems of the United Kingdom."[46] This desire to involve Canada more intimately in Commonwealth defence planning may explain why an offer to train British pilots had been interpreted as an offer to train Canadian pilots for the British air force.

It may also explain why, after the Canadian Government had rejected the Robb plan, the British persisted. In September Sir Francis Floud submitted another proposal, still based on the premise that the pilots would be recruited in Canada.[47] A fuller proposal was submitted in December which detailed the division of the costs between the two governments but which again involved training Canadian pilots.[48] This was after the Munich crisis and King was prepared to bend slightly. He was now ready to expand the training facilities in Canada for Canadian pilots although these pilots were still destined for the R.C.A.F. or would remain in Canada as part of the R.C.A.F. reserve. This would mean, however, that if war came Canada would at least have the training facilities and a reserve of pilots for the common cause. His only concession to Great Britain was to renew the offer he had made in the House in July to train some British pilots in these Canadian training bases.[49]

The message finally sank in. In January 1939 the British Government noted "with regret" that its latest proposal had been unacceptable but was "most grateful for the renewed offer of the Canadian government" and asked to discuss the details.[50] By April Mackenzie was able to inform the House of Commons that an additional six million dollars had been provided for training pilots in Canada and that fifty British pilots would be admitted to the training programme.[51] But three years had gone by since the British had first raised the question of training British pilots in Canada and at least six months had been lost by the British refusal to believe that King meant what he said. The first British recruits were scheduled to arrive in Canada in September 1939; by that time the war had intervened and the project had been cancelled.[52]

III

The three-way negotiations for trade agreements between Great Britain, the United States, and Canada were also more prolonged than King had anticipated. At the Imperial Conference of 1937 he had favoured an Anglo-American agreement, firm in his liberal conviction that freer trade was the most effective response to the depression and would also link Britain and the United States more closely. An agreement could also have a wider impact on international relations; economic recovery in these two countries would permit trade concessions to European countries and this "economic appeasement" might save the world from war. The United States, however, was certain to ask for reduced British tariffs on items for which the British Government had guaranteed Canada a margin of preference by the Ottawa Agreements of 1932. If Canadian preferences were to be reduced, Canada expected some compensation, either from Great Britain or the United States. It had therefore been agreed at the Imperial Conference that discussions would be accelerated if officials from the three countries met together for triangular trade discussions.[53] Preliminary negotiations had begun in October 1937.

Mackenzie King, like Neville Chamberlain and Cordell Hull, had talked of the prospective agreement in idealistic terms, with frequent rhetorical references to making sacrifices for the cause of international harmony. The negotiations, however, were difficult and prolonged because each government faced the political necessity of negotiating a trade agreement which promised its country some economic benefits. The public talk of sacrifice contrasted sharply with the hard bargaining that went on in private. Each of the negotiating teams was inclined at times to accuse the others of refusing to make any concessions, and Skelton's acid comment on one occasion that "somebody else besides ourselves should show a little readiness to make concessions for the good of the world"[54] was doubtless echoed on other occasions by British and American officials. At times it even seemed that the talks would be broken off. King had confidently expected the agreements to be ready in time to include the necessary tariff changes in the 1938 budget. Instead, it was November before the treaties were signed.

Mackenzie King was kept informed of the situation by Skelton but the details were entrusted to Norman Robertson of the Department of External Affairs, who spent most of the summer of 1938 in Washington.[55] There was no way in which King could be closely involved because the triangular balancing of interests was so complex. The item of lumber, which proved to be the thorniest problem, will serve as an illustration of the difficulties. The Americans wanted British tariffs reduced on Douglas fir and other lumber exports, which meant that Canada would have to agree to a reduction in its margin of preference in the British market. This would be unpopular in British Columbia but the lumbering interests there might be satisfied if at the same time the United States would remove its excise tax on lumber imported from Canada.[56] The British Government raised objections because its tariff schedules did not include a separate classification for Douglas fir; if it created a special category the Baltic countries might protest that this was a devious way to avoid the "most-favoured-nation" clause in their trade agreements with Britain. The Americans, for their part, argued that their concessions to Canadian lumber in the Canadian-American agreement of 1935 had been more than generous and that they would have to have the consent of American lumber interests before going any farther.[57] As Skelton drily observed, if both the British and Americans were afraid to ruffle any feathers, "Canada would be licked before she started."[58] In April Hull informed the American Ambassador in London that the British and the Canadians were both being intransigent and that "no satisfactory solution is as yet in sight."[59]

By September most of the other items had been resolved but Skelton reported that "the lumber situation . . . is still very indefinite as proposal after proposal had broken down."[60] By this time, at the suggestion of the Canadians, the discussions were centred on the possibility that the British might reduce their tariff on all timber beyond a certain length. This would achieve the desired objective without openly establishing a separate classification because Douglas fir was usually exported in longer lengths than Baltic timber. The British negotiators were reluctant but eventually concluded that this was feasible. When the Americans in turn agreed to reduce their excise tax on Canadian lumber imports, the Canadian negotiators were satisfied and this item was finally settled.[61]

Mackenzie King knew only the broad outlines of the negotiations on lumber and the hundreds of other items under consideration. His only direct intervention came in mid-September 1938, late in the negotiations, when Canada was being pressed to make last-minute concessions. The British Government indirectly let it be known that negotiations might break off if Canada did not yield and that the Canadians would therefore be responsible for a major setback to improved Anglo-American relations. Coming at the time of the Czechoslovakian crisis this was a serious matter. King checked with Skelton, who in turn consulted Robertson in Washington, and was told that the Canadian negotiators felt that the British were really to blame for the impasse.[62] Robertson was therefore instructed to hold firm and the British were informed that the Canadian Government would not "be stampeded into making unwarranted concessions or to deciding in undue haste."[63] In the end it was the British who gave way.

The final details were ironed out by mid-September and Robertson then returned to Ottawa to report in person to Mackenzie King. The agreements he described were a complex adjustment of the triangular trade relations between the three countries. In broad outline Canada had conceded some of its preferential advantages in the British market, had reduced its tariff on American manufactured goods to approximately the same level as before the Bennett tariff increases, and in exchange had gained easier access to the American market for a wide range of primary products. King concluded that his confidence in Robertson and the other Canadian negotiators was fully justified. There was something for each region: British Columbia would be able to export lumber to the United States; the prairies had the tariff reductions on American manufactures which they had been clamouring for; central Canada would benefit from lower American tariffs on minerals, newsprint, and dairy products; and even the Maritimes would pay lower duties on fish exported to the United States which would more than compensate for the reduced margin of preference for their apples in the British market. King's immediate reaction was that the agreement "was even better than I thought it would be possible to have it."[64]

King's colleagues were equally pleased when they heard the details. Some of them were less than enthusiastic about certain tariff reductions which would affect industries in their ridings—Lapointe regretted the lower tariff on boots and shoes and Euler objected to the reduced protection for furniture—but all agreed that the Canadian negotiators had done well and that the agreement was "a great achievement."[65]

Mackenzie King gave full credit to "the skilful negotiations" of the Canadian officials and to their lucid presentation to Cabinet of "the most intricate and involved and complicated matter."[66] But he was also prepared to take some personal satisfaction from the results. As he explained to an English friend at the end of the year:

Having been on the inside of the negotiations pretty much from the beginning, and knowing what had to be said and done, not only here but to a certain extent in England and the United States, I think I can honestly say that but for the stand which, on occasions I took pretty courageously, and in the teeth of strong opposition, neither one of those agreements would be in existence today. If I never do anything else in my life, I still feel it will be worthwhile living to make the contribution I was privileged to make towards more friendly and closer relations between these three parts of the English-speaking world.[67]

The British and American negotiators may well have felt that at times the Canadians were more interested in driving a hard bargain that in improving Anglo-American relations. King could legitimately claim, however, that no trade agreement would have been possible if he had not been prepared to reduce some of Canada's preferential advantages in the British market. He could also hope that the agreements would bring Great Britain and the United States closer together in a world where friends were important.

Friendly relations had become more important than ever because late in August, when the trade negotiations were still at a critical stage, Hitler threatened to invade Czechoslovakia. The Sudeten crisis in May had seemed to King at the time to make war almost inevitable but he had been reassured by subsequent events. He had been encouraged by Runciman's mission to Prague in July, hopeful that he would persuade Czechoslovakia to make concessions and that this would improve Anglo-German relations.[68] By the end of August, however, the despatches from London made it clear that the Czechoslovakians were being stubborn and that this might well mean war.[69]

King hoped that the Czechs would yield to Hitler's demands because he knew what the consequences would be if they resisted. Hitler would send troops to the aid of the Sudeten Germans and Great Britain would be drawn into the war to punish the aggressor. King also knew what his decision as Prime Minister would have to be. As he told Ian Mackenzie and C. G. Power, who happened to be visiting him at Kingsmere on August 31, just after the latest ominous despatch had arrived: "I would stand for Canada doing all she possibly could to destroy those Powers which are basing their action on *might* and not on *right*, and that I would not consider being neutral in this situation for a moment."[70]

Mackenzie King was sure what his decision would have to be but he also dreaded the probable reaction. He believed that the majority of Canadians would accept the decision and, indeed, would insist on being at Britain's side. He was certain, however, that other Canadians would be opposed. This meant that if war came the country would be divided and the Liberal party shattered. King saw no solution. Even without conscription, even without an expeditionary force, he saw no possibility of a consensus, no chance of holding the Liberal party together. Everything he had worked for—the unity of the party, his version of national unity, and his own political career—seemed fated to end in disaster. His nightmare might become a reality.

The reaction of some of his close associates in the first days of the Czechoslovakian crisis seemed to confirm his worst fears. Skelton, his closest adviser on foreign affairs, argued that Canada should remain neutral. Skelton had no illusions that Hitler or Mussolini could be trusted.

In March 1938 he had described them as "two paranoiacs loose [in Europe] and with their hands on the levers of war, one imagining that he was a Roman Caesar and the other that he was an Aryan God."[71] But Skelton did not believe that German ambitions in eastern Europe were a threat to Canadian security. As he wrote to King in a personal memorandum early in September: "The contention that if Germany gets control of the Danube she will next gobble up Canada might frighten children in Canada. Even children in Europe would laugh at it. We are the safest country in the world—so long as we mind our own business."[72] This argument for neutrality would be rejected by the majority of Skelton's compatriots but his reaction did suggest that even in English Canada there would be some opposition to Canadian participation.

The probable reaction of French Canadians was even more disturbing. They would accept participation reluctantly if they accepted it at all. If King's French-Canadian colleagues approved of the decision and appealed to their compatriots to support the government, there was a chance. But would they approve? Power, in his conversation with King at Kingsmere at the end of August, was dubious. He agreed that neutrality was politically impossible and that the government would have to declare war but he thought the French-Canadian Ministers would resign in protest. If there was to be a government at all, it would have to be a coalition government, kept in office by English-Canadian Liberals and Conservatives. King could argue that this would be disastrous for Quebec but he could not even be sure that Lapointe would be influenced by this argument.[73] The probability was that the Liberal party—and the country—would be more deeply divided than in 1917.

This prospect was so shattering that Mackenzie King, for the first time in his life, lost hope. He was used to political crises and the threat of divisions within the party and in the past he had always responded, had decided what had to be done, had tried to impose his will on his colleagues, and, no matter how trying the situation, had always shown remarkable reserves of energy and stamina. A European war over Czechoslovakia, however, seemed so certain to split the party and the nation asunder that King was crushed. On the eve of his talk with Power he had dreamt fitfully of the Beauharnois scandal, the other great crisis in his political career, and had lain awake most of the night "thinking of what should be done in the way of meeting Parliament, arranging for eventualities, etc., forthwith."[74] The next night he could not even think of the future because he was laid low by an attack of sciatica. For the next two weeks he was confined to his bed at Kingsmere with a full-time nurse. It was the illness of a man who could not cope with the situation.

King still had enough resilience to deal with other urgent affairs of state. The commissioner for the Bren gun inquiry had just been appointed and King summoned sufficient energy to revise the terms of reference to avoid any implication that the government had anything to hide.[75] Skelton visited King's bedside to keep him informed of the latest despatches from London, of Robertson's reports on the trade negotiations at Washington, and to report on the Cabinet meetings in Ottawa. King was also able to dictate letters and the daily diary entries and to receive brief visits from Joan Patteson and other friends. But there was no doubt that King was seriously ill. As he explained to Skelton: "For the fortnight past, the pain continued to be such that I would not manage more than 3 or 4 hours of sleep a night, notwithstanding the presence of a nurse . . . to help in relieving the pain at times. I have [only] been able in the last day or two to get to and from the bathroom." Even King realized that his illness, real as it was, was nonetheless linked to the European crisis. He could discuss affairs with Skelton, as he explained, but he did not feel he could "possibly undertake to discuss any controversial matter."[76]

King gradually recovered. On September 19 he was well enough to move back to Laurier House and for the next few days talked with some of his colleagues over the telephone, read the despatches and newspapers on the events in Europe, was briefed by Robertson on the trade agreement, caught up with his correspondence, and worried about the future of his government. He was adjusting to the situation and was once more assessing possibilities and weighing alternatives. Even a war-time coalition, which had once seemed to be the ultimate disaster, was no longer ruled out "if cleavages in the party or developments in time made it necessary."[77] But King was not yet back to normal. He could talk to his colleagues individually but he could not face a Cabinet meeting.

His will to survive owed something to events in Europe. The expected attack on Czechoslovakia had not occurred and with every rumour of a negotiated settlement King could almost convince himself "that Hitler has enough chivalry and sincerity of purpose" to save Europe—and Canada—from war.[78] The next despatches from London would dash his hopes but at least negotiations did continue. And in King's mind what gradually emerged was the significance for Canadians of Chamberlain's role as a peacemaker. On September 23 King noted in his diary that "Chamberlain has been fighting the battle of those who wish to avoid war at all costs." Even if he failed, the situation in Canada might not be as desperate as it had seemed three weeks earlier. Many Canadians who would have been reluctant to be at Britain's side might now agree that Chamberlain had done everything that was possible and that Britain's cause was just.[79] For the first time since the beginning of the Czechoslovakian crisis King saw a ray of hope. By the afternoon of September 23 he had surmounted his personal crisis. He suddenly decided to call Skelton to ask him to arrange a special Cabinet meeting. Once more he was able to face his colleagues and discuss the government's policy.

It was a solemn occasion. King opened the meeting by saying that he "was pretty clear as to the issue and the stand Canada should take but would like members of the Council to express their minds first." He then asked each in turn for his opinion. There was general agreement among the Ministers present that Canada should be at Britain's side if war came. Power even reported that prominent French Canadians, including Cardinal Villeneuve, had surprised him by their reaction; they had been impressed by Chamberlain's efforts to appease Hitler, and Power now "believed the Quebec opinion would be much less antagonistic than he had hitherto thought." Power's opinion was encouraging but neither Lapointe nor Cardin was present at this Cabinet meeting. Lapointe's position was obviously of crucial importance but he had left to attend the League Assembly at Geneva just before King's illness and King could only guess at his reaction.

The Ministers who were present had agreed that Canada would be at Britain's side. The more pressing question was what steps the government should take in the meantime. Should it announce, as King phrased it, "that Canada would not stand idly by and see modern civilization ruthlessly destroyed." If the government said nothing and Hitler could not be appeased, the Opposition would argue that Canada, by not supporting Chamberlain, had encouraged Hitler to believe that the Dominions would remain neutral. On the other hand, if the government spoke out, it might be interpreted as a reversal of the policy of no commitments and of the promise that Parliament would decide. Ilsley strongly favoured "an immediate public statement." Gardiner, who was equally convinced that Canada should participate, preferred to wait. Norman Rogers suggested consulting the British Government on whether such an announcement was desirable. Only Michaud of New Brunswick argued for assembling Parliament first. Most Ministers, however, seem to have waited for a lead from the Prime Minister. King then explained that his first impulse was to make the announcement forthwith but that he did not intend to act impulsively. It might be enough to inform the press that the government had met to discuss the situation and that it was keeping in close touch with events. In any case he would have to consult Lapointe before any decision could be made.[80]

King immediately cabled Lapointe. The reply arrived the next day.

Lapointe knew that Canadian participation would be inevitable if war broke out. As a loyal Liberal his major concern was to persuade his compatriots to accept the decision when it came. He cabled:

Cannot see that any statement should be made, prior to an outbreak of war. Situation in important parts of Canada extremely delicate and requires most careful handling. Public opinion will have to be prepared, not aroused by irrevocable steps. . . . Immediate cause of war namely minority problems in central Europe not of a nature to enthuse our people. Submit that Parliament should be summoned, if war declared, and no definite commitment made meanwhile.

But Ernest Lapointe was not exercising a veto. He knew that the English-Canadian reaction could not be ignored and he had confidence in the political judgment of his colleagues. Almost twenty years of association with King had also convinced him that his opinion would receive careful consideration. In a moving conclusion to his cable he left the final decision to King:

I do not see how I can advise any course of action that would not only be opposed to personal convictions and sacred pledges to my own people but would destroy all their confidence and prevent me from carrying weight and influence with them for what might be essential future actions. Please consider these views and submit them to colleagues before reaching final decision. God help you. I still strongly feel that conflagration shall be avoided.[81]

Mackenzie King seems to have expected and even anticipated this reply. He did mention Lapointe's response in his diary,[82] but there is no record of any further discussion in Cabinet. King's statement to his colleagues that he did not intend to act impulsively had really reflected a decision not to make any public declaration. For him it was enough to know that the government would be united in favour of participation if Britain went to war. Nonetheless it is revealing that he did not comment at length in his diary on the reaction of his colleagues or on Lapointe's reply. He seems almost to have taken it for granted that there would be no serious opposition. His conclusion that the government would survive had preceded his decision to meet his colleagues.

His own personal crisis was quickly forgotten. Two days later, on September 25, when he took a Sunday drive to Kingsmere for tea, his confidence was fully restored and even nature seemed to be on his side: "I have never seen Kingsmere look more beautiful. The sun was bright and warm, the leaves in many parts turning gold and red. The distant blue, very clear and distinct. All quiet and peaceful. It was a lovely scene, and it refreshed me greatly to have this vision restored."[83]

For the next few days King followed the turbulent events with extraordinary detachment. He found Hitler's speech on Monday "more moderate than I had anticipated" but "felt the frightful menace of the totalitarian states"; Hitler's apparent determination to invade Czechoslovakia left "no ray of hope." On Tuesday Chamberlain announced that war would be inevitable if Hitler was intent on world domination but offered to go to Germany once again in a last desperate effort to preserve peace. King found Chamberlain's speech "deeply moving, very chivalrous" but he was not optimistic; a despatch from the British Government later that day warned that the German invasion might begin the next day. King read the despatch and Chamberlain's address to his colleagues and proposed that he announce that the Canadian Government fully supported the position of the British Prime Minister. Senator Dandurand feared that this was a commitment to war but neither he nor Cardin objected directly to the suggestion.[84] King therefore issued a press release approving Chamberlain's statement, promising that Parliament would be called if war broke out, and appealing to Canadians "to avoid creating controversies and divisions that might seriously impair effective and concerted action when Parliament meets."[85]

On Wednesday King learned that Hitler had agreed to meet with Chamberlain, Daladier, and Mussolini at Munich on Thursday, September 29. He spent a restless night and occupied himself the next day with dictation and reading reports. Finally at 8:00 o'clock that evening, it was announced that an agreement had been reached. King did not wait for the details; it was enough for him that there would be no war. He knelt in prayer, called Joan Patteson to tell her the good news, and then called Skelton to say that he wanted to send an immediate message to Chamberlain. The cable was an expression of "unbounded admiration at the service you have rendered mankind. . . . On the very brink of chaos, with passions flaming, and armies marching, the voice of Reason has found a way out of the conflict which no people in their heart desired, but none seemed able to avert."[86]

This rhetorical outburst was a measure of King's relief. He had no qualms about the way he had handled the crisis. His reference in his press release to "effective and concerted action" if Parliament was assembled had been the closest he had ever come in public to suggesting a policy of participation in a European war, but King was convinced that he had struck the right note. He believed that Canadian imperialists had been reassured by his firmness and that French Canadians had been reassured by his restraint.[87] King may have exaggerated his influence on Canadian opinion during the crisis; some English-Canadian newspapers had been critical that he had not stood "foursquare with the Mother Country" before Munich[88] and some French-Canadian newspapers had regretted his refusal to affirm his neutrality.[89] Now that the crisis was over, however, there was no doubt that King's compatriots shared his view of the final settlement. To Canadians, the German occupation of Sudetenland was a small price to pay for peace.

But Mackenzie King had learned something from the crisis. He had learned that even the most cautious political tactics might not be enough to keep Canada united. "The probability of having to meet Parliament with Europe at war was a nightmare," he wrote to a former colleague. "I believe I would have found it possible to keep the Cabinet united though Heaven alone knows to what discussions, in and out of Parliament, the whole business might have led."[90] Mackenzie King had no reservations about any eastern European settlement which saved him from such a nightmare. Munich, however, had been a close thing and something would have to be done to prepare Canadians for a future crisis which might have a different ending.

CHAPTER SIXTEEN

CANADA GOES TO WAR

UNDER NORMAL CIRCUMSTANCES 1939 would have been an election year, with the government concentrating on domestic measures which would ensure the renewal of its mandate for another term. There was much to be done because in western Canada the Liberal party was on the defensive and in central Canada the federal Liberals still faced the opposition of Hepburn and Duplessis. Circumstances, however, were not normal. Domestic issues would not be forgotten but Munich had altered the usual political priorities. In 1939, even for a government planning an election, foreign policy would overshadow all other concerns. A crescendo of crises in Europe brought the possibility of a holocaust ever closer and, although there would still be fleeting moments when King could hope that Britain would find a way to keep out of the war, after Munich he could no longer risk waiting on events. Canadians would have to be psychologically prepared for a war which now seemed probable and for a war in which Canada would be a participant.

Mackenzie King still did not believe that his compatriots would agree in advance to be at Britain's side. Any prior declaration of imperial solidarity would be interpreted by some as a colonial response, as an admission that British foreign policy was automatically Canada's foreign policy. King would make no formal commitment until hostilities began. But the government would have to make Canadians more aware that Canada's participation was probable and, if possible, to reconcile them to this probability. King still found time to pay some attention to domestic issues but until September 1939 his dominating concern was to prepare Canadians for the decision that might have to be made and to persuade the doubters that Canadian participation would be in the national interest.

I

Late in October 1938, after the Munich crisis, King and O. D. Skelton went on a three-week Caribbean cruise with brief stops in Bermuda and Jamaica. Both men needed a rest and, officially at least, affairs of state were left behind while they read travel-books or took long walks on the deck or along the seashore. Even on a holiday, however, they could not forget the fateful significance of the recent crisis. On a number of occasions they came back to the crucial issue of Canadian self-interest and the related question of the value of the Commonwealth connection. King might talk of "the richness of the inheritance of the partnership in the British Empire" but Skelton was not impressed. He "did not feel that the British connection meant anything except the possibility of being drawn into European wars" and from this he drew the logical conclusion that Canada should adopt a policy of neutrality.[1]

These debates would not change Canadian foreign policy. Skelton might argue with his Minister but as a civil servant he would carry out whatever policy the government adopted. King's record of their discussions, however, does illustrate the unlikelihood of Canadians reaching any consensus in advance on Canada's obligations as a member of the Commonwealth. King and Skelton had much in common—they shared many of the same liberal values, they agreed on the importance of Canadian autonomy, they gave the same priority to national unity, and they respected each other—yet even they could not agree. In spite of their shared attitudes and opinions the two men had different concepts of what kind of nation Canada was or should be. Canadian identity for King rested on British political traditions and this identity depended on a continuing association with Britain, whereas for Skelton Canada would find its true identity as an independent North American nation, cut off from the outmoded traditions of an older Europe. No arguments, however logical, would modify their views.

In any discussion of the national interest Canada's relations with the United States could not be ignored. Mackenzie King's attitude towards the United States was ambivalent. In spite of his respect for British political institutions he shared the American disdain for British snobbery and class distinctions. In mid-November, for example, when he was once more a guest at the White House for the official signing of the trade agreements, he commented on how much easier it was to chat with Roosevelt than with British officials.[2] He was pleased but not surprised when Cordell Hull and other Americans spoke warmly of the Canadian negotiators, who had "fought hard for their own rights" but were always frank, and then described the British negotiators as difficult and sometimes unpleasant to deal with. When King later repeated these comments to Lord Tweedsmuir, the Governor General refused to concede that the British might be at fault. The explanation, according to him, was that the American officials were jealous because "their opposite numbers in England were so perfectly trained & that they knew more about trade matters than the Americans did." King thought that this "is typical of the English attitude." In his opinion, "the Americans are equal in every particular to their opposite numbers in Britain."[3]

But this sense of cultural affinity with the Americans and this respect for their competence did not undermine King's concern for Canadian identity. He saw the United States as a friendly power and he favoured closer relations but he also saw it as a foreign power, pursuing its own self-interest. Such a powerful neighbour was a potential threat to Canadian autonomy and King was wary of American influence, however well-intentioned. This pragmatic view of Canadian-American relations was for King yet another justification for maintaining the ties with Britain. The alternative to the Commonwealth association, he told Skelton, was greater dependence on the United States, and of the two he had more confidence in Canada's autonomy within the Commonwealth.[4]

Mackenzie King knew that many Canadians did not share his view of the Commonwealth and that national unity could not be achieved by attempting to convert them to his version of Canadian identity. English-Canadian attitudes ranged from the North American nationalism of Skelton to the "ready, aye ready" colonialism of leading Conservatives. As for French Canadians, few placed much value on the British connection. No arguments for a Canadian foreign policy which tried to combine Canadian autonomy and Canadian obligations to Great Britain would create a national consensus. King would have to rely, as always, on the deeply felt commitment to the survival of Canada and on the willingness of liberal-minded Canadians to accept a compromise policy rather than a policy they preferred but which other Canadians would not accept. King did not believe that his compatriots would agree to support Britain under all circumstances but in the special case of Britain being involved in a major war, where her survival seemed at stake, he was sure the majority would insist on being at Britain's side. He believed that this was the right policy and he also hoped that liberal-minded Canadians, whatever their misgivings, could be persuaded to accept it. His efforts to avoid prior commitments and his guarantee that the final decision on participation would be made by Parliament had been designed to keep this option open. Now that war seemed more imminent, however, he felt that this was not enough. He would have to avoid "the one-sided view . . . which ignored the possibility of Canada being at war when Britain was at war,"[5] and take positive steps to convince Canadians that being at Britain's side in a major European war was the only alternative which was consistent with national unity.

King's first attempt to educate his compatriots was surprisingly inept. The session opened in January 1939 and King, wasting no time, raised the issue in his opening address. His argument was that a debate over Canadian participation was really irrelevant because the decision would not be made by Canadians. Any foreign power that declared war on Great Britain would also consider that it was at war with the rest of the Commonwealth. He quoted Laurier's dictum of 1910, that "if Britain is at war, we are at war and liable to attack," and argued that this was still an inescapable fact. King went on to explain that the Canadian Parliament would decide on the extent of Canadian participation but his major point was that Canada would inevitably be involved.[6]

King apparently hoped that this would clear the air but it was soon obvious that he had misjudged the sentiments of many of his compatriots. Indignant correspondents wrote to ask him what Canadian autonomy meant if a declaration of war against Britain automatically involved Canada. Was Canada still a British colony?[7] Even Ernest Lapointe protested that Canadian status within the Empire had changed since Laurier's day and that by the Statute of Westminster a declaration of war by the British government did not commit Canada.[8] These objections did not necessarily refute Laurier's dictum. Canada might not be officially at war but if a belligerent did not recognize Canadian autonomy, Canada might still be attacked. J. T. Thorson, a Liberal member from Manitoba, produced a more effective rebuttal. He introduced a private bill to eliminate the possible confusion over Canadian status by declaring that Canada would only become a belligerent on the recommendation of the Canadian Government, thus making it possible for foreign powers to recognize Canadian neutrality.[9] The bill never got beyond second reading but it did show that national unity would not be achieved by arguing that participation was inevitable. King had hoped to avoid controversy but instead he had drawn attention to Canada's anomalous status.

Neither Canadian status nor Canadian foreign policy had been clarified when, on March 15, German troops marched into Prague. Hitler's occupation of the rest of Czechoslovakia could not be defended as righting the wrongs of the Versailles Treaty or as admitting Germans to the Reich. It was a flagrant case of unwarranted aggression. Even Neville Chamberlain, the man of peace, denounced the invasion and drew the conclusion that his policy of appeasement had failed.[10] Skelton promptly warned King of the ominous implications. Chamberlain, he wrote, had shown a sincere desire for peace but "now his anger may drive him far in the other direction." And he reminded King that Chamberlain, "born and bred in a Tory imperialist school," would expect the rest of the Commonwealth to follow his lead.[11]

Mackenzie King knew that Hitler was the threat to European peace but even after Munich he could not believe that Hitler was irrational. He would surely weigh the consequences of his acts. In February King had sent him a personal communication to remind him that "war between the great powers of Europe" would destroy everything he had accomplished in Germany and to repeat his warning that if Britain became involved in a European war so would Canada and probably the United States as well.[12] Hitler had not replied but his occupation of Czechoslovakia in March was almost answer enough.

King was deeply disturbed because the invasion of Czechoslovakia again raised the spectre of a European war. He decided that he would have to explain his foreign policy more forthrightly than he had ever dared before. Again he felt twinges of sciatica before reaching this decision but there was no repetition of his illness at the time of Munich; his sleep was only disturbed for one night.[13] He would have to "make clear Canada's determination to stand with other democracies in opposing aggression and attempts at domination of the world by force."[14] When his statement was drafted he first read it to his colleagues and was agreeably surprised to find that "such criticism as was made was mostly in the nature of not being outspoken enough."[15]

On March 20, in the House of Commons, King publicly rejected isolationism. The statement which the Cabinet had approved still insisted that Parliament would decide but the government's recommendation to Parliament was no longer in doubt: "If there were a prospect of an aggressor launching an attack on Britain, with bombers raining death on London, I have no doubt what the decision of the Canadian people and parliament would be." By an oversight, however, the typed page with this declaration was missing when King read the statement in the House. He immediately apologized and asked for a delay until the missing page was located. Fortunately Skelton still had an earlier draft on which the revisions had been made. King then decided that the confusion would draw so much attention to this section of his speech that another sentence should be added to make the government's position even more explicit. Skelton protested that the proposed addition was unnecessary but when King consulted Lapointe "he saw my point at once and did not question it or demur." The clinching sentence, which appeared in the statement King finally read to the House, expanded on his oblique reference to the decision of the Canadian people and Parliament if Britain was attacked:

"We would regard it as an act of aggression, menacing freedom in all parts of the British Commonwealth." There was still the qualification that Canada would not be involved in a dispute over trade or prestige "in some far corner of the world" but the government's policy of defending Britain in a major European war seemed clear enough.[16]

The reaction to King's statement showed how deeply Canadians were still divided. Lapointe "supposed there would be hell to pay for it but it could not be helped."[17] He was right. The French-Canadian press talked ominously of French Canadians withdrawing their support from the government which now spoke openly of participating in a European war.[18] The English-Canadian press, in contrast, regretted that King had not been more forthright. Some English-language newspapers conceded that the attitude of the French-Canadian minority could not be ignored but others berated the government for confining itself to the defence of Britain instead of affirming Canada's support for British policies.[19] A resolution introduced by Hepburn in the Ontario Legislature was even more disturbing. It demanded immediate action by all parts of the Empire to support Britain; it was passed without a dissenting vote.[20]

Canadians had little time to adjust to King's clarification of Canadian foreign policy, however, because within a week British foreign policy had abruptly shifted. The British Government, now that appeasement had failed, decided to rely on force. Sir Samuel Hoare even talked of reviving the League of Nations and military sanctions, an idea which King rightly described as "evidence of hopeless floundering in present situation."[21] Chamberlain did not flounder but his reaction was even more disturbing. He had yielded to Hitler at Munich and Hitler had betrayed him. He would not yield again. He announced that Britain would fight if Hitler's next move threatened the independence of Poland. If Poland was to be defended Britain would have to construct a European alliance against Hitler, but Chamberlain, in his haste to take a firm stand, had not waited.[22] He had also neglected to consult or even to inform the Dominions of his new policy.

Mackenzie King was horrified. Only a few short months before Chamberlain had been ready to sacrifice Czechoslovakia for world peace. Now he was promising to fight to defend a country which could not be described as democratic and which two weeks earlier had helped to dismember what had been left of Czechoslovakia. King could still not believe that the eastward expansion of Germany was a direct threat to British security and he shuddered at "the thought of great Powers being brought into wars over wretched little States in the Balkans."[23] He was even more disturbed because he realized that any effective guarantee for Poland would depend on Russian support. If Britain went to war to defend Poland, with communist Russia as its ally, how would Canadians react? Would they be prepared to stand at Britain's side under these circumstances?[24]

Mackenzie King did not try to reverse Chamberlain's policy. He deplored it but he accepted it as a *fait accompli*. His immediate concern was to prevent a domestic crisis. Under these circumstances there could be no talk of inevitable involvement or of being automatically at Britain's side, but nor could there be any suggestion of neutrality. For four days he worked on a statement on foreign affairs, a statement which could not satisfy everybody but which, he convinced himself, was "well balanced from the point of view of holding the country together in facing a very difficult and critical situation."[25]

His two-hour speech was delivered on March 30. It was essentially an appeal to Canadians to keep calm and to rely on the government to act in the national interest. The government would recommend and Parliament would decide but in the final analysis, he argued, "our country's decisions on such vital matters, now or later, will depend on deeper forces, they will depend on the thoughts and feelings of the people."[26] King then tried to reassure Canadians that the government understood and respected their feelings and that all points of view would be weighed before any recommendation was made. He acknowledged that Canada's relations with the United States were important, that its concern for the United Kingdom was a vital factor, and that even the League had not failed completely. Canadian isolationists were not forgotten; one striking passage expressed a sympathetic understanding of their viewpoint: "The idea that every twenty years this country should automatically and as a matter of course take part in a war overseas for democracy or self-determination of other small nations, that a country which has all it can do to run itself should feel called upon to save, periodically, a continent that cannot run itself, and to these ends risk the lives of its people, risk bankruptcy and political disunion, seems to many a nightmare and sheer madness."[27]

The speech was an effective summary of Canadian attitudes but it did not go on from there to suggest a consensus or to say what the government intended to do. War might come and Canada might have to participate but in the meantime Canadians should be patient and tolerant, confident that the government was aware of their sentiments and would weigh them carefully if a decision had to be made. As J. S. Woodsworth commented later in the debate: "the Canadian nationalist, the imperialist, the League of Nations collectivist, the North American, the belligerent militarist—all will find some crumbs of comfort."[28]

There was one specific promise. If war did come, King announced, there would be no conscription. "One strategic fact is clear: the days of great expeditionary forces of infantry crossing the oceans are not likely to recur." Canada's contribution to a European war would be primarily economic. "One political fact is equally clear: in a war to save the liberty of others, and thus our own, we should not sacrifice our own liberty or our own unity." The government would have to direct the economy and would rigidly control profits but "conscription of men for overseas service" would not be necessary or desirable. "So long as this government is in power, no such measure will be enacted."[29] Here was the crumb of comfort which might make participation tolerable to French Canadians.

Ernest Lapointe spoke the next day. His speech was also an appeal for national unity but he addressed his compatriots directly. As he had explained to King, he "proposed to go very much farther than I had gone."[30] He rejected conscription because it would shatter Canadian unity; he would never be a member of a government which introduced conscription and would oppose any government which enforced it. But Lapointe also warned French Canadians that participation short of conscription might be inevitable. Could any member of the Commonwealth remain neutral if Britain was at war? The constitution provided no clear answer but in any case constitutional arguments were irrelevant. The harsh reality was that Canada would not be neutral. Canadians would not close their ports to British shipping, intern British naval vessels and sailors, prohibit Canadians from enlisting in British forces, or forbid voluntary donations to support the British war effort. Neutrality would mean the equal and impartial treatment of belligerents on both sides. "I ask any of my fellow countrymen," he challenged, "whether they believe seriously that this could be done without a civil war in Canada."[31]

Mackenzie King was immensely impressed by Lapointe's courage. He felt a twinge of regret that his own speech had been less direct but he told himself that both he and Lapointe had done what was necessary:

If I had made the speech Lapointe made the party might have held its own with the Jingoes in Ontario but would have lost Quebec more or less entirely. If he had made the speech I did, he might have held Quebec, but the party would have lost heavily in Ontario and perhaps some other parts on the score that Quebec was neutral in its loyalty. Together, our speeches constituted a sort of trestle sustaining the structure which would serve to unite divergent parts of Canada, thereby making for a united country.[32]

The three-day debate did show that, at least within the House of Commons, the government's prescription for national unity on foreign affairs was effective. R. J. Manion, in his first session as Leader of the Opposition, might have been expected to seize the opportunity to outline a distinctive Conservative foreign policy as an alternative to King's plea to wait on events. He had certainly been aggressive and partisan in his attacks on the government's domestic policies.[33] His position on external affairs, however, proved to be almost indistinguishable from that of the government. He believed that when Britain was at war Canada was at war but he too insisted that "the extent of participation must be decided by parliament." And he also agreed that there should be no conscription.[34]

Manion supported the government's policy because he too was concerned with national unity and his analysis of the political situation had led him to the same conclusion. He knew that he did not have the confidence of the financial interests which traditionally supported the Conservative party and that neither Bennett nor Meighen had much respect for his political talents. But he was confident that he could confound his critics. If he could win the election his detractors would be silenced. He had already invited H. H. Stevens to rejoin the party over the objections of some of his colleagues.[35] His major objective, however, was to win the confidence of French Canada.

Manion was convinced that he could win seats in Quebec. The Liberal government, he believed, was losing support because of its failure to resolve Canada's economic problems. He believed that he was projecting the image of a leader who could lead. In Quebec he could rely on the support of the former Conservatives in the Union Nationale and he hoped to have Duplessis as an ally in the next federal election. The only obstacle was the French-Canadian suspicion of Tory Imperialism. "This little man King," he wrote to a supporter, "is hoping I suppose that I shall say something that will get him back right in Quebec."[36] He supported King's foreign policy because he too wanted a policy which French Canadians could accept.

The other parties in the House also conceded that the government's position was logical. J. S. Woodsworth agreed that "the maintenance of Canadian unity is perhaps the greatest contribution Canada can make to the peace of the world" and that King's refusal to commit himself in advance was probably necessary.[37] William Hayhurst, speaking for Social Credit, applauded "some clear-cut statements by the Prime Minister" and commended his "adroitness" at not saying more.[38] Even the dissident French-Canadian Liberals were obviously influenced by the promise that there would be no conscription. Maxime Raymond and Wilfrid Lacroix were still opposed to participation under any circumstances but Lacroix went out of his way to express his confidence that there would never be conscription "as long as the King-Lapointe government is in power."[39]

The debate, in the words of T. C. Douglas, the C.C.F. member for Weyburn, showed "a remarkable unanimity in all parts of the House on certain broad principles of foreign policy."[40]

There was less agreement outside of the House. The politicians were more aware of the need for compromise than many of their compatriots. French Canadians generally welcomed the guarantee that there would be no conscription but this did not necessarily mean that they accepted voluntary military commitments. Some of them even assumed that no conscription meant that Canadian participation would mean no more than allowing English Canadians to fight for Britain.[41] The divergent attitudes in Canada could be seen in the reactions to Lapointe's speech. It was widely acclaimed but not always for the same reasons. Newspaper headlines in French Canada stressed his opposition to conscription; in English Canada the headlines announced that he had rejected neutrality as an option.[42] Canadians were becoming more reconciled to the possibility of participation but there was no consensus on the nature or the extent of such an involvement.

II

Statements on foreign policy might help to prepare Canadians psychologically but military preparations were also essential. Munich had convinced King that defence expenditures would have to be sharply increased. In November 1938 the Chiefs of Staff had proposed that the ten-year plan for the armed forces should be telescoped into five years: "In my own mind," King commented, "what was proposed seemed reasonable and almost necessary in world situation such as we know exists today. I doubt if the Cabinet will so view it, and I imagine both Dunning and Lapointe will be against such large expenditures."[43]

When the Cabinet did discuss expenditures early in December King "found it difficult to get colleagues and Mackenzie himself to come to full grips with the situation."[44] There was less opposition to higher expenditures than King had expected; "even Quebec members felt that considerable increases in estimates were necessary and would be approved." Part of the difficulty was that Mackenzie was not clear about the existing state of the armed forces or how additional funds should be spent. He obviously depended on his officials for both information and advice. Some of King's colleagues suspected that these officials were planning for an overseas expeditionary force and they gave Mackenzie a difficult time. King finally took the initiative and proposed almost arbitrarily that the defence expenditures should be doubled from thirty-five to seventy millions on condition that half the defence budget would be spent on the air force. His colleagues accepted the emphasis on air power but insisted on limiting army expenditures more rigidly and the government finally agreed on defence estimates of sixty million dollars.[45] In January 1939, in response to ominous despatches from London, they agreed to place defence orders in the United States immediately, even before the House had approved the estimates. King did take the precaution of explaining the situation privately to Manion, who readily promised not to embarrass the government on this issue.[46]

The increased defence estimates were debated in May. There was little opposition, in contrast to the debate of 1937. The Conservatives supported the increase as a step in the right direction although they suggested that even sixty millions was little enough.[47] The C.C.F. no longer opposed defence expenditures on principle; they had no objections if the money was for home defence.[48] Maxime Raymond and Wilfrid Lacroix still argued that Canada was in no danger and that the money could only be for overseas intervention,[49] but other French-Canadian backbenchers were now prepared to support the government's policy. They argued that Canada must be able to defend itself and they discounted the possibility of overseas commitments because they had confidence in King and Lapointe.[50] Events in Europe had helped to reconcile Canadians to these increased expenditures but the government had provided some leadership. The defence budget had been tripled within three years without provoking a political crisis.

Hitler's persecution of Jews created another political problem for the government in 1939. Mackenzie King shared the ambivalence of many of his contemporaries towards Jews; he thought of them as aggressive and clannish and disturbingly prominent in international finance, although at the same time he deplored any overt discrimination against them. His first reaction to the Jewish refugee question was that Canada had no responsibility. Jewish organizations and civil liberties groups in English Canada had demanded the admission of refugees but French Canadians had objected to any increased immigration, especially of Jews.[51] In March 1938, at the time of the Austrian *Anschluss*, King had seen national unity as an excuse for inaction; "my own feeling," he wrote, "is that nothing is to be gained by creating an internal problem in an effort to meet an international one."[52] After Munich, however, Hitler's intensified persecution of Jews was less easily ignored. King was influenced in part by the tragedy of the Jews, brought home to him in conversations with Lawrence Freiman, a prominent Ottawa Jew, and with Abraham Heaps and Samuel Factor, both respected Members of Parliament.[53] He also noted, however, that Great Britain and the United States were admitting refugees and that it would be embarrassing if Canada did not co-operate.[54] In November 1938 he decided that Canada should do her part even though it was "going to be difficult politically."[55]

King tried to persuade his colleagues by stressing the government's moral obligation. "The time has come," he told them, "when, as a Government, we would have to perform acts that were expressive of what we believed to be the conscience of the nation, and not what might be, at the moment, politically most expedient."[56] Norman Rogers and T. A. Crerar warmly supported him but Lapointe and Cardin "looked glum."[57] The eventual policy showed more expediency than King would have admitted. The onus was shifted to the provincial governments by asking them how many Jewish refugees they would admit. Those who were admitted would still have to satisfy the existing immigration regulations although Crerar, the responsible Minister, assured King that these regulations would be interpreted liberally.[58]

III

In spite of King's overriding concern for the international situation in 1939, western Canada could not be ignored. Prairie farmers had welcomed the tariff reductions in the 1938 trade agreement with the United States but by then they had a new grievance related to wheat marketing and the fate of the Canadian Wheat Board. The government had begun discussing its wheat marketing policy in the summer of 1938 and J. G. Gardiner had optimistically promised a scheme which would virtually eliminate the Wheat Board and restore the open market. He made valiant efforts to persuade the west to accept his proposals but by the end of the year he had made little progress. Any modification of the scheme which might satisfy wheat growers was seen by many of his Cabinet colleagues as yet another federal subsidy for the west. The arguments within Cabinet were so acrimonious that King almost despaired of any solution. The legislation, when it was finally presented in March 1939, was a compromise which satisfied nobody.

The Liberal government had inherited the Wheat Board from Bennett and had adopted the policy of selling the board's wheat as quickly as possible without forcing down world wheat prices.[59] Each fall the government had set the price which the board would offer for the new wheat crop but each year this had been lower than the open-market price and the board had not made any purchases. By the summer of 1938 the Wheat Board had disposed of its holdings and the government had been faced with a decision about the future of the board and the role of the government in wheat marketing.

Mackenzie King had assumed from the beginning that wheat marketing should be left to private enterprise and that the Wheat Board should disappear as soon as its holdings had been sold. In the summer of 1938, however, world wheat production was high and it was expected that wheat prices would fall sharply. Western farmers wanted the board to set a price which would ensure a reasonable return for their 1938 crop even if open-market prices dropped. King was in a quandary. As he commented in his diary in June 1938: "A very difficult problem, the choice being between retaining Wheat Board with prospect of Government purchasing and price-fixing becoming a permanent policy, and finding a way to get rid of the Board without completely prejudicing the position of the party . . . In politics one has to consider all sides of the question and all factors in the equation."[60]

King had temporized by agreeing to "a continuation of the Board because of exceptional circumstances" but he had relied on the assurance from Gardiner that within a year the government would have a permanent policy which would end government intervention in wheat marketing.[61] The government still had to decide on the Wheat Board price for the 1938 crop. Gardiner wanted eighty-seven and a half cents a bushel, the board price for the previous year, but some of the eastern Ministers vehemently objected. W. D. Euler bluntly insisted that anything higher than seventy cents "would be taxing the rest of the country to help the wheat growers of the west to make their profits." King intervened to plead for the farmers and a price of eighty cents was finally adopted.[62] This proved to be higher than the open-market price and the board handled the entire crop of almost three hundred million bushels. The cost to the government amounted to some sixty million dollars when the board eventually sold the wheat.[63]

In the meantime Gardiner tried to devise a permanent policy. Gardiner, like King, believed that wheat marketing should be left to private enterprise. He believed he could convince western farmers that in the long run they could not expect to get more than the world price for their wheat. Other countries would object to dealing with a government marketing monopoly and would buy their wheat elsewhere, and the rest of Canada would not subsidize wheat prices indefinitely. His proposal was a return to the open market with the government intervening only if prices dropped to an abnormally low level. Initially he talked of a guaranteed floor of sixty or even fifty cents a bushel.[64] In brief, Gardiner was proposing that, barring an unexpected catastrophe, there would be no Wheat Board and no government support for the price of wheat.

Gardiner knew that the western farmers had more faith in a Wheat Board and a guaranteed price than in free enterprise. To make his proposal more attractive he supplemented it with a plan for insurance against crop failures. Farmers were to pay a one-cent levy on all the wheat they sold and the money would go to those whose crops had failed; the payments would be based on their wheat acreage to a maximum of five hundred dollars.[65] The scheme was not based on any actuarial studies and in practice the levy would have to be supplemented by government subsidies to cover the payments but it was at least an improvement over the odious system of relief.[66] Gardiner's combined proposals guaranteed an emergency floor price for farmers who harvested a crop and insurance payments for those who did not.

The western farmers were not convinced. They had no objection to the insurance scheme but the virtual elimination of the Wheat Board was a different matter. Farmers' organizations argued that European countries had tariffs and quotas which eliminated free competition and that wheat sales already involved negotiating with state agencies. Gardiner regretfully reported to King that most farm leaders would welcome a permanent government monopoly for the marketing of Canadian wheat. If the government was not prepared to go that far they insisted that the Wheat Board should guarantee a minimum price that would at least cover the costs of production.[67]

Both King and Gardiner were reluctant to admit defeat. Gardiner defended his scheme at a Cabinet meeting in January 1939 and King optimistically concluded that most colleagues "generally favoured the broad plan."[68] By March, however, he was having second thoughts. Western Liberals told him the party would lose the west unless the Wheat Board price was at least seventy cents,[69] and when the Cabinet discussed the proposals in detail the other western Ministers told the same story. Unfortunately, some of the eastern Ministers opposed even Gardiner's proposal because they objected to any price support for wheat. King was at a loss: "Crerar," he recorded, "decidedly of one view. Dunning, of another. Gardiner, of yet another. Euler opposed to all three. Ilsley unable to agree on any of the three. I frankly confess that while I thought I understood the problem at one time, I had now come [sic] so confused as to not be able to say what the consensus of view was, or to give any decision that seemed to be at all representative." For the moment he decided to rely on the advice of Gardiner who "knows the West as well as anyone."[70]

The legislation was finally introduced in the House late in March. The crop insurance, known as the Prairie Farm Assistance Act, encountered no opposition. The Wheat Board Amendment Act, which set the minimum price at sixty cents, was a different matter.[71] A flood of telegrams and petitions flowed in from the west denouncing the measure. King quickly concluded that Gardiner had been wrong and that "this legislation if it carries will cost us many seats in Western Canada."[72] His colleagues were slower to respond. Cabinet discussions continued through April with "Gardiner very definitely set in his own way, and Euler and Ilsley equally so in theirs." At the end of the month King finally intervened. The choice, he argued, was to accept Gardiner's proposals with a seventy-cent minimum or to drop the insurance scheme and approve an even higher minimum. Gardiner threatened to resign if the insurance scheme was rejected. Ilsley still objected to any minimum price: "To Ilsley," King recorded, "I said that I felt sure once he saw what was back of the whole discussion, namely, a desire to support western industry in the teeth of changed world conditions as affecting western Canada through markets closing, and population being practically engaged in the one industry, that he would see the reasonableness of meeting the situation this year in a way that would tide over the worst."[73] When the Wheat Board bill was reintroduced for second reading in mid-May the minimum price had been raised to seventy cents.[74] Even this concession did not satisfy some wheat producers. Five western Liberals voted against the bill on second reading.[75] "It was not bad," King consoled himself, "considering how difficult the measure and legislation has been."[76]

King had averted a major political crisis but he had not achieved his original objective of reducing the federal role in the marketing of wheat. He had now agreed to a support price slightly above the world price, which meant that the Wheat Board would probably acquire the entire 1939 crop. King regretted this extension of government intervention and still thought of the Wheat Board as an emergency measure while wheat prices were abnormally low but his sensitivity to political pressures and his search for a consensus had led him in the right direction. Government marketing was the logical response in a world where importing countries had established quotas.

The 1939 budget was a further illustration of King's capacity to adapt to changing political conditions. The year before he had reconciled himself to deficit financing in spite of his philosophical commitment to a balanced budget, justifying the expenditures as a response to a temporary emergency and intending to balance the budget as soon as the emergency was over.[77] But if King had been reluctant to accept a more positive economic role for the federal government he did not fret after the decision had been made. In December 1938, when Dunning summarized the financial position of the government, King learned that the deficit would be larger than he had expected but he made no plea for rigid retrenchment for the coming year because he saw no purpose in provoking another Cabinet crisis. In any case, increased defence estimates would make a balanced budget impossible. "We must realize," he commented, "that while actually not at war, the world is in a war-like state and that we must make expenditures to meet the situation."[78]

The defence estimates, however, were as much an excuse as an explanation for the projected deficit in 1939. When Dunning presented his budget in April his summary of the previous year showed that Canada had not yet recovered from the 1937 recession. Relief costs and railway deficits had exceeded his estimates and the deficit, which he had forecast as twenty-three million, had been thirty million dollars. But even though Dunning saw signs of economic recovery, he did not try to reduce the deficit for the next year by increasing taxes. Even the special measures in 1938 to stimulate economic activity—in housing, municipal improvements, and mining—were extended. His estimated deficit for 1939 was sixty million dollars. And this time he made no apologies for an unbalanced budget. Dunning still assumed that the economy would only be back to normal when private investment provided enough jobs but in his budget speech he openly relied on Keynesian arguments to justify the federal deficit: "In these days, if the people as a whole, and business in particular, will not spend, the governments must. It is not a matter of choice but of sheer social necessity."[79] Dunning had come a long way since 1935 when his definition of fiscal responsibility had been to prevent raids on the federal treasury.

Mackenzie King had also evolved. He had reconciled himself to deficit financing in 1938 and now he accepted it without any apparent misgivings. He showed little interest in the preparation of the 1939 budget and his comments on the budget speech had more to do with Dunning's personality than his fiscal policy: "Lapointe and I were highly amused at his [Dunning's] little vanities, dressed up with spats on, wearing morning suit with a flower in his buttonhole, but what was most amusing was the presence on his desk of two separate glasses—one with water, the other, a dark coloured glass which, when he began to speak, we all came to see was whisky and soda. A little bottle of pills or pellets also laid out. All these taken at intervals during the time of speaking." King had no sympathy for his Minister of Finance. He was convinced that Dunning had become a hypochondriac and that he wanted out of politics before the next election. "Once he is through with this session and gets a good position, he will be, if I am not mistaken, all right for many a day to come."[80] King did not speak during the budget debate. This, however, was only because he was absent from the House. The King and Queen arrived in Canada in mid-May and for the next month Mackenzie King was Minister in Attendance to Their Royal Majesties, leaving his colleagues to wind up the business of the parliamentary session.

IV

King had proposed a royal tour of Canada in 1937 while attending the coronation and had even suggested that the tour might also include a brief visit to the United States.[81] He believed that the unprecedented presence of a British monarch in North America would strengthen the emotional ties of Canadians to the Commonwealth and would benefit Anglo-American relations. But King was also aware of the partisan advantages; it would do no harm to show that the Tories had no monopoly on loyalty to the Crown.[82] May 1939 had seemed the most convenient time for the visit; the King's schedule was open and he would be safely back in England before the Canadian federal election, which was expected in the fall. The trip was almost cancelled in the spring of 1939 because of the European situation but, finally, on May 17, the King and Queen landed in Quebec City.

Mackenzie King had already been deeply involved in the preparations for the tour. One of his major concerns was to ensure that all arrangements were consistent with Canada's autonomous status within the Commonwealth and that there was no hint of colonial inferiority. No members of the British Government were to accompany the King and Queen; Mackenzie King, as the head of the King's government in Canada, would be the only Privy Councillor. The absence of precedents created some complications. What, for example, was the role of the Governor General, the King's representative in Canada, when the King himself was present? Lord Tweedsmuir was prepared to keep out of the limelight but he thought that at least he should be allowed to great Their Majesties on their arrival. King strongly objected to the idea of the Governor General taking precedence over the Prime Minister on such a significant occasion and it was finally agreed that Tweedsmuir would board the royal vessel before it docked, pay his respects to the royal couple, and then remain on board while Their Majesties disembarked.

The proposed visit to the United States raised even more complex constitutional issues. Mackenzie King had first assumed that the King would be accompanied on this part of his tour by the British Foreign Secretary and was not even sure that he would go south of the border.[83] As the visit drew nearer, however, he convinced himself that his absence would be interpreted by the American press as "placing Canada in a subordinate position."[84] British officials saw no need for anybody except the British Ambassador to be in attendance and had the temerity to suggest to King that the American State Department agreed with them.[85] King promptly wrote to Roosevelt to ask him if the Canadian Prime Minister would be welcome.[86] The President immediately telephoned King to say that he took it for granted that King would come, and that he would tell the British Ambassador.[87] The word did get to the British Government for, early in April, a letter arrived, signed by His Majesty, asking King to accompany him to Washington as Minister in Attendance. King confided to the House of Commons that he "felt greatly honoured" by this invitation although he modestly declined any personal credit. It was intended, he was sure, as a recognition of Canada's status as a nation within the British Commonwealth.[88]

King was not only interested in the symbolic affirmation of Canadian autonomy. He paid meticulous attention to the most minor details of the tour. He was shocked, for example, to learn that the flowers for the reception in Quebec were to be blue. He saw it as a Tory plot and had the colour scheme changed to red.[89] King also saw an opportunity to improve his relations with the provincial premiers. At Quebec he arranged to have Maurice Duplessis ride with him in the procession to the Lieutenant-Governor's residence. It was his first meeting with Duplessis and he was not impressed. 'He had nothing intelligent to say all day," King noted in his diary and, what was worse, as they passed the enthusiastic crowds he had the bad taste to keep repeating that "these people were going to vote for him." Nevertheless King tried to be friendly and felt that "we got along fairly nicely."[90] Things went better in Toronto where King arranged to have the Hepburn children presented to Their Majesties. King was sure that the special attention he paid to Hepburn had either "paved the way for the end of the discord" or would give King "the inside running if he begins to participate in a bitter way."[91]

In Edmonton King had another opportunity to be generous to an opponent. Aberhart and Bowen, the Lieutenant-Governor, had not been on speaking terms since Bowen had reserved Aberhart's legislation and Aberhart had closed Government House. Mackenzie King discovered that the Premier had not even been invited to the Lieutenant-Governor's reception and tea in the Legislative Buildings; as Bowen lamely explained to King, he had "had to limit the numbers." King explained the situation to the

King and Queen and again arranged to have the Aberhart children presented to the royal couple. The monarch and his Prime Minister were by
this time on easy terms. King recorded that "when I spoke to the King, he
asked me whether I was trying to get him [Aberhart] within the fold. I
replied: no but that I was anxious to avoid him becoming too much of a
broncho."[92]

The arrangements for the three-day visit in Ottawa were the direct
responsibility of the federal government and Mackenzie King organized
a busy schedule. The King gave royal assent to some bills, confiding later
to his Prime Minister that he found the Canadian House of Commons
"extraordinarily well behaved." There was also the formal dinner at
Government House, the trooping of the colours, the unveiling of the War
Memorial, the laying of the cornerstone of the new Supreme Court Building, a private luncheon at Laurier House, the Governor General's garden
party, and a dinner for all the Senators and Members of Parliament. And
always, as the King and Queen passed through the streets in their open
landau, they had to acknowledge the flag-waving and cheering crowds.

Mackenzie King was too occupied with details to enjoy himself. His
only embarrassment at Ottawa was his own neglect of his friends. Joan
and Godfroy Patteson had not been able to attend the luncheon at Laurier
House because Godfroy was ill. King had later taken his own sister and
Joan to the garden party but had rushed off to take his position beside the
King and had forgotten to make any arrangements to have them presented.
Joan was deeply disappointed and King felt very guilty. It was only after
leaving Ottawa, and after a number of long-distance telephone calls, that
he was able to arrange for Joan and Godfroy to travel to Niagara Falls to
meet the King and Queen on their return trip from western Canada.[93]

Their Majesties quickly adjusted to the novelty of a North American
tour; it was easy to respond to such an enthusiastic welcome. King George
had begun the tour firm in his sense of duty and determined to meet his
responsibilities. At first he had shown signs of nervousness, worrying
about details and irritated by any confusion or delays in the daily schedule.
As the tour progressed he showed a growing confidence, stimulated by the
huge and obviously enthusiastic crowds. Even where there were no scheduled stops people drove for miles to catch a glimpse of the King and Queen
waving from the balcony of their private car as the royal train slowed
down. The cheers were not all for the King. Queen Elizabeth was always
at his side, proud of her husband but warmly attractive, always smoothing
out difficulties and charming everybody she met at the endless series of
luncheons, dinners, receptions, stone-layings, and unveilings. She even
appeared to enjoy the informality of North Americans and recounted with

312

pleasure how Senator Rufus Pope, then in his eighties, had told her at a reception in Ottawa that he was of old Loyalist stock and would be loyal to her "till hell froze over."

Mackenzie King, in spite of his fretting, was also stimulated by the tremendous success of the tour. He knew that there were mutterings that he was neglecting his duties as Prime Minister. J. W. Dafoe had caustically commented in private that King had probably not read any despatches because "his mind is running on really important things such as—well let's say the kind of pillow the Queen will rest her head on as she travels through Canada."[94] The Conservatives, in their turn, had drawn up a list of examples where King had made sure that the Liberal party received the benefits of the publicity given to the royal tour.[95] But King could ignore the muted criticisms because of the extraordinary response of Canadians in all parts of the country. As he later told Vincent Massey: "During the first two weeks of the Royal Tour I could hardly talk with anyone; during the last fortnight, however, I felt entirely different. Being free from the worry of Parliament, the trip proved to be, in fact, a rest notwithstanding its many strenuous features."[96]

American crowds were no less enthusiastic when Their Majesties visited the United States. Protocol was almost forgotten because Franklin Roosevelt made a point of being informal. The luncheon at the White House was a family meal and even at the formal dinner that evening the President defied the rules by proposing toasts to the "Great Gentleman" and the "Gallant and Gracious Lady."[97] The royal party visited New York and the World's Fair and then drove to Hyde Park, where the informality extended to a picnic lunch with hot-dogs. Mackenzie King noted that later that evening, after the three men had discussed the international situation, Roosevelt put his hand on the King's knee and told him: "Young man, it's time for you to go to bed."[98]

The President also made a point of stressing his close relations with Mackenzie King. According to King's account, "he told the King repeatedly that he and I understood each other perfectly and worked together on all matters of mutual relationship," even describing King as the "official interpreter" between Great Britain and the United States.[99] Roosevelt knew King would be flattered but it is probably true that he preferred to communicate directly with King and to avoid the red tape of diplomatic channels.

The royal tour then visited the Maritimes and ended at Halifax in mid-June. Both King George and Queen Elizabeth expressed their gratitude to Mackenzie King in a touching farewell on board the *Empress of Britain*. Even the sun shone brightly that day as Their Majesties set sail for Europe.

It was an appropriate end to a visit which as King noted "had surpassed all expectations."[100] Canadians in all parts of the country had given the royal couple an enthusiastic welcome and, in so doing, had shared in an un-precedented national experience. "Never before," the American Minister in Ottawa reported to the President, had he "witnessed an event of more decided effect on the psychology of the people."[101] Both national unity and the Commonwealth ties had been strengthened by the tour.

V

Mackenzie King was sure that the royal visit had contributed to a sense of unity but he was too cautious to exaggerate the results. When a jour-nalist asked him if the tour would make Canadians more inclined to parti-cipate in a war for freedom, he conceded that the response to Their Majes-ties suggested an affirmative answer but warned that nothing could be taken for granted. He still thought that "everything would depend on the issue as it finally came to shape itself."[102] The issue would soon take shape.

King had been planning a fall election and on June 22, at the first Cabinet meeting after his return to Ottawa, he found his colleagues unan-imously favourable" to the idea. They felt sure of victory because, as Lapointe expressed it, the voters would recognize that there was really no alternative government.[103] By mid-July the prospects seemed even more encouraging. Ernest Lapointe had done little to organize the party in Quebec but Quebec, in any case, was no problem and C. G. Power could take care of the election details there. King recorded on July 20 that the reports from the rest of the country were all favourable: "Ilsley and Michaud seem to feel that the Maritimes are satisfactory. Crerar ditto regarding the West. As to Ontario they all feel we should go ahead regard-less of the attitude of the Ontario government; that the people were really with us."[104] His plan, therefore, was to dissolve Parliament in mid-Sep-tember and to hold the election on October 23. It seemed an auspicious date to King because it was the anniversary of his return to Parliament in 1919 as Leader of the Opposition and of his taking office as Prime Minister in 1935.[105]

The Cabinet discussions had underlined King's main reason for want-ing an election. Victory seemed certain. His colleagues had shown some concern about Hepburn's attitude but nobody had been worried about the Conservative party. Manion had signally failed to win the confidence of his followers or to give his party a sense of direction. He himself talked optimistically about winning if only the issue of foreign policy could be

314

forgotten but his strategy of moderation had only accentuated the divisions within the party. Arthur Meighen, expressing the sentiments of many prominent English-Canadian Conservatives, deplored the policy of yielding to "the French Canadian nationalistic viewpoint" in the name of unity and argued that the only result was that "Quebec today is hectoring and intransigent to a degree never known before." He saw no hope of conciliation—"nothing that will produce national unity"—and his preferred solution was to declare Canada's commitment to the British cause and to show French Canadians that "it is the will of Canada."[106] French-Canadian Conservatives, on the other hand, were urging Manion to go farther in his concessions to Quebec. Manion could only ask bitterly why his French-Canadian colleagues insisted on talking only about foreign policy and why they expected him to go even farther than the government. "Between the extremists down there and the extremists up here," he expostulated, "it is almost an impossibility for a Leader to do anything at all."[107] His pleas to his followers to ignore the issue of participation only showed that the division within the Conservative party was sharper than ever.

To most people it was clear that the European situation could not be ignored. Even King's choice of an election date had been influenced by his assessment of events in Europe. October 23 might be an anniversary but he would have preferred an earlier date. King had decided, however, that a European war, if it came, would come in August or early September because no aggressor would want a winter campaign. A September election would mean that Parliament would be dissolved for this crucial period and King and his colleagues might have to declare war without being able to call on the House of Commons to confirm the decision. An October election would delay dissolution until the danger was past or the decision had been made.[108]

A much less significant event was also delayed for the same reason. Adolf Hitler had not replied to King's plea in February to follow the path of peace and progress but in July he did thank King tardily for his letter and went on to invite "a number of Canadian students and officers to a three weeks' stay in Germany" as his guests.[109] German relations with Poland were at a crisis at the time, with Hitler threatening to seize the port of Danzig, but King was still reluctant to give up hope. The invitation might be a conciliatory gesture. King expressed great interest to the German Consul and even toyed with the idea of going to Germany himself.[110] But he made no snap decision. Three days later he informed Neville Chamberlain of the invitation, although by then there was no thought of going himself.[111] Chamberlain encouraged King to take the invitation seriously; "any friendly gesture from that quarter" should be welcomed.[112]

King finally decided to suggest November as a suitable date, after the immediate danger of war had passed and after the October election.[113]

The month of August was a time of anxious waiting. Mackenzie King still looked for encouraging signs but feared that the die was already cast. On August 21 he confided in his diary: "My only hope is in Hitler himself, that he really does not want unnecessarily to destroy human life and that he may stop short of world conflict, but with Japan, Italy and Germany together in secret conclave it is hard to believe that plans are not already made for simultaneous attacks in the Orient & Europe—a ghastly and appalling situation."[114] War was brought even closer the next day with the announcement of the Nazi-Soviet Pact, which left Poland isolated and vulnerable. "Curiously enough," King commented, "I felt instantly a sense of relief, the first relief I have had in days." King's reaction reflects his primary concern for the situation in Canada. If war came, Russia would now be on the other side.[115] Canadians and especially French Canadians would respond more willingly to a call to fight for freedom if the communists were also the enemy.

King made no attempt to influence events in Europe. He had no thought of giving the British Government any advice. European nations had already taken sides and the British Government had made its commitment; King could only watch as events unfolded.[116] His only intervention in European diplomacy was a last-minute appeal to Hitler and the President of Poland on August 25 to have recourse "to every possible peaceful means to effect a solution."[117] Hitler did not reply.

At home, the Canadian Government did take some steps to prepare for war. King had told a group of industrialists in June that he welcomed any British orders for munitions and that the government would assist them to obtain contracts;[118] when the delegation of Canadian manufacturers left for England in August it was accompanied by Canadian defence officials. King also had Orders-in-Council prepared for imposing censorship and interning enemy aliens if war broke out[119] and initiated plans for organizing the Cabinet into committees to deal more efficiently with the decisions which war would bring.[120] On August 25 the Cabinet agreed to place orders in the United States of up to seven million dollars for airplanes, financed by Governor General's warrants.[121]

These last-minute preparations, however, still seemed less important to King than the political responsibility of keeping Canada united. On August 23 he issued a statement on his own initiative to reassure Canadians that the government was prepared for any emergency, that it could take any necessary action under the War Measures Act, and that Parliament would be recalled immediately if war began. When Cabinet met next day his colleagues did not protest but King felt "there was not, however, the outspoken approval I would have liked to have had."[122] His reaction was to ask each Minister in turn, as he had at the time of Munich, what the government's policy should be. All were agreed on participation. Rogers favoured an announcement that Canada supported Britain's efforts for peace and would support Britain in war if these efforts failed. Ilsley and Mackenzie felt even more strongly that an immediate declaration of support for Britain was necessary; "that the people wanted the government to say now what the country would do." The Quebec Ministers, including Power, were still not prepared to issue "a blank cheque to Great Britain," and Lapointe appealed to his colleagues to "say and do nothing which would divide the country." King then drafted another statement for the press which his colleagues formally approved. The statement merely declared that the government was prepared for any eventuality and was united. There was no hint of what the united view of the government was.[123]

The continuing negotiations over Danzig and the Polish Corridor in the last week of August still gave King some hope that a peaceful solution would be found, but by then he clearly expected the worst. On Wednesday, August 30, he warned his colleagues to stay in Ottawa over the next weekend.[124] On Friday morning, September 1, King was awakened at 6:30 a.m. with the news that Poland had been invaded. By then it was almost an anti-climax.

The Cabinet met at 9:00 o'clock. Every Minister was present. There were no preliminaries. King merely read the Orders-in-Council which had already been prepared. Parliament was to be summoned for the following Thursday. In the meantime Canada would be in a state of apprehended war, the War Measures Act would be in effect, the armed forces would be mobilized, and censorship would be imposed. King also read a proposed press release which Lapointe had already approved: "In the event," it read, "of the United Kingdom becoming engaged in war in the effort to resist aggression, the Government of Canada has unanimously decided, as soon as Parliament meets, to seek its authority for effective cooperation by Canada at the side of Great Britain. Meanwhile necessary measures will be taken for the defence of Canada."[125] The commitment to be at Britain's side, which came two days before Britain declared war, provoked no comment. The Cabinet was united. King then read the statement to the waiting journalists and was back at Laurier House in time for a brief rest before lunch.[126]

The next major step was to demonstrate that Parliament was also united. King was confident of the outcome. The issue of participation which during the Munich crisis had seemed to him a threat to national unity no longer seemed controversial. The House met on September 7. On Saturday, September 9, it approved the government's decision to be at Britain's side without the necessity of a formal division. Early next morning the King accepted the advice of his Canadian Government and Canada was officially at war.

The support for participation, impressive as it was, was still hedged with qualifications. The declaration of war said nothing about the nature or the extent of Canadian participation. The C.C.F. party supported participation but it was deeply divided over Canada's contribution to the war. When the national council had met on September 6 J. S. Woodsworth had advocated neutrality but his plea had been rejected by a majority vote. A compromise was then proposed; the C.C.F. party would support the war but its support would be limited to economic aid and would not include sending troops to Europe. Even this compromise was not a unanimous decision.[127] The issue cut so deep that Woodsworth resigned as party leader and M. J. Coldwell spoke for the party in the debate in the House. The Conservative party was also divided. G. H. Héon, speaking as a French-Canadian Conservative, expressed his firm determination to support Britain and France short of conscription;[128] J. E. Lawson of York South promptly rose to express his objection to this qualification.[129] Three French-Canadian Liberals—Maxime Raymond, Liguori Lacombe, and Wilfrid Lacroix—opposed the policy of their party, arguing that participation would lead to heavy sacrifices of men and money and would eventually destroy national unity.[130] The government and the nation had avoided a major confrontation over the decision to go to war but the war itself would still test the fabric of a nation which had not yet decided what participation meant.

EPILOGUE

MACKENZIE KING was now the head of a war-time administration. It was not easy to know how he would respond to his new responsibilities. In December 1939 he would be sixty-five years old and the pressures of war-time leadership would test the physical resources of a man who was already becoming conscious of his age. For the last year or two he had referred more frequently in his diary to fatigue, backaches, and the occasional night when he had not slept soundly. But King had already made some adjustments. He was more careful now to conserve his energy by avoiding unnecessary appointments, by resting during the day, and by delegating more responsibility to his colleagues. And King was still remarkably healthy; he had kept his weight down, his blood pressure was normal, and he had the stamina to concentrate intently for prolonged periods when he considered it necessary. Certainly he showed no sign of declining mental alertness, no tendency to forget or to overlook the many factors, personal or regional, which needed to be considered before a decision was made. Most important of all, the war restored King's waning enthusiasm for the burden of political leadership.

Mackenzie King's paramount commitment to politics had already led to gradual changes in the pattern of his life. During his last four years in office he had narrowed his interests more and more and had paid less attention to non-political activities. He rarely attended social functions that were not related in some way to politics and, although he still maintained his correspondence with long-time friends, he wrote less frequently and made fewer efforts to sustain these personal associations. Nothing was allowed to interfere with his primary responsibilities.

King was so jealous of his time that he almost resented it when his friends came to Ottawa. In July 1939 Julia Grant had visited him at Kingsmere for four days but it had been Julia's idea and King, in his diary at least, showed no enthusiasm. Only a few years before the two had shared an interest in psychical phenomena and had expressed intense

319

sentiments of personal affection.[1] In 1939, however, King felt he could no longer afford distractions from his duty. According to his diary he told Julia that his life must be devoted to serving Canada and, possibly to make the point more bluntly, had "told her that I doubted if I should ever marry now that I was 65 & that if I did it would not be out of Canada." On the day of her departure King noted that Julia had stayed longer than he had expected and that "while the visit was enjoyable, it was a strain throughout."[2]

Violet Markham had arrived from England two weeks later. Violet had been generous to King in the past, had always shown an interest in King's political career, and there was no danger of an encroachment on King's private life.[3] Even Violet's visit, however, was almost an unwelcome imposition on his time. "Instead of being thoroughly stimulating and inspiring, as I had hoped the visit would be," he commented, "it has been rather depressing and has left me a bit fatigued and exhausted."[4]

The only sustaining friend was Joan Patteson. A day rarely went by when King did not see Joan or talk to her on the telephone. He discussed everything with her—his health, his social activities, his speeches, his political problems, and the latest confidential despatches from London—and Joan was always attentive and her comments and suggestions were always welcomed. She was a wise and gracious woman, which was important for King, and she also respected and admired him, which was also important, but Joan was unique because she combined these virtues with a selfless devotion to King's convenience. She was always prepared to adapt her life to fit into King's schedule and seemed to ask nothing in return. Even when visitors like Julia Grant or Violet Markham arrived, Joan looked after the arrangements, made sure there were flowers in their rooms, and entertained them when King had work to do or wanted to rest.

King took Joan's devotion for granted although even he recognized, for example, that she might have felt some resentment or even jealousy during Julia Grant's visit. "The first few days," he noted in his diary after Julia's departure, "have been a little trying for her but she has risen above all the feelings that were natural enough. I would not let her be hurt for worlds—and she has not been—in thought, word or deed." At the same time he knew he could rely on the Pattesons not to intrude on his time or to complicate his life; they "are always so considerate," he went on, "they never take undue advantage in any way of our friendship or presume upon it."[5] For King it was an ideal relationship and for the rest of his life his friendship with Joan would ease his loneliness and isolation.

Earlier in 1939, however, there had been signs that Mackenzie King was finding the continuing pressure of politics a burden. Over the last few years he could see few positive accomplishments; his major efforts had been to avert disaster, to avoid disunity. The party and the nation had survived but survival was a limited goal. His conviction in 1935 that Liberal fiscal and trade policies would end the depression had been gradually eroded by four years of continuing unemployment. King had blamed Bennett for many of Canada's problems and he had confidently expected to restore national harmony and a renewed sense of national purpose, but his hopes had narrowed until, four years later, his ambition went little farther than trying to stay in office. His efforts just to hold the party and the nation together, the seemingly endless succession of regional confrontations, and the constant search for half-measures and compromises had taken their toll of King's commitment to politics.

Under these circumstances it was not surprising that King had occasionally wondered about the future and had even questioned how much longer he wanted to continue in politics. In April 1939, for example, he had noted in his diary that "I did a thing which I seldom do, which was to build a sort of castle in the air with regard to the future." Even on this occasion, however, he had not thought of quitting politics entirely. His castle in the air had been to turn over the leadership to a younger man while he stayed on as Minister for External Affairs.[6] Usually he was more realistic. Politics might seem wearing and frustrating but it was the only thing that gave him any satisfaction and, in his words, "to go into the life of silence, congenial as it would be, would be to desert the real purpose of my life." Even partial retirement was unthinkable; he could never have accepted a subordinate position in any government. He would stay on as leader because nothing else could give him a sense of "real purpose." The decision to stay on was easily justified. There was nobody to take his place, nobody who could keep the party and the nation united: "I am," he commented in February 1939, "proceeding on the basis that short of health itself being undermined, I will continue to do the thing that is less pleasing to myself because of what I see in it, in the way of obvious duty, and the belief that, however inadequate in a multitude of ways, I nevertheless can help to keep Canada on a steadier keel than possibly any other one likely to succeed at the present time."[7]

King's declining enthusiasm for politics could also be seen in his tendency to postpone decisions. By 1939 some of his senior colleagues wanted to retire and a major reconstruction of the Cabinet was overdue, but King preferred to wait, at least until after the expected election. Ernest Lapointe was one who was attracted by "the life of silence." Lapointe had been depressed by the success of Duplessis' appeals to the anti-communist and nationalist sentiments of his compatriots and his health had been affected. It was difficult for King to imagine a Liberal government without Lapointe at his side but in this case his affection for his colleague outweighed his self-interest. In the summer of 1938 he had taken the initiative to tell Lapointe that if he wanted to retire he could have whatever post he wanted: the Supreme Court, the Lieutenant-Governorship of Quebec, or the Senate.[8] Lapointe had made no decision at the time but after Munich, to King's "great surprise and delight, he told me he intended to stay on through the next campaign but was doing so 'only for me'".[9] Even then the partnership would not end because Lapointe proposed to go to the Senate and as Liberal leader there would still be a member of the Cabinet.[10]

King had not shown the same concern for Charles Dunning, who had also talked of retirement. Dunning had brought strength to the government in 1935 because the leading Canadian industrialists approved of his financial orthodoxy. By 1938, however, Dunning was less important to King because the Liberal party could count on the support of the financial and industrial interests even if Dunning left.[11] King had always resented Dunning's unconcealed ambition to become leader of the Liberal party and his assumption that he was at least as well fitted for that post as the present incumbent; now that Dunning was less important to the government King showed his feelings by his private comments about Dunning's vanity and by the absence of any sympathy for Dunning's health. But King did not want to face a major reorganization of his Cabinet. When Dunning, doubtless affected by his declining influence within the government and his unsatisfactory relations with the Prime Minister, had offered to resign in August 1938, King had persuaded him to stay on.[12] In July 1939 Dunning formally submitted his resignation but again King had persuaded him to stay, at least until after the expected election.[13] King was postponing any Cabinet changes because he felt reluctant to face difficulties until they were unavoidable.

In September 1939 with the outbreak of war, however, King's mood suddenly changed. Politics no longer seemed an endless effort to avoid disaster because the war gave him a renewed sense of purpose. His career now seemed to have a larger meaning because the unity of the government and of the nation would be a contribution to a higher cause—the fight for freedom in a menaced world. The political problems were fundamentally the same—the need to conciliate, to find the appropriate compromises, and to persuade liberally-minded men to accept them—but the will to apply his political talents and his experience was restored. The day-dreams about retirement were forgotten and King once more concentrated on the immediate tasks of political leadership.

Thus, within a few days of Hitler's invasion of Poland, King reorganized his Cabinet. He had already thought of J. L. Ralston as Dunning's successor. Ralston had retired from active politics in 1935 and was reluctant to return but he had told King in August 1939 that "if war came he would be ready to enter the Government or perform any service I [King] might wish him to perform."[14] On September 5, in response to a summons from King, Ralston was in Ottawa; the next day Dunning's resignation was formally accepted and Ralston was sworn in as Minister of Finance. King had already decided that Ian Mackenzie was a liability; he shunted Mackenzie to a minor portfolio and moved Norman Rogers to the Department of National Defence. There would be less procrastination now that the war gave King a clearer sense of purpose.

The difference in King's attitude was so apparent that even his friends were surprised. Violet Markham had found him jaded and exhausted when she had visited him in July and had expressed grave concern about his health.[15] Four months later she learned from Lord Tweedsmuir that King was a changed man. "I was afraid," wrote the Governor General, "that with his old Liberal hatred of war he might find the subconscious strain too great. On the contrary, he is ten years younger, active, vigorous, cheerful."[16] It was at least an encouraging sign for a man who now faced the burdens of war-time leadership.

Many Canadians, however, still had reservations about King as the leader of a nation at war. It was not so much a question of his age or his commitment to politics as his style of leadership. He did not project the image of a man who could rouse the patriotic sentiments of his compatriots, who could both inspire and symbolize the determination and the spirit of sacrifice of a nation at war. Even his political talent for compromise seemed inappropriate for a leader who would have the responsibility for sending Canadians to their death on European battlefields and for organizing the nation for victory.

But although Mackenzie King was not an inspiring or charismatic figure, he did have talents and qualities which might be more appropriate for leadership in a country which did not see the war as a holy crusade. In a Canada still unprepared for total war and still deeply divided over the full meaning of participation, a clarion call for patriotic sacrifices would have fallen on many deaf ears and a militant Prime Minister dedicated to winning the war at all costs would have provoked bitter opposition. King still saw Canada as an association of diverse cultural, regional, and economic groups; he still saw his task as strengthening this association by fostering a sense of national partnership. His twenty years as Liberal leader suggest that this image of Canadian society, the prism through which King saw the Canadian spectrum, bore a close relation to political reality. And in September 1939 this national diversity had not magically disappeared. The partnership could not be taken for granted. Mackenzie King's experience, his political sensitivity, his style of leadership, and his overriding concern for national unity had not been outmoded by the declaration of war.

NOTE ON SOURCES

THE MACKENZIE KING COLLECTION at the Public Archives of Canada is the central source for this study. The King Papers include his extensive correspondence, state papers, successive drafts of his speeches, the memoranda prepared for him on a wide range of topics, as well as more personal documents such as his financial and medical records. Mackenzie King's diary is an invaluable supplement to this material. It has daily entries for the entire period, written in longhand in the earlier years but more frequently dictated to his secretary after he returned to office. King recorded many of his activities in great detail and the diary is a unique source of information on political events and on his personal life; he had an excellent memory and his accounts of interviews, meetings, or sittings in the House are selective but usually reliable. He is much less trustworthy when he discusses his own motives but he does unconsciously reveal his own preconceptions and his image of himself. Few public figures are as well documented.

A number of other private papers were consulted, including those of R. B. Bennett, J. W. Dafoe, R. B. Hanson, Ernest Lapointe, R. J. Manion, Arthur Meighen, and H. H. Stevens at the Public Archives of Canada, C. A. Dunning, N. P. Lambert, C. G. Power, and Lord Tweedsmuir at Queen's University Archives, F. D. Roosevelt at Hyde Park, and the papers of Floyd Chalmers in his personal possession.

The major printed sources were the *House of Commons Debates*, the reports of various Royal Commissions and Parliamentary Committees, and other state papers. The most useful secondary sources, including books, articles, and theses, are referred to in the footnotes.

NOTES

All manuscript collections are in the Public Archives of Canada unless otherwise indicated. The initials W.L.M.K. refer to William Lyon Mackenzie King, and correspondence including them may be found in the King Papers.

INTRODUCTION

1 W.L.M.K., *Industry and Humanity* (Boston and New York, 1918), p. 14.
2 W.L.M.K. to Bernard Rose, July 17, 1929.
3 *Proceedings of the First National Convention of the Twentieth Century Liberal Association of Canada*, Ottawa, June 2, 3, 1933.
4 *The Liberal Way: The First Liberal Summer Conference* (Toronto, 1933), p. 273.
5 Address to First Assembly of the National Federation of Liberal Women of Canada, April 18, 1928.
6 R. J. Manion, *Life is an Adventure* (Toronto, 1936), p. 289.
7 *Ibid.*, p. 290.
8 Vancouver *Sun*, Oct. 3, 1932.
9 Queen's University Archives, Norman Lambert, Diary, April 8, 1934.
10 W.L.M.K., Diary, July 20, 1932.
11 *Ibid.*

CHAPTER ONE
THE OTTAWA TRADE AGREEMENTS

1 W.L.M.K., Diary, Dec. 5, 1931.
2 See H. Blair Neatby, *W. L. Mackenzie King*, II: *1924–1932* (Toronto, 1963), p. 396.
3 *Can. H. of C. Debates*, May 9, 1932, p. 3454.
4 *Report of Imperial Economic Conference* (London, 1932), p. 67.
5 The importance of this question is outlined in a preliminary document prepared by the British officials, "Memorandum on the evils of monetary instability," Meighen Papers, Vol. 164, pp. 100956–69. The minutes of the sub-committee on Monetary and Financial Questions can be found in RG 19, E2(f), Vol. 27.
6 Ian M. Drummond, *Imperial Economic Policy 1917–1939* (Toronto, 1974), pp. 209–18.
7 Bennett Papers, R. B. Bennett to F. D. L. Smith, Feb. 20, 1932, p. 115309.
8 The list is in the Bennett Papers, pp. 113054–61. It runs to more than one hundred pages but the length of the list is misleading.
9 *Ibid.*, R. B. Bennett to J. E. Walsh, General Manager, Canadian Manufacturers' Association, July 11, 1932, p. 113405.
10 Drummond, *Imperial Economic Policy*, 219.
11 Bennett's bullying approach was described by Bennett himself in an extraordinary

conversation with Grant Dexter in the washroom of the Rideau Club. Dafoe Papers, A. G. Dexter to J. W. Dafoe, Oct. 16, 1932.
12 Bennett Papers, R. B. Bennett to Walter Runciman, July 27, 1932, p. 113447.
13 *Ibid.*, S. Baldwin to R. B. Bennett, Aug. 8, 1932, p. 115235.
14 *Ibid.*, R. J. Manion to R. B. Bennett, Aug. 16, 1932, reporting a conversation with L. Amery, p. 118760.
15 Bennett Papers, R. B. Bennett to Governor General, telegram, Aug. 16, 1932, Box 826, F. S. Chalmers file.
16 Iain McLeod, *Neville Chamberlain* (New York, 1962), p. 161, quoting from Chamberlain's diary, Aug. 15, 1932.
17 *Report of Imperial Economic Conference*, 1932, p. 158.
18 Keith Feiling, *The Life of Neville Chamberlain* (London, 1946), p. 213.
19 McLeod, *Neville Chamberlain*, p. 161.
20 Feiling, *The Life of Neville Chamberlain*, p. 215.
21 Douglas Annett, *British Preference in Canadian Commercial Policy* (Toronto, 1948), p. 68.
22 On the results of the Conference see W. K. Hancock, *Survey of British Commonwealth Affairs.* II: *Problems of Economic Policy, 1918–1932* (London, 1937), and Drummond, *Imperial Economic Policy.* For the impact on the Canadian economy see *Report of Royal Commission on Dominion-Provincial Relations*, I (Ottawa, 1940), p. 159, and A. E. Safarian, *The Canadian Economy in the Great Depression* (Toronto, 1959), pp. 69, 133.
23 Diary, July 30, 1932.
24 *Ibid.*, March 5, 1932.
25 *Can. H. of C. Debates*, April 26, 1932, pp. 2378–88.
26 W.L.M.K. to Sir William Mulock, June 27, 1932.
27 Diary, July 30, 1932.
28 W.L.M.K. to J. C. Elliott, Aug. 18, 1932.
29 Diary, Aug. 31, 1932.
30 W.L.M.K. to J. J. Duffus, Aug. 20, 1932.
31 Ian Mackenzie to W.L.M.K., Sept. 2, 1932.
32 W.L.M.K. to Mitchell Hepburn, Aug. 29, 1932.
33 Mitchell Hepburn to W.L.M.K., Aug. 24, 1932.
34 Diary, Sept. 7, 1932. Vincent Massey's "memorandum," Sept. 8, 1932, which summarized the discussions, is much less hostile to the agreements than King wanted to be.
35 *Canadian Annual Review*, 1933 (Toronto, 1934), p. 32.
36 Diary, Oct. 3, 1932.
37 *Can. H. of C. Debates*, Oct. 10, 1932, p. 39.
38 *Ibid.*, Oct. 10, 1932, pp. 44–7.
39 Diary, Oct. 10, 1932.
40 *Ibid.*, Oct. 12, 1932.
41 *Ibid.*
42 *Ibid.*, Oct. 13, 1932.
43 *Ibid.*, Oct. 14, 1932.
44 J. L. Ralston to W.L.M.K., Oct. 16, 1932, Ralston's italics.
45 *Can. H. of C. Debates*, Oct. 17, 1932, pp. 256–92.
46 Diary, Oct. 17, 1932.
47 Manion Papers, R. J. Manion to James Manion, Oct. 22, 1932.
48 Dafoe Papers, N. Lambert to J. W. Dafoe, Oct. 19, 1932.
49 *Can. H. of C. Debates*, Nov. 3, 1932, p. 837.
50 Diary, Nov. 25, 1932.
51 *Ibid.*, Nov. 27, 1932.
52 *Ibid.*, Dec. 30, 1932.

CHAPTER TWO
THE NEW LIBERALISM

1 W.L.M.K. to Violet Markham, Jan. 28, 1933.
2 W.L.M.K. to Charles G. Dunlop, July 8, 1933.
3 W.L.M.K., Diary, May 25, 1934.
4 *Can. H. of C. Debates*, Feb. 27, 1933, p. 2498.
5 W.L.M.K. to J. T. Thorson, Jan. 31, 1933.
6 See H. Blair Neatby, *W. L. Mackenzie King*, II: *1924–1932* (Toronto, 1963), pp. 395–7.
7 J. G. Gardiner to W.L.M.K., Oct. 5, 1932.
8 Diary, Jan. 30, 1933.
9 *Can. H. of C. Debates*, Oct. 10, 1932.
10 W.L.M.K. to T. A. Crerar, Jan. 24, 1933.
11 W.L.M.K. to Robert Hunter, Nov. 15, 1933.
12 W.L.M.K. to T. A. Crerar, Jan. 24, 1933.
13 Dafoe Papers, J. W. Dafoe to N. W. Rowell, Sept. 30, 1932.
14 V. Massey, Memorandum, Sept. 8, 1932.
15 Diary, Sept. 8, 1932.
16 Senator Lambert in an interview with the author on May 4, 1960 recalled that when this issue was discussed King turned to Ralston to say that, as Liberal financial critic in the House, he would have to explain the position of the party because he himself didn't understand what was involved.
17 Norman Rogers to W.L.M.K., Dec. 26, 1925.
18 *Ibid.*, March 24, 1933.
19 *Ibid.*, Nov. 23, 1930; see also Feb. 23, 1933. Rogers publicly challenged theories of provincial rights in "The Compact Theory of Confederation," Canadian Political Science Association *Proceedings*, 1931, pp. 205–30, and "The Genesis of Provincial Rights," *Canadian Historical Review*, XIV, March 1933, 9–23.
20 Norman Rogers to W.L.M.K., April 25, 1932.
21 N. M. Rogers, *W. L. Mackenzie King* (Toronto, 1935), suggests that A. F. W. Plumptre also contributed to this memorandum.
22 C. A. Curtis, Memorandum on a Central Bank for Canada [no date].
23 Vincent Massey to W.L.M.K., Aug. 31, 1932; Feb. 6, 1933.
24 W.L.M.K. to Vincent Massey, Feb. 13, 1933.
25 Diary, Feb. 1, 1933.
26 *Can. H. of C. Debates*, Feb. 1, 1933, pp. 1687–93.
27 Diary, Feb. 8, 1933.
28 *Ibid.*, Feb. 9, 1933.
29 *Ibid.*, Feb. 10, 1933.
30 See *Can. H. of C. Debates*, Feb. 27, 1933, pp. 2509–11 for King's presentation of the Liberal platform.
31 Diary, Feb. 15, 1933.
32 Earl Lawson, *Can. H. of C. Debates*, Feb. 2, 1933, p. 1746.
33 *Mail and Empire*, Nov. 10, 1932, cited by J. S. Woodsworth, *Can. H. of C. Debates*, Feb. 1, 1933, p. 1688.
34 Diary, Feb. 27, 1933.
35 *Can. H. of C. Debates*, Feb. 27, 1933, p. 2505.
36 *Ibid.*, p. 2498.
37 W.L.M.K. to J. K. Blair, March 25, 1933.
38 Diary, March 29, 1933.
39 *Ibid.*, Nov. 8, 1932.
40 *Ibid.*, March 6, 1933.

41 *Ibid.*, July 21, 1933.
42 *Ibid.*, Nov. 24, 1933; W.L.M.K. to Beatrix Robb, March 29, 1934.
43 Dafoe Papers, Vincent Massey to J. J. Dafoe, April 3, 1933.
44 *The Liberal Way: The First Liberal Summer Conference* (Toronto, 1933), p. ix.
45 Diary, March 31, 1933.
46 W.L.M.K. to Ernest Lapointe, Aug. 30, 1933.
47 Diary, Sept. 8, 1933. For Moley's speech, see *The Liberal Way*, pp. 241–50.
48 *The Liberal Way*, p. 277.
49 *Iibid.*, p. 284.
50 Manion Papers, R. J. Manion to James Manion, Jan. 21, 1933.
51 *Can. H. of C. Debates*, March 21, 1933, pp. 3204–27.
52 *Ibid.*, March 24, 1933, p. 3381.
53 *Ibid.*, April 4, 1933, p. 3710.
54 W.L.M.K. to Norman Rogers, April 3, 1933.
55 Diary, April 11, 1933.
56 *Canadian Annual Review*, 1933 (Toronto, 1934), p. 26.
57 An undated copy of this letter is in the Meighen Papers, p. 091676.
58 *Can. H. of C. Debates*, Feb. 24, 1933, pp. 2249–64.
59 *Ibid.*, Feb. 24, 1933, pp. 2465–72.
60 See Neatby, *Mackenzie King*, II, 398–9.
61 *Can. H. of C. Debates*, March 27, 1933, p. 3445.
62 Diary, March 27, 1933.
63 *Report of Royal Commission on Transportation* (Ottawa, 1932), p. 14.
64 J. W. Dafoe to W.L.M.K., Sept. 14, 1933.
65 Diary, Sept. 13, 1932.
66 *Ibid.*, March 9, 1933.
67 *Ibid.*, March 1, 1933.
68 *Can. H. of C. Debates*, March 9, 1933, p. 2853.
69 *Ibid.*, March 9, 1933, pp. 2860–2. See also Manion Papers, R. J. Manion to James Manion, Jan. 10, 1935.
70 *Ibid.*, March 9, 1933, p. 2863.
71 A. W. Currie, *Economics of Canadian Transportation* (Toronto, 1959), pp. 457–9.
72 *Can. H. of C. Debates*, Feb. 14, 1933, p. 2102.
73 *Ibid.*, May 24, 1933, p. 5371.
74 *Ibid.*, May 24, 1933, p. 5372.
75 W.L.M.K. to W. M. Martin, Dec. 30, 1932.
76 W.L.M.K. to J. T. Thorson, Jan. 16, 1932.
77 Diary, June 18, 1932.
78 W.L.M.K. to J. G. Gardiner, Sept. 10, 1932; W.L.M.K. to Ian Mackenzie, Sept. 21, 1932.
79 W.L.M.K. to Sir Charles Starmer, Feb. 24, 1933.
80 John E. Sinclair to W.L.M.K., Dec. 26, 1932.
81 W.L.M.K. to J. G. Gardiner, Nov. 14, 1933.
82 *Can. H. of C. Debates*, Feb. 20, 1933, p. 2253.
83 *Ibid.*, p. 2266.
84 Diary, Feb. 20, 1933.
85 *Can. H. of C. Debates*, May 1, 1933, p. 4433.
86 Diary, July 20, 1933.
87 W.L.M.K. to Norman Rogers, March 18, 1933.
88 T. A. Crerar to W.L.M.K., June 30, 1933.
89 W.L.M.K. to J. G. Gardiner, March 25, 1933.
90 Diary, July 29, 1933.
91 *Ibid.*, Aug. 17, 1933.
92 *Ibid.*, July 19, 1933; W.L.M.K. to J. C. Elliott, Aug. 24, 1933.

93 E. M. Macdonald to W.L.M.K., Aug. 23, 1933.
94 See Margaret Ormsby, *British Columbia: A History* (Toronto, 1958), pp. 451–3 for an account of this election.
95 W.L.M.K. to Ian Mackenzie, Oct. 4, 1933.
96 See Margaret Ormsby, "T. Dufferin Pattullo and the Little New Deal," in *Canadian Historical Review*, XLIII, Dec. 1962, 277–297.
97 J. G. Turgeon to W.L.M.K., Nov. 13, 1933.
98 W.L.M.K. to T. D. Pattullo, Nov. 3 and 4, 1933.
99 W.L.M.K. to T. Reid, Nov. 17, 1933.
100 W.L.M.K. to Violet Markham, Dec. 11, 1933.
101 W.L.M.K. to Ian Mackenzie, Nov. 14, 1933.
102 W.L.M.K. to Violet Markham, Dec. 11, 1933.
103 Diary, Dec. 31, 1933.

CHAPTER THREE
PRE-ELECTION MANŒUVRES

1 Manion Papers, R. J. Manion to James Manion, Jan. 12, 1934.
2 *Ibid.*, May 8, 1934.
3 *Can. H. of C. Debates*, Jan. 29, 1934, p. 58.
4 *Ibid.*, Jan. 30, 1943, p. 62.
5 R. J. Manion, *ibid.*, Feb. 13, 1934, p. 518.
6 *Can. H. of C. Debates*, March 22, 1934, p. 1740.
7 W.L.M.K., Diary, March 27, 28, 1934; *Can. H. of C. Debates*, March 26, 1934, pp. 1815–26.
8 *Can. H. of C. Debates*, April 18, 1934, p. 2267.
9 *Ibid.*, April 23, 1934, p. 2445.
10 Bennett Papers, R. B. Bennett to A. S. Bellingham, March 5, 1934, p. 63460.
11 *Ibid.*, R. B. Bennett to J. A. McLeod, June 1, 1933, p. 62215.
12 *Ibid.*, R. B. Bennett to Robert Reid, May 23, 1934, p. 63793.
13 *Can. H. of C. Debates*, Jan. 30, 1934, p. 84.
14 *Ibid.*, Feb. 22, 1934, pp. 824–6.
15 For a detailed discussion of the origins of the Bank of Canada Act and the debate in the House of Commons, see Linda M. Grayson, "The Formation of the Bank of Canada" (unpublished Ph.D. thesis, University of Toronto, 1974).
16 *Can. H. of C. Debates*, Feb. 22, 1934, p. 840.
17 Diary, Feb. 27, 1934.
18 W.L.M.K. to W. E. Rundle, Feb. 3, 1934.
19 Diary, Feb. 7, 1934.
20 *Ibid.*, March 1, 1934.
21 *Can. H. of C. Debates*, March 8, 1934, p. 1285.
22 *Ibid.*, June 21, 1934, p. 4152.
23 *Ibid.*, June 27, 1934, pp. 4363–4.
24 *Ibid.*, p. 4357.
25 *Ibid*, June 21, 1934, p. 4168.
26 Diary, June 22, 1934.
27 *Can. H. of C. Debates*, June 22, 1934, pp. 4241–3.
28 See Marc La Terreur, *Les tribulations des Conservateurs au Québec* (Québec, 1973), pp. 49–54.
29 *Canadian Annual Review*, 1934 (Toronto, 1935), p. 82.
30 *Can. H. of C. Debates*, June 4, 1934, p. 3639.
31 *Ibid.*, June 5, 1934, p. 3664.

32 Diary, April 2, 1934.
33 *Ibid.*, April 10, 1934.
34 *Can. H. of C. Debates*, April 19, 1934, pp. 2332–52.
35 *Ibid.*, June 6, 1934, p. 3727.
36 A. C. Hardy to W.L.M.K., April 20, 1934; N. W. Rowell to W.L.M.K., May 11, 1934.
37 *Can. H. of C. Debates*, April 19, 1934, p. 2354.
38 *Ibid.*, May 4, 1934, p. 2814.
39 Diary, June 7, 1934.
40 Quoted in J. R. H. Wilbur, "H. H. Stevens and the Antecedents of the Reconstruction Party, 1930–1935" (unpublished M.A. Thesis, Queen's University, 1961).
41 *Can. H. of C. Debates*, Feb. 19, 1934, p. 729.
42 *Ibid.*, June 30, 1934, p. 4581.
43 For details on the C.C.F. in Ontario, see G. L. Caplan, *The Dilemma of Canadian Socialism: the C.C.F. in Ontario* (Toronto, 1973); L. Zakuta, *A Protest Movement Becalmed: A Study of Change in the C.C.F.* (Toronto, 1964); Margaret Stewart and Doris French, *Ask No Quarter* (Toronto, 1959).
44 For a discussion of the Liberal coalition, see Neil McKenty, *Mitch Hepburn* (Toronto, 1967), Chap. 5.
45 A Darrach to W.L.M.K., Jan. 2, 1931.
46 See McKenty, *Mitch Hepburn*, pp. 22–7.
47 Diary, Nov. 5, 1930.
48 *Ibid.*; W.L.M.K. to W. R. P. Parker, Nov. 6, 1930.
49 Harry Johnson to W.L.M.K., Dec. 2, 1930.
50 See McKenty, *Mitch Hepburn*, pp. 35–8 for a description of the convention.
51 W.L.M.K. to M. Hepburn, Dec. 17, 1930.
52 *Ibid.*, Dec. 18, 1930.
53 W.L.M.K. to W. A. R. Slater, April 8, 1933.
54 Toronto *Mail and Empire*, Dec. 18, 1930.
55 W.L.M.K. to M. Hepburn, May 24, 1934.
56 Diary, June 25, 1934.
57 W.L.M.K. to M. Hepburn, July 12, 1934.
58 W.L.M.K. to E. C. Drury, July 7, 1934.
59 Diary, June 25, 1934.
60 W.L.M.K. to E. C. Grant, Oct. 18, 1934.
61 J. G. Gardiner to W.L.M.K., June 28, 1934.
62 Diary, June 21, 1934.
63 Ottawa *Citizen*, June 20, 1934.
64 W.L.M.K. to Ian Mackenzie, Aug. 16, 1934.
65 W.L.M.K. to W. A. Fraser, July 16, 1934.
66 W.L.M.K. to V. Massey, July 17, 1934.
67 E. A. Carroll to W.L.M.K., July 18, 1934.
68 Ottawa *Journal*, Sept. 17, 1934.
69 V. Massey to W.L.M.K., July 28, 1934.
70 Diary, Aug. 3, 1934.
71 *Ibid.*, July 28, 1934.
72 H. H. Stevens, *Deplorable Conditions in Some Businesses Revealed*, dated July 27, 1934.
73 *Canadian Annual Review*, 1934, p. 39.
74 *Winnipeg Free Press*, Aug. 7, 1934.
75 Dafoe Papers, J. W. Dafoe to J. S. McLean, Aug. 16, 1934.
76 Ian Mackenzie to W.L.M.K., Aug. 17, 1934.
77 *Winnipeg Free Press*, Sept. 15, 1934.
78 Toronto *Star*, Sept. 20, 1934.

79 Diary, Sept. 17, 1934.
80 Ottawa *Citizen*, Sept. 25, 1934.

CHAPTER FOUR
BEYOND POLITICS

1 W.L.M.K. to James Malcolm, July 18, 1934.
2 W.L.M.K., Diary, Jan. 9, 1934.
3 *Ibid.*, Dec. 7, 1933.
4 *Ibid.*, July 31, 1934; also July 24, Aug. 6, 14, 21, 1934.
5 W.L.M.K. to Mrs Lambert, Feb. 9, 1934.
6 For King's first séances with Mrs Wreidt see H. Blair Neatby, *W. L. Mackenzie King, II: 1924–1932* (Toronto, 1963), pp. 406–9; C. P. Stacey, *A Very Double Life: The Private World of Mackenzie King* (Toronto, 1976), pp. 160–70.
7 Diary, Aug. 16, 1934; J. E. Hatt to W.L.M.K., Aug. 14, 1934.
8 Diary, Aug. 30, 1934.
9 *Ibid.*, Aug. 28, 1934.
10 For a discussion of this relationship see Neatby, *Mackenzie King*, II, 198–9; Stacey, *A Very Double Life*, pp. 118–138.
11 Diary, Dec. 17, 1933.
12 *Ibid.*, May 12, 1934.
13 *Ibid.*, not transcribed, March 9, 1934.
14 *Ibid.*, not transcribed, May 10, 1934.
15 *Ibid.*, June 4, 1934.
16 *Ibid.*, June 3, 1934.
17 *Ibid.*, June 12, 1934.
18 *Ibid.*, June 20, 1934.
19 *Ibid.*, July 1, 1934.
20 *Ibid.*, July 5, 1934.
21 *Ibid.*, July 5, 1934; these and other table-rapping experiences are described in Stacey, *A Very Double Life*, pp. 171–89.
22 *Ibid.*, Oct. 2, 1934.
23 King had marked the margin of his copy of W. H. R. Rivers, *Conflict and Dreams* (London, 1932), where Freud's theory of wish fulfilment is discussed.
24 Diary, not transcribed, Feb. 24, 1934.
25 *Ibid.*, not transcribed, March 30, 1934.
26 *Ibid.*, not transcribed, March 3, 1934.
27 See F. A. McGregor, *The Rise and Fall of Mackenzie King* (Toronto, 1962) and R. M. Dawson, *W. L. Mackenzie King, I: 1874–1923* (Toronto, 1958), for numerous examples of this reaction.
28 See Dawson, *Mackenzie King*, I, 264–5.
29 Diary, not transcribed, Jan. 18, 1934; *ibid.*, Jan. 7, 1935.
30 *Ibid.*, Dec. 11, 1934.
31 *Ibid.*, July 6, 1934.

CHAPTER FIVE
THE NEW CONSERVATISM

1 R. J. Manion Papers, R. J. Manion to James Manion, May 8, 1934.
2 *Ibid.*, R. J. Manion to R. B. Bennett, Aug. 25, 1934.
3 *Ibid.*, A. A. Allan to R. J. Manion, Nov. 6, 1934.
4 *Ibid.*, R. J. Manion to A. A. Allan, Nov. 7, 1934.
5 H. H. Stevens to R. B. Bennett, Oct. 30, 1934. The full correspondence was released

to the press and was later published as *Can. H. of C. Sessional Paper*, No. 98, 1935.
6 Toronto *Star*, Nov. 1, 1934.
7 Ottawa *Journal*, Oct. 30, 1934.
8 Toronto *Globe*, Nov. 6, 1934.
9 Ottawa *Journal*, Nov. 21, 1934.
10 Montreal *Gazette*, Dec. 5, 1934.
11 J. E. Elliott to W.L.M.K., Nov. 23, 1934.
12 S. W. Jacobs to W.L.M.K., Dec. 6, 1934.
13 W.L.M.K. Diary, Nov. 29, 1934.
14 H. R. L. Henry to Henry Moyle, Nov. 20, 1934.
15 Conservative Cabinet Ministers reported this to King in private conversations and King interpreted some private remarks by Bennett as confirmation; Diary, March 5, June 20, 1935.
16 *Can. H. of C. Debates*, April 11, 1934, p. 2046.
17 *Ibid.*, April 13, 1934, p. 2163.
18 *Canadian Annual Review*, 1934 (Toronto, 1935), p. 36.
19 See, for example, J. W. Dafoe Papers, W. J. Major to J. W. Dafoe, Sept. 26, 1934; A. W. Roebuck to J. W. Dafoe, Nov. 8, 1934.
20 *Foreign Relations of the United States, 1933*, III, Memorandum of U.S. Secretary of State, Nov. 20, 1933, p. 51; *ibid.*, 1934, I, Memorandum of U.S. Secretary of State, Feb. 8, 1934, p. 845.
21 See Arthur M. Schlesinger, Jr, *The Age of Roosevelt: The Coming of the New Deal* (Boston, 1959), pp. 255–9.
22 *Foreign Relations of the United States, 1934*, I, J. D. Nickerson, Memorandum, Aug. 7, 1934, p. 845.
23 *Ibid.*, W. D. Herridge to Cordell Hull, Nov. 14, 1934, p. 856.
24 *Ibid.*, W. D. Robbins to Cordell Hull, Nov. 21, 1934, pp. 859–63.
25 *Ibid.*, William Phillips, Memorandum, Dec. 1, 1934, p. 871.
26 Franklin D. Roosevelt Library, Hyde Park, Roosevelt Papers, W. D. Robbins to F. D. Roosevelt, Dec. 18, 1934, P.S.F. Canada folder.
27 Diary, Dec. 18, 1934.
28 Quoted in *Can. H. of C. Debates*, Jan. 21, 1935, from a speech of Nov. 27, 1934.
29 Diary, Dec. 5, 1934.
30 *Ibid.*, Dec. 18, 1934.
31 Dafoe Papers, J. W. Dafoe to Mary McGeachy, Dec. 31, 1934.
32 Bennett Papers, W. D. Herridge to R. B. Bennett, April 12, 1934, pp. 184946–57.
33 *Ibid.*, Aug. 20, 1934, p. 185006–14.
34 This strategy is not outlined in Herridge's correspondence at the time but is clearly implied in subsequent letters when he complains that Bennett has ruined everything by not calling the election in the spring of 1935. Bennett Papers, W. D. Herridge to R. Finlayson, April 6, 1935, pp. 184719–21; Manion Papers, W. D. Herridge to R. J. Manion, May 23, 1935.
35 First radio broadcast, Jan. 2, 1935. The broadcasts were later published in a pamphlet, "The Premier Speaks to the People."
36 Second radio broadcast, Jan. 4, 1935.
37 Third radio broadcast, Jan. 7, 1935.
38 Fourth radio broadcast, Jan. 9, 1935.
39 Fifth radio broadcast, Jan. 11, 1935.
40 For Bennett's comments see Michiel Horn, ed., *The Dirty Thirties* (Toronto, 1972), pp. 598–9.
41 Manion Papers, R. J. Manion to James Manion, Jan. 10, 1935.
42 C. H. Cahan to W.L.M.K., Dec. 16, 1935. See also Cahan Papers Additional, C. H. Cahan to Hector McInnis, Oct. 18, 1935.
43 Montreal *Gazette*, Jan. 4, 1935.

44 Diary, Jan. 2, 1935.
45 *Ibid.*, Jan. 9, 1935.
46 *Can. H. of C. Debates*, Jan. 17, 1935, p. 3.

CHAPTER SIX
DEALING WITH THE NEW DEAL

1 Manion Papers, W. D. Herridge to R. J. Manion, May 23, 1935. C. H. Cahan told King late in February that this had been Bennett's plan; Diary, Feb. 27, 1935.
2 W.L.M.K., Diary, Jan. 11, 1935.
3 *Ibid.*, Jan. 18, 1935.
4 *Can. H. of C. Debates*, Jan. 21, 1935, p. 35.
5 *Ibid.*, p. 49.
6 *Ibid.*, p. 59.
7 Manion Papers, R. J. Manion to James Manion, Jan. 28, 1935.
8 *Can. H. of C. Debates*, Jan. 24, 1935, p. 187.
9 *Ibid.*, Jan. 29, 1935, p. 280.
10 Diary, Jan. 30, 1935.
11 *Ibid.*, Feb. 18, 1935.
12 *Ibid.*, Feb. 20, 1935.
13 *Can. H. of C. Debates*, Feb. 21, 1935, p. 1087.
14 *Ibid.*, Feb. 8, 1935, pp. 632–45.
15 Diary, Feb. 9, 1935.
16 Manion Papers, R. J. Manion to James Manion, March 4, 1935.
17 *Can. H. of C. Debates*, March 11, 1935, p. 1572.
18 *Ibid.*, p. 1573.
19 Diary, March 13, 1935.
20 *Can. H. of C. Debates*, March 22, 1935, pp. 1960–89.
21 *Ibid.*, March 26, 1935, p. 2121.
22 Manion Papers, R. J. Manion to W. D. Herridge, April 8, 1935.
23 Diary, March 14, 1935.
24 *Can. H. of C. Debates*, April 8, 1935, pp. 2504–12.
25 W.L.M.K. to Sir Herbert Samuel, April 20, 1935.
26 Manion Papers, R. J. Manion to James Manion, March 22, 1935.
27 *Ibid.*, W. D. Herridge to R. J. Manion, March 22, 1935.
28 Diary, April 27, 1935.
29 *Ibid.*, April 30, 1935.
30 *Ibid.*, Jan. 3, 1935.
31 *Ibid.*, Feb. 3, 1935.
32 N. M. Rogers, *W. L. Mackenzie King* (Toronto, 1935).
33 Diary, May 11, 1935.
34 W.L.M.K., *Industry and Humanity* (rev. ed., Toronto, 1935), p. xii.
35 Diary, May 26, 1935.
36 W.L.M.K. to Julia Cantacuzene, Aug. 18, 1935.
37 Diary, May 8, 1935.
38 *Ibid.*, May 24, 1935.
39 *Ibid.*, May 25, 1935.
40 *Ibid.*, May 26, 1935.
41 *Ibid.*, July 10, 1932.
42 *Ibid.*, July 27, 1932.
43 *Canadian Annual Review*, 1935 and 1936 (Toronto, 1937), p. 8.
44 Toronto *Globe*, June 5, 1935; Manion Papers, R. J. Manion to H. A. Bruce, June 6, 1935.

45 *Canadian Annual Review*, 1935 and 1936, p. 8.
46 Manion Papers, R. J. Manion and R. B. Bennett, Feb. 14, 1935.
47 *Ibid.*, R. J. Manion to James Manion, June 3, 1935.
48 *Report of Royal Commission on Price Spreads* (Ottawa, 1937), pp. 248–75.
49 *Ibid.*, pp. 143–99.
50 *Ibid.*, pp. 124–42.
51 *Ibid.*, p. 274.
52 *Can. H. of C. Debates*, June 11, 1935, pp. 3508–11.
53 An amendment to the Industrial Disputes Investigation Act did extend the powers of the Minister to order an enquiry into an industrial dispute but it was argued that anything further was beyond the jurisdiction of the federal government. *Ibid.*, May 29, 1935, p. 3155.
54 *Can. H. of C. Debates*, June 11, 1935, pp. 3508–11.
55 *Ibid.*, May 29, 1935, p. 3167.
56 "The Premier Speaks to the People," fourth radio broadcast, see above p. 87.
57 Diary, Jan. 10, 1935.
58 *Ibid.*, Feb. 13, 1935.
59 *Ibid.*
60 *Report of Royal Commission on Price Spreads*, pp. 276–87.
61 *Ibid.*, pp. 288–307.
62 Diary, May 20, 1935.
63 W.L.M.K. to Norman Rogers, May 28, 1935.
64 *Can. H. of C. Debates*, June 19, 1935, p. 3801.
65 *Ibid.*, pp. 2801–3811.
66 Dafoe Papers, Grant Dexter to J. W. Dafoe, June 3, 1935.
67 Diary, June 19, 1935.
68 *Ibid.*
69 Vernon C. Fowke, *The National Policy and the Wheat Economy* (Toronto, 1957), p. 249.
70 The sequence of decisions can be traced in the lengthy correspondence between R. B. Bennett and John I. McFarland in the Bennett Papers.
71 Diary, June 7, 1935.
72 C. D. Howe to W.L.M.K., Jan. 10, 1935; T. A. Crerar to W.L.M.K., Jan. 26, 1935.
73 *Can. H. of C. Debates*, June 14, 1935, n. 3648.
74 A. B. Hudson to W.L.M.K., Feb. 23, 1935.
75 Diary, March 6, 1935.
76 *Ibid.*, June 10, 1935.
77 *Ibid.*
78 Diary, June 12, 1935.
79 *Can. H. of C. Debates*, June 12, 1935, p. 3574.
80 *Ibid.*, p. 3578.
81 *Ibid.*, June 13, 1935, p. 3633.
82 Special Committee on Bill 98, 1935, *Minutes of Proceedings and Evidence*, pp. 224, 268.
83 Diary, July 3, 1935.
84 *Ibid.*, July 5, 1935.
85 *Ibid.*

CHAPTER SEVEN
KING OR CHAOS

1 E. N. Rhodes and Arthur Sauvé went to the Senate; Alfred Duranleau was named to the Quebec Superior Court, and Hugh Guthrie went to the Board of Railway Commissioners.

2 Manion Papers, R. J. Manion to James Manion, Sept. 29, 1935. For a more pessimistic view see R. J. Manion to James Manion, Aug. 10, 1935.
3 Press release of Bennett's radio broadcast of Sept. 11, 1935.
4 Toronto *Globe*, Sept. 10, 1935.
5 Press release of Bennett's radio broadcast of Sept. 11, 1935.
6 Press release of Bennett's radio broadcast of Sept. 14, 1935.
7 G. M. Lefresne, "The Royal Twenty Centers" (honours essay, Royal Military College, 1962), defends the administration of these relief camps; Ronald Liversedge, *Recollections of the On to Ottawa Trek* (Toronto, 1973), sees no redeeming features in these "slave camps."
8 A record of this interview and other documents is printed in Liversedge, *Recollections of the On to Ottawa Trek*.
9 *Sessional Paper No. 422*, 1935; R. B. Bennett to J. G. Gardiner, June 27, 1935.
10 *Ibid.*, Sept. 11, 1935.
11 Toronto *Globe*, Sept. 24, 1935.
12 Manion Papers, R. J. Manion to R. B. Bennett, Sept. 1, 1935.
13 H. H. Stevens, "The Issues as I see them," *Maclean's Magazine*, Sept. 15, 1935; *Canadian Annual Review*, 1935–1936 (Toronto, 1937), p. 65.
14 Press release of Bennett's radio broadcast of Sept. 14, 1935.
15 *Foreign Relations of the United States, 1935*, II, J. C. H. Bonbright, "Memorandum," Aug. 14, 1935, p. 19.
16 N. Robertson, "Memorandum on Trade Negotiations between Canada and the United States," Oct. 26, 1935; *Foreign Relations of the United States, 1935*, II, N. Armour, "Memorandum," Sept. 21, 1935, p. 22.
17 Windsor *Daily Star*, Sept. 10, 1935.
18 Ottawa *Journal*, Sept. 16, 1935.
19 Ottawa *Citizen*, Oct. 13, 1935.
20 Harry Anderson to W.L.M.K., Sept. 14, 1935; Frank Fowler to N. P. Lambert, Sept. 7, 1935.
21 There is an extensive literature on the Social Credit movement in Alberta. William E. Mann, *Sect, Cult and Church in Alberta* (rev. ed Toronto, 1972), discusses the religious background; C. B. Macpherson, *Democracy in Alberta: Social Credit and the Party System* (Toronto, 1953), analyses the economic structure underlying the party system in the province; John A. Irving, *The Social Credit Movement in Alberta* (Toronto, 1959), concentrates on Aberhart and his evangelism.
22 Grant Dexter, "Mr. King," *Maclean's Magazine*, Nov. 15, 1935.
23 W.L.M.K. to W. A. Fraser, July 13, 1935.
24 These speeches were distributed as a campaign pamphlet entitled "Mackenzie King to the Canadian People, 1935."
25 Ottawa *Citizen*, Aug. 8, 1935.
26 Toronto, *Globe*, Aug. 15, 1935.
27 "Mackenzie King to the Canadian People, 1935."
28 W.L.M.K. to Norman Rogers, Aug. 23, 1935; W.L.M.K. to J. B. McBride, Aug. 30, 1935.
29 *Winnipeg Free Press*, Sept. 23, 1935.
30 W.L.M.K. to M. F. Hepburn, Aug. 6, 1935.
31 W.L.M.K. to Archer Martin, May 18, 1935.
32 W.L.M.K., Diary, April 3, 1935.
33 For a discussion of finances see J. L. Granatstein, "Financing the Liberal Party, 1935–1945," in M. Cross and R. Bothwell, eds., *Policy by other Means: Essays in Honour of C. P. Stacey* (Toronto, 1972), pp. 181–99.
34 See above, p. 67.
35 Diary, May 10, 1926.
36 N. P. Lambert, Diary, May 10, 1935.

37 Diary, May 10, 1935.
38 *Ibid.*, May 31, 1935.
39 W.L.M.K. to A. C. Hardy, Aug. 21, 1935.
40 W.L.M.K. to C. B. Howard, Aug. 19, 1935.
41 N. P. Lambert to W. F. Kerr, Aug. 12, 1935.
42 W. B. Herbert to N. P. Lambert, Aug. 29, 1935; J. C. Davis to W.L.M.K.,
   Sept. 13, 1935.
43 W.L.M.K. to N. P. Lambert, Sept. 21, 1935; W.L.M.K. to C. A. Dunning,
   Sept. 26, 1935.
44 Ottawa *Citizen*, Sept. 5, 1935.
45 J. C. Davis to N. P. Lambert, Sept. 17, 1935; Frank Fowler to N. P. Lambert,
   Sept. 17, 1935.
46 W.L.M.K. to L. Chevrier, Aug. 22, 1935.
47 Manion Papers, R. J. Manion to James Manion, Sept. 29, 1935.
48 W.L.M.K. to Ernest Lapointe, Sept. 8, 1935.
49 "Mackenzie King to the Canadian People, 1935."
50 W.L.M.K. to Harry Anderson, Aug. 10, 1935.
51 Halifax *Chronicle*, Sept. 5, 1935.
52 Ottawa *Citizen*, Oct. 1, 1935.
53 Diary, Oct. 5, 1935.
54 Victoria *Daily Times*, Sept. 28, 1935.
55 N. P. Lambert, Diary, Aug. 28, 1935.
56 London *Advertiser*, Aug. 16, 1935.
57 Quebec *Chronicle-Telegraph*, Sept. 9, 1935.
58 Press release of R. B. Bennett's radio broadcast, Sept. 6, 1935.
59 Howard A. Scarrow, *Canada Votes* (New Orleans, 1962), gives a detailed breakdown of the election results. He lists the following percentages for the popular vote
   (with 1930 figures in brackets): Liberals 44.9 (45.5); Conservatives 29.6 (48.7);
   Reconstruction 8.7; C.C.F. 8.9; Social Credit 3.9. If the Independent Liberal vote is
   included the Liberal popular vote would be almost 47 per cent. For a contemporary
   analysis of the election results see Escott Reid, "The Canadian Election of 1935—and
   after," *American Political Science Review*, XXX, Feb. 1936, pp. 111–21.
60 *Can. H. of C. Debates*, July 29, 1931, p. 4278.

CHAPTER EIGHT

THE REINS OF OFFICE

1 W.L.M.K. to M. F. Hepburn, July 12, 1934.
2 W.L.M.K., Diary, Nov. 26, 1920.
3 For a fuller discussion of King's relations with his senior French-Canadian colleague
   see H. B. Neatby, "Mackenzie King and French Canada," *Journal of Canadian
   Studies*, XI, Feb. 1976, pp. 3–13.
4 The King diary gives a full account of Cabinet formation. There is also a detailed
   study by F. W. Gibson, "The Cabinet of 1935," in F. W. Gibson, ed., *Cabinet
   Formation and Bicultural Relations* (Ottawa, 1970).
5 Diary, June 10, 1935.
6 Queen's University Archives Dunning Papers, C. A. Dunning to J. A. Cross,
   Dec. 27, 1932.
7 *Ibid.*, C. A. Dunning to M. Gervin, Jan. 9, 1935.
8 *Ibid.*, C. A. Dunning to E. M. Macdonald, Feb. 15, 1935.
9 *Ibid.*, R. L. Borden to L. A. Taschereau, Oct. 17, 1935; see also W.L.M.K. to
   R. L. Borden, Nov. 20, 1935.
10 Diary, June 10, 1935.

11 *Ibid.*, Oct. 18, 1935.
12 *Ibid.*, Oct. 22, 1935.
13 *Ibid.*, Oct. 17, 1935.
14 *Ibid.*, Oct. 22, 1935.
15 M. F. Hepburn to W.L.M.K., Oct. 21, 1935.
16 W.L.M.K. to M. F. Hepburn, Oct. 22, 1935.
17 Diary, Oct. 17, 1935.
18 *Ibid.*, Oct. 22, 1935.
19 *Ibid.*, Oct. 23, 1935.
20 Diary, Aug. 7, 1930.
21 See, for example, Vincent Massey, *What's Past is Prologue* (Toronto, 1963), p. 135.
22 Diary, Sept. 11, 1929.
23 O. D. Skelton to W.L.M.K., Oct. 23, 1935.
24 Diary, Oct. 25, 1935.
25 G. P. de T. Glazebrook, *A History of Canadian External Relations* (Toronto, 1950), pp. 371–3.
26 Secretary of State for External Affairs to Dominions Secretary, Sept. 3, 1935, reprinted in A. I. Inglis, ed., *Documents relatifs aux relations extérieures du Canada/ Documents on Canadian External Relations*, V: *1931–1935* (Ottawa, 1973), pp. 381–2.
27 Prime Minister to Advisory Officers, Oct. 9, 1935, *ibid.*, p. 386.
28 Advisory Officer to Secretary of State for External Affairs, Oct. 9, 1935, *ibid.*, pp. 386–7.
29 Note by O. D. Skelton on telephone conversation with R. B. Bennett, Oct. 10, 1935, *ibid.*, p. 391.
30 Acting Secretary of State for External Affairs to Advisory Officer, 9 Oct. 1935, *ibid.*, p. 386.
31 The best study of this incident is R. Bothwell and J. English, "Dirty Work at the Crossroads: New Perspectives on the Riddell Incident," Canadian Historical Association, *Historical Papers 1972*, pp. 263–85.
32 Cited in R. A. Mackay and E. B. Rogers, *Canada Looks Abroad* (Toronto, 1938), p. 346.
33 Diary, Oct. 25, 1935.
34 *Ibid.*, Oct. 2, 1935.
35 *Can. H. of C. Debates*, Feb. 8, 1932, pp. 29–30.
36 Diary, May 24, 1934.
37 *Ibid.*, Oct. 25, 1935.
38 Jean Bruchési, "A French-Canadian view of Canada's foreign policy," in *Canada, The Empire and the League* (Toronto, 1936), p. 143.
39 Diary, Oct. 29, 1935.
40 The press release is reprinted in MacKay and Rogers, *Canada Looks Abroad*, pp. 346–8.
41 Diary, Oct. 29, 1935.
42 For details on the "Riddell incident" see Bothwell and English, " 'Dirty Work at the Crossroads.' " For a more favourable interpretation of Riddell's actions, see John A. Munro, "The Riddell Affair Reconsidered," *External Affairs*, Oct. 1969. Riddell gives his version of these events in *World Security by Conference* (Toronto, 1947).
43 Cited in Bothwell and English, " 'Dirty Work at the Crossroads,' " p. 275.
44 O. D. Skelton to L. Beaudry, Nov. 26, 1935, reprinted in Inglis, ed., *Documents on Canadian External Relations*. V: *1931–1935*, p. 410.
45 King Papers, L. Beaudry to O. D. Skelton, Nov. 28, 1935; Diary, Nov. 29, 1935.
46 MacKay and Rogers, *Canada Looks Abroad*, p. 347.
47 See, for example, Dafoe Papers, N. W. Rowell to J. W. Dafoe, Dec. 2, 1935; J. B. Coyne to T. A. Crerar (copy), Dec. 7, 1935.

48 *Ibid.*, T. A. Crerar to J. B. Coyne (copy), Dec. 3, 1935.
49 Ottawa *Citizen*, Dec. 7, 1935.
50 Diary, Dec. 11, 1935.
51 *Ibid.*, Oct. 22, 1935.
52 N. Armour to Cordell Hull, Oct. 24, 1935; reprinted in *Foreign Relations of the United States, 1935*, II, pp. 28–30.
53 N. Armour to Cordell Hull, Oct. 24, 1935; reprinted in *ibid.*, p. 29.
54 Diary, Nov. 4, 1935.
55 N. A. Robertson, "Trade Negotiations between Canada and the United States," Oct. 26, 1935.
56 *Ibid.*
57 King had a high opinion of Dana Wilgress and H. A. McKinnon, the two negotiators who had arrived in Washington a few days before King and Skelton; Diary, Oct. 31, 1935.
58 *Ibid.*, Nov. 8, 1935.
59 *Ibid.* Roosevelt had apparently overlooked his authority to reduce the excise tax on articles on which the tariff was being reduced.
60 For a study of the agreement from the U.S. perspective see Richard N. Kottman, *Reciprocity in the North Atlantic Triangle, 1932–1938* (Ithaca, 1968), Chap. III.
61 Diary, Nov. 8, 1935.
62 *Ibid.*, Nov. 11, 1935.
63 *Ibid.*, Nov. 9, 1935.
64 *Ibid.*, Nov. 8, 1935.
65 King Papers, J. E. R[ead], "Memorandum on Parliamentary action in respect to Canada-United States Trade Agreement," Nov. 13, 1935; O. D. Skelton to W.L.M.K., Nov. 12, 1935.
66 Diary, Nov. 15, 1935.
67 See King Papers, R. L. Fredenburgh, "Memorandum on the Canada-United States trade agreement," Dec. 21, 1935.
68 See Hume Wrong to W.L.M.K., Nov. 22, 1935 for an analysis of U.S. reactions to the agreement.
69 For a discussion of this conflict within the Roosevelt administration see A. M. Schlesinger, Jr, *The Age of Roosevelt: The Politics of Upheaval* (Boston, 1960), pp. 255–9.
70 O. D. Skelton to W.L.M.K., Dec. 30, 1935. See also King Papers, "Summary of discussions between representatives of some Canadian distillers and U.S. Departments of Treasury and Justice," April 23, 1936.
71 Memorandum by Economic Adviser, Jan. 30, 1936; reprinted in *Foreign Relations of the United States, 1936*, I, 800; O. D. Skelton to W.L.M.K., March 12, 1936; Hume Wrong to W.L.M.K., March 21, 1936.
72 Cordell Hull, *Memoirs* (New York, 1948), I, 206–7.
73 W. Aberhart to W.L.M.K., Oct. 16, 1935.
74 Dominion-Provincial Conference 1935, *Record of Proceedings* (Ottawa, 1936), p. 10.
75 *Ibid.*, pp. 8–9.
76 *Ibid.*, p. 11.
77 Diary, Dec. 9, 135.
78 King Papers, Harry Baldwin, "Memorandum on Unemployment Relief, 1930–35, Administration and Control," Nov. 30, 1935.
79 Dominion-Provincial Conference 1935, *Record of Proceedings*, p. 48.
80 W.L.M.K. to J. G. Ross, Nov. 30, 1935.
81 See H. Blair Neatby, *W.L. Mackenzie King, II: 1924–1932* (Toronto, 1963), p. 235.
82 Dominion-Provincial Conference 1935, *Record of Proceedings*, p. 12.
83 Diary, Dec. 26, 1935.
84 *Ibid.*, Dec. 19, 1935; N. Ward, ed., *The Memoirs of Chubby Power* (Toronto,

1966), pp. 338–42.
85 Dominion-Provincial Conference 1935, *Report of Proceedings*, p. 64.

CHAPTER NINE
THE LIBERAL RESPONSE TO THE DEPRESSION

1 W.L.M.K., Diary, March 30, 1936; see also R. B. Bennett, *Can. H. of C. Debates*, March 30, 1936, p. 1580.
2 *Can. H. of C. Debates*, March 30, 1936, p. 1572.
3 *Ibid.*, p. 1570.
4 Bernard Rose to W.L.M.K., Feb. 17, 1936.
5 Diary, April 4, 1936.
6 Diary, April 7, 1936. The statements which provoked this outburst appear in *Can. H. of C. Debates*, April 7, 1936, pp. 1889, 1907.
7 *Can. H. of C. Debates*, April 3, 1936, p. 1787.
8 Diary, April 8, 1936.
9 *Ibid.*, March 14, 1936.
10 *Ibid.*, April 4, 1936.
11 *Ibid.*, March 30, 31, 1936.
12 E. R. Chevrier to W.L.M.K., April 15, 1936, enclosure.
13 *Can. H. of C. Debates*, May 14, 1936, pp. 2295–6.
14 See M. A. Ormsby, "T. Dufferin Pattullo and the little New Deal," *Canadian Historical Review*, XLII, Dec. 1962, pp. 277–297.
15 W.L.M.K. to T. D. Pattullo, April 11, 1936; telegram, April 29, 1936.
16 Diary, April 7, 1936.
17 C. Cockroft to C. A. Dunning, March 12, 1936. The correspondence was later published in *Can. H. of C. Debates*, April 1, 1936, pp. 1683–7.
18 Diary, March 18, 1936.
19 *Can. H. of C. Debates*, April 1, 1936, p. 1687.
20 See J. R. Mallory, *Social Credit and the Federal Power in Canada* (Toronto 1954), pp. 128–35.
21 Diary, Dec. 11, 1935.
22 *Ibid.*, March 25, 1936.
23. *Ibid.*, March 25, 28, 30, 1936.
24 V. Massey to W.L.M.K., April 3, 1936; L. B. Pearson to W.L.M.K., April 9, 1936.
25 C. A. Dunning to William Aberhart et al., May 1, 1936; T. D. Pattullo to C. A. Dunning, May 2, 1936; William Aberhart to C. A. Dunning, May 12, 1936.
26 Diary, April 25, 1936.
27 *Ibid.*, May 14, 15, 1936.
28 *Can. H. of C. Debates*, May 14, 1936, p. 2800.
29 *Ibid.*, p. 2839.
30 Diary, May 14, 20, 1936.
31 Diary, June 23, 1936.
32 The proposals are printed in P. Gérin-Lajoie, *Constitutional Amendment in Canada* (Toronto, 1950), pp. 301–2. For an assessment of the proposals see G. Favreau, *The Amendment of the Constitution in Canada* (Ottawa, 1965).
33 *Can. H. of C. Debates*, April 22, 1936, p. 2077.
34 T. A. Crerar to W.L.M.K., April 28, 1936.
35 Diary, April 29, 1936.
36 *Can. H. of C. Debates*, May 1, 1936, pp. 2362–91.
37 A. K. Cameron to C. A. Dunning, May 5, 1936.
38 *Can. H. of C. Debates*, May 5, 1936, pp. 2503–25.
39 *Ibid.*, May 6, 1936, p. 2569.

40 *Ibid.*, p. 2688.
41 Diary, April 30, May 5, 1936.
42 *Ibid.*, April 30, 1936.
43 *Can. H. of C. Debates*, June 19, 1936, pp. 3897–903.
44 *Ibid.*, p. 3922.
45 Diary, Jan. 17, 1936.
46 *Ibid.*, April 22, 1936.
47 *Can. H. of C. Debates*, June 1, 1936, p. 3286.
48 *Ibid.*, June 16, 1936, p. 3781.
49 *Ibid.*, p. 3752.
50 Diary, June 16, 1936.
51 *Can. H. of C. Debates*, April 27, 1936, pp. 2178–86.
52 *Ibid.*, p. 2202.
53 Diary, July 7, 1936.
54 *Can. H. of C. Debates*, March 24, 1936, pp. 1412–16.
55 *Ibid.*, p. 1426.
56 Diary, Nov. 19, 1936.
57 *Ibid.*, March 30, 1936; see also Diary, 17 Feb. 1936.
58 *Ibid.*, Aug. 5, 1936.
59 *Ibid.*, Oct. 31, 1935.
60 *Can. H. of C. Debates*, March 27, 1936, p. 1553. The partisan debate had begun two days before, pp. 1440–64.
61 Diary, March 25, 1936.
62 *Ibid.*, Aug. 19, 1936.
63 *Ibid.*, Aug. 27, 1936.
64 W.L.M.K. to Vincent Massey, Aug. 4, 1936.
65 Bennett Papers, Alice Millar to George S. Robinson, March 20, 1936.

CHAPTER TEN

CANADA AND THE EUROPEAN VORTEX

1 James Eayrs, *In Defence of Canada*. II: *Appeasement and Rearmament* (Toronto, 1965), p. 51.
2 W.L.M.K., Diary, March 7, 1936.
3 *Ibid.*, March 13, 1936.
4 W.L.M.K. to Secretary of State for Dominion Affairs, March 17, 1936.
5 Diary, March 13, 1936.
6 *Can. H. of C. Debates*, March 23, 1936, p. 1933.
7 Diary, March 23, 1936.
8 Keith Feiling, *The Life of Neville Chamberlain* (London, 1946), p. 296.
9 O. D. Skelton to W. A. Riddell, Feb. 29, 1936.
10 W.L.M.K. to Thomas Vien, April 11, 1936.
11 Diary, June 11, 1936.
12 *Can. H. of C. Debates*, June 18, 1936, pp. 3862–73.
13 Diary, June 18, 1936.
14 *Can. H. of C. Debates*, June 18, 1936, pp. 3873–9.
15 *Ibid.*, p. 3897.
16 Diary, June 23, 1936.
17 *Ibid.*, March 7, 1936.
18 W.L.M.K. to Duke of Montrose, Aug. 10, 1936.
19 The speech is reprinted in R. A. Mackay and E. B. Rogers, *Canada Looks Abroad* (Toronto, 1938), pp. 363–9.
20 W.L.M.K. to Henri Bourassa, Oct. 2, 1936.

341

21 W.L.M.K. to Lord Tweedsmuir, Oct. 2, 1936.
22 *Winnipeg Free Press*, Oct. 1, 1936. For an analysis of the press reaction see Eayrs, *In Defence of Canada*, II, 39–40.
23 Dafoe Papers, J. W. Dafoe to J. A. Glen, Oct. 22, 1936.
24 Diary, Sept. 9, 1936.
25 *Ibid.*, Sept. 29, 1936.
26 *Ibid.*, Nov. 3, 1936.
27 See, for example, W.L.M.K. to J. L. Counsell, Aug. 8, 1936; to Duke of Montrose, Aug. 10, 1936; to Tweedsmuir, Oct. 2, 1936; to J. D. Rockefeller, Jr, Oct. 6, 1936.
28 Diary, Oct. 13, 1936.
29 *Ibid.*
30 *Ibid.*
31 *Ibid.*, Sept. 20, 1936.
32 *Ibid.*, Sept. 20, 24, 1936.
33 *Ibid.*, Oct. 1, 1936.
34 *Ibid.*, Oct. 26, 1936.
35 *Ibid.*, Sept. 20, Oct. 26, 1936.
36 *Ibid.*, Feb. 20, 1936.
37 *Ibid.*, Oct. 19, 1936.
38 *Ibid.*, Oct. 25, 1936.
39 *Ibid.*, Oct. 23, 26, 1936.
40 *Ibid.*, Oct. 27, 1936.
41 John Evelyn Wrench, *Geoffrey Dawson and Our Times* (London, 1955), p. 343.
42 See *Can. H. of C. Debates*, Feb. 15, 1937, p. 899 for a table of annual defence expenditures.
43 See C. P. Stacey, *Six Year of War* (Ottawa, 1955), pp. 6–8.
44 A. J. P. Taylor, *English History 1914–1945* (Oxford, 1965), p. 383.
45 Vincent Massey to W.L.M.K., March 13, 1936.
46 *Can. H. of C. Debates*, March 10, 1936.
47 Diary, March 10, 1936.
48 Gwendolen Carter, *The Commonwealth and International Security* (Toronto, 1947), pp. 253–5.
49 O. D. Skelton to W.L.M.K., March 26, 1936.
50 Diary, Aug. 26, 1936.
51 *Ibid.*, Aug. 26, 1936.
52 Stacey, *Six Years of War*, p. 11.
53 Diary, Sept. 10, 1936.
54 *Ibid.*, Oct. 23, 1936.
55 *Ibid.*, Nov. 24, 1936.
56 *Ibid.*, Dec. 16, 1936.
57 *Ibid.*, Dec. 18, 1936.
58 *Ibid.*
59 *Ibid.*, Nov. 28, 1936.
60 This despatch of Nov. 27, 1936 has not been released by the British government although Prime Minister Baldwin referred to it in Great Britain, *H. of C. Debates*, Dec. 10, 1936, p. 2191.
61 Diary, Nov. 28, 1936.
62 W.L.M.K. to Stanley Baldwin, Nov. 29, 1936.
63 W.L.M.K., press release, Dec. 4, 1936.
64 *Can. H. of C. Debates*, Jan. 18, 1937, p. 39. The message was dated Dec. 8, 1936.
65 W.L.M.K. to Sir Francis Floud, Dec. 8, 1936; Sir Francis Floud to W.L.M.K., Dec. 9, 1936; W.L.M.K. to Sir Francis Floud, Dec. 9, 1936; Sir Francis Floud to W.L.M.K., Dec. 10, 1936.
66 Diary, Feb. 4, 1936.

67 W.L.M.K. to Violet Markham, Feb. 1, 1937.
68 Montreal *Gazette*, Dec. 7, 1936; Toronto *Globe and Mail*, Dec. 12, 1936; Toronto *Telegram*, Dec. 15, 1936.
69 Diary, Jan. 20, 1937.
70 *Ibid.*, Dec. 16, 1936.

CHAPTER ELEVEN
PORTENTS OF DISUNITY

1 W.L.M.K. Diary, Jan. 20, 1937.
2 O. D. Skelton to W.L.M.K., April 20, 1937.
3 *Can. H. of C. Debates*, Feb. 25, 1937, p. 1211.
4 Diary, Feb. 23, 1937.
5 *Ibid.*
6 *Can. H. of C. Debates*, Feb. 25, 1937, p. 1238.
7 *Ibid.*, March 2, 1937, p. 1391.
8 *Ibid.*
9 T. A. Thompson, *Can. H. of C. Debates*, March 3, 1937, p. 1451.
10 C. R. Evans, *ibid.*, March 11, 1937, p. 1709.
11 Diary, Jan. 20, 1937.
12 Eugene Forsey to W.L.M.K., Feb. 14, 1937.
13 H. C. Engelbrecht and F. C. Hanighen, *Merchants of Death: A Study of the International Armaments Industry* (London, 1934); G. Seldes, *Iron, Blood and Profits* (New York, 1934).
14 Diary, Nov. 15, 1928.
15 W.L.M.K. to David Carnegie, April 20, 1935.
16 Diary, Nov. 24, 1936.
17 W.L.M.K. to Ian Mackenzie, Dec. 29, 1936; O. D. Skelton, "Report of Interdepartmental Committee on Armaments Problems," Jan. 21, 1937.
18 *Can. H. of C. Debates*, Feb. 15, 1937, p. 905.
19 *Ibid.*, Jan. 25, 1937, pp. 237–43.
20 *Ibid.*, Feb. 15, 1937, p. 890.
21 *Can. Senate Debates*, Jan. 19, 1937, pp. 7–8.
22 *Can. H. of C. Debates*, Feb. 9, 1937, p. 702.
23 *Ibid.*, March 25, 1937, p. 2218.
24 *Ibid.*, Feb. 16, 1937, p. 1927.
25 For a more recent study of the attitudes of French-Canadian M.P.s see David Hoffman and Norman Ward, *Bilingualism and Biculturalism in the House of Commons*, Documents of the Royal Commission on Bilingualism and Biculturalism (Ottawa, 1970).
26 Diary, Feb. 10, 1937.
27 These interventions appear in *Can. H. of C. Debates*, Feb. 15, 16, and 18, 1937; Pierre Gauthier, Liguori Lacombe, Wilfrid Lacroix, and Maxime Raymond opposed the increase in the estimates.
28 Diary, Feb. 17, 1937.
29 *Can. H. of C. Debates*, Feb. 19, 1937, p. 1058.
30 E. J. Tarr, "Canada in World Affairs," *International Affairs*, XVI, Sept.–Oct. 1937, p. 686, E. J. Tarr, a Winnipeg lawyer, was a leading member of the Canadian Institute of International Affairs.
31 Diary, Feb. 19, 1937.
32 *Ibid.*, Feb. 11, 1937.
33 For a discussion of debt adjustment legislation, see J. R. Mallory, *Social Credit and the Federal Power in Canada* (Toronto, 1954), Chap. VI.

34 Meighen Papers, Arthur Meighen to Judge Montague, Feb. 12, 1938, 96354–5.
35 Mallory, *Social Credit and the Federal Power in Canada*, p. 100.
36 See W. J. Turnbull to W.L.M.K., "Memorandum on Alberta Debt Legislation," Nov. 21, 1936.
37 J. B. McBride to W.L.M.K., Sept. 5, 1936.
38 *Financial Post*, Sept. 19, 1936; for comments from the British press see L. B. Pearson to W.L.M.K., Nov. 6, 1936.
39 Diary, Sept. 10, 1936.
40 W.L.M.K. to W. A. Buchanan, Sept. 6, 1936.
41 G. H. Van Allen to R. J. Deachman, enclosed in R. J. Deachman to W.L.M.K., Sept. 18, 1936; see also C. Campbell to W.L.M.K., Nov. 20, 1936; W. A. Buchanan to J. G. Gardiner, Sept. 2, 1936, enclosed in J. G. Gardiner to W.L.M.K., Sept. 6, 1936.
42 J. G. Gardiner to W.L.M.K., Nov. 7, 1936; *Can. H. of C. Debates*, March 30, 1937, pp. 2296–311.
43 J. G. Gardiner to W.L.M.K., Nov. 1, 1936.
44 S. Bates, *Financial History of Canadian Governments* (Ottawa, 1939), p. 254.
45 Diary, Dec. 15, 1936.
46 *Can. H. of C. Debates*, Feb. 25, 1937, p. 1232.
47 Diary, Dec. 16, 1936.
48 *Ibid.*, Jan. 8, 1937.
49 W. C. Clark to R. L. Fredenburgh, Nov. 30, 1936.
50 C. A. Dunning to W.L.M.K., Dec. 16, 1936, enclosing *Report on the Meetings of the National Finance Committee*, Dec. 9, 10, and 11, 1936.
51 *Can. H. of C. Debates*, Jan. 26, 1937, p. 288.
52 H. Blair Neatby, *W. L. Mackenzie King*, II: *1924–1932* (Toronto, 1963), p. 223; J. G. Gardiner to W.L.M.K., Feb. 8, 1937.
53 T. D. Pattullo to W.L.M.K., Dec. 14, 1936.
54 *Can. H. of C. Debates*, Jan. 26, 1937, p. 270.
55 See *ibid.*, p. 274 and p. 279 for the opinions of Lapointe and King.
56 Diary, Jan. 28, 1937.
57 *Can. H. of C. Debates*, Feb. 1, 1937, p. 425.
58 C. A. Dunning to W.L.M.K., Dec. 16, 1936; enclosing *Report . . . of the National Finance Committee*, Dec. 9, 10, and 11, 1936.
59 Ian Mackenzie to W.L.M.K., Jan. 9, 1937, enclosing T. D. Pattullo to Ian Mackenzie, Jan. 4, 1937.
60 Diary, Feb. 16, 1937.
61 *Ibid.*, July 21, 1937.
62 *Can. H. of C. Debates*, Feb. 16, 1937, p. 923.
63 H. V. Nelles, *The Politics of Development* (Toronto, 1975), pp. 429–64.
64 M. F. Hepburn to Norman Lambert, Nov. 12, 1936.
65 Queen's University Archives, N. P. Lambert, Diary, Nov. 16, 1936.
66 Diary, Jan. 6, 7, 1937.
67 Nelles, *The Politics of Development*, p. 480.
68 Cordell Hull to Norman Armour, Feb. 26, 1936; Norman Armour "Memorandum," May 19, 1936; printed in *Foreign Relations of the United States, 1936*, 837, 844.
69 Diary, Feb. 24, 1937.
70 Norman Armour to Cordell Hull, March 2, 1937, *Foreign Relations of the United States, 1936*, p. 169.
71 Diary, March 4, 1937.
72 *Ibid.*
73 *Ibid.*, March 5, 1937.
74 *Ibid.*
75 Cordell Hull, *Memoirs*, I, 527; see also Cordell Hull to W.L.M.K., April 2, 1937.

76 Diary, March 5, 6, 1937; W.L.M.K. to F. D. Roosevelt, March 8, 1937.
77 Hull, *Memoirs*, I, 528.
78 W.L.M.K. to F. D. Roosevelt, March 8, 1937; see also W.L.M.K. to Cordell Hull, April 23, 1937.
79 Diary, March 8, 1937.
80 *Ibid.*, March 18, 20, 1937.
81 *Ibid.*, March 16, 1937.
82 *Ibid.*, March 23, 1937.
83 *Can. H. of C. Debates*, March 24, 1937, p. 2114.
84 Neil McKenty, *Mitch Hepburn* (Toronto, 1967), p. 105.
85 *Ibid.*, p. 108.
86 For a discussion of Hepburn's relations with these men see Brian Young, "C. George McCullagh and the Leadership League," *Canadian Historical Review*, XLVII, Sept. 1966, 201–26; McKenty, *Hepburn*; I. M. Abella, *Nationalism, Communism, and Canadian Labour: The CIO, the Communist Party, and the Canadian Congress of Labour* (Toronto, 1973); Nelles, *The Politics of Development*.
87 Diary, April 13, 1937.
88 For a fuller account of Hepburn's activities see McKenty, *Hepburn*, pp. 104–15.
89 For the reaction in Ontario see *ibid.*, 115–21.
90 Diary, April 13, 1937.
91 *Ibid.*, May 5, 1937.
92 *Ibid.*, April 15, 1937.
93 T. A. Crerar to M. F. Hepburn, March 5, 1937.
94 Diary, April 8, 1937.
95 *Ibid.*, April 13, 1937.
96 M. F. Hepburn to W.L.M.K., April 13, 1937.
97 W.L.M.K. to M. F. Hepburn, April 13, 1937.
98 Diary, April 14, 1937.
99 M. F. Hepburn to W.L.M.K., April 15, 1937.
100 Diary, April 15, 1937.
101 McKenty, *Hepburn*, p. 125.
102 Diary, June 4, 1937.

CHAPTER TWELVE

A FORAY INTO EUROPEAN DIPLOMACY

1 W.L.M.K., Diary, April 20, 1937.
2 *Ibid.*, May 4, 1937.
3 *Ibid.*, April 24, 1937; Toronto *Star*, May 3, 1937; Montreal *Star*, May 5, 1937.
4 Diary, May 12, 1937.
5 *Ibid.*, May 12, 1937.
6 Imperial Conference 1937, "Minutes of Meeting of Principal Delegates," May 21, 1937.
7 Diary, May 26, 1937.
8 Imperial Conference 1937, "Minutes of Meeting of Principal Delegates," June 7, 1937.
9 The successive versions of the statement in the King Papers have marginal comments by King and O. D. Skelton. See also Sir Maurice Hankey to W.L.M.K., June 5, 1937, and King's own version of a possible statement, June 6, 1937. The discussions occurred at the meetings of the Principal Delegates on June 1, 7, 8, 9, 1937.
10 O. D. Skelton to W.L.M.K., March 29, 1937; Diary, April 15, 1937.
11 Imperial Conference 1937, "Meeting of Principal Delegates," May 24, 1937; the

quotation is from Savage of New Zealand.
12 *Ibid.*
13 Diary, June 8, 1937; W.L.M.K., Memorandum on Report of Committee on Munitions and Food Supplies, June 8, 1937. See also H. Duncan Hall, *North American Supply* (London, 1955), pp. 7–8.
14 Diary, June 10, 1937.
15 Imperial Conference 1937, "Minutes of Meeting of Principal Delegates," June 10, 11, 1937.
16 Ian Mackenzie to W.L.M.K., May 17, 1937.
17 W.L.M.K. to H. J. Plaxton, Sept. 12, 1936.
18 Imperial Conference 1937, *Summary of Proceedings* (London, 1937), May 14, 1937, 51–2.
19 Diary, May 26, June 4, 7, 1937.
20 Imperial Conference 1937, "Minutes of Meeting of Principal Delegates," May 27, 1937; Diary May 27, 1937.
21 Imperial Conference 1937, *Summary of Proceedings*, p. 15.
22 Kingsley Martin, "Is the British Empire in Retreat?" *Yale Quarterly*, autumn 1937.
23 W.L.M.K. to George Morang, Sept. 29, 1937.
24 *Can. H. of C. Debates*, March 24, 1938, p. 1652.
25 Foreign Office 372/3202/T9371, Minutes of F. H. Cleobury, June 12, 1937; cited in Norman Hillmer, "The Pursuit of Peace: Mackenzie King and the 1937 Imperial Conference," in J. O. Stubbs and J. R. English, eds., *Mackenzie King: Twelve Essays* (Toronto, in preparation).
26 Diary, May 24, 1937.
27 *Ibid.*
28 "Notes of a discussion at the Board of Trade on Tuesday, 1 June 1937, at 3:00 p.m. on the Anglo-American Trade Negotiations."
29 "Notes of a Meeting held at the Board of Trade on Monday, 7 June 1937, at 5:15 p.m. on the proposed Anglo-American Trade Agreement"; Diary, June 7, 1937.
30 Diary, June 11, 1937.
31 *Ibid.*, May 26, 1937.
32 *Ibid.*, June 3, 1937.
33 *Ibid.*, June 15, 1937.
34 *Ibid.*, June 4, 1937.
35 *Ibid.*, June 15, 1937.
36 *Ibid.*, May 26, 1937.
37 *Ibid.*, June 15, 1937.
38 *Ibid.*, June 29, 137. His version of the interview is confirmed by the notes taken by his secretary, E. A. Pickering. See also W.L.M.K. to Neville Chamberlain, July 6, 1937; W.L.M.K. to Anthony Eden, July 6, 1937.
39 W.L.M.K. to Lord Tweedsmuir, July 10, 1937.
40 Ottawa *Citizen*, July 3, 1937.
41 London *Times*, July 3, 1937.
42 Diary, July 8, 1937.
43 *Can. H. of C. Debates*, April 1, 1938, p. 1932.
44 Diary, July 9, 1937.
45 W.L.M.K. to Viscount Greenwood, Oct. 6, 1937.

CHAPTER THIRTEEN
THE PROVINCIAL CHALLENGE TO
NATIONAL UNITY

1 W.L.M.K., Diary, Oct. 18, 1937.

2 C. B. Macpherson, *Democracy in Alberta: Social Credit and the Party System* (Toronto, 1953), p. 159.
3 Cited in Harold J. Schultz, "The Social Credit Back-bencher's Revolt, 1937," *Canadian Historical Review*, XLI, March 1960, p. 2.
4 *Canadian Annual Review*, 1937 and 1938 (Toronto, 1939), pp. 479–80.
5 Schultz, "The Social Credit Back-bencher's Revolt,' p. 15.
6 Macpherson, *Social Credit in Alberta*, p. 177.
7 J. R. Mallory, *Social Credit and the Federal Power in Canada* (Toronto, 1954), pp. 72–3.
8 *Ibid.*, p. 73–5.
9 On the history of disallowance see G. V. LaForest, *Disallowance and Reservation of Provincial Legislation* (Ottawa, 1955); Mallory, *Social Credit and the Federal Power in Canada*, Chap. II; E. A. Forsey, "Disallowance of Provincial Acts, Reservation of Provincial Bills, and the Refusal of Assent by Lieutenant-Governors since 1867," *Canadian Journal of Economics and Political Science*, IV, Feb. 1938, 47–59. Some legislation, which conflicted with British Imperial policies, had also been disallowed but this problem was eliminated in 1931 by the Statute of Westminster.
10 For the report of the Minister of Justice on the Alberta Mineral Taxation Act see LaForest, *Disallowance and Reservation of Provincial Legislation*, pp. 75–6.
11 *Can. H. of C. Debates*, Feb. 4, 1936, p. 177. Lapointe was referring to his report on the Ontario Statutes which cancelled the power contracts.
12 Diary, Aug. 5, 1937.
13 *Ibid.*, Aug. 6, 1937.
14 *Ibid.*; Report of Minister of Justice, Aug. 10, 1937.
15 W.L.M.K. to W. Aberhart, Aug. 11, 1937.
16 W. Aberhart to W.L.M.K., Aug. 16, 1937.
17 Diary, Aug. 17, 1937.
18 W.L.M.K. to W. Aberhart, Aug. 17, 1937.
19 Diary, Aug. 17, 1937.
20 The reactions of local newspapers in Alberta were reproduced in the Calgary *Herald*, Sept. 8, 1937.
21 See for example his long and discursive letter to W.L.M.K., Aug. 26, 1937.
22 Mallory, *Social Credit and the Federal Power in Canada*, p. 77.
23 *Ibid.*, pp. 77–9.
24 Lapointe did tell the House that "there were no instructions sent to the lieutenant-governor of Alberta" but this was only technically true. The Lieutenant-Governor informed Lapointe on Oct. 3, 1937 that he intended to reserve the bills. The federal government had already decided that the legislation should be reserved (Diary, Sept. 28, 1937) but when the Lieutenant-Governor took the initiative Lapointe merely replied, on Oct. 4, 1937, that he had "no objections to your reserving all four bills mentioned."
25 W. Aberhart to W.L.M.K., Oct. 12, 1937. The request to refer the power of reservation to the Supreme Court was suggested later; W. Aberhart to W.L.M.K., Nov. 5, 1937.
26 Diary, Oct. 28, 1937.
27 *Ibid.*, Aug. 17, 1937.
28 *Ibid.*, Aug. 19, 25, 1936; see also Philippe Roy to W.L.M.K., Oct. 27, 1937.
29 Diary, Dec. 18, 1936.
30 E. A. Forsey, "Canada and Alberta: The Revival of Dominion Control over the Provinces," *Politica*, June 1939; reprinted in E. A. Forsey, *Freedom and Order* (Toronto, 1974), pp. 177–205.
31 R. Rumilly, *Histoire de la province de Québec*, XXXVI, p. 116.
32 *Can. H. of C. Debates*, March 30, 1937, pp. 2293–6.
33 Lapointe Papers, E. Lapointe to L'Abbé M. Papineau, mars 15, 1937. The volumi-

nous correspondence on communism in the Lapointe Papers shows the concern felt by French Canadians at this time.

34 Ian Mackenzie to W.L.M.K., July 28, 1937; W. J. Turnbull to W.L.M.K., memorandum, July 19, 1937; Diary, July 28, 1937.
35 Diary, July 27, 1937.
36 Ottawa *Citizen*, Aug. 13, 1937.
37 Ottawa *Journal*, Oct. 6, 1937.
38 Diary, Oct. 5, 1937.
39 *Ibid.*, Oct. 3, 4, 5, 1937.
40 *Ibid.*, Oct. 3, 1937; see also Dec. 17, 1937.
41 *Ibid.*, Oct. 7, 9, 1937.
42 W.L.M.K. to H. A. Bruce, Sept. 29, 1937; W.L.M.K. to M. F. Hepburn, Oct. 8, 1937.
43 M. F. Hepburn to W.L.M.K., Oct. 12, 1937.
44 Diary, Oct. 13, 14, 1937.
45 F. G. Sanderson to W.L.M.K., Oct. 20, 1937, enclosing a memorandum of his conversation with Hepburn on Oct. 13, 1937.
46 M. F. Hepburn to W.L.M.K., Oct. 18, 1937.
47 Diary, Oct. 22, 1937.
48 Tweedsmuir to W.L.M.K., Oct. 27, 1937, enclosing H. A. Bruce to Tweedsmuir, Oct. 27, 1937.
49 Neil McKenty, *Mitch Hepburn* (Toronto, 1967), p. 143.
50 Diary, Nov. 21, 24, 1937.
51 McKenty, *Hepburn*, p. 145.
52 M. F. Hepburn to W.L.M.K., Nov. 25, 1937.
53 W.L.M.K. to J. S. Norris, Aug. 14, 1937.
54 Diary, Nov. 25, 1937.
55 *Ibid.*, Nov. 26, 1937.
56 *Ibid.*, Nov. 29, 1937.
57 McKenty, *Hepburn*, p. 146.
58 Montreal *Gazette*, Dec. 18, 1937; Toronto *Star*, Dec. 18, 1937.
59 Toronto *Globe and Mail*, Dec. 22, 1937.
60 Diary, Dec. 18, 1937.
61 W.L.M.K., press release, Dec. 20, 1937.
62 McKenty, *Hepburn*, p. 151.
63 Diary, Nov. 9, 1937; Toronto *Globe and Mail*, Nov. 10, 1937.
64 There is a lengthy correspondence between King and the provincial Premiers on this issue, some of which is published in *Can. H. of C. Sessional Paper*, June 25, 1940. King refused to table the bill until the constitution was amended, although he did promise that the provinces would be consulted on the details of the legislation; W.L.M.K. to T. D. Pattullo, March 2, 1938.
65 *Can. H. of C. Debates*, Jan. 21, 1937, p. 62.
66 See above, p. 200.
67 Diary, April 21, May 9, 1937.
68 E. A. Pickering, Memorandum, July 21, 1937.
69 Diary, April 13, 14, July 21, 1937.
70 *Ibid.*, July 22, 1937.
71 *Ibid.*, Aug. 13, 1937. Judge Rinfret resigned within a few months and was replaced by Joseph Sirois, a Laval law professor; P.C. 2880, Nov. 18, 1937.
72 Order-in-Council P.C. 1908, Aug. 14, 1937.
73 See, for example, Edmonton *Journal*, Winnipeg *Tribune*, Montreal *Star*, Aug. 16, 1937; Edmonton *Bulletin*, Regina *Star*, Ottawa *Journal*, Québec *Le Soleil*, Aug. 17, 1937; Calgary *Herald*, Montreal *Gazette*, Montréal *Le Devoir*, Aug. 20, 1937.
74 *Canadian Forum*, Oct. 1937.

75 Winnipeg *Tribune*, Oct. 23, 1937.
76 Edmonton *Journal*, Nov. 8, 1937.
77 For a discussion of French-Canadian attitudes to Dafoe see Dafoe Papers, J. W. Dafoe to R. R. Carman, Nov. 5, 1937.
78 W. Aberhart to W.L.M.K., Aug. 26, 1937.
79 Toronto *Telegram*, Aug. 17, 1937.
80 Montreal *Gazette*, Dec. 10, 1937.
81 *Canadian Annual Review*, 1937 and 1938, p. 218.
82 Diary, Aug. 16, 1937.
83 *Ibid.*, Dec. 10, 1937.
84 McKenty, *Hepburn*, p. 157.
85 T. D. Pattullo to W.L.M.K., Dec. 17, 1937.
86 Diary, Nov. 29, 1937.
87 *Canadian Annual Review*, 1937 and 1938, p. 17.
88 Diary, Dec. 20, 1937.
89 *Ibid.*, Dec. 21, 1937.
90 *Ibid.*, Jan. 22, 1938.
91 National Employment Commission, *Final Report* (Ottawa, 1938), p. 49.
92 Diary, Jan. 23, 1938.
93 *Ibid.*, Jan. 22, 1938.
94 *Ibid.*, Jan. 25, 1938.

CHAPTER FOURTEEN

THE RELUCTANT ASSERTION OF FEDERAL
LEADERSHIP

1 W.L.M.K., Diary, Nov. 12, 1937.
2 *Ibid.*, Jan. 12, 1938.
3 W.L.M.K. to each Minister, Jan. 12, 1938.
4 C. D. Howe to W.L.M.K., Jan. 15, 1938; see also replies of J. G. Gardiner, Jan. 17, 1938, F. Rinfret, Jan. 19, 1938, J. L. Ilsley, Jan. 20, 1938, E. Lapointe, Jan. 22, 1938, P. J. A. Cardin, Jan. 25, 1938.
5 See replies of C. G. Power, Jan. 15, 1938, Ian Mackenzie, Jan. 19, 1938, N. M. Rogers, Jan. 19, 1938.
6 T. A. Crerar to W.L.M.K., Jan. 19, 1938.
7 W.L.M.K. to T. A. Crerar, Jan. 21, 1938.
8 Diary, Jan. 25, 1938.
9 The main estimates for 1937–8 which had been tabled in the House on Jan. 19, 1937, had totalled $410,465,397; the main estimates for 1938–9, tabled on Feb. 3, 1938, came to $418,968,457.
10 J. S. Woodsworth, *Can. H. of C. Debates*, March 2, 1938, p. 971.
11 J. M. Turner to W.L.M.K., March 26, 1938.
12 *Can. H. of C. Debates*, March 28, 1938, pp. 1745–6; Margaret Ormsby, *British Columbia: A History* (Toronto, 1958), p. 467.
13 The committee guidelines are outlined in E. A. Pickering, Memorandum, April 1, 1938.
14 Diary, April 1, 1938.
15 W. E. Leuchtenberg, *Franklin Roosevelt and the New Deal* (New York, 1963), p. 249.
16 Diary, April 14, 1938.
17 *Ibid.*, April 25, 1938.
18 *Ibid.*, May 4, 1938.

19 *Ibid.*, May 2, 1938.
20 *Ibid.*, May 5, 1938.
21 Rogers' views on the economic role of government are expressed in the *Nova Scotia Submission on Dominion-Provincial Relations* (Halifax, 1934) and in "One Path of Reform," *Canadian Forum*, Dec. 1934. He argued for a strong federal role in "the Genesis of Provincial Rights," *Canadian Historical Review*, XIV, March 1933, 9–23. His views on fiscal policy when he entered the federal government were outlined in *Can. H. of C. Debates*, Feb. 17, 1936, pp. 240–6. King concurred in these views and described Rogers' speech as "an excellent bit of reasoning and exposition," Diary, Feb. 18, 1936.
22 National Employment Commission, *Final Report* (Ottawa, 1938), Section I.
23 *Ibid.*, p. 28.
24 *Ibid.*, p. 52.
25 Diary, May 5, 1938.
26 *Ibid.*, May 16, 1938.
27 *Ibid.*, April 4, 1938.
28 *Ibid.*, May 5, 16, 1938.
29 *Ibid.*, May 16, 1938.
30 The National Housing Act also offered federal loans to encourage local authorities to provide low-rental housing. The initiative for this section came from Clifford Clark, the Deputy-Minister of Finance, who had a special interest in both the economic and social benefits of subsidized housing for low-income families. This clause was a dead letter because no applications for low-rental projects were ever submitted. Under the other sections of the Act for the seventeen months from August 1938 to December 1939 8000 units received loans with the coverage loan being $3300. For a thirty-four month period under the Dominion Housing Act, from October 1935 to July 1938, some 5000 units had received federal assistance, with $4000 as the average loan. See report of operation of Act in Department of Finance files, R.G. 19, E2(f), vol. 15.
31 Diary, May 20, 1938.
32 *Ibid.*, June 8, 1938.
33 *Ibid.*, June 13, 1938.
34 For the budget speech see *Can. H. of C. Debates*, June 16, 1938, pp. 3893–928.
35 Diary, June 22, 1938.
36 *Ibid.*
37 *Can. H. of C. Debates*, June 23, 1938, p. 4201. The dissident Liberal was H. Leader, representing Portage la Prairie.
38 Diary, June 23, 1938.
39 *Can. H. of C. Debates*, March 7, 1938; Diary, March 7, 1938.
40 Diary, May 13, 1938.
41 *Can. H. of C. Debates*, June 7, 1938, p. 3619.
42 *Ibid.*, June 10, 1938, p. 3735.
43 *Ibid.*, p. 3740.
44 Diary, June 10, 1938.
45 *Can. H. of C. Debates*, June 14, 1938, p. 3831–5; June 16, 1938, pp. 3933–47.
46 *Ibid.*, July 1, 1935, pp. 4453–4.
47 Hanson Papers, R. B. Hanson to H. A. Allison, July 19, 1938. For the debate on the resolutions see the verbatim report of the convention proceedings in the Bennett Papers, Box 837.
48 See M. LaTerreur, *Les Tribulations des conservateurs au Québec* (Québec, 1973), for Bennett's "incomprehension" of French Canada.
49 The Conservatives had held Argenteuil, a riding with a large English-Canadian population, in February 1938. In Lotbinière in Dec. 1937 and again in St. Henri in January 1938 there were no official Conservative candidates and the Liberal

opponents ran as Independents.
50 Bennett Papers, Maurice Dupré to R. B. Bennett, Dec. 13, 1936.
51 *Ibid.*, Verbatim report of convention proceedings, Box 837.
52 Toronto *Globe and Mail*, July 8, 1938.
53 J. L. Granatstein, *The Politics of Survival: The Conservative Party of Canada, 1939–1945* (Toronto, 1967), pp. 10–18.
54 Diary, July 6, 1938. Manion had been a Liberal until he joined the Union Government in 1917.
55 *Ibid.*, July 7, 1938.
56 W.L.M.K. to Lord Tweedsmuir, Dec. 31, 1935.
57 Diary, Aug. 30, Sept. 1, 1937.
58 J. W. Pickersgill to A. D. P. Heeney, Oct. 17, 1938.
59 Personal interview with J. W. Pickersgill, June 16, 1970. See also J. W. Pickersgill, *My Years with Louis St. Laurent* (Toronto, 1975), pp. 8–10.
60 A. D. P. Heeney, *The Things that are Caesar's: Memoirs of a Canadian Public Servant* (Toronto, 1972), pp. 37–49.
61 D. Pattullo to W.L.M.K., April 23, 1938.
62 Diary, April 26, 1938. See also O. D. Skelton, Memorandum, April 26, 1938.
63 Memorandum of meeting between Canadian Government and Mr. Pattullo and his colleagues, Sept. 26, 1938; D. Pattullo to W.L.M.K., Oct. 17, 1938; A. D. P. Heeney, Memorandum, Nov. 9, 1938.
64 O. D. Skelton to W.L.M.K., May 8, 1939.
65 *Can. H. of C. Debates*, June 2, 1938, p. 3459; June 6, 1938, pp. 3588–9.
66 *Ibid.*, May 31, 1938, pp. 3427–8.
67 Ormsby, *British Columbia*, p. 468.
68 Diary, June 20, 1938.
69 W.L.M.K. to T. D. Pattullo, July 12, 1938.
70 For the court decisions see J. R. Mallory, *Social Credit and the Federal Power in Canada* (Toronto, 1954), 84–90.
71 Diary, March 4, 1938.
72 See Mallory, *Social Credit and the Federal Power in Canada*, Chap. VI, for an analysis of this debt-adjustment legislation.
73 E. A. Pickering to W.L.M.K., June 6, 1938, reported 124 requests for disallowance from Boards of Trade, Chambers of Commerce, corporations, and individuals, 78 of them from Alberta. There were 175 letters opposing disallowance, all of which came from Alberta and all but 10 from Social Credit groups.
74 Meighen Papers, A. Meighen to J. T. M. Anderson, May 24, 1938; Bennett Papers, F. W. Turnbull to R. B. Bennett, June 9, 1938.
75 Diary, June 8, 1938.
76 *Ibid.*, May 18, 1938.
77 *Ibid.*, June 9, 1938.
78 Report of the Minister of Justice, June 13, 1938.
79 *Canadian Annual Review*, 1937 and 1938 (Toronto, 1939), p. 475.
80 J. W. Pickersgill, "Notes on the Padlock Law," April 19, 1938.
81 *Can. H. of C. Debates*, Feb. 1, 1938, pp. 76, 95–6.
82 Diary, July 5, 6, 1938.
83 *Ibid.*, July 6, 1938.
84 W. T. Turnbull to W.L.M.K., April 26, 1938; Diary, April 29, 1938; H. D. Angus to W.L.M.K., July 3, 1938; T. C. Davis to J. G. Gardiner, Dec. 10, 1938.
85 Diary, May 2, 1938.
86 Toronto *Globe and Mail*, May 3, 1938; for a fuller discussion of Hepburn's relations with the commission, see R. M. H. Alway, "Hepburn, King and the Rowell-Sirois Commission," *Canadian Historical Review*, XLVII, June 1967, 113–41.
87 Ottawa *Citizen*, Aug. 12, 1938.

88 Toronto *Telegram*, March 15, 1938; Toronto *Globe and Mail*, July 18, 1938; Toronto *Telegram*, Aug. 8, 1938.
89 Toronto *Globe and Mail*, Aug. 8, 1938; Ottawa *Citizen*, Oct. 10, 1938; see also Windsor *Star*, Nov. 5, 1938; Toronto *Globe and Mail*, Nov. 14, 1938; Toronto *Star*, Nov. 26, 1938.
90 Memorandum of U.S. State Department, March 17, 1938, published in *Correspondence relating to Kenogami (Long Lake) Project and Export of Electrical Power* (Ottawa, 1937). See also Franklin D. Roosevelt Library, Hyde Park; Roosevelt Papers, Frank Walsh to F. D. Roosevelt, Dec. 12, 1937.
91 Cordell Hull to Herbert Marler, May 28, 1938, published in *Foreign Relations of the United States, 1938*, II, p. 177.
92 O. D. Skelton to W.L.M.K., Aug. 17, 1938.
93 Speech of Aug. 18, 1938, published in *The Public Papers and Addresses of Franklin D. Roosevelt, 1938* (New York, 1941), VII, 497.
94 O. D. Skelton to W.L.M.K., Aug. 19, 1938.
95 Ottawa *Journal*, Aug. 25, 1938.
96 M. F. Hepburn to W.L.M.K., Aug. 19, 1938.
97 Roosevelt Papers, Frank P. Walsh, Memorandum, Sept. 1, 1938.
98 W.L.M.K. to M. F. Hepburn, Aug. 30, 1938; M. F. Hepburn to W.L.M.K., Sept. 21, 1938.
99 Neil McKenty, *Mitch Hepburn* (Toronto, 1967), pp. 163–8.
100 Diary, Nov. 15, 1938.
101 *Ibid.*, Nov. 21, 1937.
102 *Ibid.*, Dec. 8, 1937.
103 *Ibid.*, Dec. 8, 1938.
104 Toronto *Star*, Dec. 12, 1938.
105 Toronto *Telegram*, Dec. 13, 1938.
106 *Ibid.*
107 Diary, Dec. 13, 1939.
108 F. G. Sanderson to W.L.M.K., Dec. 17, 1938.

CHAPTER FIFTEEN
ON THE EDGE OF THE VORTEX

1 W.L.M.K. Diary, March 14, 1938.
2 See above, p. 224.
3 Diary, Feb. 20, 21, 1938.
4 *Ibid.*, March 8, 1938.
5 *Ibid.*, March 11, 1938.
6 *Ibid.*
7 Diary, April 11, 1938.
8 *Ibid.*, May 10, 1938.
9 *Ibid.*, May 23, 1938.
10 *Ibid.*, May 24, 1938.
11 *Can. H. of C. Debates*, May 24, 1938, p. 3178.
12 *Ibid.*, pp. 3182–4.
13 *Ibid.*, pp. 3221–3.
14 *Ibid.*, pp. 3190, 3219.
15 *Ibid.*, p. 3211.
16 *Ibid.*, pp. 3212–21.
17 *Ibid.*, April 1, 1938, p. 1938.

18 Diary, Nov. 12, 1937; Ian Mackenzie to W.L.M.K., Jan. 19, 1938; *Can. H. of C. Debates*, March 24, 1938, p. 1648.
19 Diary, March 24, 1938.
20 See above, p. 217.
21 *Report of the Royal Commission on the Bren Machine Gun Contract* (Ottawa, 1938), p. 47.
22 Ian Mackenzie to Vincent Massey, Oct. 19, 1936.
23 See *Report of the Bren Gun Commission* for details of the contracts.
24 *Maclean's Magazine*, Sept. 1, 1938.
25 Diary, Sept. 14, 1938.
26 *Report of the Bren Gun Commission*, pp. 45–6.
27 *Ibid.*, p. 51.
28 *Can. H. of C. Debates*, Feb. 2, 1938, p. 538.
29 *Ibid.*, Feb. 6, 7, 9, 1939. The matter was also referred to the Public Accounts Committee but it failed to report before the end of the session.
30 *Can. H. of C. Debates*, Feb. 9, 1939, pp. 794, 797.
31 Diary, Feb. 9, 1939.
32 Ian Mackenzie to W.L.M.K., Sept. 4, 1936.
33 E. A. Pickering, Memorandum, Sept. 11, 1936.
34 Diary, May 13, 1938. See James Eayrs, *In Defence of Canada. II: Appeasement and Rearmament* (Toronto, 1965), pp. 92–3, for an extensive excerpt from the diary of this interview.
35 Diary, May 13, 1938.
36 *Can. Senate Debates*, June 14, 15, 22, 1938. See also Sir Francis Floud to W.L.M.K., June 22, 1938; W.L.M.K. to Sir Francis Floud, June 24, 1938.
37 *Can. H. of C. Debates*, July 1, 1938, p. 4528.
38 Diary, July 1, 1938.
39 *Can. H. of C. Debates*, July 1, 1938, p. 4529.
40 Diary, July 1, 1938.
41 *Can. H. of C. Debates*, July 1, 1938, p. 4531.
42 Diary, July 5, 1938.
43 L. R. Laflèche to Ian Mackenzie, Aug. 5, 1938.
44 Diary, Aug. 10, 1938.
45 *Ibid.*, Aug. 9, 1938.
46 C.A.B. 23/94, June 30, 1938; cited in Keith Middlemass, "The Effect of Dominion Diplomacy on British Foreign Policy, 1937–38" in *Institute of Commonwealth Studies*, Collected seminar papers on the Dominions between the Wars, Oct. 1970–March 1971, mimeographed.
47 Sir Francis Floud to W.L.M.K., Sept. 3, 1938.
48 Sir Gerald Campbell to W.L.M.K., Dec. 9, 1938.
49 Diary, Dec. 15, 1938; W.L.M.K. to Sir Francis Floud, Dec. 31, 1938.
50 Sir Gerald Campbell to W.L.M.K., Jan. 10, 1939.
51 *Can. H. of C. Debates*, April 26, 1939, pp. 3253, 3259.
52 Eayrs, *In Dence of Canada*, II, 103.
53 See above, p. 221.
54 R.G. 25, Box 746, 167, Vol. 5, O. D. Skelton to Norman Robertson, Aug. 24, 1938.
55 Norman Robertson's principal associates were Dana Wilgress of the Department of Trade and Commerce and Hector McKinnon of National Revenue.
56 Sir Herbert Marler to O. D. Skelton, April 2, 1938; O. D. Skelton to Sir Herbert Marler, April 4, 1938.
57 N. Robertson to O. D. Skelton, April 5, 1938.
58 O. D. Skelton to W.L.M.K., April 8, 1938.
59 Secretary of State to Ambassador in United Kingdom, April 9, 1938, published in *Foreign Relations of the United States, 1938*, II, pp. 25–6.

60 R.G. 25, Box 727, 167, Vol. 8, O. D. Skelton, "Memorandum for the Prime Minister," Sept. 6, 1938.
61 R.G. 25, Box 727, 167, Vol. 11, N. Robertson to O. D. Skelton; the agreement covered lumber ten or more inches in width and fifteen or more feet in length.
62 Diary, Sept. 14, 1938.
63 R.G. 25, Box 747, 167, Vol. 10, O. D. Skelton to Norman Robertson, Sept. 15, 1938.
64 Diary, Sept. 26, 1938.
65 Ibid., Sept. 27, Nov. 8, 1938.
66 Ibid., Sept. 26, 1938.
67 W.L.M.K. to Mrs. James Carrothers (née Violet Markham), Jan. 3, 1939.
68 Diary, July 28, 1938.
69 Ibid., Aug. 26, 31, 1938.
70 Ibid., Aug. 31, 1938.
71 O. D. Skelton, "Canada and Foreign Policy," March 30, 1938. This was the draft for King's speech in the House in May but because of the critical situation King eliminated this phrase; Can. H. of C. Debates, May 24, 1938, pp. 3175–90.
72 O. D. Skelton, "Central European Situation," Sept. 11, 1938.
73 Diary, Aug. 31, 1938.
74 Ibid.
75 Ibid., Sept. 7, 1938.
76 R.G. 25, Box 747, 167, Vol. 10, W.L.M.K. to O. D. Skelton, Sept. 10, 1938. King himself, after his retirement, when he was planning his memoirs, linked this illness with the Munich crisis; W.L.M.K., Personal Memoirs, "Chapter re health," March 22, 1950.
77 Diary, Sept. 13, 1938.
78 Ibid., Sept. 21, 1938.
79 Ibid., Sept. 23, 1938.
80 Ibid.
81 Lapointe Papers, E. Lapointe to W.L.M.K., Sept. 24, 1938.
82 Diary, Sept. 24, 1938.
83 Ibid., Sept. 25, 1938.
84 Ibid., Sept. 27, 1938.
85 Press release, Sept. 27, 1938.
86 W.L.M.K. to Neville Chamberlain, Sept. 29, 1938.
87 Diary, Sept. 28, 1938.
88 Toronto Globe and Mail, Sept. 15, 1938; see also Vancouver Province, Sept. 16, 1938; Financial Post, Sept. 24, 1938.
89 Montréal Le Devoir, Sept. 19, 1938; Québec, L'Action Catholique, Sept. 20, 1938.
90 W.L.M.K. to E. M. Macdonald, Oct. 1, 1938.

CHAPTER SIXTEEN
CANADA GOES TO WAR

1 W.L.M.K., Diary, Oct. 24, 1939.
2 Ibid., Nov. 17, 1938.
3 Ibid., Nov. 19, 1938.
4 Ibid., Oct. 24, 1938.
5 Ibid., Jan. 16, 1939.
6 Can. H. of C. Debates, Jan. 16, 1939, p. 52.
7 T. S. Ewart to W.L.M.K., Jan. 21, 1939; A. Vanier to W.L.M.K., Jan. 23, 1939; J. A. Paradis to W.L.M.K., Feb. 18, 1939.
8 Diary, Jan. 19, 1939.

9 *Can. H. of C. Debates*, Feb. 2, 1939, p. 539.
10 Neville Chamberlain's speech of Birmingham, March 17, 1939, was reprinted in the Toronto *Globe and Mail*, March 18, 1939.
11 O. D. Skelton to W.L.M.K., March 20, 1939.
12 W.L.M.K. to Hitler, Feb. 1, 1939; Diary, Jan. 31, 1939.
13 Diary, March 17, 1939.
14 *Ibid.*, March 20, 1939.
15 *Ibid.*
16 *Can. H. of C. Debates*, March 20, 1939, p. 2043; Diary, March 20, 1939.
17 Diary, March 21, 1939.
18 Montréal *Le Devoir*, March 23, 1939; Ottawa *Le droit*, March 24, 1939.
19 Toronto *Globe and Mail*, March 22, 1939; Ottawa *Journal*, March 22, 1939.
20 Quoted in *Can. H. of C. Debates*, March 31, 1939, p. 2458.
21 W.L.M.K., marginal note on O. D. Skelton, "European Situation and League of Nations," March 24, 1939.
22 Keith Feiling, *The Life of Neville Chamberlain* (London, 1946), pp. 401–4; T. Desmond Williams, "Negotiations leading to the Anglo-Polish Agreement of 31 March 1939," *Irish Historical Studies*, X, 1956–7.
23 Diary, March 21, 1939.
24 *Ibid.*, March 21, April 25, 1939.
25 *Ibid.*, March 30, 1939.
26 *Can. H. of C. Debates*, March 30, 1939, p. 2426.
27 *Ibid.*, p. 2419.
28 *Ibid.*, p. 2443.
29 *Ibid.*, p. 2426.
30 Diary, March 31, 1939.
31 *Can. H. of C. Debates*, March 31, 1939, pp. 2467–9.
32 Diary, March 31, 1939.
33 *Can. H. of C. Debates*, Jan. 16, 1937, pp. 37–49; March 7, 1939, pp. 1616–17; March 14, 1939, pp. 1906–9.
34 *Ibid.*, March 30, 1939, pp. 2436, 2441.
35 Stevens Papers, R. J. Manion to H. H. Stevens, Dec. 23, 1938; Hanson Papers, R. B. Hanson to R. J. Manion, Dec. 15, 1938.
36 Manion Papers, R. J. Manion to J. A. Clark, March 25, 1939.
37 *Can. H. of C. Debates*, March 30, 1939, p. 2443.
38 *Ibid.*, pp. 2449–50.
39 *Ibid.*, April 3, 1939, p. 2527.
40 *Ibid.*, p. 2517.
41 L. A. Taschereau to W.L.M.K., April 1, 1939; Québec *Le Soleil*, March 31, April 1, 1939.
42 Montréal *Le Devoir*, Québec *Le Soleil*, Montreal *Gazette*, Ottawa *Journal*, Toronto *Globe and Mail*, April 1, 1939.
43 Diary, Nov. 14, 1939.
44 *Ibid.*, Dec. 2, 1938.
45 *Ibid.*, Dec. 16, 1938.
46 *Ibid.*, Jan. 30, 1939.
47 *Can. H. of C. Debates*, R. J. Manion, May 12, 1939, p. 3970; W. A. Walsh, May 13, 1939, p. 4029.
48 *Ibid.*, C. G. MacNeil, May 13, 1939, p. 4037; Agnes MacPhail, May 13, 1939, p. 4040.
49 *Ibid.*, May 12, 1939, p. 3992; May 13, 1939; p. 4034.
50 *Ibid.*, J. Francœur, May 12, 1939, p. 3980; E. Roberge, May 16, 1939, p. 4146.
51 F. H. Soward, *Canada and World Affairs: The Pre-War Years* (Toronto, 1941), pp. 165 ff.

52 Diary, March 29, 1938.
53 *Ibid.*, Nov. 13, 1938.
54 *Ibid.*, Nov. 17, 1938.
55 *Ibid.*, Nov. 13, 1938.
56 *Ibid.*, Nov. 24, 1938.
57 *Ibid.*, Nov. 22, 1938.
58 *Ibid.*, Dec. 1, 21, 1938, Jan. 12, 1939. The arrival of some 3000 Sudeten Germans in the spring attracted some attention; the brief debate in the House showed more concern about admitting communists or taking away the livelihood of Canadians than sympathy for the refugees: *Can. H. of C. Debates*, March 9, 1939, pp. 1697–9.
59 See above, p. 167.
60 Diary, June 21, 1938.
61 *Ibid.*, June 23, 1938.
62 *Ibid.*, July 26, 1938.
63 Vernon C. Fowke, *The National Policy and the Wheat Economy* (Toronto, 1957), p. 267.
64 J. G. Gardiner to W.L.M.K., June 28, 1938; J. G. Gardiner to W.L.M.K., Nov. 15, 1938, enclosing address of Nov. 3, 1938, to Annual Meeting of Saskatchewan Cooperative Wheat Producers Limited.
65 *Can. H. of C. Debates*, May 5, 1939, p. 3647.
66 Fowke, *The National Policy and the Wheat Economy*, p. 293.
67 J. G. Gardiner to W.L.M.K., Sept. 10, 1938.
68 Diary, Jan. 31, 1939.
69 *Ibid.*, March 20, 1939.
70 *Ibid.*, March 21, 1939.
71 *Can. H. of C. Debates*, March 27, 1939, p. 2279.
72 Diary, April 5, 1939.
73 *Ibid.*, April 25, 1939.
74 *Can. H. of C. Debates*, May 10, 1939, p. 3842.
75 *Ibid.*, May 11, 1939, p. 3903. The five Liberals were H. R. Fleming, H. Leader, J. A. MacMillan, W. R. Motherwell, and W. J. Ward.
76 Diary, May 11, 1939.
77 See above, p. 257.
78 Diary, Dec. 9, 1938.
79 *Can. H. of C. Debates*, April 25, 1939, p. 3146.
80 Diary, April 25, 1939. Charles Dunning did retire in September 1939 and then had an active and successful business career. He died in 1959.
81 Diary, May 5, June 11, 1937.
82 *Ibid.*, June 6, 1938.
83 *Ibid.*, Dec. 6, 1938.
84 *Ibid.*, Jan. 11, 1939.
85 *Ibid.*, Feb. 28, 1939.
86 W.L.M.K. to F. D. Roosevelt, March 3, 1939.
87 Diary, March 4, 1939.
88 *Can. H. of C. Debates*, April 24, 1939, p. 3103.
89 Diary, April 25, 1939.
90 *Ibid.*, May 17, 1939.
91 *Ibid.*, May 22, 1939.
92 *Ibid.*, June 2, 1939.
93 The details of the Ottawa visit are based on *ibid.*, May 19–21, 1939.
94 Dafoe Papers, J. W. Dafoe to George Ferguson, March 19, 1939.
95 Manion Papers, "Memorandum re Royal Visit," no date.
96 W.L.M.K. to Vincent Massey, Aug. 15, 1939.
97 Diary, June 8, 1939.

98 Franklin D. Roosevelt Library, Hyde Park, Roosevelt Papers, D. C. Roper to F. D. Roosevelt, July 5, 1939.
99 Diary, June 10, 11, 1939.
100 *Ibid.*, June 15, 1935.
101 Roosevelt Papers, D. C. Roper to F. D. Roosevelt, July 5, 1939.
102 Diary, May 27, 1939.
103 *Ibid.*, June 22, 1939.
104 *Ibid.*, July 20, 1939. Most of King's correspondents also predicted a Liberal victory; A. D. P. Heeney to W.L.M.K., July 7, 1939.
105 Diary, July 26, 1939.
106 Meighen Papers, Arthur Meighen to J. S. McLean, Feb. 21, 1939.
107 Manion Papers, R. J. Manion to S. Gobeil, July 28, 1939; see also R. J. Manion to Georges Héon, Aug. 1, 1939.
108 Diary, Aug. 11, 1939; see also *ibid.*, July 26, 1939.
109 E. Windels to W.L.M.K., July 21, 1939.
110 Diary, July 21, 1939.
111 W.L.M.K. to Neville Chamberlain, July 24, 1939.
112 Neville Chamberlain to W.L.M.K., Aug. 7, 1939.
113 Diary, Aug. 11, 1939. James Eayrs, *In Defence of Canada*. II: *Appeasement and Rearmament* (Toronto, 1965), pp. 77–8, describes this incident but suggests that King was naïve and that only good luck saved him from the blunder of accepting the invitation.
114 Diary, Aug. 21, 1939.
115 *Ibid.*, Aug. 22, 1939.
116 *Ibid.*; see also W.L.M.K. to R. Dandurand, July 13, 1939.
117 The full text is reprinted in Eayrs, *In Defence of Canada*, II, 79.
118 Diary, June 28, 1939.
119 J. F. MacNeill to W.L.M.K., July 20, 1939, enclosing Report of Committee on Emergency legislation.
120 A. D. P. Heeney to W.L.M.K., Aug. 24, 1939.
121 Order-in-Council PC 2389, Aug. 25, 1939.
122 Diary, Aug. 24, 1939.
123 *Ibid.*
124 Diary, Aug. 30, 1939.
125 W.L.M.K., press release, Sept. 1, 1939.
126 Diary, Sept. 1, 1939.
127 Walter Young, *The Anatomy of a Party: The National C.C.F., 1932–61* (Toronto, 1969), pp. 92–6; Kenneth McNaught, *A Prophet in Politics: A Biography of J. S. Woodsworth* (Toronto, 1959), pp. 305–6. The vote was 13 to 9 in favour of the resolution.
128 *Can. H. of C. Debates*, Sept. 9, 1939, pp. 83–4.
129 *Ibid.*, pp. 87–8.
130 *Ibid.*, pp. 58, 70, 75.

EPILOGUE

1 See H. Blair Neatby, *W. L. Mackenzie King*, II: *1924–1932* (Toronto, 1963), pp. 404–10.
2 W.L.M.K., Diary, July 17, 1939.
3 See R. M. Dawson, *W. L. Mackenzie King*, I: *1874–1923* (Toronto, 1958), pp. 162, 224.
4 Diary, Aug. 2, 1939.
5 *Ibid.*, July 17, 1939.

6 *Ibid.*, April 3, 1939.
7 *Ibid.*, Feb. 7, 1939.
8 *Ibid.*, May 20, 1938.
9 *Ibid.*, Nov. 29, 1938.
10 *Ibid.*, Aug. 11, 1938.
11 By 1938 even Sir Edward Beatty of the C.P.R. could be counted as a supporter of the Liberal administration; E. W. Beatty to W.L.M.K., Sept. 2, 1938. For Manion's relations with business interests see J. L. Granatstein, *The Politics of Survival: The Conservative Party of Canada, 1939–1945* (Toronto, 1967), pp. 18–22.
12 C. A. Dunning to W.L.M.K., Aug. 27, 1938.
13 C. A. Dunning to W.L.M.K., July 21, 1939; Diary, June 27, Aug. 1, 1939.
14 Diary, Aug. 12, 1939.
15 Violet Markham, *Return Passage* (London, 1953), p. 220.
16 Violet Markham, *Friendship's Harvest* (London, 1956), p. 165.

INDEX

INDEX

Abdication 171, 178–9, 183–5
Aberhart, William: elected 114; on Loan Council 159–60; W.L.M.K.'s impression of 159, 196, 225–6; and debt legislation 195–6, 266, 267; and appeal to Privy Council 266; appoints Social Credit Board 266–7; passes Social Credit legislation 226–7; on unemployment insurance 243; on Royal Commission on Dominion-Provincial Relations 245, 246; and Royal Tour 311–12
Accurate News and Information bill 230–1, 265
Action Libérale Nationale 152, 234
Alaska Highway 264
Anderson, J. T. M. 65
Angus, H. F. 244
Anschluss 273, 274, 275, 304
Armour, Norman 142

Baldwin, Stanley 20, 177, 178, 180, 182, 184, 214, 244
Bank of Canada 32–9, 50, 52–7, 87, 160, 164–5, 197
Bank Taxation bill 230–1, 265
Beatty, Sir Edward 43, 55
Beauharnois, 259, 288
Bennett, R. B.: and Imperial Economic Conference 18–21; and Ottawa Agreements 21–2, 24, 26, 84; W.L.M.K.'s opinion of 29; on inflation 31; on C.C.F. 37; response to depression (1933) 39–40; restores titles 44; on trade agreement with U.S. 46, 83–4; criticized by colleagues 51–2, 80–1; on Bank of Canada 52, 53, 55–6; on Natural Products Marketing Act 59; relations with H. H. Stevens 60–1, 68, 69, 81, 82, 100, 104; B.N.A. Act

amendment 82–3, 161, 199; New Deal broadcasts 85–8, 89; election of 1935 84, 90, 110–14; health 92, 95, 96, 100; on Royal Commission on Price Spreads 101–2; on Wheat Board 104–8; on Ethiopian crisis 122; assessment of his leadership 124–5, 154–5, 186, 260; on League sanctions 137; on aid to provinces 148, 151; on Section 98, 164; on bilingual currency 165; on railway policy 166; defends wheat policy 167; comments on 1936 session 169; on Liberal foreign policy 174, 193, 277; on 1937 budget 189; on Royal Commission on Dominion–Provincial Relations 244, 245; in 1938 session 259–60; on Commonwealth defence 281–2
Bennett New Deal 85–9, 90, 199, 243, 260
Bergman, Ingrid 179
Bilingual currency 56, 165
Blackmore, J. H. 277
Blum, Léon 176
Bowen, J. C. 311
Bracken, John 45, 116n
Bren gun 216–17, 273, 278–81
British Commonwealth air training proposals 281–3
British Commonwealth from Canadian perspective 170, 177, 213–19, 220, 276, 278, 295–7
British North America Act amendments 82–3, 151–2, 155, 157–61, 161–2, 199, 243
Bruce, H. A. 238–9
Buck, Tim 44, 164
Budget: (1932) 30; (1933) 40–1; (1934) 52; (1935) 95–6; (1936) 162–4; (1937) 187–99; (1938) 249, 250–8; (1939) 308–9